BOOKS BY

Perez Zagorin

The Court and the Country   1970

A History of Political Thought in the English Revolution   1954

The Court and the Country

The Court
and the Country

The Beginning of
the English Revolution

PEREZ ZAGORIN

Atheneum NEW YORK

1970

Copyright © 1969 by Perez Zagorin
All rights reserved
Library of Congress catalog card number: 72-104129
Printed in the United States of America by
The Murray Printing Company, Forge Village, Massachusetts
Bound by H. Wolff, New York
First American Edition

To H.S. and A.D.Z.

'Grau, teurer Freund, ist alle Theorie
Und grün des Lebens goldner Baum.'

Contents

Preface

The revolution of 1640–1660 is the highest mountain in the English seventeenth-century landscape, towering over events before and after. I have sought in the following work to add to the general understanding of the English revolution from its origins to the inception of the civil war in 1642. My aim throughout has been to penetrate the specific factors, political, social, and religious, that engendered the revolt against Charles I and determined its character and progress. Comparative considerations relative to the sixteenth–seventeenth-century revolutions in general have not been absent from my mind and are taken up especially in the first two chapters. They have been strictly subordinated, however, to the task of investigating the process of revolution in England. As far as any single theme predominates, it is the organization, tactics, principles, and ideas of the movement of opposition to the Stuart régime. I have attempted to trace these from the formation of the Country opposition in the 1620s to the emergence of the Parliamentarian party in 1641–42. The method I have chosen is as far as possible interpretative and analytic. Accordingly, when I give any connected narrative of events or transactions, as is particularly the case in chapters seven through nine, I do so in order to clarify and set in relief the themes and problems which have claimed my interest.

This book doubtless contains many weaknesses, but it would contain still more, had I not been able to draw freely on the writings of other scholars who have done significant work on the period with which I deal. The amount of research in sixteenth–seventeenth-century British history has become enormous during the past twenty years—more, indeed, than a single student can possibly control. As regards learning, originality, and suggestiveness, some of it stands on the highest level of the historical scholarship of our time. I have tried to avail myself of this to the best of my ability, and hope that my notes give an adequate indication of my indebtedness. Of the older writers, I have had frequent recourse to the great work of S. R. Gardiner.

Preface

At this date his history of England from the time of James I to the Cromwellian protectorate is perhaps more to be consulted than read. It remains indispensable, nevertheless, in the masterly scope, accuracy, and detail of its narrative, while in part, at least, its interpretation of the English conflict still continues to hold sway.

Among the manuscripts I have used, the most important is Sir Simonds D'Ewes's Journal of the Long Parliament in the Harleian manuscripts at the British Museum. D'Ewes, who represented Sudbury in the House of Commons, left an incomparable record of the Commons' transactions down to 1645. In 1923, when Professor Wallace Notestein of Yale University published an edition of D'Ewes's Journal for the period 3 November 1640–20 March 1641, he declared in the Preface: 'No private journal of Parliament during the seventeenth century, or for that matter in any century, can compare in importance with that of Sir Simonds D'Ewes.' Nearly twenty years later, Professor Willson Coates of the University of Rochester published a further edition of D'Ewes covering the period 12 October 1641–10 January 1642. I am indebted to both these editions. At present, however, though nearly a half-century has elapsed since Notestein's words, far the greater part of D'Ewes's Journal is still unpublished. This can only be described as a scandal to Anglo-American scholarship and a glaring void in the considerable body of work devoted to parliamentary history in recent years.

I have incurred numerous obligations in writing this book, which I acknowledge with gratitude. Fellowships from the Canada Council and the Social Science Research Council enabled me to do a considerable part of my research in England. At a subsequent stage, a fellowship from the Folger Library in Washington, awarded while I was visiting professor of history at the Johns Hopkins University, provided me with invaluable facilities as well as the unexcelled amenities of a great research institution. My thanks are due to the librarians and staffs of the following: the British Museum Reading Room, North Library, and Department of Manuscripts; the Public Record Office; the City of London Guildhall Record Office; Dr. Williams's Library; the Bodleian Library; the Sheffield Central Library; the Folger Library; and the libraries of McGill University, the University of Rochester, and Yale University.

To the following I express appreciation for materials they have allowed me to use: Viscount De L'Isle, for permission to read his manuscripts in the Public Record Office; the Marquess of Salisbury, for permission to read the Cecil manuscripts in microfilm deposited in the British Museum; Earl Fitzwilliam and the Trustees of Earl Fitzwilliam's Wentworth Estates Company, for permission to read the Strafford manuscripts in the Sheffield Central Library.

Preface

I also thank: Professor H. N. Fieldhouse, Academic Vice-Principal Emeritus of McGill University; Mr. Roger Ellis, Secretary of the Historical Manuscripts Commission; Dr. L. B. Wright, Director of the Folger Library, who procured at my request a microfilm of D'Ewes's Journal; Professor Willson Coates of the University of Rochester, who permitted me to use his transcript of the portion of D'Ewes's Journal from 11 January to 21 March 1642; Mr. John Bebbington, Sheffield City Librarian, who provided me with the microfilm of a document in the Strafford manuscripts; the Warden and Fellows of Wadham College, who gave me hospitality as a member of their Senior Common Room when I resided in Oxford.

I have had the assistance of my graduate students, Mrs. Susan Guralnik and Mrs. Jean Woy, in preparing this book for publication. Mrs. Claire Sundeen, who typed my manuscript, has rendered invaluable service.

I have given dates according to the 'Old Style' or Julian calendar, which still prevailed in England in the seventeenth century; by contrast, however, I have reckoned the year as beginning on 1 January, rather than, as the contemporary English usage was, on 25 March. Most of the seventeenth-century works cited were published in London. In transcribing documents, I have consistently followed the originals in all points of grammar, spelling, and syntax, except when changes became necessary for the sake of intelligibility.

P. ZAGORIN

Abbreviations

Add.	Additional manuscripts.
B.M.	British Museum.
C.J.	*Journal of the House of Commons.*
C.S.P.D.	*Calendar of State Papers Domestic.*
C.S.P.V.	*Calendar of State Papers . . . in the archives and collections of Venice. . . .*
Clarendon, *Life*	*The life of Edward earl of Clarendon written by himself,* Oxford, 1843 [bound in and paginated continuously with *The history of the rebellion*].
Clarendon, *Rebellion*	Edward earl of Clarendon, *The history of the rebellion and civil wars begun in the year 1641,* ed. W. D. Macray, 6 v., Oxford, 1888 [references are to book and paragraph].
Coates, *D'Ewes*	*The journal of Sir Simonds D'Ewes from the first recess of the Long Parliament to the withdrawal of King Charles from London,* ed. W. Coates, New Haven, 1942.
D.N.B.	*Dictionary of National Biography.*
E.H.R.	*English Historical Review.*
An exact collection	*An exact collection of all remonstrances, declarations, votes, orders, ordinances, proclamations, petitions, messages, answers, and other remarkable passages betweene the Kings most excellent Majesty and his high court of Parliament . . . December 1641 . . . untill March the 21, 1643, 1643.*

Abbreviations

S. R. Gardiner, *History*	S. R. Gardiner, *History of England from the accession of James I to the outbreak of the civil war, 1603–42*, 10 v., L., 1883–84.
Harl.	*Harleian manuscripts.*
H.M.C.	*Reports and calendars issued by the Royal Commission on Historical Manuscripts.*
Journal	Journal of the common council of the city of London, Guildhall record office.
L.	London, used in footnotes as place of publication.
L.J.	*Journal of the House of Lords.*
Notestein, *D'Ewes*	*The journal of Sir Simonds D'Ewes from the beginning of the Long Parliament to the trial of the earl of Strafford*, ed. W. Notestein, New Haven, 1923.
P.R.O.	Public Record Office.
Repertories	Repertories of the aldermanic bench of the city of London, Guildhall record office.
J. Rushworth	J. Rushworth, *Historical collections of private passages of state*, 8 v., L., 1682–1721.
S.P.	State Papers.

1

Introduction

In the middle years of the seventeenth century, a tempest of rebellions and civil wars broke over the greatest of the European monarchies and for a space engulfed them. The nations were already treading a grisly dance of death in the long war which, beginning in 1618 with the Bohemian insurrection, had gradually grown into a general conflict of the powers. Smitten by a flail of iron, the provinces of Germany and other seats of war bled under the marchings and devastations of the soldiery. Then to this sanguinary international rivalry of dynasties was added the further affliction of domestic insurrections and internal wars. Widespread revolts spanned the years of the 1640s and '50s. Scotland, England, and Ireland, the kingdoms of the Stuart, Charles I; Catalonia, Portugal, Sicily, and Naples, the realms of the Spanish Habsburg, Philip IV; France of the young Bourbon, Louis XIV: in all these lands the flocks threw off their subjection and about the princely shepherds of the people the storm winds blew, menacing their authority, threatening the loss of great domains long in possession, even endangering their thrones.

Civil disturbances, though for the most part of lesser dimension, also overtook other of the states of Europe. The Dutch republic passed through a sharp tussle with its princely family of Orange which resulted in the extinction of the latter's power and a new form of republican regime for many years. Sweden under Queen Christina was wracked simultaneously by a deep constitutional and social crisis. In the Swiss cantons a peasant Jacquerie broke out. The Ukraine, then ruled by the King of Poland, was the ground of one of the greatest serf and Cossack insurrections ever to occur in eastern Europe.

Was there an identical conjuncture of malign planets presiding at that period over the destinies of the unlucky governors of states whose influence can account for these many rebellions and disturbances? Did the latter possess a common character and result from the same set of causes? Did they belong, as it were, to a single constellation and

1

thus constitute what has been called a 'general crisis' of the seventeenth century?[1]

Contemporaries impressed by the extent of the revolts occasionally noted resemblances but were unable to go beyond this. An English writer compared the rebellion of Ireland to that of Catalonia and Portugal, while several Italians composed meagre chronicles of the civil wars of their time.[2] The councillors of Queen Christina interested themselves in news from England and France and spoke forebodingly of the 'spiritus vertiginis' abroad.[3] The Brandenburg Elector, Frederick William, accused the Estates in his recently acquired Rhenish principalities of seeking to emulate the English Parliamentarians.[4]

Such commonplaces aside, a close view of the struggles in question would show at best a series of partial parallelisms with little inner connection, rather than a general crisis.[5] Not only the rebellions against the different sovereigns, but even those within the realms of the same prince, originated and developed in almost complete independence of each other. The closest link was that between Scotland and England, where the heads of the resistance to Charles I actually established mutual relations. But no such thing happened in the Spanish empire, and the risings of Catalonia and Portugal in 1640, of Sicily and Naples in 1647, proceeded entirely separately.[6]

[1] An attempt to deal with the seventeenth-century revolutions collectively was made by R. B. Merriman, *Six contemporaneous revolutions*, Oxford, 1938. More recently there has been much discussion of the 'crisis of the seventeenth century'; cf. E. Hobsbawm, 'The crisis of the seventeenth century', *Past and present*, 5, 6 (1954), a brilliant but unconvincing account premised on the (to-say-the-least) questionable Marxian view that the crucial problem of early modern history is the transition from feudalism to capitalism. A better analysis, though also unconvincing, is H. R. Trevor-Roper's 'The general crisis of the seventeenth century', *ibid.*, 16 (1959). A symposium on the seventeenth-century revolutions is in *ibid.*, 13 (1958), and a discussion of Trevor-Roper's article by E. H. Kossmann, E. J. Hobsbawm, J. H. Hexter, R. Mousnier, J. H. Elliott, and L. Stone appears in *ibid.*, 18 (1960). The contribution by M. Roberts, 'Queen Christina and the general crisis of the seventeenth century', *ibid.*, 22 (1962), should also be read. Some of these papers previously printed in *Past and present* are now collected in *Crisis in Europe 1560–1660*, ed. T. Aston, L., 1965.
[2] H.G., *England's present distractions paralleled with those of Spaine, and other foraigne countries*, 1642; Masolino Bisaccioni, *Historia delle guerre civili di questi ultimi tempi*, Venice, 1653; G. B. Birago-Avogadro, *Delle historie memorabili che contiene le sollevationi di stato di nostri tempi*, Venice, 1653.   [3] M. Roberts, *op. cit.*
[4] F. L. Carsten, *Princes and parliaments in Germany*, Oxford, 1959, 302.
[5] Justifiable scepticism as to the 'general crisis' has been expressed by E. H. Kossmann, *Past and present*, 18 (1960), 8–11 and Q. Skinner, *E.H.R.*, LXXXI, 321 (1966), 791–5.
[6] It has been pointed out, however, that in Palermo, where the Sicilian

Introduction

Moreover, the many elements that determined the nature of these revolts also differed largely. There were significant contrasts in the groups and classes who rose, in the aims pursued by their leaders, in their programmes and ideas, as well as in the depth and intensity of the rebellions, the stages through which they passed, and their ultimate results.

The grievances, too, that produced the secret swellings and hollow gusts before the tempest varied considerably from state to state. As to these in general, we may take a hint from Francis Bacon. A thinker in an age when public order was always precarious, a councillor who had seen how the Netherlands rebellion and the French wars of religion caused mighty monarchies to totter, Bacon had reflected deeply on the causes of revolution in his time. The grounds of troubles in states, he said, are

innovation in religion; taxes; alteration of laws and customs; breaking of privileges; general oppression; advancement of unworthy persons; strangers; dearths; disbanded soldiers; factions grown desperate; and whatsoever in offending people joineth and knitteth them in a common cause.[1]

Add to this list religious persecution and provincial oppression (if Bacon's account does not already imply them) and we should have the complete repertoire of motives to sedition in the sixteenth- and seventeenth-century rebellions.

Although some of these were common to more than one state, their incidence and the circumstances in which they manifested themselves formed in every case a pattern of particular causes incommensurable with that prevailing elsewhere. Ireland, for instance, like Catalonia, found a cue to revolt in the alien rule from which it suffered. But here resemblance ended. For Ireland's subjection to England was far greater than Catalonia's to its Spanish master. If Ireland before its rebellion had been governed too hard, Catalonia had been governed too little. Sudden withdrawal of a strong arm in the one, attempts to introduce fresh pressures in the other, alike ended in revolt. In addition, while the Catholic Catalans were ruled

[1] F. Bacon, *Essays*, 'Of seditions and troubles.'

revolt broke out in May 1647, the news of the revolt of Naples two months later may have influenced the guilds and their consuls to think of overthrowing the Spanish regime. At the beginning the slogan of the Sicilian rising had been, 'Long live the King and down with the taxes and the bad Government'; cf. H. L. Koenigsberger, 'The revolt of Palermo in 1647' *Cambridge historical journal*, VIII, 2 (1945), 133, 135.

by a dynasty of the same faith as their own, the Irish felt their hardships doubled in having to endure the persecution of a heretical religion.[1]

Probably the most common condition making for rebellion in these star-crossed decades was the strain resulting from the Thirty Years War. The prolonged military operations and the maintenance of armies on a scale never before attained, necessitated crushing costs and burdens. These the beset combatants endeavoured to meet by fiscal demands and exactions which eventually provoked resistance not only from the peasants and urban poor but also from the aristocratic and privileged orders. The hatred which the cardinals Richelieu and Mazarin aroused in France, and the count-duke of Olivares in Spain, was partly a consequence of the financial expedients to which these prepotent ministers were constrained to resort. Neither for the first nor last time war, and for Spain grave defeats as well, proved to be the midwife of revolt.

Yet even the frictions generated internally by the Thirty Years War were restricted in their range. Charles I's kingdoms had no share in them. Only France and the possessions of imperial Spain were affected, and of the latter, the kingdom of Portugal and the principality of Catalonia, whose burdens were least, revolted, while Castile, the most severely exploited of all Philip IV's realms, remained quiescent.[2]

Amidst these differences and the prevalence of particular causes, one broad feature nevertheless characterized in some degree the context of nearly all the mid-century rebellions. Most of them were directed against a monarchical power which, however vulnerable at the moment of revolt because of war or other difficulties, had grown during the preceding decades more centralized, more capable of imposing its will, more uniform in controlling and disciplining all ranks of its subjects. The outstanding exception was the Dutch republic, where the process had been checked through the prosperous outcome of the rebellion against Spain. There, too, however, it was opposition to the ambition of the stadholder Prince of Orange that

---

[1] Comparing the situation of the Irish with that of the Dutch, Lord Burghley once remarked that 'the Flemings had no such cause to protest against Spanish oppression as the Irish against the tyranny of England'; cf. C. Read, *Lord Burghley and Queen Elizabeth*, L., 1960, 9. Catalonia's relation to the monarchy of Spain is described in J. H. Elliott's notable work, *The revolt of the Catalans*, Cambridge, 1963.

[2] The importance of the effects of the Thirty Years War in provoking revolution has been stressed by Mousnier and Elliott, *Past and present*, 18 (1960), 23–4, 29–30, and by H. L. Koenigsberger, 'The revolt of Palermo in 1647,' *loc. cit.*, 130; cf. also J. H. Elliott, *The revolt of the Catalans*, chs. XVII–XVIII and E. H. Kossmann, *La Fronde*, Leiden, 1954, ch. II.

led to the commotions of 1650.[1] Elsewhere in the foremost states of Europe the progress of royal authority had been in full career for more than a hundred and fifty years. Despite intervals of retrogression, that authority was increasing in all the attributes which could make its rule over its subjects an untrammelled reality. Everywhere there were groups, orders, and whole regions upon whom regal sovereignty fell as a vexation and a burden. The inherited and prescriptive privileges of assemblies of estates, the liberties of provinces and of degrees of men, were pared down, became thin and emaciated, or were rendered lifeless at the feet of the all-conquering Leviathan. And at the same time the administrative apparatus of the crowns expanded, the costs of their government rose, and expenditure for the maintenance of courts and the support of wars became more prodigal. To finance government, war, and courts, the princes challenged or obtained a taxing power that invaded their subjects' security of property. It was inevitable that so far-reaching an application of royal power among peoples not yet fully habituated to bear the yoke should give rise to popular and aristocratic reaction.

2

Such in its general complexion was the background against which the seventeenth-century revolutions took place. The investigation of their detailed similarities and differences could, of course, be extended with illuminating results. What is especially pertinent to our present purpose, however, is to observe that of all these occurrences only one, the English revolution, possesses a significance transcending the restricted national history of which it is part. By common consent the rebellion against Charles I belongs to the handful of the 'great revolutions' of Europe and the West—cataclysms which appear to mark the turning of times and to signify some fundamental change in the condition of humanity. Ranke spoke of the 'universal historical importance of these contests in Great Britain,' declaring his conviction that 'it is an event which concerns all, this shaking of the foundations of the old British state.'[2] Lord Acton called England's revolution 'the point where the history of nations turned into its modern bed' and 'the second stage on the road of revolution, which started from the Netherlands, and went on to America and France, and is the centre of the history of the modern world.'[3] More recently,

[1] P. Geyl, *The Netherlands in the seventeenth century, Part two, 1648–1715*, L., 1964, 13–19.
[2] L. von Ranke, *A history of England principally in the seventeenth century* (trans. of *Englische Geschichte*, 1859–69), 6v., Oxford, 1875, II, 331.
[3] Lord Acton, *Lectures on modern history*, L., ed. 1952, 205.

Trotsky, maker and theorist of revolution in one, found it natural, when writing his *History of the Russian revolution*, to refer to the English struggle as constituting part of a mighty succession of ideas and forms that passed through France to attain a new and higher stage of the Bolshevik conquest of power in 1917.[1]

These judgments as to the importance of the English revolution are well founded. The great revolutions are those in which the pace of change is suddenly accelerated and in which, as Macaulay wrote, 'the experience of years is crowded into hours' and 'old habits of thought and action are violently broken.'[2] Political and social conflict brought to white heat creates a forcing-house that permits every existent tendency to realize itself with startling rapidity. Programmes and shibboleths, ideas and myths, come to birth which will engross the deepest efforts not only of the present contestants but of others in time to come. Perspectives are announced which may require fifty years, a century, or longer for their fulfilment; utopias are envisioned whose being can never be seen on land or sea. In a few weeks or months, venerable monuments are overthrown before which men's forefathers had made reverential obeisance. Amidst the convulsive heavings of an enraged generation, great reforms are effected and powerful energies released which elevate the character and raise the power of the revolutionary state among the nations.

If the English alone of the seventeenth-century rebellions belongs to the category of 'great revolutions' and is thus fittingly linked with the American and French revolutions of the next century, this is because it, too, like these latter, was a decisive event in the emergence of a liberal political order in the world. In the range of its constitutional and religious experimentation, the fertility of its public discussion, and the extremity to which it was carried by the abolition of kingship and the establishment of a republic, it far exceeded the other rebellions of its time. Moreover, in longer perspective, both its practical attainments and ideal aims may be seen as expressive of the aspirations of the epoch at whose threshold it stood. Popular sovereignty; representative rule through parliamentary bodies; the accountability of kings and magistrates; the bounding of government by law; the liberty of the religious conscience; the disestablishment of all ecclesiastical dominion; individual consent to subjection as a natural and human right; written constitutions; republicanism: in short, many of

---

[1] L. Trotsky, *The history of the Russian revolution*, tr. M. Eastman, 3v., N.Y., 1936, I, 14–15, 208–9. Trotsky's references to the English revolution in this work are not always on the mark. Mr. Isaac Deutscher in his great biography of Trotsky also invokes the English revolution for comparison from time to time, with results no more consistently correct.

[2] T. B. Macaulay, *History of England*, 5v., Philadelphia, n.d., II, 451.

the principles and demands that were to subvert the European *ancien régime* made their appearance in England at some time or other between 1640 and 1660.

The wider significance here ascribed to the English revolution has been commonly acknowledged. But almost as a direct result, serious misconceptions have often arisen concerning its nature and origins. For the recognition of the revolution's place as precursor in the course of subsequent development has not infrequently been the cause of an inability to perceive how much its history was peculiar to itself and to its own immediate age.

This failure is due mainly to the influence of the Marxian theory of revolution. According to Marx and Engels, the bourgeois revolution formed a necessary general stage of the historical process leading to capitalism, so that each of its instances bore substantially the same character and resembled the others in essential respects. It thus became possible within the Marxian ambit of ideas to describe the English conflict as 'a bourgeois revolution . . . of classical type, to be closely compared with the French revolution of 1789.'[1] Inevitably, the revolution in France, owing to its thoroughness and universal scope, was taken by Marx and his followers as the model to which the interpretation of other revolutions considered 'bourgeois' could be assimilated. This was not, however, the conclusion of research, but the presupposition through which the entire subject was approached.[2] Thus, in its social origins, in the nature of the contending forces, in the stages through which it passed, the French revolution provided the pattern which, *mutatis mutandis*, was believed a sufficient explanation of the revolution in England.[3]

In consequence of this view the grossest errors and distortions have been committed. It enabled Marx to call the civil war

the victory of bourgeois over feudal property, of nationality over provincialism, of free trade over the guilds, of sub-division of property

[1] Cf. C. Hill, 'The English civil war interpreted by Marx and Engels', *Science and society*, XII, 1 (1948), which conveniently summarizes the Marxian analysis of the English revolution with appropriate citations.

[2] Cf. the apt remark of J. Plamenatz concerning the 'great error of the Marxists, which is to search hard for the causes of things before they have looked carefully at the things themselves. They know, so they think, what revolutions are, and they also know what kind of events their causes must be. This knowledge they acquire not from history but from philosophy; and their task as historians is to discover not what happened but what must have happened.' *The revolutionary movement in France 1815–1871*, L., 1952, x.

[3] The Marxian class analysis which in one form or another has dominated the historiography of the French revolution for many years is the subject of critical treatment in the recent work by A. Cobban, *The social interpretation of the French revolution*, Cambridge, 1964.

over primogeniture, of landownership over the subordination of the owner by means of the land ... of the family over family title, of industry over heroic idleness. ...[1]

In a similar way, it has allowed recent historians, despite the weight of evidence to the contrary, to speak of England in 1640 as a predominantly feudal society and to pronounce the revolution the conflict of a progressive mode of production and way of life against the trammels of a surviving feudalism.[2]

Such aberrations are a natural result of the presupposition which Marx maintained and are bound to persist while it is taken seriously. It is therefore essential to realize that there is no model of revolutions, bourgeois or other, no 'classical type,' which can yield the secret of the specific phenomenon we are studying. Comparisons otherwise instructive will lead only to error so long as they are based on the fallacious belief that a single morphological structure exists to which the explanation of events of a certain kind must necessarily conform.

In particular, as regards the English revolution, we must cast aside the categories elaborated by historians and sociologists for the revolution in France and examine it in its own right. At once vital differences appear. One of the most striking was remarked on over a century ago by the historian, Guizot, to whom the civil war was a subject of absorbing study. In an implied contrast to France he declared:

It was the peculiar felicity of England in the seventeenth century that the spirit of religious faith and the spirit of political liberty reigned together. ...

All the great passions of the human soul were thus excited and brought into action, while some of the most powerful restraints by which they are controlled remained unbroken. ...

The two parties fought with the most determined acrimony; but, in the midst of mortal struggle, they did not renounce all sentiments of order and peace. There were no sanguinary riots, no judicial massacres. There was civil war, fierce, obstinate, full of violence ... but without cynical

[1] Cited in C. Hill, 'The English civil war interpreted by Marx and Engels'' *loc. cit.*, 143.

[2] C. Hill, *The English revolution*, 3rd rev. ed., L., 1955 and 'The agrarian legislation of the Revolution,' *Puritanism and revolution*, L., 1958, 154, 156. A similar conception informs M. Dobb's discussion of the revolution in *Studies in the development of capitalism*, L., 1947, ch. IV. Cf. also 'Tercentenary number on the English revolution,' *Modern quarterly*, IV, 2 (1949) and A. Meusel, *Aus der Vorgeschichte der bürgerlichen Revolution in England, Sitzungsberichte der Deutschen Akademie der Wiss. zu Berlin, Klasse für Gesellschaftswissen*, 1954.

or atrocious excesses, and restrained by the general manners of the people within certain bounds of justice and humanity.[1]

The essential truth of Guizot's perhaps slightly hyperbolic statement is, of course, undeniable. The English revolution did not devour its own children. Neither side resorted to systematic and ideologically buttressed destruction of political enemies, and there was no 'Red' terror while the revolutionary governments were in power and no 'White' terror at the Restoration.

We could easily add further contrasts as well. Thus, we do not find among any of the opponents of Charles I a party remotely similar to the Jacobins in organization, vigilance, and ideological passion. We do not see in England the prevalence of the extravagant hopes and boundless combinations which exercised the minds of the revolutionary leaders in France. Most important of all, perhaps, we do not discover a class conflict to underlie the origins of the English revolution or to be its cause; and we observe that through political change and upheaval the social order remained unshaken at its foundations, emerging intact in the aftermath of the cataclysm on the same continuum along which it had been evolving before.

3

To cite these differences is, of course, to specify a problem. What *was* the nature of the English revolution? Why did it occur? What made it what it was? It will be our aim in the present work to answer these questions, if possible, with some precision, and to delineate the physiognomy of the revolution in its own right—not, indeed, over the full extent of its twenty years, but from its origins to the onset of the civil war, the period which witnessed the dissolution of the inherited governmental order and the inauguration of a long series of political expedients and experiments.

In order to proceed to our task, however, we must first inquire whether and how far the seventeenth century itself possessed a conception of revolution. This is a topic which historians of the rebellions and civil wars of the time have seldom considered, though it is of high interest and importance. For while we, the retrospective analysts at three centuries' distance, rightly describe English occurrences after

[1] F. Guizot, *On the causes of the success of the English revolution of 1640–1688*, L., 1850, 3, 18. Sainte-Beuve's essay on this work (*Causeries du Lundi*, 4 Feb. 1850) points out how much its judgment on the English revolution was formed in reaction against the French. It should be recalled that Guizot wrote it after the collapse of the July monarchy in 1848 and his own exile to England.

1640 as a revolution, the contemporaries and actors of these events did not—or certainly not, at any rate, in our sense. Is it not therefore apparent that a revolution initiated by men who had no thought of what *we* have come to understand by 'revolution' and, moreover, no awareness of being revolutionaries, must present, in significant respects, another character than the type of revolutionary change predominant in aftertimes? It is to this preliminary question that we here wish to address ourselves.

If we reflect on our present-day conception of 'revolution,' we shall observe that besides its having proliferated into many diverse contexts such as the economic, scientific, military, and even aesthetic, it has also acquired on its political side an enormous amplitude of meaning. It stands here for the conscious, unremitting will to transform fundamentally the condition of humanity. Far more comprehensive than rebellion, it signifies the attempt not only to overthrow a regime, but to change society. The merely 'political' does not exist for it, premissed as it is upon the complete interpenetration of the political and social realms and the controlling relevance of politics for every field of action. Its characteristic note is orientation and commitment towards the future as a history to be made in full awareness. Hence, when this conception issues forth as a deed, the latter aims at nothing less than total emancipation from the old society and creation of the new, to which end the conquest of state power is instrumental.

That this idea has not only entered deeply into the texture of modern politics, but has actually conditioned and guided the greatest revolutions of our time, is incontestable. Its materialization in world events would suffice of itself to confirm the frequently expressed conviction as to the overwhelming part which revolution has played in the history of the twentieth century.[1]

Whence, however, did such a conception derive?[2]

[1] Cf. H. Arendt, *On revolution*, N.Y., ed. 1965, Intro., and the contributions to the theory and history of revolution collected in *Revolution, Nomos*, VIII, ed. C. J. Friedrich, N.Y., 1966. Cf. also the useful survey by L. Stone, 'Theories of revolution,' *World politics*, XVIII, 2 (1966). Within the typology of revolution, what S. Neumann and C. Johnson have called the Jacobin Communist Revolution—'a sweeping fundamental change in political organization, social structure, economic property control and the predominant myth of a social order . . .' (cited in L. Stone, *op. cit.*, 163)—is, in fact, the preeminent type of revolution of this century. The description, 'Jacobin Communist,' however, is somewhat misleading, as the Nazi movement belongs to it as well. This appears with great clarity in H. Rauschning, *The revolution of nihilism*, tr. E. W. Dickes, N.Y., 1939, a work which remains fundamental for the understanding of German national-socialism.
[2] The history of the idea and terminology of revolutions has been treated by E. Rosenstock-Huessy, 'Revolution als politischer Begriff in der Neuzeit,'

Introduction

Undoubtedly, its immediate origin lay in the thought of Marx, just as it also attained its fullest development in Marxist theory, which holds as a basic proposition that 'revolutions are the locomotives of history.'[1] In becoming a practical will, as it did with Lenin and the Bolsheviks, the Marxian revolutionary idea revealed its elemental potency. The nature of its operation appears to perfection in the brilliant pages of Trotsky's *History of the Russian revolution*, permeated as the latter is by the consciousness of moulding history and the belief that 'never in all the past have the conceptions of a revolution in the minds of revolutionists approached so closely to the actual essence of the events as in 1917.'[2]

But prior to the theoretical enthronement of revolution in Marxism occurred the *fact* of the French revolution. Originating like nearly all the European revolts of the previous age in a resistance of the aristocratic order—a *révolte nobiliare*, it then rapidly grew into a vast popular movement which drove on with unexampled dynamism to extremes of violence and struggle. Here for the first time, beyond the aims of securing a constitution and specific reforms, the will to regenerate mankind became during the Jacobin ascendancy a ruling passion.[3] Amidst the colossal events through which France passed, the idea and terminology of revolution expanded and acquired an extraordinary resonance. Their new significance was symbolized in the well-known saying of the Duc de Rochefoucauld-Liancourt on the morrow of the fall of the Bastille. To Louis XVI's question,

[1] K. Marx, *The class struggles in France 1848-50, Selected works*, ed. V. Adoratsky, 2v., N.Y., n.d., II, 283; cf. K. Griewank, *op. cit.*, 270-9 and R. C. Tucker, 'The Marxian revolutionary idea,' in *Revolution, Nomos*, VIII.

[2] L. Trotsky, *op. cit.*, III, App. III, 380. Cf. also the remark, 'You may say of the Bolsheviks ... they were adequate to their epoch and its tasks; curses in plenty resounded in their direction, but irony would not stick to them—it had nothing to catch hold of.' *Ibid.*, II, vii.

[3] Cf. the numerous texts cited in J. L. Talmon, *The origins of totalitarian democracy*, N.Y., ed. 1961, pt. II.

Festgabe ... für Paul Heilborn, Breslau, 1931 and in the same writer's *Out of revolution*, N.Y., 1938, *passim*. The fullest account of the subject is K. Griewank's posthumously published *Der neuzeitliche Revolutionsbegriff*, Weimar, 1955, which, in agreement with Rosenstock-Huessy, establishes convincingly that revolution as word and concept 'ist in seiner politischen Anwendung ein Erzeugnis der Neuzeit' and 'ist ... erst möglich geworden auf Grund eines spezifisch modernen Weltverständnisses', *ibid.*, 1, 8. Cf. also A. Hatto, 'Revolution: an enquiry into the usefulness of an historical term,' *Mind*, LVIII, 232 (1949) and V. Snow, 'The concept of revolution in seventeenth-century England,' *Historical journal*, V, 2 (1962). The relation of the idea of reform to revolution and other renewal concepts is discussed by G. Ladner, *The idea of reform*, Cambridge, 1959, ch. 1.

'C'est une révolte?', the Duc replied, 'Non, Sire, c'est une révolution.'[1] Already for some of its contemporaries and participants the revolution was a *mystique*—the expression of humanity's advance into the realm of freedom. The word itself annexed this novel meaning. Adding the definite article and capitals, it was invoked as *La Révolution*. And further, as has been strikingly observed,

it now becomes one of the most individual of words, one of the most powerful. He who could say now, 'La révolution, c'est moi,' *would wield a greater, a more violent power, than had he who said,* 'L'état, c'est moi.' La Révolution, *in the minds of many, now replaces* l'état, le gouvernement, l'église, le roi. *. . . It has swept all these from their seats of authority.*[2]

From hence, too, after 1789 came the mintage of related terms such as 'revolutionary,' 'revolutionize,' and 'counter-revolutionary,' which seem not to have been in use before. Thus, the Convention's wartime decree of 10 October 1793 proclaimed the government of France to be *'révolutionnaire'* until the peace.[3] A Jacobin notable, insisting in 1793 that only severe measures could save the republic, wrote,

. . . la Révolution n'est point faite, et il faut bien dire . . . à la Convention nationale: 'Vous êtes une assemblée révolutionnaire.'[4]

To the Girondist, Condorcet, who composed a tract, *Sur le sens Du mot révolutionnaire* (1793), the word, 'revolutionary,' applied only to revolutions which have liberty as their object.[5] Presently it appeared in English dress and was used pejoratively by Edmund Burke in a diatribe against the French revolution: 'Everything is new, and according to the fashionable phrase, revolutionary.'[6]

These verbal elaborations answered to the need to describe a fresh reality. They were recognitions in the realm of language, the infallible register of men's consciousness, of a phenomenon new in human affairs—the emergence of what Tocqueville, the profoundest his-

---

[1] This is mentioned by E. Rosenstock-Huessy, *Out of revolution*, 130.
[2] H. J. Swann, *French terminologies in the making*, cited in E. Rosenstock-Huessy, *Out of revolution*, 129–30. Cf. also the account of the idea and language of revolution in France after 1789 in K. Griewank, *op. cit.*, ch. IX.
[3] Cited in J. L. Talmon, *op. cit.*, 111. The decree originated with Saint-Just.
[4] Jeanbon de Saint-André, cited in J. L. Talmon, *op. cit.*, 291–2.
[5] Condorcet remarks: 'De *révolution*, nous avons fait révolutionnaire,' and gives various acceptations of the word. He defines '*contre-révolution*' as a revolution against liberty, *Oeuvres*, 12v., Paris, 1847–9, XII, 615, 619.
[6] *Fourth letter on the proposals for peace with the regicide directory of France, 1795, Select works*, ed. E. J. Payne, new ed., 3v., Oxford, 1892, III, 261.

torian of the French revolution, called the 'revolutionary spirit' and a 'race of revolutionaries' dedicated to changing the world.[1]

4

It is the total absence of this highly charged idea of revolution born in France and elevated to a theoretical principle by Marx that we have to notice as we look back across the abyss of time to the 1640s. 'Revolution' had then another, mainly non-political meaning. If the contemporaries of Charles I's deposition used the word in a political context at all, they did so without any of the dynamic connotations it later acquired. Neither did the historiography of the seventeenth century attain to the conception of England's civil conflict as a revolution. To Clarendon, it belonged to the familiar and long-established category of rebellion, the name he gave it in his great work, *The history of the rebellion and civil wars in England*. Not until after the assimilation of post-1789 French experience, it seems, was historical thought able to grasp the revolt against Charles I's government as an authentic *revolution*. The earliest historian to do so systematically was Guizot, whose writings on the subject, begun in 1826, treated the decades 1640–60 and their antecedents for the first time as 'the English revolution.'[2]

The predominant meaning which 'revolution' possessed for the thought and language of the seventeenth and preceding centuries was astronomical. Both in Latin and the vernacular it denoted the rotation of bodies, as in the title of Copernicus's celebrated treatise, *De revolutionibus orbium coelestium* (1543). Belonging thus to a cosmological context, its chief attribute was *circularity*—motion returning to its point of origin.[3]

When occasionally historians or political writers took over the term, it retained this sense. In their usage, it signified political change proceeding cyclically and describing in its course an alternation of rise and fall of powers. Thereby it might include the notion of upheaval and turbulence, but not that of the creation of a new order of things. Machiavelli, though he hardly ever used the word, understood it in this way speaking in *The prince*, for instance, of '*tante*

[1] Cf. the valuable essay by M. Richter, 'Tocqueville's contributions to the theory of revolution,' *Revolution, Nomos*, VIII, 86–8.
[2] *Histoire de la révolution d'Angleterre depuis l'avènement de Charles Ier jusqu'a sa mort*, 2v., Paris, 1826. In his preface Guizot placed the English and French revolutions on a level, calling the former 'avant la révolution française . . . le plus grand évènement que l'Europe eût à raconter.' Cf. also R. C. Latham, 'English revolutionary thought, 1640–1660,' *History*, n.s., XXX, iii (1945), 39.
[3] Cf. V. Snow, *op. cit.*, 167–8.

revoluzioni d'Italia.' On the other hand, his customary expression for changes in states was the neutral *mutazione* or some variant thereof like *alterazione* or *variazione.*[1] So far was Machiavelli from the later idea of revolution that he declared the only salutary *alterazioni* in republics to be those that bring them back (*riducano*) to their founding principles.[2] Jean Bodin in his *De republica* (1576) likewise characterized the transformation of states merely as *conversio, alteratio,* or *changement* in the French version, terms which his English translator of 1606 rendered simply as 'change.'[3]

In the seventeenth century the astronomical sense of revolution still prevailed over any other. Hence, even as applied to politics, instead of betokening the event which engenders a new political order, revolution, by a curious irony, described the opposite: the return of the cycle of change to its beginning, or else the reversals and overturnings attendant on the cycle. And this conception was often tinged with a pessimistic implication of fatality, as though the rotations of human affairs were subject to the same irresistibility as the orbits of the planets.

In just such a way did a seventeenth-century lover of antiquity refer to 'The revolution of families now wholly extinguished' and confess that

The supreme powers have framed all sublunary things transitory and subject to revolution.[4]

Some writers, with the cyclical image in mind, called the Stuart restoration of 1660 a 'revolution.' Alluding to Charles II's re-establishment on the throne, Thomas Hobbes declared:

I have seen in this Revolution a circular Motion of the Sovereign Power, through two Usurpers, from the late King to this his Son . . . where long may it remain![5]

---

[1] *Il principe*, c.26; *Discorsi*, III, vii ('*mutazioni dalla libertà alla servitù*'), viii ('*alterare una republica*'); cf. K. Griewank, *op. cit.*, ch. IV.

[2] *Discorsi*, III, 1.

[3] *De republica*, IV, c. 1, 2, translated into English by Richard Knolles, *The six books of a commonweale*, 1606.

[4] Robert Reyce, *The breviary of Suffolk*, 1618, ed. F. Hervey, L., 1902, 2. Cf. also Chief Justice Crewe's well-known lament over the passing of families in the Oxford peerage case of 1625: '. . . time hath his revolution; there must be a period and an end to all temporal things . . . an end of names and dignities. . . . For where is Bohun? Where's Mowbray? Where's Mortimer? . . . nay, which is more, and most of all, where is Plantagenet? They are intombed in the urns and sepulchres of mortality.' C. H. Firth, *The House of Lords during the civil war*, L., 1910, 7.

[5] *Behemoth*, in F. Maseres, *Select tracts*, L., 1815, pt. 2, 652.

Introduction

The diplomat, Sir William Temple, spoke similarly of 'the revolution of England in the year sixty. . . .' The associated aspect of overturning is suggested by another of Temple's remarks concerning the Dutch republic invaded by Louis XIV in 1672:

> . . . *such a greatness, and such a fall of this State, seem revolutions unparalleled in any story. . . .*[1]

The analogous thought appears in the few instances where mid-century writers termed the civil conflicts of their time 'revolutions'. They intended no more by the expression than reversals or a *peripeteia* of state. An Italian account of the Neapolitan rising bore the title, *Le rivolutioni di Napoli*.[2] After Charles I's deposition, the English political theorist, Anthony Ascham, published a work called *Of the confusions and revolutions of governments* (1649).[3] Another tract of the 1650s, *Of the origin and progress of the revolution in England*, presupposed the cyclical character of political change both in its title and in its author's reference to 'the strange revolutions we have seen.'[4]

Unrelated to 'revolution' and possessing an entirely different import was 'rebellion.' The former, with its rooted associations in the image of cosmic motion, was an occurrence, not an act. 'Rebellion,' on the other hand, referred indisputably to human conduct; and since it denoted treasonable resistance to authority, it bore the taint of illegality and sin. Hence, none of the rebels of the age admitted to being such. All pleaded grounds of law or religion to repel the accusation from themselves. This was equally true of Charles I's opponents, of the French Fronde, and of the revolt of the Catalans.[5] John Locke, in justifying the right of rebellion, went so far as to turn the charge of rebel against bad rulers. It is they, he said, who incur the responsibility of rebellion by illegal actions contrary to the ends for which government is ordained.[6]

[1] Sir William Temple, *Works*, 4v., L., 1757, I, 57, 59.

[2] Alessandro Giraffi, *Le rivolutioni di Napoli*, Venice, 1647; cf. also in the same sense an account of the Catalan rebellion by Luca Assarino, *Le rivolutioni di Catalogna*, Bologna, 1648.

[3] On Ascham, cf. P. Zagorin, *A history of political thought in the English revolution*, L., 1954, 64–7. Cyclical conceptions with a strong note of pessimism are a prominent feature of Ascham's political ideas.

[4] Matthew Wren, *Of the origin and progress of the revolution in England*, in J. Gutch, *Collectanea curiosa*, Oxford, 1781, 170.

[5] Recent historians of the Fronde and the Catalonian rebellion have stressed the conservatism and appeal to law of both these revolts; cf. P. Doolin, *The Fronde*, Cambridge, 1935, xii–xiii; E. Kossmann, *La Fronde*, ch. I; J. H. Elliott, *The revolt of the Catalans*, 549.

[6] *Two treatises of government*, ed. P. Laslett, Mentor ed., N.Y., 1965, ch. XIX, par. 227.

The Court and the Country

The event in the seventeenth century that contributed most to infuse the idea of revolution with an enduring political content was James II's deposition and the enthronement of William and Mary.[1] To contemporaries, 1688 was a 'revolution' and such it remained to posterity as well.[2] Yet here also, despite the establishment of a new royal line, the concept still preserved its attribute of circularity. Locke, in the preface to his *Two treatises of government*, published in 1690, called King William 'our Great Restorer,' thereby sufficiently indicating how he viewed the revolution. In the *Two treatises* themselves, now known to have been written mainly before 1688, the term only occurs twice, and exclusively in its cyclical sense, as in the allusion to 'the many Revolutions . . . seen in this Kingdom, in this and former Ages. . . .'[3]

On the same premiss the revolution was represented by its makers as a restoration. The Convention Parliament of 1689, which laid the foundation of the revolution settlement, took care to avoid any suggestion of innovation. Although in fact a revolutionary body, in form its work was conservative. It professed only to restore and preserve the laws and liberties violated by a law-breaking King.[4] This enabled Burke a century later to boast of the finality of the revolution of 1688 and of its close continuity with the historic past.[5]

5

The foregoing account has shown that revolution had not yet become a fundamental and actuating concept of politics in the seventeenth century. Not till 1688 did it even possess itself of a definite political meaning. Only thereafter did it also begin to acquire for the contemporary mind a close and invincible connection with liberty. Even at this stage, however, the idea of revolution remained devoid of dynamism and attached to its restorationist premiss. There was paradox, too, in the fact that 1688, a substitution of rulers accomplished peacefully with the least possible breach of continuity, should

[1] Cf. K. Griewank, *op. cit.*, 179–80.
[2] Cf. Evelyn's remark on 2 Dec. 1688, when declarations for the Prince of Orange were pouring in: 'it lookes like a Revolution,' John Evelyn, *Diary*, ed. E. S. de Beer, Oxford, 1959, 895; an earlier mention of a 'sad revolution' threatening 'this sinfull Nation,' *ibid.*, 891.
[3] *Two treatises of government*, Preface, and *Second treatise*, ch. XIX, par. 223, 225. For the dating of Locke's work, see P. Laslett's introduction, pt. III.
[4] This view appears clearly in the Declaration of Rights, 1 Will. and Mary, Sess. 2, c.2, *Statutes of the realm*, VI, 142–5; cf. also the remarks of G. N. Clark, *The later Stuarts*, 2nd ed., Oxford, 1961, 146–7.
[5] *Reflections on the revolution in France*, 1790, *Select works*, I, 18–22.

have become known as a revolution; while 1640–60, a period of violence and unprecedented innovation, did not receive the name.

But this, in turn, reflected a view of things which inevitably influenced the nature of the actual revolutions of the age. The political outlook that held so limited an idea of revolution belonged to societies still strongly bound to their traditions. It pertained to social structures dominated by aristocratic and privileged élites in whose opposition most of the significant rebellions and civil wars of the sixteenth and seventeenth centuries arose. The men of that time tended to look backward rather than forward. Conservatives at heart, they were not magnetized by an ideal of the future, and preferred to find their justifications in the precedents of the past and the wisdom of ancestors. They groped blindly towards the new, instead of boldly embracing it. The revolutions of which they were the authors occurred, as it were, behind their own backs.

We shall see these characteristics at the inception of the English revolution. The inspirers of resistance to Charles I never dreamed of being revolutionaries. They opened a course of unimaginable change contrary to their own intentions. Having promoted a civil war, they prepared the way for the momentary appearance of a radicalism which did, indeed, proclaim in political terms the goal of a new order of freedom and justice. It was a Leveller pamphleteer in 1646 who denounced Magna Charta as 'a beggarly thing, containing many markes of intollerable bondage. ...' It was the same writer who imperiously declared that

whatever our Fore-fathers were; or whatever they did or suffered, or were enforced to yield unto, we are the men of the present age, and ought to be absolutely free from all kindes of exorbitancies, molestations or Arbitrary Power. ...[1]

Here we perceive the germ of a political doctrine new to Europe which, by its appeal to reason and natural right, would at a later day help to remould the institutions of the Western peoples. But not even the Levellers could emancipate themselves completely from the myth of the past; and their thought faced backward as well in its invocation of a primitive Anglo-Saxon freedom to be restored after centuries of Norman tyranny.[2]

Outside these audacious democrats and a few fellow radicals, the only other belief in a new age to appear during the revolution took the familiar form of religious millenarianism. Expectation of a

[1] [Richard Overton], *A remonstrance of many thousand citizens*, 1646, 16, 5,
[2] Cf. C. Hill, 'The Norman yoke,' in *Puritanism and revolution*; P. Zagorin, *op. cit.*, 27–8.

supernatural reign of righteousness excited some of the Puritans in the early 1640s, and gave rise in the '50s to the Fifth Monarchy movement, which looked impatiently for the Second Coming and the rule of the saints.[1] At no time, however, did a will to secular transformation determine the revolution's course. Millenarianism, a phenomenon recurrent in Christian history, was politically sterile; while Leveller democracy was too far in advance of its age to achieve power or play a directive role.

Undoubtedly, the revolution administered a great shock to the inherited order. Yet notwithstanding, most Englishmen and their governors remained under the spell of continuity with the past. They did not wish to cut loose from the generations or to venture on a terrain bare of landmarks. This abiding trait in the political mentality of the old societies conditioned the revolution in its origins, just as it resulted at its end in the restoration of kingship.

[1] P. Zagorin, *op. cit.*, ch. VIII.

2

Social Structure and the Court and the Country

It has become a virtual axiom for the scientific study of revolutions that the latter as a general phenomenon are held to reflect a severe structural crisis in society. Insofar as this view forces inquirers to look closely at the connection between revolution and the social system, it is incontrovertible. Often, however, it is associated with the theoretical conviction (of Marxian provenance but by no means exclusively Marxist) that every revolution is necessarily a class struggle—that economic classes are the dominant collectivities whose conflict lies at the root of revolution. This, as a general proposition, is certainly false. Besides its inapplicability to other prominent cases in the sixteenth and seventeenth centuries, it cannot account for the English revolution. Hence, if the cleavage that underlay the revolt against Charles I is to be properly understood, it is essential to dispose of this opinion in regard to England together with the picture of the pre-revolutionary society on which it is based.

The question of English social structure thus presented has been widely discussed of recent years. In particular, it has figured as an issue in the brilliant display of intellectual fireworks known as the gentry controversy, perhaps the most notable historical debate of this generation. The subject of that debate, broadly stated, is the direction of social-economic change in the century preceding 1640 and the connection of the latter with the English revolution. On one side, the thesis advanced by Professor Tawney held that a large-scale shift of landed property away from the crown, the church, and aristocracy resulted in the rise to economic supremacy of a new class of gentry; and further, that it was this class, a species of 'agricultural capitalists,' whose bid for state power overthrew the monarchical regime.[1] On the other side, Professor Trevor-Roper's counter-thesis asserted that economic conditions were unfavourable to gentry

[1] R. H. Tawney, 'The rise of the gentry, 1558–1640,' *Economic history review*, XI, 1 (1941); 'Harrington's interpretation of his age,' *Proceedings of the British Academy*, XXVII, 1941.

19

prosperity from the profits of landholding alone; that far from rising, the gentry declined as a class, save for a fortunate minority who also possessed non-agrarian sources of income such as crown offices or the law; and that the revolution was the rebellion of the 'declining mere gentry' against a hated court and the system of royal benefit and patronage from which they were excluded.[1]

It is not our purpose to review the details of the gentry controversy or the large body of research and criticism it has generated. This has been done in several writings which contain effective assessments of the discussion.[2] What rather calls for notice here are the conceptual and terminological confusions respecting the social structure that still persist. Was the gentry a class? Ought it to be distinguished from, or contrasted with, the aristocracy? Did economic factors determine the form of stratification at that period? Did they determine political organization? These questions remain undecided.[3] Tawney's anatomy of the English social order was framed entirely on quasi-Marxian lines of class, and against this Trevor-Roper directed a powerful critique. His own conception, however, if closer to the realities of seventeenth-century society, runs counter to obvious facts (for it is incorrect that the revolution was the act of a declining gentry) and is therefore only slightly less unsatisfactory. Most recently, Professor Stone, after first concurring with Tawney and then modifying his views in response to criticism, has thrown a penetrating light on the social order in his magisterial study of the peerage.[4] Yet this work manages at the same time to perpetuate some of the muddle concerning social condition. It speaks of the aristocracy when it means the peerage, thus conveying the misleading suggestion that the

[1] H. R. Trevor-Roper, 'The Elizabethan aristocracy: an anatomy anatomized,' *Economic history review*, 2nd ser., III, 3 (1951); *The gentry, 1540–1640*, Cambridge, 1953.

[2] J. H. Hexter, 'Storm over the gentry,' in *Reappraisals in history*, L., 1961; C. Hill, 'Recent interpretations of the civil war,' in *Puritanism and revolution*; P. Zagorin, 'The social interpretation of the English revolution,' *Journal of economic history*, XIX, 3 (1959). A good selection of writings and documents relating to the gentry controversy is contained in Lawrence Stone (ed.), *Social change and revolution in England 1540–1640*, L., 1965, which also has a useful bibliography.

[3] It is worth noticing that similar differences over social classification and terminology exist concerning France in the seventeenth century and at the revolution; cf. R. Mousnier, 'Problèmes de méthode dans l'étude des structures sociales des seizième, dix-septième, dix-huitième siècles,' *Spiegel der Geschichte. Festgabe für Max Braubach*, ed. K. Repgen and S. Skalweit, Münster, 1964, and A. Cobban, 'The vocabulary of social history,' *Political science quarterly*, LXXI, 1 (1956) and *The social interpretation of the French revolution*, chs. II–III.

[4] *The crisis of the aristocracy 1558–1641*, Oxford, 1965; cf. also Stone's introduction to *Social change and revolution in England 1540–1640*.

two were identical although in fact the first, a broader category than the second, included the gentry as well.[1]

If we wish to grasp the relation between politics and the social system, we must take care not to use categories that are classificatory constructions and nothing more. The nature of such categories is purely artificial. However usefully they may serve certain purposes of inquiry, they do not define real collectivities whose actuality and common consciousness is attested in documents.

The failure to recognize this has been a cause of error in the gentry controversy. Much of the argument has turned on disagreements concerning the economic developments of the century. The period was evidently one that witnessed exceptional fluctuations in the composition of landed society. In the present state of knowledge it appears nearly certain that the price revolution and rising population established conditions conducive to the prosperity of landlords. There is a good deal of evidence to indicate that landed incomes, especially from the late sixteenth century on, rose steeply.[2] It is very probable that the gentry grew in numbers and wealth on the profits from land; and it is also likely that relative to the gentry, the land-holdings and wealth of the peerage somewhat declined.[3]

But if this description be correct, there is still no reason to suppose that the trends in question produced a different type of social structure than before. Nor is it the case that a classification founded on changes in the distribution of the ownership of land or wealth necessarily coincides with one that delineates real social groups. Tawney's rising gentry, Trevor-Roper's declining gentry (in this respect like the fictitious progressive landlords who, according to the

---

[1] Stone writes of the Tudor period, for instance, 'If the gentry were the ruling, the aristocracy were the governing class.' (*The crisis of the aristocracy*, 55.) The meaning of this statement is unclear and the distinction it asserts untenable. England was governed under the crown by an aristocratic order that consisted of both the titular nobility or peerage and the gentry.

[2] Cf. E. Kerridge, 'The movement of rent, 1540–1640,' *Economic history review*, 2nd ser., VI, 1 (1953); M. Finch, *The wealth of five Northamptonshire families 1540–1640, Northamptonshire record society*, XIX, 1956; A. Simpson, *The wealth of the gentry 1540–1640*, Chicago, 1961; L. Stone, *The crisis of the aristocracy*, App. XVIB.

[3] The movement of yeoman families into the lesser gentry on an unprecedented scale has been frequently remarked; cf. M. Campbell, *The English yeoman under Elizabeth and the early Stuarts*, New Haven, 1942, 34–42, and W. G. Hoskins, *Provincial England*, L., 1963, 151. The expansion of the gentry is also attested by the statistics representing the increase in the number of armigerous families and grants of knighthood; cf. L. Stone, *The crisis of the aristocracy*, 66–82 and App. III. For the financial decline of the peerage relative to the gentry, cf. *ibid.*, 129–64. W. K. Jordan, *Philanthropy in England 1480–1660*, L., 1959, 333n., has also commented on the striking numerical expansion of the gentry.

orthodox Marxian interpretation, were in conflict with a semi-feudal monarchy[1]) are at best economic abstractions. They are categories that do not reach the operative distinctions in the society nor the actual basis of its political behaviour and division.

The social system in which the revolution occurred was not based on economic classes. It was based, rather, on status, and the terms in which we must perforce delineate it—peers, gentry, yeomen, citizens, etc.—are fundamentally not economic classifications at all.[2] Indeed, none of these categories possesses a distinct economic correlate. If, for example, we refer either to economic function or source of income, then the peerage and the gentry compose a single undifferentiated body. Rising or declining, richer or poorer, ancient family or recent, all were landlords living from the rights they possessed over land, which might be materialized as rents and fines, as profits from the direct sale of agricultural commodities like wool, or as the royalty or other return on mineral resources belonging to their estates. If, on the other hand, we refer to the economic developments that occupied Tawney, then peerage and gentry would have to be alike divided, since within both some prospered by the more efficient exploitation of their estates on capitalist lines, while others did not. These categories do, it is true, imply a financial criterion in that the social sense of the sixteenth century deemed it fitting that a peer's income should exceed a knight's or an esquire's. As contemporaries

---

[1] Cf. C. Hill, *The English revolution 1640*.

[2] The concept of class is one of the most complex and disputed problems in both history and sociology. Its difficulty is increased because, as has been well-remarked, it is used 'with equal frequency and intensity, as a descriptive category, and as a symbol of demand and identification. . . .' (H. Lasswell and A. Kaplan, *Power and society*, L., 1952, 62). Marx himself, while employing it constantly, yet never defined it or provided a formal analysis of its character as a category of social description. As will be seen from the remarks that follow in the text, I have preferred to distinguish status from class as alternative types of social organization. Historically, the first precedes the second as the form of social structure in Western Europe. Classes are primarily economically-determined collectivities; they lack religious or legal sanction, and membership in them confers no special rights; moreover, the boundaries between them are undefined. Status groups differ from classes in all of these respects (cf. T. B. Bottomore, *Classes in modern society*, L., 1955, 14). The emergence of economic classes as the basis of social structure and social consciousness proceeded *pari passu* with the disintegration of the status system and the coming of industrialism. The revolutions of the sixteenth and seventeenth centuries took place in status, not class, societies. On the distinction of status and class, cf. P. Sorokin, 'What is a social class?', F. Tönnies, 'Estates and classes,' Max Weber, 'Class, status, party,' all in R. Bendix and S. Lipset (eds.), *Class, status, and power*, Glencoe, 1953; T. H. Marshall, 'The nature of class conflict,' in *Class conflict and social stratification*, ed. T. H. Marshall, L., 1938; W. G Runciman, *Social science and political theory*, Cambridge, 1963, ch. VII.

well realized, however, this conventional assumption was not infrequently falsified; and Thomas Wilson, writing in 1600, had to
observe that some knights, 'cheefe men in their Countryes both for
livinge and reputacions ... equall the best Barons and come not
much behind many Erles. ...'[1]

In reality, what the nomenclature of peers, gentry, etc., envisaged
was a system of status defined mainly by non-economic criteria such
as titles of honour, ancestry, legal and customary privilege, deference,
and service to the prince.[2] Of this system the ruling principle was
honour and the dignity attaching to way of life. The most elementary
distinction it enforced was between those who were gentlemen and
those not.[3] Around this, however, further and more complex differentiations were elaborated. It was status that conditioned men's social
awareness; equally, it was status that provided the frame of political
action. In view of the determinative influence of this type of social
organization, its basic features may be more fully depicted.

2

To the observation of the sixteenth and seventeenth centuries, society
appeared as a hierarchy of orders or degrees of men, graduated from
the prince at the top, through the peerage, gentry, and other estates,
down to the artificers, husbandmen, and labourers at the bottom.
Such was the conception everywhere implicit in the religious, didactic,
and imaginative literature of the age, and incorporated as well in
formal accounts of their society by contemporary thinkers.[4]

Writing in Henry VIII's time, Sir Thomas Elyot defined the
republica as a 'body ... compact or made of sundry estates and
degrees of men ... disposed by the order of equity and governed by
the rule and moderation of reason.' Of this body the king was head,
with magistrates under him as governors 'chosen out of that estate of

[1] Thomas Wilson, *The state of England (1600)*, ed. F. J. Fisher, *Camden
miscellany*, XVI, 1936, 23.
[2] Cf. R. Mousnier's forceful critique of the attempts to analyse the society
of the *ancien régime* on lines of economic class and his account of the actual
basis of its stratification, 'Problèmes de méthode dans l'étude des structures
sociales des seizième, dix-septième, dix-huitième siècles,' *loc. cit.*
[3] The importance of the difference between the gentleman and others has
been stressed by P. Laslett, who speaks of it as 'the exact point at which the
traditional social system divided up the population into two extremely
unequal sections.' He has confused the matter, however, by picturing the
society as composed of many status groups and only one class, that of the
gentlemen; cf. *The world we have lost*, L., 1965, ch. II.
[4] Cf. R. Mohl, *The three estates in medieval and renaissance literature*, N.Y.,
1933 and R. Kelso, *The doctrine of the English gentleman in the sixteenth
century*, Urbana, 1929.

men which be called worshipful.'[1] Thirty-five years later under Queen Elizabeth, Sir Thomas Smith divided Englishmen into the four degrees of gentlemen, citizens or burgesses, yeomen, and labourers. The gentlemen consisted of the prince, a *nobilitas maior* composed of the peerage, and a *nobilitas minor* of knights, esquires, and gentlemen *simpliciter*.[2] At the beginning of the seventeenth century Thomas Wilson employed a nearly identical classification in which the uppermost order was a two-fold *nobilitas* formed of the peerage proper and of a lesser nobility of knights, esquires, and gentlemen.[3] In James I's reign, Robert Burton, author of *The anatomy of melancholy*, characterized the society as an 'inequality of States, orders, and degrees,' appointed by God.[4] Henry Peacham, a prolific commentator on social custom, described the preeminence of noblemen and gentlemen, who were to be preferred in 'honours, offices, and other dignities of command and government.'[5] Another writer listed seven 'degrees of callings' whose three highest, respectively, were the peerage, the 'degree of Gentry called Knighthood,' and 'Gentlemen of Aunrestry. . . .'[6]

Forty years passed, the revolutionary upheaval was subsiding, but the schematism of status persisted. The political theorist, Harrington, by conviction a republican, still took it for granted that the task of government was a thing 'peculiar unto the Genius of a Gentleman.'[7] A pamphleteer at the Restoration spoke of the gentry as a dominant order that 'live plentifully and at ease upon their rents' and hold 'the command of this nation. . . .'[8] Even at the end of the century, the founders of the science of Political Arithmetic, the earliest quantitative investigation of national wealth and population, continued to analyse the social structure in terms of status. In 1685, Sir William Petty divided the kingdom for tax purposes into a number of 'orders' of which the titular nobility was first, followed by knights, esquires,

---

[1] Sir Thomas Elyot, *The book named the governor*, 1531, Everyman ed., L., 1962, 1, 12, 13.
[2] Sir Thomas Smith, *De republica Anglorum*, written 1565, published 1583, ed. L. Alston, Cambridge, 1906, 31–40.
[3] Thomas Wilson, *The state of England (1600)*, *loc. cit.*, 17. Wilson notes five divisions to Smith's four: noblemen, citizens, yeomen, artificers, and labourers.
[4] Robert Burton, *The anatomy of melancholy*, 1621, ed. A. R. Shilleto from the 6th ed., 3v., L., 1904, II, 196.
[5] Henry Peacham, *The complete gentleman*, 1622, ed. V. Heltzel, Ithaca, 1962.
[6] R. Reyce, *A breviary of Suffolk*, 56–72. Reyce's other degrees are the poor, husbandmen, yeomen, and townsmen.
[7] James Harrington, *Oceana*, 1656, ed. S. B. Liljegren, Lund and Heidelberg, 1924, 35.
[8] Cited in C. Hill and E. Dell, *The good old cause*, L., 1950 471.

and gentlemen.[1] The most elaborate classification made up to that time, however, was Gregory King's table of incomes and expenditure of all English families for the year 1688. He distinguished twenty-six 'Ranks Degrees Titles and Qualifications.' At the summit were some 16,500 families of temporal and spiritual lords, baronets, knights, esquires and gentlemen; at the foot, 849,000 families of labourers, cottagers, paupers, common seamen, common soldiers, and vagrants.[2]

We could add almost indefinitely to these illustrations, but they should suffice to show how strongly status dominated the contemporary perception of the social order. Nor should we imagine that the notion of status was merely a myth, an illusory form of consciousness, falsifying for those who thought in its categories the reality in which they lived. However it might distort by idealizing a system of inequality, it nevertheless corresponded to an objectively-given structure of distinctions. For the society itself, in its resistance to the pretensions of money and riches as such, and in the gradations of privilege and disability, authority and subordination, deference and disesteem which it incorporated, made manifest in innumerable ways that status was its effective mode of differentiation.

Both by law and common practice, every man was known not only by his name, but by his rank.[3] Esquires and gentlemen might have their names prefixed by 'Master,' while yeomen were to be called 'John' or 'Thomas,' 'Goodman Smith' or 'Goodman Coot.'[4]

Parliamentary statutes, royal proclamations, town ordinances, and gild regulations all concurred in their deference to status by confining certain apparel and recreations to particular ranks. Elizabethan proclamations, for instance, minutely prescribed the degrees of persons permitted to use satin, silk, cloth of gold, and other rich materials in their outer garments.[5] An act of 1566 regulating hat

---

[1] *The Petty papers*, ed. Lord Lansdowne, 2v., L., 1927, I, 182–4.

[2] Gregory King, *Natural and political observations*, 1696, in *Two tracts*, ed. G. E. Barnett, Baltimore, 1936, 31. Commenting on King's classification, Professor G. N. Clark has criticized it for attaching too much importance to rank as compared with wealth (*Three aspects of Stuart England*, L., 1960, 39). King, however, as his writings show, took a wide and informed interest in all matters of money, finance, and political economy; and if he differentiated the higher orders according to status (he used occupational and economic criteria for some of the middle and inferior grades), this was because the society itself did so.

[3] Cf., e.g., the act of 1413 which required that original writs in legal proceedings should contain the defendant's 'Estate or Degree, or Mystery . . .', *Statutes of the realm*, II, 171.

[4] William Harrison, *Elizabethan England* [*Description of England*, first printed in Holinshed's *Chronicle*, 1577], ed., L. Withington, L., n.d., 8, 13, 16.

[5] R. Steele, *Tudor and Stuart proclamations*, 2v., Oxford, 1910, 517, 717, 890. These proclamations were issued to enforce statutes of Henry VIII and Philip and Mary against excess in apparel.

manufacture was characteristic in ordering that no one 'under the degree of a knight, or of a lord's son' should wear a hat or cap of velvet.[1] Servants and labourers in husbandry were indicted for playing such games as bowls or football legally prohibited to their rank.[2]

Gentlemen whose status had been traduced could seek redress in the Court of Chivalry, a tribunal restored by James I after a long eclipse.[3] The court possessed jurisdiction over wrongs done to gentlemen, and during the 1630s it heard many cases in which aggrieved parties alleged that their gentility had been denied or defamed by 'scandalous words.' The procedure in such suits was for the plaintiff to bring evidence of his rank. He might do this by producing a pedigree or coat of arms, but more commonly he offered proof that he had always lived in the manner of a gentleman and was so reputed; or he might show that his father was a gentleman and known as 'Mr. Rigby,' never 'Goodman Rigby.'

The prevailing mentality accepted these distinctions as belonging to the nature of things. The general attitude was reflected in the recollections of a seventeenth-century clergyman, a yeoman's son, looking back to his childhood in the reign of Charles I. 'Freeholders' daughters,' he said,

were then confined to their felts, pettiecoates and waistcoates, crosse handkerchiefs about their neckes, and white cross-clothes upon their heads. . . . Tis true the finest sort of them wore gold or silver lace upon their wastcoates, good silk laces (and store of them) about their pettiecoates, and bone laces . . . about their linnens. But the proudest of them (below the gentry) durst not have offered to weare an hood, or a scarfe . . . noe, nor soe much as a gowne, till her wedding day. And if

[1] F. E. Baldwin, *Sumptuary legislation and personal regulation in England*, Baltimore, 1926, 210. The statutes of apparel were repealed in 1604, *ibid.*, 249.

[2] Cf. indictments in 1621 and 1637, *Nottinghamshire county records*, ed. H. H. Copnall, Nottingham, 1915, 52. The inferior orders were confined to archery and sports believed necessary to condition them for martial action.

[3] G. D. Squibb, *The high court of chivalry*, Oxford, 1959, chs. III, XII. The Long Parliament abolished the Court of Chivalry (the Earl Marshal's court) in 1641 as having no foundation in law. Five years later, however, it appointed a successor commission composed of the earl of Northumberland and other lords and members of the Commons to prevent 'Abuses in Heraldry' and the wrongful assumption of arms (C. H. Firth and R. Rait, *Acts and ordinances of the interregnum*, 3v., L., 1911, I, 838–9). 'The Parliamentarians,' writes the court's historian, 'numbered many armigerous men in their ranks and the prospect of heraldic chaos can have held no attraction for them.' G. D. Squibb, *op. cit.*, 68.

any of them had transgressed these bounds, she would have been accounted an ambitious foole.[1]

From the same angle a gentleman of Kent in 1642 defended his intention to marry beneath his status:

There is one objection, which I doubt not but in the course of my life I shall heare often, and that is my Mistress was a Yeoman's daughter; True itt is her father was a Yeoman, but such a Yeoman as lived in his house, in his company, and in his sportes and pleasures like a gentleman . . . and . . . hee bred his daughter . . . mayntaining her 4 yeares at schoole, amongst other gentlemen's daughters, at the same costs and charges. . . .

He added—a striking remark, in view of the impending civil war—'. . . my former highlie esteeming of politicall nobilitie I now reckon amongst the follies of my youth.'[2]

The highest places in the status system belonged to the peerage and gentry, which were separate ranks. Each of these was further differentiated internally in accordance with such factors as age of title and family eminence, crown office, territorial or neighbourhood importance, size of landed income, and opulence in the aristocratic way of life. Except for titles and the order of precedence they conferred, these were informal criteria: but they effectually stratified landed society, giving rise within the latter to an uppermost layer of lords and greater gentry of particular distinction and prestige.

At the same time, however, peerage and gentry together constituted an aristocratic order. Of this aristocracy, the peerage formed a hereditary nobility recognized by law, while the gentry did not. The peerage thus enjoyed legally sanctioned privileges peculiar to itself, among which was the right to be summoned by individual writ to sit in the House of Lords. But in a social, if not a legal sense, the gentry was also a nobility. It was the English equivalent of the lesser nobilities of the continental states, as appears plainly from contemporary descriptions of it as a *'nobilitas minor.'*[3]

Beneath the aristocratic order came the middle and low degrees. Their inferiority was founded on the practice of occupations or

[1] *The life of Adam Martindale . . . by himself*, ed. R. Parkinson, *Chetham society*, IV, 1845, 6–7. This was written in 1685.

[2] *The Oxinden letters, 1607–1642*, ed. D. Gardiner, L., 1933, 278, 279.

[3] Cf. *supra*, 24 and A. R. Wagner, *English genealogy*, Oxford, 1960, 89. Bacon declared in his Star Chamber speech of 1618 that 'here in England are noblemen and gentlemen incorporated' and alluded to knights and gentlemen as *'minores nobiles,'* *Works*, ed. J. Spedding, D. Heath, and R. Ellis, 14v., L., 1859–74, XIII, 303.

functions lacking in honour. In rural society were many yeomen freeholders and copyholders of substance—men who might employ a little agricultural labour and who gained a profitable living from the land. Although deemed a worthy status, they were not gentlemen because they engaged in manual pursuits and attained their prosperity by thrifty ways incompatible with the leisure and display of gentry existence.[1]

In urban society, trade disqualified its practitioners from the status of gentleman. A small minority of merchants might acquire grants of arms, put 'gent.' after their names, or receive knighthoods. The prevailing attitude, however, refused to acknowledge such persons as authentic gentlemen and as a rule classified the mercantile part of the community among the 'citizens and burgesses.'[2]

As for the remaining and still lower levels of the status structure, which of course meant the great majority of the kingdom, their position was summarily defined as having

no voice nor authoritie in our common wealth, and no account is made of them but onelie to be ruled, and not to rule other. . . .[3]

Sir Thomas Smith's words, written in 1565, were equally applicable seventy-five years later when the Long Parliament met. In this category—'lowe and base persons,' according to Smith—he placed day labourers, poor husbandmen, copyholders, many merchants and retailers, and all artificers.[4] At the end of the next century, Edmund Burke, goaded to fury by French revolutionary levelling, expressed the same sentiments:

The occupation of a hair-dresser, or of a working tallow-chandler, cannot be a matter of honour to any person—to say nothing of a number of other more servile employments. Such descriptions of men ought not to suffer oppression from the state; but the state suffers oppression if such as they, either individually or collectively, are permitted to rule.[5]

A type of social organization so congruent with the past in which

---

[1] Cf. Sir Thomas Smith's account of yeomen, *op. cit.*, ch. 23, and the authoritative discussion of yeoman status in M. Campbell, *op. cit.*, ch. II. In current usage the yeoman was in the next degree above husbandman and was a prosperous small farmer, whether he held by freehold tenure of 40s. p.a., as the law defined him, or by copyhold tenure.

[2] Cf. *infra*, ch. V for a fuller discussion of this subject.

[3] Sir Thomas Smith, *op. cit.*, 46.

[4] *Ibid.*, 46.

[5] *Reflections on the revolution in France, Select works*, II, 58.

for centuries lordship of the soil had been the title to authority—so buttressed, too, by law and custom, so rooted in current values, so sanctified by religion as the terrestrial analogy of God's cosmos: this was a resistant and perdurable thing. Under the impact of the economic changes of the pre-1640 century, it responded to new pressures, but was far from being displaced. In England its barriers had never been impassable, and the higher reaches of the status hierarchy were not quasi-castes, as the French *noblesse* tended to be. Loosened by inflation and lubricated by wealth, the structure became less rigid, circulation within it more frequent and rapid.

Contemporaries attributed the accelerated mobility to riches. Robert Burton's jaundiced comment was characteristic:

Thy great great great grandfather was a rich citizen, and then in all likelihood a usurer, a lawyer, and then . . . a Country Gentleman, and then he scraped it out of sheep.[1]

That the heralds of the College of Arms took bribes from aspirants to gentility in return for granting them coat armour contrived under the pretence of antiquity was well known.[2] The relentless social ambition of a climbing age effected a broadened definition of the gentleman. The trend was indicated by Smith's observation that 'gentlemen . . . be made good cheape in England'; and he did not consider the English way amiss that a man who 'can live idly . . . without manuall labour, and will beare the port, charge and countenaunce of a gentleman,' should be accounted one. Thus the university graduate, the student at the Inns of Court, the practitioner of a liberal profession, could style themselves gentlemen.[3] In England, wrote Thomas Fuller in 1642 in his essay on the yeoman, 'the temple of honour is bolted against none. . . .'[4]

What should be obvious, nevertheless, is that the new wine of riches flowed into the old bottles of status. For while the minimal condition for gentility became more easily attainable and the financial buoyancy of the age enabled families to rise in larger numbers, this did not alter the social framework. The status system remained intact and, as before, to belong to the higher orders meant to be or to become of a certain quality and to live in a certain way. The gentleman was still preeminently one 'extracted from ancient and worshipful parentage.' His ambit continued to be landed society. He displayed the hospitality, apparel, recreations of a gentleman and

[1] Robert Burton, *op. cit.*, II, 159.
[2] A. R. Wagner, *op. cit.*, 112.
[3] Sir Thomas Smith, *op. cit.*, 39–40.
[4] Thomas Fuller, *The holy state*, L., ed. 1840, 91.

married according to his rank.[1] It was incumbent on him to show a 'bountifuller liberalitie than others, and keepe about him idle servauntes, who shall doe nothing but waite upon him.'[2] In short, he exhibited the 'ancient characters of true Gentry,' and as the exemplar of an aristocratic ethos, was expected to be 'more affable, courteous, gently disposed . . . of a more magnanimous, heroical, and generous spirit' than the '*vulgus hominum*.'[3]

3

Where status constitutes the prevailing mode of stratification, there also exists a socially sanctioned inequality of living standards between the degrees of men as well as a great inequality of political rights and privileges. But these differentiations are able to survive because such a society tends to develop in its members the type of mentality appropriate to their place in the general scheme. The assumption is assiduously maintained that each order contributes to the welfare of the body politic and that the superior legitimately utilize the inferior for the benefit of all. No provision is made for any bargaining respecting status itself or the marked distinctions it entails. The lower orders, the ruled, must accept their subordination. For them there is virtually no middle course between complete acquiescence and outright rebellion.

Social criticism, of course, issues in abundance from preachers and publicists and is occasionally capable of penetrating insights. Almost invariably, however, its assumptions are fixed within the inherited scheme of inequality, which it seldom questions. Criticism reserves its severest condemnation for the defections of the respective estates from their duties and obligations to the commonweal and one another; it stigmatizes alike the insubordination of the low and the acquisitiveness of the high; if it recommends measures of reform besides the moralist's change of heart, their purpose is to enable the various estates to maintain their way of life within the customary system.[4]

In this profoundly unequal society—it is the society in which the sixteenth and seventeenth revolutions occurred—the power of political and constitutional initiative, of manoeuvre, of obstruction, is

---

[1] *Ibid.*, ch. XL, 'The true gentleman.'

[2] Sir Thomas Smith, *op. cit.*, 40.

[3] Robert Burton, *op. cit.*, II, 165.

[4] On social criticism and the defections of estates, cf. R. Mohl, *op. cit.*, chs. VII–IX and H. C. White, *Social criticism in popular religious literature of the sixteenth century*, N.Y., 1944. A sign of changing times in the sixteenth century was that the remedies proposed against prevailing evils often took the form of legislation.

largely restricted at the outset of any struggle to the superior orders. They are the community's governors under the prince; and if we speak henceforth of a governing or dominant class, we shall mean by this the persons who occupy the aristocratic and the privileged sectors of the status hierarchy. These possess in special measure an ascendancy over the rural countryside and its inhabitants; they hold the higher and more honorific offices bestowed by the prince; they are present with influential voice in the assemblies of estates which the prince convokes when he wishes to consult or tax his subjects;[1] their social and political importance entitles them to deference from even the wealthiest *bourgeoisie* and the magistrates of the town corporations.

Thus, when a conflict destined to rend the body politic occurs, its inception is inevitably dominated by the action, the manoeuvres, and the fissions of members of the governing class. Uprisings of the inferior and contemned, such as peasant insurrections, for instance, break out as a rule with sudden violence and are quickly suppressed by the united power of an affrighted society. In some of the greatest rebellions of the age, however, the throne-shaking movements that become protracted civil wars, nobilities and aristocracies take a leading part. These alone possess the authority to draw other orders of men into resistance against divinely appointed sovereigns.

In the French and Netherlands revolts of the sixteenth century, it was seigneurial Protestantism and the adherence of members of the high nobility, such as the princes of the house of Bourbon, the Montmorency family, and William of Orange, that made the Calvinist parties so formidable. The French Huguenot leaders, wrote the Venetian envoy, were 'tutti gentiluomini onorati, e di sangue nobile.' If the reformed churches provided the organizational discipline and sustaining faith in these struggles, the nobility provided the military cadres and political direction. It was no accident, either, that the Calvinists' justification of rebellion was commonly couched in aristocratic terms, placing in aristocracies of 'inferior magistrates' the right and duty to resist tyrannous kings.[2]

The phenomenon of governing class opposition was equally conspicuous in some of the mid-seventeenth-century rebellions. The

---

[1] The relations of assemblies of estates to the society of legalized privilege and inequality is discussed by O. Hintze, 'Typologie der ständischen Verfassungen des Abendlandes,' *Gesammelte Abhandlungen*, 3v., Leipzig, 1941, I.
[2] Cf. H. G. Koenigsberger, 'The organization of revolutionary parties in France and the Netherlands,' *Journal of modern history*, XXVII, 1 (1955) and R. M. Kingdon, 'The political resistance of the Calvinists in France and the Low Countries,' *Church history*, XXVII, 3 (1958). The dissemination of Calvinism within the French social structure is described in L. Romier, *Le royaume de Catherine de Médicis*, 2v., Paris, 1922.

revolt of Catalonia would have been impossible without the concurrence of the native aristocracy and its disaffection from the government in Madrid.[1] Members of the nobility appeared in the forefront of the Scottish Covenanters' resistance to Charles I.[2] In France, the initiators and chiefs of the Fronde were officials of the King's sovereign courts, princes of the blood, and persons belonging to the highest aristocracy.[3] It has been shown as well that French peasant outbreaks of the earlier seventeenth century were frequently inspired by local officials and noblemen; the latter were able to instigate a resistance of diverse strata to the fiscality of the royal regime.[4]

So, too, *mutatis mutandis*, the case was in England. The fundamental cleavage of the decades before the civil war was that which opened *within* the dominant class between the crown and its adherents on the one side, and its opponents on the other. Around this widening split, all the various conflicts in the kingdom gradually became polarized. The antagonism was thus not a lateral one between the orders of society; it was vertical, by degrees dividing the peerage, the gentry and the merchant oligarchies of the towns. At last it drew in also the unprivileged and normally inarticulate mass of men.

As the cleavage grew, the opposing sides acquired names. They began to be called the Court and the Country. The appearance of these terms was of great symptomatic importance. It was a sign of recognition by politically conscious Englishmen of the bitter struggle developing in their midst. It was a sign as well of the progressive deterioration of the unity of the governing class around the crown.

In the strife of the Court and the Country—if diffuse, yet real, not fictitious, collectivities—the English revolution had its origins. And the names themselves are of moment. For when understood they reveal to us how the contemporary mind saw the schism that completely transformed public life between Queen Elizabeth's death and the meeting of the Long Parliament. We shall therefore consider the evolution and meaning of this political terminology, in order that we may then pass in the next chapters to an account of the substance of what it represented.

[1] J. H. Elliott, *The revolt of the Catalans*, 485–6.
[2] S. R. Gardiner, *History*, VII, 304–5, 313.
[3] E. Kossmann, *La Fronde*, chs. II, V.
[4] Cf. R. Mousnier, 'Recherches sur les soulèvements populaires en France avant la Fronde,' *Revue d'histoire moderne et contemporaine*, V (1958). This is a critique of B. Porchnev, *Les soulèvements populaires en France de 1623 à 1648* (Moscow, 1948) Paris, 1963. See on the controversy concerning these risings the review by M. Prestwich, *E.H.R.*, LXXXI, 320 (1966), 565–72.

To begin with the Country: this was the label most commonly applied to the opposition to the crown before the civil war.[1] Occasionally other terms, such as 'patriots' and 'parliamentarians,' were employed,[2] but 'Country' was becoming current in the 1620s and appears to have been in fairly wide use by the commencement of Charles I's reign.[3] Its emergence reflected the hardening of political differences in these final years of King James and the first of his son. A coalescence of several meanings with subtle overtones and connotations, the name throws a flood of light on the opposition movement's self-conception and the impression it made on the political scene.

The oldest use of the word, dating apparently from the fourteenth century, signified 'county,' and it continued to retain this sense for centuries. Somewhat later, it acquired the further meaning of rural and distant from cities and courts, instances of which occur from the sixteenth century on.[4]

By Queen Elizabeth's time, its meaning as 'county' was becoming fused—doubtless because of the rapid development of parliament at this period—with the general idea of representation and the public interest. Members of the Commons now talked of their duty to their 'Countries' or 'Country.' Thus, when the Privy Council sequestered Strickland in 1571 for his conduct in the House, it was protested 'in regard of the Country, which was not to be wronged,' the debarred member being not a private person but the representative of a multitude. In the monopolies debate of 1601, a member referred to the heavy grievances suffered by the 'Town and Country for which I serve. . . .' When a subsidy was under consideration in 1593, the poverty of 'the Country' was adduced, and a member declared, '. . . our Countries are poor, and we must respect them that sent us hither.'[5] In 1621, Edward Alford, one of the most vocal of the

---

[1] Cf. also P. Zagorin, 'The Court and the Country: a note on political terminology in the earlier seventeenth century', *E.H.R.*, LXXVII, 303 (1962).

[2] For 'patriots,' cf., e.g., the description of Sir Henry Neville's conduct in the parliament of 1610, when he was said to have 'ranged himself with those Patriots that were accounted of a contrary faction to the Courtiers . . .', *H.M.C. Buccleuch*, I, 102. 'Parliamentarians'—'*li parlamentarii*'—occurs frequently in the Venetian despatches, e.g., *C.S.P.V. 1623–25*, 568, 574, ibid., *1625–26*, 298, 425.

[3] The currency of 'Country' was first pointed out by W. Notestein, 'The winning of the initiative by the House of Commons,' *Proceedings of the British Academy*, XI, 1924–25, 152n. Cf. also D. H. Willson, *The privy councillors in the House of Commons*, Minneapolis, 1940, 122–3.

[4] *Oxford English dictionary*, s.v., 'Country.'

[5] S. D'Ewes, *A compleat journal of the . . . House of Commons throughout the*

Country opposition, complained that parliament 'had given away our two subsidies and donne no good for our Countrie. . . .'[1] Four years later, a tax proposal in Charles's first parliament was criticized, said a news writer, 'by three or four of the principall speakers who usually stand stiffest for the country. . . .'[2]

Besides the meanings already illustrated, there was also another conception, very familiar in the seventeenth century, of the Country as a mode of existence to be favourably contrasted with the Court. It was implied, for instance, in a remark of the third earl of Southampton, a peer who had gained sad experience of courts as the friend and fellow conspirator of the earl of Essex and who belonged to the opposition in the parliament of 1621. He wrote from his mansion at Titchfield in December 1623:

I have been wholy a country man and seldom seen either the Court or London. . . . In this life I have found so much quiet and content, that I thinke I should hardly ever brooke any other; sure I am I envy none.[3]

Calidore in *The Faerie Queene* expressed the same feeling when he resolved to

> *set his rest amongst the rusticke sort*
> *Rather than hunt still after shadowes vaine*
> *Of courtly favour fed with light report*
> *Of every blast. . . .*[4]

An amusing tract by Nicholas Breton, *The Court and Country* (1618) treated this theme by comparing the two modes of life.[5] Breton, of course, had no intimate knowledge of courts, and his standpoint was solidly burgher rather than aristocratic. He elaborated, however, a conception of the country as the symbol of simplicity and wholesome pleasures based on religion and respect for tradition. Against this he set the court with its sophistication and search for novelty, its moral and financial dangers. There was no suggestion in

[1] *Commons debates 1621*, ed. W. Notestein, F. Relf, H. Simpson, 7v., New Haven, 1935, III, 435n.

[2] *Commons debates in 1625*, ed. S. R. Gardiner, *Camden society*, n.s., 1873, 155–6.

[3] C. C. Stopes, *The life of Henry, third earl of Southampton*, Cambridge, 1922, 449.

[4] Book VI, canto x, 2.

[5] Printed in *Inedited tracts, Roxburghe library*, 1868.

---

whole reign of Queen Elizabeth, 2nd ed., L., 1693, 175, 645, 646, 490, 491; cf. L. F. Brown, 'Ideas of representation from Elizabeth to Charles II,' *Journal of modern history*, XI, I (1939).

Breton's writing that the two might also stand for opposed political positions, but such a view was already emerging in parliamentary affairs.

There the types of Court and Country first represented the distinction between men officially connected with the Court and royal government and private members not resident in the capital. In 1587, a Puritan member zealous for reformation chided the privy councillors in the Commons for their lack of initiative on this important subject and told them:

> . . . *if any of the inferior sort here amongst us do happen in some zeal to overstrain himself, surely ye that are honorable . . . ought in equity to bear with them, because the fault is in yourselves. . . . It is wondered at . . . that simple men of the country should be so forward; and it doth amaze us in the country that wise men of the Court should be so backward. . . . Is it fault in a private man to be too busy and can it be excused in a Councillor to be too sleepy?*[1]

By the middle years of James I's reign, the unconnected member had passed through a metamorphosis. He now appeared as the honest, disinterested country gentleman, an ideal aura about him. When the privy councillors preparing for the parliament of 1621 were considering how to forestall a general outcry against monopolies, they decided that

> *the most convenient way will be, if some grave and discreet gentlemen of the country, such as have least relation to the court, make at fit times some modest motions touching the same. . . .*[2]

A speaker in the parliament of 1625 described himself as 'neither Courtier nor Lawyer but a plaine Countrey Gentleman;' apparently this description was held to be a sure warrant of a man's candour and lack of prejudice.[3] In 1626, a paper of advice drawn up by Sir Dudley Digges on the King's relations with parliament told Charles to put his trust in these members:

> . . . *if Your Majesties Grave Counsellours, such as are reverenced for their worth, shall make known your engagements and your wants, the honest Countrie knights . . . will soone shew their Affections. . . .*[4]

---

[1] Cited in J. E. Neale, *Elizabeth I and her parliaments 1584–1601*, L., 1957, 150.
[2] F. Bacon, *Works*, XIV, 146.
[3] *Commons debates in 1625*, 158. The speaker was the oppositionist, Sir Robert Phelips.
[4] P.R.O. S.P. 16/19, no. 107.

The Court and the Country

All these intimations and aspects of 'Country' were closely inter-woven in its use as the name of the opposition. It referred at one and the same time both to those who on grounds of public interest actively resisted the Court and those who, lacking any connection with the Court, would stand for their 'Country.' Sir John Eliot, a leader of the Country, employed it indiscriminately in both senses. Writing of a debate in the Commons he declared that '. . . it was begun by a gentleman of the Countrie . . . unexpected to the Cour-tiers. . . .'; and alluding to the small attendance in the House on a certain occasion, he remarked, 'ther were hardlie threescore in the house, & of these, countrimen not the most.' His description of the parliament of 1625 contrasted the 'Courtiers' with the 'Countrie,' the antagonists, as he conceived it, in the political struggle.[1]

Evidently Eliot's view was widespread, for in the parliament of 1626 Sir George Goring

tooke exception how the name of Courtyer was a woyrd of faccion, and how he thought that Courtyers were as honest men as any . . . in the house and did interest themselves as much in the good of the State.'[2]

In 1629, the Chancellor of the Duchy, Sir Humphrey May, was provoked into telling the House, 'I wish we heare noe more of the distinction between Courtiers and country gentlemen . . .'[3]

In similar fashion, peers opposed to the King were sometimes known as 'country lords.' Thus did Lord Robartes call them, who was of their number.[4] Lord Savile, an oppositionist who went over to the Court, was regretfully spoken of as 'one of the stoutest Lords in all England for the countrey . . . at first. . . .'[5] The oppositionist, Sir Anthony Weldon, complained of the courtiers' insolence 'to any Country Nobleman, that was not in the Court favour.'[6] A sym-pathetic portrait of the first Lord Spencer, an opposition peer whose wealth came from sheep, depicted him as one that

made the Countrey a vertuous Court, where his Fields and Flockes broughte him more calme and happie contentment, than the various and mutable dispensations of a Court. . . . and when he was called to the

---

[1] Sir J. Eliot, *Negotium posterorum*, ed. A. Grosart, 2v., p.p., 1881, I, 75, 118, II, 49.
[2] Cited in D. H. Willson, *op. cit.*, 213n.
[3] *Commons debates, 1629*, ed. W. Notestein and F. Relf, Minneapolis, 1921, 236.
[4] J. L. Sanford, *Studies and illustrations of the Great Rebellion*, L., 1858, 496.
[5] R. Baillie, *Letters and journals*, ed. D. Laing, 3v., *Bannatyne Club*, 1841, I, 348.
[6] Cited in G. E. Aylmer, *The King's servants*, L., 1961, 463.

Senate, was more vigilant to keep the Peoples Liberties from being a prey to the incroaching power of Monarchy, than his harmless and tender Lambs from Foxes and ravenous Creatures.[1]

The term, 'Country,' thus suggested that the men it designated were persons of public spirit, unmoved by private interest, untainted by court influence and corruption—representatives, in short, of the highest good of their local communities and the nation in whose interest they, and they only, acted. It described those members of parliament who believed that

being chosen for the Country, they are to be all for the Country, for the Liberty of the Subject, for the freedome of Speech, & to gain as much and as many Priviledges for the Subject from the King, as is possible. And if they stand stiffely out in the deniall of Subsidies, to save their owne & their Countries purses, then they are excellent Patriots, good Commonwealthsmen, they have well & faithfully discharg'd the trust reposed in them by their City or Country.[2]

Between men of this political tendency and the court only hostility could prevail. Hence, according to Thomas Fuller, 'The country hath constantly a blessing for those for whom the court hath a curse.'[3] Equally, it was the conviction of the political writer, Henry Parker, that '. . . we have ever found enmity and antipathy betwixt the Court and the country. . . .'[4] Clarendon often expressed his awareness of the differences between the two, and when narrating his peaceful life before the Long Parliament, he wrote of himself: 'As he had . . . many friends in court, so he was not less acceptable to many great persons in the country, who least regarded the court, and were least esteemed by it. . . .'[5]

But despite the political significance of the name, it cannot be likened with any accuracy to a modern party title, any more than those associated in or related to the Country can be supposed to have constituted a party in the modern sense. A man could be 'of the Country,' or 'for the Country,' but nowhere at this period is the

[1] Arthur Wilson, *The history of Great Britain*, 1653, 162–3.
[2] [Anon.], *A true presentation of forepast parliaments*, 1629, B. M. Lansdowne, 213, f. 162.
[3] *The church history of Britain*, 1655, ed. J. Nichols, 3v., L., 1842, III, 350. This remark appears under the year 1627, in Fuller's account of Archbishop Abbott, whose 'averseness to . . . court-designs' incurred the King's displeasure.
[4] Henry Parker, *Observations upon some of his majesties late answers and expresses*, 2nd ed., 1642, 11.
[5] *Life*, 931.

expression, 'country party,' met with, such as came into use later in the century during the reign of Charles II.[1] The word was both vaguer and less determinate than a modern party name and far more comprehensive in its possible reference. Indeed, its pronounced implication of general interest, and the absence of any explicit association with the idea of party, show how reluctant the men of the time still were to acknowledge the legitimacy of self-constituted organizations coming into being to pursue political ends of their own.[2] Had Eliot, Pym, Phelips, or other opposition leaders in parliament been willing to concede that the Country was anything like a party at all, it could only have been in the exalted sense laid down many years later by Lord Bolingbroke when he stated that

A country party must be authorized by the voice of the country. It must be formed on principles of common interest. It cannot be united and maintained on the particular prejudices . . . or . . . particular interests of any set of men whatsoever. It is the nation, speaking and acting in the discourse and conduct of particular men. . . .[3]

'Court,' the term for the crown's adherents, may be dealt with quite summarily. It was the customary collective designation of the monarch, his residence, council, officials, and courtiers.[4] But coupled as a label with Country, it meant that the King, his councillors, officials, and supporters had become the recognized partisans in a political struggle. Thus, Sir Henry Spelman, the great antiquarian, disclaimed any intention of studying the calamitous history of the parliaments of his own time lest the results should 'displease both Court and Country. . . .'[5] In 1640, a Kentish candidate for election to the Short Parliament was warned that a rival '. . . hath endeavoured . . . to poyson the good opinion the Country hath of you, by professinge . . . howe diligent & eager a servant you were for the Court. . . .'[6] Lord Digby declared after the outbreak of the civil war that he had hoped

[1] Cf. G. Burnet, *History of my own time*, pt. I, *The reign of Charles II*, ed. O. Airy, 2v., Oxford, 1897, I, 489, II, 82n.; H. C. Foxcroft, *A supplement to Burnet's history*, Oxford, 1902, 99n., 151, 258; D. Ogg, *England in the reign of Charles II*, 2v., 2nd ed., Oxford, 1955, II, 477, 526–7. On the persistence of Court and Country as political divisions, cf. K. Feiling, *History of the Tory party 1660–1714*, Oxford, 1924, 145, 277.
[2] Cf. C. Robbins, 'Discordant parties: a study of the acceptance of parties by Englishmen,' *Political science quarterly*, LXXIII, 4 (1958).
[3] Lord Bolingbroke, *A dissertation on parties*, Works, 5v., L., 1754, II, 68.
[4] *Oxford English dictionary*, s.v., 'Court.'
[5] Cited in J. G. Pocock, *The ancient constitution and the feudal law*, Cambridge, 1957, 120–1.
[6] Sir John Sedley to Sir Edward Dering, B. M. Stowe 743, f. 140.

for a reconciliation which would make 'The Court and the Country ... to be all of a piece. ...'[1] Related to 'Court' was 'courtier,' mentioned by Pym and Eliot in connection with parliamentary affairs with the implication that the defenders of royal policy were dependents of the crown.[2] Another less frequent term for the crown's supporters was 'royalist,' used as early as 1612 by Francis Bacon,[3] and from time to time also in the Venetian dispatches.[4]

The appearance of *Court* and *Country* as political descriptions signalized the enlarging conflict within the upper ranks of English society. It meant that the organic body politic of the sixteenth century was in process of dissolution and that the bonds which had so intimately united the prince and his subjects in the governing class were falling away. No longer could the King and Court stand as the highest unchallenged expression of an integral authority. Royal power was forced into a certain isolation when it took shape as the Court, one side of the deepening division in political and public life. At the same time, the vagueness and imprecision of 'Court' and 'Country' reflected the transitional character of political affairs from the 1620s onwards, as well as the loose and somewhat unstable composition of the antagonistic groupings. But a new relationship of power in the state was in prospect. What Lord Bolingbroke said of a country party was soon to come to pass:

... whenever such a party finds it difficult to prevail, our constitution is in danger; and when they find it impossible, our constitution must in fact be altered.[5]

[1] *The Lord George Digbie's apologie*, 1643, 11.
[2] Sir John Eliot, *op. cit.*, I, 75, II, 49; *Commons debates 1621*, IV, 281.
[3] Bacon to King James, May 1612: '... I was a perfect and peremptory royalist, yet ... never one hour out of credit with the lower house. ...', *Works*, XI, 280. The word also occurs in the same connection in the first Lord Brooke's *Life of ... Sir Philip Sidney, Works*, 4v., ed. A. Grosart, p.p., 1870, IV, 187, which was written in James's reign.
[4] *C.S.P.V. 1628–29*, 580; *ibid., 1632–36*, 256 ('*Realisti*').
[5] *Op. cit.*, II, 66.

3

The Court

In an age of personal monarchy, when the prince ruled as well as reigned and his favour conferred riches or power, all roads of advancement led to the Court. The Court was a lottery of fortune. There, ambition might achieve its furthest ends and disaster, political and financial, overwhelm the unlucky.

Kingship was not conceived merely abstractly. It was incarnated in the ruler's person, the sun whose warming rays fructified the body politic. 'The fountain of honour is the king,' wrote Bacon, 'and the access to his person continueth honour in life, and to be banished from his presence is one of the greatest eclipses of honour that can be.'[1] The sovereign possessed a sacral character. 'Ye are Gods,'—so said the Scripture of kings, an image James I liked to invoke and on which the seventeenth century, pondering its meaning, reared an imposing structure of exegesis and commentary.[2] The *mystique* of kingship was expounded in the thought of the theologian and the lawyer. It was blazoned forth with a deep and solemn pomp in the coronation rite. It was vivified in the services of the church in the prayers and homilies. Rebellion was the compound of all sins, civil war the worst of evils.[3] The King's touch could cure, so that common men hastened to his presence to beseech the mysterious gift. On Good Friday 1639, despite the gathering wave of resistance to Charles I's rule, two hundred persons attended on him at York Cathedral to receive his touch.[4] Regality was the sustaining principle of order in the state, the prince's fitness to govern the condition of its peace and well-being. What the prince did, who were the recipients of his

[1] Cited in F. H. Anderson, *Francis Bacon*, Los Angeles, 1962, 46.
[2] Psalm 82.6; cf. *The political works of James I*, ed. C. H. McIlwain, Cambridge, 1918, 307.
[3] Cf. Homily XXI, 'Against disobedience and wilful rebellion,' ed. 1623, reprinted in *Certain sermons or homilies*, Oxford, 1840. Article XXXV of the Thirty-nine Articles authorized the homilies to be read in the churches. Canon XLVI of the Canons of 1604 required them to be read on any Sunday when there was no sermon.
[4] F. Drake, *Eboracum*, 2v., ed. 1788, I, 156.

bounty or ill will, 'who loses and who wins; who's in, who's out;'[1]—
these topics provided the talk and cynosure of the body politic.

A throng of ministers, courtiers, officials, and servants belonged to
the Court, for the latter in the broadest sense embraced all the organs
of central and regional government, all who had to do with the
ceremonial position of the monarch as the fountain of honour and
head of his people, and all who served him as the greatest landowner
and chief feudal lord of the realm. Thus, the Privy Council, the
secretaries of state with their staff, the diplomatic personnel, and
great departments such as the Exchequer and Court of Wards were
part of the Court; so were the courts of common law and equity and
the prerogative tribunals—the Star Chamber and the High Commission; so too were the King's household and the households of the
Queen and the Prince of Wales. Beyond the seat of government at
London, the Court swept out to include officials in every area of the
kingdom: receivers of royal revenue and feodaries of the Court of
Wards in the counties; persons connected with the Admiralty, the
customs, the Duchy of Lancaster, the Councils of the North and in
Wales; keepers and surveyors, constables, stewards, and under-officers
of royal castles, manors, and forests. All these, in the capital and in the
countryside, were the ministers, officials, and servants of the prince,
receiving by his authority the fees and perquisites of their places.[2]

What was *not* part of the Court was the structure of county
government. The sheriffs, the justices appointed to the commission
of the peace, the lords lieutenants and their deputies, were unpaid
officers of the crown. The men serving these places were the more
important members of the governing class for whom the county was
a natural sphere of public activity. They undertook their functions as
a duty to prince and community and because of the prestige associated with such offices in landed society. Some of the incumbents
might also, of course, be of the Court: the lords lieutenants, for
instance, were usually peers or privy councillors, like Viscount
Wentworth, who in the 1630s was at the same time President of the
Council of the North, Lord Deputy of Ireland, and lord lieutenant of
Yorkshire.[3] On the county notables and municipal magistracies
depended local administration, civil and military, and the execution
of the crown's mandates.[4]

[1] *King Lear*, V, 3, 1. 15.
[2] Cf. the account of the personnel of governmental institutions at the time
of Charles I by G. E. Aylmer, *The King's servants*, ch. 2.
[3] Cf. Wentworth's letter to his deputy lieutenants of Yorkshire, W. Knowler,
The letters and dispatches of the earl of Strafforde, 2v., L., 1739, II, 284–5.
[4] Cf. the accounts of the process and personnel of county government by
W. B. Willcox, *Gloucestershire . . . 1590–1640*, New Haven, 1940 and T. G.
Barnes, *Somerset 1625–1640*, Cambridge, 1961.

The Court and the Country

The seat of a royal power so essentially personal in its nature and so frequently capricious in its operation, the Court was a scene of ceaseless competition for the prizes obtainable by the favour of the King and those who possessed his confidence.[1] Hobbes's analysis of human nature might have been taken thence, where life was a race and envy, joy, and sorrow the passions of the participants as they advanced or fell behind in the contest. The privy councillors advised the ruler in an individual capacity, not as a body endowed with a common voice. At the pinnacle of the Court, they were themselves rivals for the high offices and grants that would increase their wealth and multiply the suitors who crowded their doors. They formed factions that might be associated with differences of policy, but whose principal aim was to extend their influence over the King and form an exclusive channel for the receipt and distribution of the ensuing rewards.

Almost everything at the Court was done by means of patronage and intermediaries. This was the normal accompaniment both of the concentration of personal power in the monarch and of the differentiation and subordination of ranks in society at large. Patronage existed not only in the Court but in the relations between the more and the less powerful everywhere. Government was not conducted by an administrative bureaucracy trained in loyalty to an abstract state, discharging its functions in conformity with objective norms, and recruited according to fixed and impersonal criteria of competence. The King exercised his authority through such instruments as he pleased. To obtain a favourable decision in any business, much depended on the propitiation and support of those with influence. It was essential to gain the countenance of ministers, courtiers, favourite, or of persons near to them.

Moreover, the prevalence of status as the mode of stratification entailed the result that an acknowledged personal dependence should exist between those in authority and their inferiors. At a remoter time, such dependence had commonly rested on a tenurial basis; later, in the decaying feudalism of the fifteenth century, it took the form of good lordship and retainership.[2] By the end of the sixteenth century, though the forms of dependence were much vaguer, the latter still remained a potent factor. It now manifested itself as patronage and influence. Persons desiring success in a suit or advancement attached themselves to men of rank in order to obtain their recommendation. 'The gentleman that shall present these lines'—so went a letter in 1637 from the earl of Dorset to the Lord Deputy of

[1] Cf. J. E. Neale, 'The Elizabethan political scene,' *Proceedings of the British Academy*, XXXIV, 1948.
[2] Cf. W. H. Dunham, *Lord Hastings' indentured retainers*, New Haven, 1955.

Ireland, Viscount Wentworth, craving the latter's favour for a friend
—'... is the descendant of a family that hath for three descents
depended on mine. His father, grandfather and now himselfe have
ever been owned by us ... more out of there own inclination then any
benefitt ... myself be able to deserve.'[1] In this way, clients and
followings would form around the great and the powerful. A peer or
great official who controlled some parliamentary seats might obtain a
small following as a result. A landlord of broad possessions with
places of profit to grant in the administration of his estates might
have numerous dependents in his neighbourhood, while his influence
could extend over scores or even hundreds of freeholders. A minister
would always be sought out by petitioners wanting his backing. In
using their influence on behalf of dependents, men in great place
enhanced their own standing and proclaimed the advantage their
good will conferred.[2]

Inevitably, the nature of Court life evoked ambivalent attitudes in
all who had to do with it. A veteran courtier dismissed from the
service of the Prince of Wales, the future Charles II, declared, 'Were
I to live a thousand years I would never sett my foott within a court
againe, for there is nothing in itt butt flattery and falshood.'[3] Dependence frequently led to humiliation and patient merit was often
spurned. At the age of forty-six, Francis Bacon, still unsuccessful in
his pursuit of office, petitioned his cousin, the earl of Salisbury,
James I's chief minister, for the Solicitor's place—though he knew,
he said, 'how mean a thing I stand for. ... For ... it is not the thing
it hath been.' He reminded Salisbury of his hopes, 'your Lordship
being pleased to tell me, during the course of my last service, that you
would raise me; and that when you had resolved to raise a man, you
were more careful of him than himself. ...' Bacon obtained his
desire, but after Salisbury's death, he affirmed that his relation to the
minister had been that of 'a hawk tied to another's fist, that mought
sometimes bait and proffer but could never fly.'[4]

The 'aulical faculty' requisite to success in the Court came far short
of the standard of conduct demanded by a moralist. Sir Robert
Naunton, a cold-eyed observer of court ways, Master of the Wards
under James and Charles, told of the saying of one of Elizabeth's

[1] Strafford MSS., v. 22, no. 136.
[2] On the role of patronage under Elizabeth and in the early Stuart period,
cf. J. E. Neale, 'The Elizabethan political scene,' *loc. cit.*; W. T. MacCaffrey,
'Place and patronage in Elizabeth politics,' *Elizabethan government and
society*, ed. S. T. Bindoff, J. Hurstfield, and C. Williams, L., 1961; D.
Mathew, *The social structure in Caroline England*, Oxford, 1948, 4–6.
[3] *The autobiography of Anne, Lady Halkett*, ed. J. G. Nichols, *Camden
society*, n.s., XIII, 1875, 30. The remark was made by Will Murray.
[4] *Works*, X, 296–7, XI, 279.

peers '(and it did him no good), That he was none of the *Reptilia*, intimating that he could not creep on the ground, and that the Court was not his element.' Another courtier, an unfortunate Deputy of Ireland, was 'a person who loved to stand too much alone, and on his own legges . . . a fault . . . incompatible with the wayes of Court and favour.'[1] Elizabeth's favourite, the earl of Leicester, was noted by Sir Henry Wotton, another Jacobean commentator on court practices, to be 'a great Artizan of Court,' one who did 'nothing by chance nor much by affection.'[2] Bacon's essays contained sombre reflections on the nature of courtly advancement. 'All rising to great place,' he wrote, 'is by a winding stair. . . .' The rising

is laborious . . . and it is sometimes base; and by indignities men come to dignities. The standing is slippery, and the regress is either a downfall, or at least an eclipse, which is a melancholy thing.[3]

Although tradition idealized the courtier-type as the incarnation of high virtues, the reality was commonly otherwise.[4] Sir John Harington, having spent years in a frustrated quest for the prizes of courtiership under Elizabeth and James, held that 'He that thryveth in a Courte must put halfe his honestie under his bonnet. . . .'[5] The poet, Wither, an opposition sympathizer, wrote in 1628:

> *The Court is fraught with bribery, with hate,*
> *With envie, lust, ambition, and debate;*
> *With fawnings, with fantasticke imitation,*
> *With shamefull sloth, and base dissimulation.*
> *True Virtue's almost quite exiled thence. . . .*[6]

A treatise on courts composed in the reign of Charles I pictured the courtier as driven by ambition and avarice to

contrive strange plotts, basely serve others turnes and use all . . . artifices to compasse his projects; and this is the reason hee putte himselfe to the sea of the court, hoping by that voyage to gett the golden

---

[1] Sir R. Naunton, *Fragmenta regalia*, 1641, *Harleian miscellany*, 12v., L., ed. 1811, V, 137, 140.
[2] Sir H. Wotton, *A parallel betweene Robert, late earle of Essex, and George, late duke of Buckingham, Reliquiae Wottonianae*, 3rd ed., L., 1672, 162.
[3] 'Of great place.' Cf. also the essays, 'Of followers and friends' and 'Of suitors.'
[4] Cf. the account of the literature of English courtiership in J. E. Mason, *Gentlefolk in the making*, Philadelphia, 1935, ch. VII.
[5] *Nugae antiquae*, ed. H. Harington, 3v., L., 1779, II, 153.
[6] G. Wither, *Britain's remembrancer*, 1628, 195–6.

Peru, and to finde out a Magelan advancement. . . . There is noe
Machiavilian politie which he diveth not into . . . nor sordid actions
which he doth not accomplish. . . . [Courtiers] nourishe Oppositions and
factions to make the pathe more facill for their endes. . . . Theire Motto
is; Qui nescit dissimulare nescit vivere. . . .[1]

The Court was not known for loyalty or disinterested friendship.
'. . . a cashiered Courtier,' said Bishop Williams after Charles I
dismissed him as Lord Keeper, 'is an Almanack of the last Year,
remembered by nothing but the great Eclipse.'[2] The declension of a
courtier or minister was the signal of an imminent redistribution of
places of profit. On the disgrace of the earl of Somerset, King James's
favourite, Viscount Lisle, commander of the English garrison at
Flushing, was informed by a dependent, 'Undoubtedly their will be
by this man's fall manye good things in his Matys. guifte againe. I
beseache your Lordship take this Occation . . . to move for sumthing
for me unto his Maty.' Naturally, the author of this request hoped
too that 'this great man's fall will rayse your Lordship and some of
your nobell friendes to your just and worthye demerits. . . .'[3]

Despite the dangers of the Court, every man of rank understood
the importance of having good connections there. Lord Burghley
advised his son, Robert:

Be sure to keep some great man thy friend, but trouble him not for
trifles. Compliment him often with many, yet small gifts, & of little
charge. And if thou hast cause to bestow any great gratuity, let it be
something which may be daily in sight. Otherwise, in this ambitious age,
thou shalt remain like a hop without a pole, live in obscurity, & be made
a foot-ball for every insulting companion to spurn at.[4]

Widely circulated, Burghley's precept was frequently cited by
aristocratic fathers in the seventeenth century. Sir John Holles, later
earl of Clare, addressed the same counsel to his heir, as did the earl
of Derby, who added, however, that 'Court friendship is a cable that
in storms is ever cut.' The chief thing, he asserted, was that his heir
should look well to his estate: for 'though a friend at court be . . .
better than a penny in the purse, yett keepe your owne estate & a

---

[1] Edward Payton, *A discours of Court and courtiers*, 1633–4, B. M. Harl.
3364, ff. 29–30. Dedicated to the young duke of Lennox, this writing preserves, despite its strictures, the idealistic tradition of courtier literature.
[2] J. Hacket, *Scrinia reserata*, L., 1693, pt. II, 26.
[3] *H.M.C. De L'Isle and Dudley*, V, 340, 344 (Sir John Throckmorton to Lord
Lisle, Nov. 1615).
[4] Printed in F. Peck, *Desiderata curiosa*, L., ed. 1779, Bk. I, 49.

penny to spare, & you will create friends in court or countrey at any time.'[1] The earl of Huntingdon recommended his son to go to the Court for brief visits no more than once or twice yearly: 'I should be sorry that you should like a court life too well, for it is but a *splendida miseria. . . .*'[2]

If some got wealth in the Court, others squandered it. Viscount Wentworth impressed his youthful nephew and ward, Sir William Savile, with the financial risks to be run there:

. . . think not of putting yourself into Court before you be thirty years of Age at least, till your Judgment be so awakened, as that you may be able to discover and put aside such Trains, as will always infallibly be laid there for Men of great Fortunes, by a Company of Flesh Flies, that ever buzze up and downe the Palaces of Princes; and this let me tell you, I have seen many men of great Estates come young thither and spend all, but did I never see a good Estate prosper amongst them that put itself forward before the Master had an Experience and Knowledge how to husband and keep it. . . .[3]

A Court life, often extremely costly, could make deep inroads on a man's fortune. The Kentish baronet, Sir William Twysden, left his son a heavily encumbered inheritance because of his extravagant expenditure at Court.[4] The earl of Carlisle, another of James I's favourites, had tasted the royal bounty to the extent of many thousand pounds; yet so great was his outlay that in 1622 he complained that he could not subsist without further help from the King. At his death in 1636 his debts were said to exceed £120,000.[5] The pursuit of office put the earl of Newcastle into debt for £40,000. In 1633 he told Wentworth that debt and disappointment made him resolve to press his suit no longer: 'It is better to give over in tyme wth some losse than lose all. . . .'[6] The position and success of Court luminaries, like that of the glittering figures in the cinema capitals of the twentieth century, depended so much on spectacular spending and dazzling consumption that men of large inherited estates might

---

[1] *The letterbook of Sir John Holles, H.M.C. Portland*, IX, 6; *Stanley papers*, pt. iii, *Chetham society*, LXX, 1867, 45; F. Peck, *op. cit.*, Bk. XI, 443.
[2] *H.M.C. Hastings*, IV, 333, II, 70–1.
[3] *The earl of Strafforde's letters*, I, 169–70.
[4] F. W. Jessup, *Sir Roger Twysden*, L., 1965, 11–12, 19–21.
[5] Carlisle, then still Viscount Doncaster, to Buckingham, B.M. Harl. 1581, ff. 335–8; *C.S.P.V. 1632–36*, 558.
[6] *The earl of Strafforde's letters*, I, 101–2; G. E. Cokayne, *Complete peerage*, rev. ed., 13v., L., 1910–49, *s.v.*, 'Newcastle, 1st earl.' In 1638 the earl's ambition was finally gratified when the King appointed him governor of the Prince of Wales.

well think it prudent not to venture themselves in the Court's dangerous waters.[1]

Beyond all these considerations, great rising and an eminent career in the Court were attended by envy, hatred, and faction. 'Happy the favourite,' wrote Fuller, 'that is raised without the ruin of another.'[2] The actors on the Stuart political scene long retained the memory of the rivalry between the Essex and Cecil factions and of Essex's fall and execution at the setting of Queen Elizabeth's reign. The reigns of James and Charles likewise witnessed the disgrace of such Court personages as the earls of Somerset and Suffolk, Bacon, and Bishop Williams, whose calamity pointed up the perils incident to high office. The weightiest words on the subject were those Sir Edward Stanhope addressed in intimate friendship to Viscount Wentworth, vainly imploring the nobleman not to accept the Irish deputyship then dangling before him. 'How manye men,' Stanhope warned,

> ... *have endeavored to sease on the hyghest and most honorable places in the state, and having reached their desiered prey, before they could feed enough to satisfye their exorbitant appetites, have miserably fallen ... into disgrace and infamye. ... How many have purchased their owne ruin att a deare rate ... by contracting for the greate and burthensom offices of the Kingdom? ... How many greate officers in our times made, in our times unmayde agayne. ... Som thrust out by heade and shoulders, some led out ... som for pleasing others, som for being corrupt, som for integritye ... soe have greate offices bin purged, and the officers, som with detestation and infamye eiected, som like excrements that every man avoyds both sight and sence of. ... And yet how many competitors have striven whoe shall succeede, and then the next that fills itt is the next (before warme in itt) that leaves itt for another.*[3]

This foreboding letter was penned in 1631. Ten years later, with the spectacle of Wentworth's disastrous end before his eyes, Stanhope could only have exclaimed, 'O my prophetic soul!'

2

The Court's resources for gratifying the hope of preferment were of diverse kinds. They ranged from the bestowal of titles and places of

[1] This point has been stressed by M. Finch, *Five Northamptonshire families*, 63.
[2] T. Fuller, *op. cit.*, LXVI, 'The favourite.'
[3] P. Zagorin, 'Sir Edward Stanhope's advice to Thomas Wentworth, Viscount Wentworth, concerning the deputyship of Ireland: an unpublished letter of 1631,' *Historical journal*, VII, 2 (1964), 316–17.

honour, through rewards of land or money, grants of valuable fiscal privileges under the royal prerogative, such as monopolies and customs farms, miscellaneous rights in the crown's gift that could be a source of profit to their recipients, and appointment to office. The commonest aim, however, of the seeker after advancement was office, which might also afford access to other benefits obtainable in the Court. We shall therefore confine our attention to the nature and significance of office.[1] In particular, we shall wish to consider how far officials constituted a *bloc* committed to the support of the King's power and whether they were a body socially distinct from men without Court affiliation.

The fundamental feature determining the nature of office in the seventeenth century was that the latter was usually a species of property which belonged to its occupant in the same way as did his land. This characteristic derived from feudal times, when public functions of all sorts were granted out to private men as property to be held on certain terms. Despite the lapse of centuries, offices preserved this peculiarity. Both they and the emoluments pertaining to them were regarded as a form of freehold from which their possessors could not be legally disseized.[2] The King, according to Bacon, 'can no more take away the profits of a man's office, than . . . the profits of his land.'[3]

To be sure, the tenure specified in grants of office varied. A sampling, for instance, from the reign of Charles I contains offices conferred for life, for two lives, for thirty-one years, during pleasure, during good behaviour, and hereditarily in a few cases where the grant was made to a man and his heirs.[4] The principle of life tenure, however, had steadily gained ground in the royal service since the fifteenth century, so that by the seventeenth the majority of offices, including occasionally even such high political appointments as the secretaryship of state, appear to have been granted for life.[5] Many

---

[1] Office in England in the earlier seventeenth century is the subject of comprehensive treatment in G. E. Aylmer's *The King's servants*; cf. also his paper, 'Office holding as a factor in English history, 1625–42,' *History*, XLIV, 152 (1959).

[2] Cf. the account of the legal position of office as property in Sir W. Holdsworth, *A history of English law*, 13v., L., ed. 1922–52, I, 246–8.

[3] F. Bacon, *Works*, XIII, 295; instances of contemporary legal opinion to the same effect respecting office and its profits are given in Sir W. Holdsworth, *op. cit.*, I, 260 and J. Wilson, 'Sir Henry Spelman and the Royal Commission on Fees 1622–1640,' *Studies presented to Sir Hilary Jenkinson*, Oxford, 1957, 467.

[4] These specimens are taken at random from grants of office under the privy seal printed in T. Rymer, *Foedera*, 20v., L., 1704–32, XIX, *passim*.

[5] On the tenure of offices, cf. G. E. Aylmer, *The King's servants*, 106–25; A. F. Havighurst, 'The judiciary and politics in the reign of Charles II,' pt. I,

office holders thus enjoyed great security in their places. An objectionable official with life tenure might be interdicted from exercising his functions, but to remove him was extremely difficult.[1] The easiest way was to procure a candidate as his successor who would offer a pecuniary inducement sufficient to make him relinquish his place voluntarily.

The usual means of obtaining office were purchase and patronage. These were not mutually exclusive, as patronage was often exercised in behalf of someone who wished to buy an office in which other competitors were interested. It was also possible to succeed to an office by acquiring the reversion; and if an official owned the reversion to his place, he could bequeath it to an heir. Through the device of reversions, a hereditary element was introduced into the crown service, resulting in an association between certain families and offices or departments that might last for generations, like that of the Fanshawes, Osbornes, and Crokes with the Exchequer.[2]

Although legally the buying and selling of offices was forbidden—at any rate in the law courts and revenue departments—the prohibition was ineffectual and trafficking in office a common occurrence.[3] Wither adverted bitterly to the practice in 1628:

> *Nor will this Iland better dayes behold,*
> *So long as offices are bought and sold.*
> *Nor shall I ever think that any one,*
> *Much cares, what right or injury be done,*
> *That buyes or sels an Office. . . .*[4]

[1] Officials appointed for life could be removed only if convicted of high treason or of contravening the act of 1552 against the sale of offices. The latter, however, seems to have been nearly a dead letter.

[2] Cf. G. E. Aylmer, 'The officers of the Exchequer, 1625–1642,' *Essays in the economic and social history of Tudor and Stuart England*, ed. F. J. Fisher, Cambridge, 1961, 172–4.

[3] Sir W. Holdsworth, *op. cit.*, I, 246–8, 250–1, has summarized the legislation concerning venality of office. There is a brief account of the practice in England in K. Swart, *Sale of offices in the seventeenth century*, The Hague, 1949, ch. III. Cf. also the discussion and instances in D. Mathew, *The Jacobean age*, L., 1938, 209–15 and G. E. Aylmer, *The King's servants*, 225–39.

[4] G. Wither, *Britain's remembrancer*, 189.

Law quarterly review, LXVI (1950), 64–5; and J. C. Sainty, 'The tenure of offices in the Exchequer,' *E.H.R.*, LXXX, 316 (1965). Sainty has commented on the increase of life tenure in office and has attributed the phenomenon to the growing replacement of clerical by lay officials. As regards the secretaryship of state, F. M. G. Evans declares that the office was granted during pleasure and the salary for life (*The principal secretary of state*, Manchester, 1923, 211). Sir George Calvert, however, was appointed for life in 1619 (*C.S.P.D. 1619–23*, 14).

The character of such a transaction in the upper reaches of the crown's service may be illustrated from the attempt by Sir Dudley Carleton, ambassador in Holland, to purchase one of the two secretaryships of state in 1624. The office was held by Sir George Calvert, appointed for life in February 1619. Carleton, who had been seeking further preferment for some time, was informed that Calvert wished to retire because of ill-health and would sell his place for £6,000. The price seemed reasonable, as the secretary's office was said to be worth £2,000 *per annum* and £7,000 and £8,000 had been offered for it prior to Calvert's appointment. Naturally, the King would have to sanction an arrangement by which one of his secretaries left to make way for another. But Carleton was unlucky. He was passed over on Calvert's resignation and the office obtained by Sir Albertus Morton, Clerk of the Privy Council. On the latter's death a few months later, the secretaryship went to Sir John Coke, a client of the King's favourite, the duke of Buckingham. Carleton was told that he had been denied promotion because he had fixed his dependence on persons averse to Buckingham and all his undertakings.[1]

In contemporary France, venality of offices, however strongly deplored, was an established policy of the crown and a regular source of the King's revenue.[2] This was not the case in England. While both James I and Charles I sometimes sold offices, they did not institutionalize the practice; nor was it mainly the crown that profited from the sale of places in its service. The beneficiaries were the courtiers and ministers who used their influence for money. In addition, officials themselves also profited from venality. Some of them possessed in right of their office the gift of appointment to subordinate posts in their departments: this was a feature of certain offices, for instance, in the law courts and the Exchequer. Naturally, the officials enjoying this privilege commonly exercised it only in favour of one prepared to offer a good bargain. The gains thus made were a recognized item in the profits of office.

Salaries, generally fixed long before the seventeenth century, were small and usually represented the least part of office-holders' income. Far more important were the various perquisites, the scheduled fees exacted from those using their services, and confidential gratuities and bribes. The latter kinds of payment were the inevitable consequence

---

[1] The details of this transaction may be followed in *C.S.P.D. 1619–23*, 14, ibid. *1623–25*, 231, 450, 457, 472, ibid. *1625–26*, 100. Carleton had actually tried to win Buckingham's support by sending him from the continent a costly gift of marble for his building. Carleton later achieved his ambition, becoming, as Viscount Dorchester, Secretary of State in 1629.

[2] Cf. R. Doucet, *Les institutions de la France au XVIe siècle*, 2v., Paris, 1948, I, ch. XVIII and R. Mousnier, *La vénalité des offices sous Henri IV et Louis XIII*, Rouen, 1945.

of low official remuneration. The earl of Dorset, Chamberlain to the Queen, asserted during a Star Chamber suit in 1635 in which an officer stood accused of fraud that 'he did not think it a crime for a Courtier that comes up to Court for His Majestie's service, and lives at great expence in his attendance, to receive a reward to get a business done by a great man in Power. . . .'[1] Dorset's remark merely reflected the current attitude, which maintained a tenuous distinction between the permissible present or *douceur* and the impermissible bribe, thus tolerating practices which a later age would unhesitatingly pronounce corrupt.

Besides irregular gifts and rakeoffs, there was a steady tendency for the fees demanded by officials to increase in size and number.[2] The proprietary conception of office doubtless encouraged incumbents to make what gains they could. Wither blamed their extortions on the system of venality:

> *It is a sum of money that prefers*
> *To ev'ry place; and that makes knaves, and sharks,*
> *Of Sergeants, Waiters, and of Under-clarks.*
> *This maketh Registers, in ev'ry Court,*
> *And other Ministers, so much extort:*
> *This makes them seek out knots, demurs, delayes,*
> *And practise many unapproved wayes,*
> *To make up that which foolishly they paid:*
> *. . . .*[3]

In the parliament of 1621 there was a strong protest against exactions by officials: Bacon's impeachment as Lord Chancellor on the charge of bribery was connected with this outcry. In 1610 criticism of the rapacity of office-holders had resulted in the first of a series of royal commissions to investigate excessive fees in offices. Although these commissions functioned intermittently until 1640 and gathered a large quantity of information on the malpractices of officials, they appear to have done little to reform the abuses complained of by parliamentary orators.[4]

It has been pointed out that the payments which officials took

---

[1] J. Rushworth, II, 313.
[2] Cf. the fees taken in the Court of Wards and Liveries, H. E. Bell, *An introduction to the history and records of the Court of Wards & Liveries*, Cambridge, 1953, 36.
[3] *Britain's remembrancer*, 190–1.
[4] Cf. J. Wilson, 'Sir Henry Spelman and the royal commission on fees 1622–1640,' *loc. cit.* and the less favourable verdict on these commissions by G. E. Aylmer, 'Charles I's commissions on fees, 1627–1640,' *Bulletin of the Institute of Historical Research*, XXXI, 83 (1958) and *The King's servants*, 182–203.

beyond their remuneration from the crown were in effect an indirect tax levied on the public to finance the costs of administration. The royal government was thus spared the necessity of having to draw on its own hard-pressed income to raise its servants' pay, grown totally inadequate in the seventeenth century after decades of inflation.[1] Of the economic significance of this *de facto* transfer of costs by the monarchy there can be little question. An estimate for the early 1630s suggests its magnitude. At that time, when Charles I's ordinary annual revenue averaged about £618,000, the fees and gratuities of officials have been reckoned at between £250,000 and £400,000. A sum that may possibly have exceeded 40 per cent of ordinary revenue was thus paid, in lieu of crown remuneration, as an indirect tax to officials by the persons who, for whatever reasons, used their services.[2]

It must not be supposed, however, that office was in itself a high road to fortune, for the places in which spectacular gains were possible were relatively few. Families such as Cecil, Montagu, Villiers, Feilding, Goring, Wentworth, and Weston, who established peerages on the riches acquired through office or favour in the Court were not typical of the official class as a whole. The enormous sums, licit and illicit, which Robert Cecil, first earl of Salisbury, realized by his ministerial posts under King James as Treasurer, Master of the Wards, and Secretary of State were most exceptional—an Eldorado to which only a tiny minority could hope to gain admittance.[3]

Moreover, office was desired for diverse reasons and incumbents treated it in various ways. It might be wanted to provide a regular income—a consideration which, in the absence of an organized system of pensions and annuities, often entered into the purchase of offices and reversions.[4] When Sir Henry Wotton, thrice ambassador to Venice, returned from his last embassy in 1623, he sought an office on which to live. By Buckingham's intercession he obtained the provostship of Eton. This gave him security in his old age (he was then fifty-six), though besides his residence and perquisites, his stipend came to only £140 per annum.[5] On the other hand, office

[1] Cf. J. Hurstfield, *The Queen's wards*, L., 1958, 348.

[2] These figures come from G. E. Aylmer, *The King's servants*, 246–8. Aylmer's estimate of ordinary revenue appears to have been taken from Gardiner, *History*, X, App. I.

[3] Cf. L. Stone, 'The fruits of office: the case of Robert Cecil, first earl of Salisbury, 1596–1612,' *Essays in the economic & social history of Tudor and Stuart England.*

[4] D. Mathew, *The Jacobean age*, 209–10, has stressed this aspect of office.

[5] L. P. Smith, *The life and letters of Sir Henry Wotton*, 2v., Oxford, 1907, II, 284, I, 200–1, 204–5. Wotton also received a pension of £200 *p.a.* from the King in 1611 which was increased in 1632 to £500. He owned two reversions which he surrendered to Buckingham in exchange for the office of Provost of Eton.

might be desired as a form of investment to yield a high return on capital. Such a purpose probably actuated Paul D'Ewes, the father of the parliamentary diarist, Sir Simonds D'Ewes, to buy a Six Clerks office in the Court of Chancery for nearly £5,000 in 1607: the elder D'Ewes kept the place for twenty-three years, realizing about £32,500 from it.[1]

In contrast to officials who wanted a regular income or a return on capital, others used their position like entrepreneurs. Richard Boyle exploited his offices in Ireland with such success that he made a great fortune and secured Irish peerages for himself and two of his sons.[2] Sir Arthur Ingram was another who became extremely rich by exploiting office and other devices of profit obtainable in the Court.[3]

Some aspirants looked for office only as a means to further promotion. A feodary's place in the Court of Wards was described as one '. . . not of profit, but rather an introduction to better fortunes.'[4] At the other extreme, office was sought for its political importance and honorific status as much as for its pecuniary value. Great places like that of Lord Treasurer, Lord Admiral, Lord Chamberlain, and Lord Steward were of this kind. The occupants of these in the seventeenth century were privy councillors *ex officio*: personages, it was said, 'by place and office soe interested in the businesses of state as they are of the Councell.'[5]

Since office was frequently property and commonly viewed in that light, its rationale was not exclusively one of service to prince or public. This circumstance was profoundly important for the political consequences of office holding. Undoubtedly, so far as concerned high officials in the executive, the legal departments, and the household, the aspect of service to their royal master would be prominent: though most of them, too, were keenly interested in their private enrichment. But in general, the idea of office as a trust entailing the disinterested performance of public duties was little developed. Rather, the usual concern in office was primarily with its pecuniary side, and only secondarily with its public features. Hence office-holders did not necessarily favour the royal government's policy or

[1] *The autobiography and correspondence of Sir Simonds D'Ewes*, ed. J. O. Halliwell, 2v., L., 1845, I, 179.
[2] Cf. T. O. Ranger, 'Richard Boyle and the making of an Irish fortune, 1588–1614,' *Irish historical studies*, IX (1957) and *Lismore papers*, ed. A. B. Grosart, 10v., pp., 1886–8, II, 239.
[3] Cf. A. F. Upton, *Sir Arthur Ingram*, Oxford, 1961.
[4] *C.S.P.D. 1629–31*, 373. Bishop Goodman took a more favourable view of a feodary's office; cf. G. Goodman, *The court of James I*, ed. J. S. Brewer, 2v., L., 1839, I, 271.
[5] Cf. E. R. Turner, *The Privy Council of England in the seventeenth and eighteenth centuries*, 2v., Baltimore, 1927, I, 77.

invariably feel themselves obliged to support it. Considerations of this sort had little to do with the motives of most seekers and occupants of Court places. In parliament's conflict with the King after 1640, some officials remained neutral, while others, if they did not adhere to parliament, nevertheless complied with it. A prudent care for their stake in office might lead them to such a course. The official of the posts in Durham who declared during the protectorate of Oliver Cromwell that he had bought his place in 1637 for £120 and intended 'to be true to any government established' expressed a view easily comprehensible in revolutionary times.[1] The Long Parliament itself was sensible of the claims of office-holders and disposed to give them compensation if their places were extinguished by its reform measures.[2]

Notwithstanding the great patronage resources at the crown's disposal and the many motives inducing men to the Court, the latter was a much less solid body politically than might be expected. In the intermediate ranks of the royal service were men who belonged to the Country opposition or were in some way related to it.[3] Even courtiers and ministers in the highest positions, however, were not always steady in their adherence to the King's policies. Factional differences and personal rivalries often caused them to hinder crown measures underhand and give covert support to oppositionists. Bacon warned James I of the evil consequences of Court disaffection. As long as turbulent spirits, peevish Puritans, and popular men, he said, should be able when opposing the King's causes to 'have a retreat . . . in the favour of some great person, let his Majesty look for nothing but tempest.'[4] In the parliament of 1614, the earl of Northampton, a privy councillor, incited a member to denounce the favour shown by the King to the Scotsmen at Court.[5] Great peers and councillors such as the third earl of Pembroke, who was Chamberlain and afterwards Lord Steward, and his brother and heir, the fourth earl, who also became Chamberlain, did not hesitate to abet oppositionists. Intent on extending their personal power against competitors, they gave their countenance at different times both to the Country leaders and to those who were discontented in the Court. The fourth earl was reputed a protector of the Puritans, and had the habit of 'speaking frankly of the oversights of the Court that he might not be thought a slave to it.'[6]

[1] J. Thurloe, *State papers*, 7v., L., 1742, IV, 283.
[2] Cf. the pensions which the Houses assigned to be paid to the officers of the Court of Wards, abolished in 1646, H. E. Bell, *op. cit.*, 160–1.
[3] Cf. *infra*, ch. IV.   [4] *Works*, XII, 188–9.
[5] Cf. T. L. Moir, *The addled parliament of 1614*, Oxford, 1958, 138, 140.
[6] Clarendon, *Rebellion*, I, 122, VI, 399; *C.S.P.V. 1636–39*, 571. Pembroke's steward at Baynard's Castle, Nathan Walworth, was certainly a Puritan; cf.

In parliament men with Court connections did not form a disciplined group always ready to follow the lead of councillors and ministers. The parliamentary transactions of the time were studded with episodes in which members of the lower House who enjoyed office or favour either acted independently or refused to rally behind the government's spokesmen. Bacon asserted that one of the great problems of political management was the 'drawing of that body of the house which consisteth of courtiers and the K[ing's] servants to be . . . sure and zealous for the K[ing] and not fearful or popular.'[1] In the parliaments of 1621 and 1625, the opposition received support from many who held offices.[2] After the Long Parliament met, a number of officials in great or profitable places abandoned the Court and went over to its enemies. In short, not all attached to the Court were deeply or unalterably committed to it; not all officials who enjoyed advancement there would remain loyal in the struggle for power that impended.

When we turn to the social basis of the Court, nothing stands out to distinguish the members in its intermediate and highest regions from the dominant class as a whole. Socially speaking, they were more or less homogeneous with the general body of gentlemen who governed England. As a rule, their family origins lay in the gentry.[3] Economic interests in the land, kinship, and neighbourhood associations linked them with their fellows of the aristocratic order who lacked Court connection. Like the latter, they usually owned landed properties out of which they derived a portion of their income. Together with the latter, they might be appointed to the commission of the peace. If they left office, it was to the land they went and in landed society that they took, or aspired to take, their place.

In these respects there was no perceptible difference between the peers, knights, and gentlemen in Court offices and their counterparts in the Country opposition. Of course, the fortunate insiders who profited from monopolies and other crown rewards thereby acquired pecuniary interests not shared beyond the favoured circle. But the dislike these parasitic devices of enrichment provoked was not a

[1] *Works*, XI, 366.
[2] Cf. W. F. Mitchell, *The rise of the revolutionary party in the House of Commons*, N.Y., 1957, 90 and J. N. Ball, 'Sir John Eliot at the Oxford parliament, 1625,' *Bulletin of the Institute of Historical Research*, XXVIII, 78 (1955), 115. D. H. Willson, *The privy councillors in the House of Commons 1604–1629*, also gives numerous instances of the disunity and disaffection of courtiers and officials in the Commons.
[3] Cf. the social description of Charles I's officials in G. E. Aylmer, *The King's servants*, ch. 5.

The correspondence of Nathan Walworth and Peter Seddon, ed. J. S. Fletcher, *Chetham society*, CIX, 1880.

manifestation of social antagonism. It was simply the reaction of men who saw the King's power and resources used for purposes they condemned, or who perhaps in an occasional instance envied the opportunities beyond their reach. The conflict between the Court and the Country was therefore not rooted in social or economic contradictions. Fundamentally, it expressed a *political* opposition among the governing and wealthy members of the society, divided by their attachment or hostility to the operation of the authority and prerogative power of the crown.

Because the Court and the Country were formations within the governing class, no rigid barrier separated the two. It was possible, therefore, for men connected with the Country to pass over to the Court. All that was necessary was a political change of front. A number of instances of this kind took place in the 1620s and '30s, just as the reverse movement occurred afterwards when the Court collapsed in 1640–1.

Sir Dudley Digges, for example, was a prominent opponent of the crown in the House of Commons and in 1626 served as one of the House's managers in its impeachment of the duke of Buckingham. But having shown his disapproval of the opposition's conduct at the parliamentary dissolution of 1629, he obtained the reversion to the important office of Master of the Rolls, actually succeeding to the place in 1636.[1] William Noy, a great lawyer in his day, took a similar course. Conspicuous as an oppositionist in the parliaments of the 1620s, he made a political turnabout, became the King's Attorney-General in 1731, and lived to devise the execrated ship money tax.[2] Another instance was Sir Henry Yelverton, who was first an oppositionist and then, on obtaining the King's good will, became successively Solicitor-General and Attorney-General. Next, a quarrel with Buckingham caused his disgrace and in 1621 he attacked the favourite when called before the House of Lords to give evidence on monopolies. Four years later he pleaded to be restored to favour, and having made his political peace, was appointed a judge of the Court of Common Pleas.[3]

But the most momentous of political reversals was that accomplished by Sir Thomas Wentworth, later famous as Viscount Wentworth and earl of Strafford. Member of an important Yorkshire family, heir to a baronetcy and a great estate, Wentworth did not require Court infusions to supplement his fortune. The earlier part of

---

[1] Gardiner, *History*, VI, 99; *C.S.P.D. 1627–28*, 2, *ibid. 1629–31*, 392; *D.N.B.*, *s.v.*

[2] *D.N.B.*, *s.v.*

[3] Gardiner. *History*, IV, 22–3, 111–15; *C.S.P.D. 1623–25*, 461; *D.N.B.*, *s.v.*

his public career was a record of opposition and of slights from the King. By his second marriage in 1624 to Arabella Holles, daughter of the earl of Clare, he was related as well to a prominent opposition family. Wentworth's actions in the parliament of 1625 incurred the disfavour of both Charles I and Buckingham. In consequence, he and other Country spokesmen were pricked as sheriffs to render them ineligible for election to the House of Commons in the following year.[1] This disqualification, Lord Clare wrote him, 'me thinkes . . . putts a marke of estimation uppon you & your fellowes, for perseqution is oftner a sumtome of virtu, then reward.'[2] In 1626 he suffered the further humiliation of being summarily dismissed from his dignity as *custos rotulorum* of the Yorkshire commission of the peace.[3] A year later, when the King exacted a forced loan from his subjects, Wentworth appeared amongst the principal resisters, being summoned by the Council and committed for his defiance.[4] The climax of his political association with the Country came in the parliament of 1628, where he virtually led the House of Commons in its efforts to secure the liberties of the subject.[5]

Yet throughout his years of opposition, Wentworth repeatedly sought admission to the Court. He aspired to a peerage, sued for office, and tried unavailingly to make a bargain of support with the favourite, Buckingham. Then in July 1628, shortly after the close of the parliamentary session in which he had distinguished himself, he attained his aim. He received a peerage and several months later was appointed President of the Council of the North. To this high place was added in 1632 the great office of Lord Deputy of Ireland.[6]

Did Wentworth, then, adhere to the Country from conviction, or because he wished to become so considerable in opposition that the King would think him a personage worth gaining for the Court? The answer must remain uncertain. What is undeniable, however, is that if he held any principles, his conduct was no less marked by mercenary self-interest and lack of scruple. These traits appeared fully in his political *volte-face*, whose nature is revealed in the letter sent him in 1631 by his intimate and kinsman, Sir Edward Stanhope. In this extraordinary communication, from which we have already cited,

[1] Cf. Sir Arthur Ingram's letter, *The earl of Strafforde's letters*, I, 28.
[2] Strafford MSS., v. 22, no. 53.
[3] *The earl of Strafforde's letters*, I, 36.
[4] *Ibid.*, I, 37–8.
[5] C. V. Wedgwood, *Thomas Wentworth first earl of Strafford*, L., 1961, ch. V.
[6] Wentworth's approaches to the Court are summarized in P. Zagorin, 'Sir Edward Stanhope's advice to Thomas Wentworth, Viscount Wentworth, concerning the deputyship of Ireland,' *loc. cit.*, 301–2.

Stanhope conveyed the truth of Wentworth's entry to the Court.[1] He there drew an imaginary picture of the voice of malice speaking of Wentworth to Charles I as follows:

Sir you have bin of late pleased to cast a speciall eye of Royall favor on Sir Thomas Wentworth. Why, I know not, unless itt hath bin to with draw him (beinge but a private Gentleman, which maks the wonder greater) from his vyolent and refractory courses against you and your iust designs, which rather should have provoked you to have showred downe tempests of your displeasure on his disobedient head and heart. But you whoe have ever desiered more to shew mercye and win favor then to inforce by vyolence . . . have honored him by creatinge him a Baron . . . and a Peere of the Realme. . . . being perswaded by the Duke of Buckingham (whoe receaved his informatione from the Lord Treasurer [Sir Richard Weston] that undertooke to reduce him to a mylder temper and make him his creature). . . .[2]

Wentworth thus abandoned the Country for the King's service on his agreeing to become the duke of Buckingham's dependent—a transaction in which the Treasurer Weston, another of Buckingham's clients, was the intermediary. In this way did he enter the path to preferment and power. And so, too, did destiny set him on the course which led him thirteen years later to Tower Hill and the executioner's axe, the most hated minister in three kingdoms.

3

It was in 1616 that George Villiers, the future Buckingham, began his career as favourite. Supported by the affection of two kings, he rose to the meridian of power, there to shine in blazing splendour until the knife of an assassin extinguished his light. With his beauty of

[1] Both H. F. Kearney (*Strafford in Ireland*, Manchester, 1959, 27–8) and C. V. Wedgwood (*op. cit.*, 68) connect Wentworth's entry into the Court with the reorientation of English policy towards Spain. According to them, Wentworth disliked the war against Spain, begun in 1624, and as soon as the government started to veer towards peace and friendship with Spain in 1628, he had no further reason to continue his political opposition. This explanation of his conduct appears to me implausible and I know of no convincing evidence to support it.

[2] P. Zagorin, 'Sir Edward Stanhope's advice to Thomas Wentworth, Viscount Wentworth, concerning the deputyship of Ireland,' *loc. cit.*, 314. C. V. Wedgwood alludes briefly to this letter (*op. cit.*, 122), thirty-five folio pages in length, which the present writer first published in 1964 from the Strafford MSS. Inexplicably, she fails to quote from it or to observe its significance for the comprehension of Wentworth's personality and political career.

person and his adeptness in the complimenting ways of courts, the youthful Villiers became the recipient of the most lavish gifts both James I and Charles I could bestow. A golden shower of wealth and offices descended on him. Swift promotion through the peerage brought him in 1623 to the culminating honour of the dukedom of Buckingham. By King James's aid he secured an earl's daughter for his wife. The rays of princely benefaction fell equally on his kindred and dependents, fructifying them with titles of nobility and grants of money, land and office. Never did a subject wield greater influence or grow to such prodigious height under the sun of royal favour.[1]

Buckingham's domination formed an epoch of critical importance in the pre-history of the revolution. It deformed the workings of the King's government and the patronage system. It sowed disaffection in the Court and was a prime cause of enmity on the political scene. It brought the royal regime into hatred and contempt. To the favourite's ascendancy must be ascribed in no small measure the decline of the crown's moral authority—an authority indispensable to government which, once lost, can hardly ever be recovered.

With all his sway over affairs, Buckingham had no real policy or extended aims. Unlike his contemporary ministers, Richelieu and Olivares, his predominant purpose in the use of power was to aggrandize himself and his dependents. Both the maxims of statecraft and the examples of prudent rulers warned princes to beware of permitting any subject a monopoly of rewards and influence.[2] Thus had Elizabeth governed, and in her greatest indulgences to favourites she took care to balance her generosity to one by the countenance she gave to another.[3] But James and Charles were neither as strong nor shrewd as the great Queen. The result was that they allowed Buckingham to secure virtually complete control of the higher administration and the machinery of patronage, thereby inflicting incalculable harm upon the monarchy.

Of all the organs of authority, the Council was the most important. The nerve and brain of regal power, on its right functioning the effectiveness of the King's government depended, and every episode of feeble or uncertain rule in the previous century had been connected with its impairment or debility. The establishment of Buckingham's

[1] *D.N.B.*, *s.v.*, 'George Villiers, first duke of Buckingham' and cf. also the sketch of Buckingham's rise and relation to the King by G. P. V. Akrigg, *Jacobean pageant*, Cambridge, 1962, ch. XVII and M. A. Gibb, *Buckingham*, L., 1935.

[2] Cf. Charles V's so-called political testament of 1543 to his son, Philip II, in K. Brandi, *The Emperor Charles V*, tr. C. V. Wedgwood, L., 1939, 490–2.

[3] Cf. the observations of Sir R. Naunton, *Fragmenta regalia*, *loc. cit.*, V, 123–5, and of Fulke Greville, Lord Brooke, *The life of . . . Sir Philip Sidney*, *Works*, IV, 176, 181.

dominion was quickly followed by the Council's decline. Privy Councillors became his mouthpieces or feared to express their views. The Council toiled at routine business, while great matters were reserved for private consultation between the King and favourite.[1] This condition, prevalent in James I's later years, continued after Charles I's accession. In the first Council meeting of the new reign, the earl of Arundel, a Privy Councillor since 1616, protested against the Council's exclusion from affairs, but to no avail.[2] With perfect justification did the Venetian envoy write in a *relazione* of England that 'There was no longer any Council' since Buckingham alone 'with three or four creatures constituted it.'[3]

While rendering the Council impotent, Buckingham also fastened his grip on key positions in the King's government. The machinery of promotions and favour in the Court could operate with full political advantage to the crown only if its fruits were not at the disposal of a single faction. Some rough parity, at least, between rivals was essential. But under the favourite's rule, the system of patronage which sustained the Court suffered the severest distortion. The principal levers were in his hands. It was him, not the King, whom suitors had to propitiate for benefits sought, and him whom they must thank for what was received. He alone could open the door to offices of importance in the royal service. The resentment his control aroused only made his hold the tighter, lest his enemies dislodge him from his eminence. Thus, what ought to have been a powerful asset in the strength of the crown became a source of weakness; and while the Country opposition denounced him, in the bitter words which Tacitus used of Sejanus, as a man 'audax, sui obtegens . . . superbus . . . clientes suos provinciis adornare,'[4] the Court itself was divided and some of its great personages disaffected.

For himself, Buckingham obtained a collection of honourable offices providing rich opportunities for influence and the gratification of dependents. During his primacy he became Master of the Horse; Lord Admiral; Lord Warden of the Cinque Ports; Warden, Chief Justice, and Justice in Eyre of the forests this side of Trent; Constable of Windsor Castle; and Chancellor of the University of Cambridge. He held, besides, a place in the royal household as Gentleman of the Bed Chamber. To diminish criticism, he resigned his wardenship of the Cinque Ports shortly before his death to the earl of Suffolk, 'a mean spirited man, his creature and humble servant. . . .'[5] When the

---

[1] *C.S.P.V. 1621–23*, 229, *ibid., 1625–26*, 603, *ibid., 1626–28*, 22, 128.
[2] *Ibid., 1625–26*, 12, 21.   [3] *Ibid., 1625–26*, 603.
[4] This expression was quoted by Sir John Eliot in a speech during the impeachment proceedings against the duke in 1626; cf. J. Rushworth, I, 355.
[5] *C.S.P.V. 1628–29*, 213.

Lord Steward's place fell vacant in 1625 through the death of the duke of Richmond, he was urged by his dependent, the Lord Keeper, Bishop Williams, to take it for himself. 'It keeps you,' Williams pointed out,

in all Changes and Alterations of years, near the King; and gives unto you all the Opportunities of Accesses, without the Envy of a Favourite. . . . It gives you Opportunities to Gratifie all the Court, great and small, Virtute Officii . . . which is a thing better accepted of, and interpreted, than a Courtesie from a Favourite; because in this you are a Dispenser of your own, but in the other (Say many envious men) of the King's Goodness. . . .[1]

Buckingham, however, had sufficient restraint to let this dignity go to the earl of Pembroke, the Lord Chamberlain, in an ineffectual attempt to purchase the latter's support.[2]

In addition to these places, the duke enjoyed lucrative royal grants and gifts of land. In 1623, his income exceeded £15,000 per annum. A sinecure in the Court of King's Bench alone yielded £4,500, while a grant on the customs of Ireland gave him £3,100 and an Exchequer pension £1,000. His lands in five counties produced nearly £6,000 more.[3]

The royal service, furthermore, was staffed with his clients, and his correspondence a tale of sycophantic requests for his favourable notice.[4] The Secretaries of State, Sir John Coke and Viscount Conway, made their careers by his patronage and were wholly at his bidding.[5] The Lord Keeper, Bishop Williams, rose in the same way, and lost his post after he fell into disfavour.[6] He was succeeded by Sir Thomas Coventry, still another dependent.[7] Sir Lionel Cranfield

---

[1] *Cabala*, 3rd ed., L., 1691, 280–1.
[2] Cf. *C.S.P.V. 1625–26*, 500, 515.
[3] These figures are taken from a report made in July 1623 by commissioners whom Buckingham appointed to ascertain his estate; cf. P.R.O. S.P. 14/149, no. 91. His expenses, made high by the requirements of Court display, almost equalled his income. They amounted to £14,700, £3,000 of which was spent on housekeeping, £2,500 on charges at Court, £2,000 on servants' wages and pensions, £1,200 on the stable, £1,500 on wearing apparel, and £2,000 on private expenses for rewards. Letters to Buckingham on the care of his estate are contained in B.M. Harl. 1581, *passim*.
[4] Cf. the letters in B.M. Harl. 1580, 1581, and *Fortescue papers*, ed. S. R. Gardiner, *Camden society*, n.s., I, 1871.
[5] For Coke, cf. *C.S.P.V. 1625–26*, 168, and D. Coke, *The last Elizabethan*, L., 1937. Conway's letters and references to the duke are those of client to patron; cf. *C.S.P.D. 1627–28*, 224, 225, 434.
[6] J. Hacket, *op. cit.*, pt. II, 24.
[7] *C.S.P.V. 1625–26*, 238.

became Master of the Court of Wards and was promoted to Treasurer and the earldom of Middlesex with Buckingham's support.[1] Sir Richard Weston's advancement in the royal service also occurred under his auspices.[2] The Admiralty was filled with his creatures, Sir James Bagg, Vice-Admiral in Cornwall, subscribing himself in letters as the duke's 'humble servant and slave.'[3] Prominent courtiers like George Goring furthered their aims as his dependents. '. . . I so sucked in debt from my cradle,' Goring told Buckingham, 'as I never knew what freedom was. . . . with hope and my eyes well fixed upwards I have as your Lo:p sees yet lived.'[4] To ambitious gentlemen who aspired to noble titles, the duke became a broker, procuring peerages for them at a price. Clerical careerists besought his aid. By the duke's 'sole procurement,' said Bishop Laud, 'I am made a Governour [in the Church].'[5] '. . . one blast of your Breath,' Bishop Field of Llandaff prayed, 'is able to bring me to the Heaven where I would be. . . .'; the bishop meant the see of Ely or of Bath and Wells.[6] What Lord Keeper Williams told the favourite was not far from the truth: 'Lett all our Greatness depend . . . upon youres, the true Originall. Lett the kinge be Pharao, youre self Joseph, and lett us com after as your halfe Brethren.'[7]

Buckingham's unprecedented sway aroused intense antagonism, but as James continued, despite all criticism, to support the duke, the latter became a heavy liability to the crown and a prime cause of political enmity. In the Court the strongest resentment was felt towards the man who engrossed the favour of two princes, the setting and the rising sun, King James and Prince Charles. The duke of Richmond, Lord Steward and a cousin of the monarch, strove to unseat Buckingham from the royal affections.[8] During the second session of the parliament of 1625, the earls of Arundel and Pembroke consulted frequently with members of the Commons against him.[9] In the 1626 parliament, Pembroke employed his territorial influence and his office of Warden of the Stannaries to elect opponents of Buckingham and the Court. The first to call for the duke's impeachment in

---

[1] B.M. Harl. 1581, ff. 89–90; *Cabala*, 263; cf. also R. H. Tawney, *Business and politics under James I*, Cambridge, 1958, 125–6.

[2] B.M. Harl. 1581, ff. 202, 204.

[3] *C.S.P.D. 1627–28*, 444, 447.

[4] B.M. Harl. 1580, f. 405.

[5] *Cabala*, 108.

[6] *Ibid.*, 111.

[7] *Ibid.*, 263.

[8] *Letters of John Chamberlain*, ed. N. E. McClure, 2v., Philadelphia, 1940, II, 542. Richmond's dislike is seen in a letter sent in 1623 to Lord Herbert, ambassador in France, P.R.O. Powis MSS. 30/53/10, f. 165.

[9] Sir Arthur Ingram to Wentworth, November 1625, *The earl of Strafforde's letters*, I, 28.

this parliament was a member returned to the Commons with Pembroke's aid.[1] There is no doubt that Charles I's difficulties with parliament were acutely aggravated because of the support discontented courtiers gave the Country leaders in their attacks on the duke and his measures.

Once, and once only, did Buckingham try to win over the Country opposition by identifying himself with a popular policy. Successful at first, the attempt ended in failure, an episode that pointed up the complexity of the political scene before public differences hardened beyond any likelihood of reconciliation.

As early as 1621, the favourite had been persuaded to make a tentative move to mollify his antagonists. On the advice of a kinsman who suggested that he 'oblige the Puritans, and lay a groundwork for his own security, if tempests should arise,'[2] he secured the appointment of John Preston, a clergyman who was spiritual guide to some of the principal Puritan gentry, as Prince Charles's chaplain.[3] Compounding this good office, he then assisted Preston the next year to become Master of Emmanuel College, Cambridge. Preston's promotion was the first step towards a tactical alliance between the Court and the Country. It was not till 1624, however, in consequence of a sharp reversal in the King's foreign policy, that a *rapprochement* became possible.

King James had long pursued a Spanish marriage for his son, and with it also the chimerical hope of Spain's assistance for the restoration of the Palatinate, his son-in-law's principality occupied by the Catholic-Imperialist forces at the beginning of the Thirty Years War. In 1623, Buckingham and Charles journeyed to Madrid to press the long-discussed marriage treaty in person—an imprudent venture, exposing the prince to unnecessary danger, which aroused strong criticism at home. English opinion, in any case, heartily disliked the proposed alliance, as it saw in Spain the national enemy and the supreme menace to continental Protestantism. At Madrid negotiations proved unsuccessful. Buckingham, therefore, to remove the odium they brought on him, resolved to sponsor a fresh policy. He returned from Spain determined to end the Spanish connection with parliament's backing and to make a French marriage alliance instead. This was an objective the Country opposition could support. The result of the agreement was seen in the parliament of 1624, where the

---

[1] *C.S.P.D. Addenda 1625–49*, 112–13; *H.M.C. Mar and Kellie, Supplementary*, 237; V. Rowe, 'The influence of the earls of Pembroke in parliamentary elections 1625–41,' *E.H.R.*, L, 198 (1935), 247–8.
[2] T. Ball, *Life of John Preston* in S. Clarke, *A general martyrologie*, L., 1677, pt. 2, 49–50.
[3] Cf. Christopher Hill's essay on Preston in *Puritanism and revolution*, ch. 8.

duke and Charles, who concurred in the new line, found themselves for the first and only time exponents of a policy that parliament endorsed.[1]

On behalf of the Country leaders in the House of Commons, Buckingham pressed the unwilling King for concessions. James, he insisted, should allow him to 'assure some of them underhand' that their advice for a war with Spain and a grant of money for this purpose would be accepted. He further told the monarch of the fear 'that when your turns are served, you will not call them together again to reform abuses. . . . and the making of laws for the good government of the country. . . .' James must therefore show himself in love with parliaments, and to prove his sincerity must permit a parliamentary committee to supervise the expenditure of moneys raised for the war.[2] Throughout this time, the duke was in cordial association with principal men of the opposition, and together with the Prince an advocate of all popular courses.[3] 'I did never see,' wrote an old Scottish courtier, '. . . onye Parliament lyke to it, whitche dois evrye daye grate upone the King's prerogative soe mutche. . . . It is verrye strange to see the Prince goe on soe in applawding all or the most pairt of their doeings, whitche . . . monye thinks he shall never recover againe. . . .'[4]

Buckingham and the opposition got their war. Negotiations were started for a match with France which led the next year to Charles's marriage to Henrietta Maria, sister of Louis XIII. Parliament was permitted freely to debate foreign policy matters and to impeach the unpopular Treasurer, the earl of Middlesex, who fell out of the duke's good graces because he disliked the break with Spain on grounds of economy. Parliament's Subsidy Act trenched deeply on the King's prerogative, giving the lower House supervision of the collection and expenditure of the money voted for the war.[5] But notwithstanding these concessions, the agreement with the Country did not last. The oppositionist leaders and the Commons, wanting a sea war accom-

---

[1] An account of the short-lived alliance between Buckingham and the Country is given in I. Morgan's biography of John Preston, *Prince Charles's Puritan chaplain*, L., 1958; cf. also J. F. Maclear, 'Puritan relations with Buckingham,' *Huntington Library quarterly*, XXI, 1 (1957).

[2] *Hardwicke state papers*, 2v., L., 1778, II, 466, 467–8. A similar letter of advice to James from the earl of Carlisle (*Cabala*, 197–8) seems also to be connected with Buckingham's strategy.

[3] Cf. his letters to Sir Robert Phelips, *Cabala*, 314–15, and Richard Knightley, *Fortescue papers*, 196–7.

[4] The earl of Kellie to the earl of Mar, May 1624, *H.M.C. Mar and Kellie, Supplementary*, 200.

[5] Cf. the act in J. R. Tanner, *Constitutional documents of the reign of James I*, Cambridge, 1930, 374–9 and the remarks of C. Roberts, *The growth of responsible government in Stuart England*, Cambridge, 1966, 39–40.

panied by penetration of Spain's American empire, showed themselves unprepared to support the cost of land hostilities on the continent. In addition, their suspicion of Buckingham remained invincible. The love of the Puritans 'is yet but green towards [you],' Bacon had informed the duke. '. . . there are a great many that will magnify you and make use of you for the . . . putting the realm into a war, which will after return to their old bias.'[1] Bacon's forecast proved correct, and the period immediately following Charles I's accession saw the liaison of the Court and the Country draw to an end. In the first parliament of the reign, the strain became great during the second session as the Country leaders opposed further money grants and conditioned for religious and other reforms.[2] By the time the parliament of 1626 met, the alliance lay in ruins and Buckingham confronted the prospect of impeachment.

The destruction of the political *rapprochement* was at the same time also of considerable consequence for the Church of England. Previous to this, Buckingham's policy of conciliating the Puritans made it uncertain that the Arminian and high-church party[3] would be allowed to prevail in the Anglican establishment.[4] The duke gave his support to silenced Puritan ministers,[5] and Preston even went so far as to broach a project for solving the crown's financial difficulties by the confiscation of episcopal lands. There were reports, too, that Charles I would appoint Preston Lord Keeper in succession to Bishop Williams.[6] In February 1626, while parliament was sitting, Buckingham sponsored a conference at his London house where a number of theologians publicly debated the merits of the Arminian position. Preston was one of the disputants, but the Calvinistic divines failed to convince the duke; indeed, their opponents had the best of the argument.[7] After this, Puritan influence swiftly waned, while the oppositionists' attack in parliament on Buckingham and

---

[1] *Works*, XIV, 442.

[2] Cf. the speeches of Sir N. Rich and Sir R. Phelips in H. Hulme, *The life of Sir John Eliot*, L., 1957, 89, and J. N. Ball, 'Sir John Eliot at the Oxford Parliament, 1625,' *loc. cit.*

[3] The nature of the Arminian movement in the church is discussed below in ch. VI.

[4] The persistent anxieties of high-church clergymen at this period appear in Richard Montague's letters to John Cosin; cf. *Correspondence of John Cosin*, ed. G. Ornsby, *Surtees society*, LII, 1869, 98, 100, 103.

[5] The eminent ministers, John Dod and Arthur Hildersam, were permitted to resume preaching, I. Morgan, *op. cit.*, 42 and Dr. Williams's Library, Morrice MSS., G., f. 841.

[6] J. Hacket, *op. cit.*, pt. I, 204; G. Burnet, *op. cit.*, I, 27–8.

[7] This conclusion can be drawn from a reading of the debate in J. Cosin, *The sum and substance of conferences lately had at York House, Works*, ed. J. Sansom, 5v., Oxford, 1843–5, II.

the King's policy removed all further incentive to conciliate the Puritans. Preston himself, according to his contemporary biographer, '... finding that his standing at Court was undermined ... resolved upon Buttresses to underprop him in the Countrey.'[1] It was now that Bishop Laud, who enjoyed Buckingham's patronage, was able to consolidate his own and the intolerant Arminian ascendancy over ecclesiastical affairs. Thus, the resumption of the conflict between the Court and the Country gave the administration of the church to men as responsible as any for provoking revolution.

The next three years witnessed the aggravation of political and religious division, while the King's governmental methods aroused growing resistance. The levying of loans and taxes widely regarded as illegal, imprisonment of the crown's opponents, general hatred of the favourite—these provoked what by 1629 was very nearly a revolutionary situation.[2] Military failure added to the regime's discredit. Operations against Spain were signally unsuccessful and war with France, begun in 1627 in support of the Huguenots, equally so. In August 1628 Buckingham was assassinated. The following March Charles dissolved his third parliament in an atmosphere of bitterest animosity. Henceforth he determined to rule without summoning again a body he had found to be unmanageable. He adhered to this resolution until the Scottish rebellion, breaking out in 1638, led on to its eventual denouement in the convening of the Long Parliament and the rout of the Court.

4

In the decade before the revolution, the King did nothing to remove the causes of his subjects' discontents. At home he showed himself altogether unforeseeing of the dangerous weather that lay close ahead. Abroad, his policy aimed at avoiding any undertakings which he could not sustain without parliamentary assistance. To this end he made peace with France in 1629, with Spain in 1630. The ministers managing affairs had all enjoyed Buckingham's patronage. None succeeded to the duke's position, however, and Charles never again gave his unreserved friendship to anyone. Sir Richard Weston, appointed Lord Treasurer in 1628 and subsequently created earl of Portland, was the leading minister, the one, it was stated, 'who moves all the wheels of this government as he pleases. ...' Joined with him was his colleague, Lord Cottington, Chancellor of the Exchequer and Master of the Court of Wards.[3] These men were clever politicians, in

[1] T. Ball, *Life of John Preston, loc. cit.*, pt. 2, 108. Preston died in 1628.
[2] Cf. *infra*, 110–11.
[3] *C.S.P.V. 1629–32*, 588, ibid., *1632–36*, 55–6.

no wise statesmen, agile enough on the slippery paths of the Court, but unfit to steer a state should waves run high. On Portland's death in 1635, Archbishop Laud became the most considerable person in the Privy Council. The archbishop's importance was the most conspicuous sign of the increase of clerical influence in the Court that contributed so much to envenom politics and estrange even the crown's supporters.

Translated from London to the archbishopric of Canterbury in 1633, Laud already possessed control of the church because of the King's confidence in him and the displeasure into which his predecessor, Archbishop Abbott, had fallen. Once primate, he was able to place the full resources of his metropolitan authority behind his ecclesiastical programme. This was inspired by the grand conception of a national church, uniform in worship and doctrine, acknowledging its affinities with the historic Catholicism of Rome but purged of Rome's errors, and submissive to God's vicegerent, the King, and to God's spiritual representatives, the bishops. Such a uniformity, however, resting on clericalism and ceremonialism, could not be attained: both Puritan opposition and the prevailing moderate Anglicanism of the laity forbade it. But the archbishop had no indulgence for those who differed. Personally insecure, troubled by fears that he would fall out of favour, he detested every challenge to his position.[1] Thus when he met resistance, he pursued his goal by means of the whip, the pillory, and the prison. To English Protestantism he became what the Counter-Reformation was to the Protestantism of the continent. His pressures for a church order towards which most of his countrymen were antipathetic brought both himself and the royal regime into odium.

And the weight of Laud's power was felt in other matters besides religion. '. . . this is the great man,' said a courtier of him in 1635, 'made now of the Commissioners of the Treasury and the First of the Junto of Foreign Affairs, and in the greatest esteem with his Majesty of any in my observance.'[2] He took a conspicuous part in the Court of Star Chamber. He was active on the commission to investigate enclosures. In 1636 his influence secured the appointment of his episcopal colleague, Juxon, Bishop of London, as Treasurer. He was, indeed, a ubiquitous presence in the King's government. Charles trusted Laud for his reverence of monarchy, his loyalty, and his lack of opportunism. So great a political role permitted an ecclesiastic was

---

[1] The deeper recesses of Laud's personality are glimpsed in his diary, printed in *Works*, ed. W. Scott and J. Bliss, 7v., Oxford, 1847–60, III. Cf. also the sketch of his life by S. R. Gardiner in *D.N.B.*, *s.v.* and H. R. Trevor-Roper, *Archbishop Laud*, L., 1940.

[2] Sir T. Roe to the Queen of Bohemia, *C.S.P.D. 1635*, viii.

unprecedented since the Reformation. It touched the nerve of English anti-clericalism and prepared the storm of condemnation that was about to break upon the church.

Ablest of the King's ministers during the 1630s was Wentworth. With all his defects of character and vision, he alone of those in the Court had perhaps some quality of greatness in him. His imperious nature, his heroic energy, and his proconsular confidence in the invulnerability of the King's power made him a formidable royal servant.[1] In office he distinguished himself at once by his capacity and rigour. Lacking the politic pliability of weaker men, he suffered no hindrance to the crown's authority or to himself as its instrument. '. . . this is an arrogance grown frequent now-a-days,' he declared, that

every ordinary man must put himself in balance with the King. . . . Silly wretches! Let us not deceive ourselves. . . . The ground whereupon Government stands will not so easily be washed away, so as the sooner we unfool ourselves of this error, the sooner we shall learn to know ourselves, and shake off that self-pride, which hath to our own esteem represented us much bigger, more considerable, than indeed there is cause for.[2]

As a minister Wentworth did not fail to exploit his position to enrich himself greatly; in 1637 his annual income, by his own account, was £27,000.[3] But at the same time he strove unsparingly to render the crown independent and powerful. He was resolved that the King must conquer what he called 'The universal Distemper of this Age, where the Subjection nestles itself too near the Sovereignty, where we are more apt wantonly to dispute the Powers which are over us than in former times.'[4] That he himself had but recently exemplified this same distemper, irony, of course, can hardly overlook. Nevertheless, only Archbishop Laud among the other councillors was actuated with equal inflexibility by the same purpose, and the two men were united in a policy of Thorough, as they named it. The

---

[1] Wentworth's best biography is C. V. Wedgwood's, *op. cit.*, which gives an absorbing account of his life and career; cf. J. P. Cooper's review in *E.H.R.*, LXXIX, 311 (1964). Suggestive observations will also be found in H. D. Traill, *Strafford*, L., 1889 and D. Mathew, *The age of Charles I*, L., 1951, ch. VI.

[2] *C.S.P.D. 1631–33*, xxv.

[3] So Wentworth told his friend, Lady Carlisle, *H.M.C. De L'Isle and Dudley*, VI, 90. On Wentworth's financial dealings, cf. J. P. Cooper, 'The fortune of Thomas Wentworth, earl of Strafford,' *Economic history review*, 2nd ser., XI, 2 (1958).

[4] *The earl of Strafforde's letters*, II, 161.

injustices each committed in his official career were to bring the day of reckoning upon them both. In the Council Wentworth was disliked and resented for his arrogance, energy, and success. He was incapable of forming a faction of his own, so that despite Laud's friendship and support, he remained isolated in the Court.[1] 'I procure daily so many Ill-Wishers,' he told the archbishop,

keep the Friends I have with so much difficulty in this rigid Way I go for my Master's Service, as almost makes Business unwelcome unto me, yet so long as I do serve, I will Thorough *by the Grace of God. . . .*[2]

When Wentworth was offered the Irish deputyship in 1631, Sir Edward Stanhope warned him that the appointment was a plot of his Court rivals, Weston and Cottington, who sought his removal from England. Eager to dissuade his friend, Stanhope described the Irish office as a burden too heavy for the shoulders of Atlas and Ireland as 'the last refuge of desperate hope . . . whither never man of eminency went, but was driven as the surest meanes of his overthrow. . . .'[3]

Nevertheless, Wentworth's record in Ireland seemed for long to defy these gloomy prognostications. He dominated the subject kingdom as none of its former governors could. Mastering every element of Irish society, he made all interests yield to the King's and not least those of the ruling English colonial minority.[4] But in the end, his severe and unscrupulous rule drove Ireland to revolt, while it convinced the Country oppositionists in England that there was no safety for them if he lived.[5]

The King himself, although conscious of Wentworth's exceptional services, remained cold and aloof towards him for a long time. Evidently something in Wentworth's forceful personality grated painfully on Charles. Twice the minister petitioned to be made an earl as a fresh sign of royal esteem, requests the King denied in chill and lapidary words.[6] As the emergency of the Scottish insurrection grew, however, Charles at length turned to Wentworth as the strongest pillar of his state. In the fall of 1639 he summoned the

[1] Cf. his remarks to the earl of Newcastle in 1638, *The earl of Strafforde's letters*, II, 174.
[2] *Ibid.*, II, 250.
[3] P. Zagorin, 'Sir Edward Stanhope's advice to . . . Viscount Wentworth, concerning the deputyship of Ireland,' *loc. cit.*, 303–6, 308.
[4] Wentworth's Irish administration is definitively treated by H. F. Kearney, *op. cit.*; cf. also T. Ranger, 'Strafford in Ireland: a revaluation.' *Past and present*, 19 (1961).
[5] The Irish rebellion is discussed *infra*, 254–9.
[6] *The earl of Stafforde's letters*, I, 331–2, II, 32.

Deputy home and shortly gave him coveted promotion as Lord Lieutenant of Ireland and earl of Strafford. Now, in the King's extremity, Strafford became the most great and trusted of councillors. It was what he had wanted all his life. Unflinchingly he took the fate of the monarchy upon his shoulders, and both he and it were to be overwhelmed in the same catastrophe.

As the 1630s drew towards a close, the King's difficulties multiplied, while the Court presented a scene of disunity and hidden discontent. Scotland was in revolt, incited by Laud's attempt to impose his ceremonialism on the Scottish church. Charles's rule in his northern kingdom was tottering, its nobility unreliable, its populace shaken by a deep tremor of hatred for the episcopal church and the royal supremacy in religion. At home money was scarce to pay the forces being raised against the Scots. None of the fiscal expedients devised since parliament last met was sufficient. Without a parliament no relief from financial stringency, no support against Scotland, would be forthcoming. But parliament was a dangerous medicine that might kill rather than cure. Everywhere in England a spirit of sullen resentment and opposition prevailed. '. . . what with Scottish brags,' wrote Laud despondently at the end of 1638, 'and desire of a Parliament, and a Puritan fashion, and a discontented subject, and a wasted estate. . . . The case at best is bad enough, not to add court divisions and jealousies.'[1]

In the cold world of the Court, distrust and rivalry between the councillors weakened the government's ability to deal with the crisis. The archbishop suspected Cottington of wanting a parliament so as to drive him from power and become Treasurer in place of Bishop Juxon.[2] The Treasurer of the Household, Sir Henry Vane, who became Secretary of State early in 1640, hated Strafford and hoped for his ruin.[3] The earl of Holland, a great courtier friend of the Queen, was thought to be cultivating his Puritan connections. He, too, was Strafford's enemy.[4] The Lord Admiral, the earl of Northumberland, one of the foremost noblemen in the kingdom, was disaffected. 'Such Incendiaries are here amongst us,' he complained of his fellow councillors, 'that . . . I do not see how we shall possibilie avoid falling into great Misfortunes. . . . To think well of the [Reformed Religion] is cause enough to make [Laud] . . . Ene-

[1] *Works*, VII, 513.
[2] *Ibid.*, VII, 568, Laud to Wentworth, May 1639.
[3] *C.S.P.D. 1639–40*, 436; Sir Edward Walker, *Historical discourses*, L., 1705, 305.
[4] Viscount Conway to Laud, June 1640, *C.S.P.D. 1640*, 278. Laud referred frequently in his letters to the enmity of Holland and Strafford, *Works*, VII, *passim*. The former was the brother of the great oppositionist peer, the earl of Warwick.

mie. . . .'[1] Although appointed in January 1640 to command against the Scots, Northumberland had no sympathy with his task. To Lord Mandeville, a Puritan oppositionist peer, he wrote excusing himself for his new employment 'against our brethren in Scotland . . . this Generallship will I feare utterly ruine my reputation, and make me be thought allmost as greate a reprobate as any Bishop. . . .'[2]

The regime faced the crisis disunited internally, surrounded from without by enmity and suspicion. The King was estranged from his subjects, though he lacked the political insight or imagination to gauge the depth of animosity against his rule. His own strong sense of kingship, the dominant idea of his life, deprived him of any comprehension of the convictions that sustained the angry energies of his opponents.

The Court's atmosphere emphasized its isolation. Its higher circles breathed an artificial air. Its theatricals with their precious, sentimental love themes were the amusement of a coterie. They induced a feeling of exclusiveness and aristocratic intimacy amongst the courtiers.[3] The poets who reflected the Court's taste flattered the King and Queen in exquisite verses conveying slight awareness of the differences in public life. The literature responsive to the Court's sensibility expressed a spirit of make-believe in such representative lines as the following by Abraham Cowley:

> *Happy who did remain*
> *Unborn till Charles's reign!*
> *Where, dreaming chymics! is your pain and cost?*
> *How is your oil! How is your labour lost!*
> *Our Charles, blessed alchemist! (Though strange,*
> *Believe it, future time!) did change*
> *The iron-age of old*
> *Into an age of gold!*[4]

Not only Cowley, but other writers like Carew, Shirley, Waller, and Davenant all fostered the illusion of a contented state in love with its royal master that was very far from the reality of the 1630s.[5]

---

[1] Northumberland to the earl of Leicester, Dec. 1639, A. Collins, *Letters and memorials of state*, 2v., L., 1746, II, 623, bracketed words in cipher.
[2] P.R.O. Manchester MSS., 30/15, no. 471.
[3] Cf. A. Harbage, *Cavalier drama*, Oxford, 1936, chs. I, II, IV and M. B. Pickel, *Charles I as patron of poetry and drama*, L., 1936, chs. III, VI, VII.
[4] *Ode in commendation of the time we live under, the reign of our gracious King Charles.*
[5] Cf. C. V. Wedgwood, *Poetry and politics under the Stuarts*, Cambridge, 1960, ch. II.

The Court and the Country

A Catholic element in the Court also promoted its remoteness from the prevailing temper. Queen Henrietta Maria was the centre of a fashionable Catholicism which the King, secure in his unswerving Anglicanism, treated with courtesy and toleration. There were aristocratic converts in Court society. Ministers such as Portland had Romanist sympathies. Catholics freely frequented the Queen's chapel at Somerset House. The King received the pope's diplomatic agents.[1] Naturally, such things aroused the dislike and mistrust of the robust Protestantism in country houses and tradesmen's shops.

Connected with this Catholic note was the impression the King conveyed as a collector and connoisseur. Charles had a keen love of art, and at a time when English taste was still provincial and little guided by knowledge, his own cultivated preferences led him to the art associated with the world of the courtly baroque and the Counter-Reformation. He admired such masters as Raphael, Titian, Caravaggio, and Rubens, the last of whom painted for him a rich glorification of Stuart kingship in the banqueting house at Whitehall.[2] This was the taste, then shared by few Englishmen, which the King exemplified in the formation of his great collections.[3] Outside the Court it could only have seemed a further manifestation of the ornate ceremonialism and subtle sensibility to be stigmatized as Romanist or crypto-Catholic.

In the portraits of Van Dyck, who worked in England under royal patronage from 1632 to his death nine years later, the image of Charles's court was enshrined forever on the eve of its passing. King, Queen, ministers, courtiers, noblemen, were represented in romantic grandeur. Elevated by the sumptuous, aristocratic imagination of the artist, the figures appear somewhat remote in their self-conscious elegance. The King gazes with a distant majesty in his equestrian portraits. The earl of Strafford and the opposition peer, Lord Warwick, both share the same withdrawn quality. The charm of the Queen and the royal children is enclosed within a cool hauteur. Van Dyck's vision was the definitive formulation of the Court's mood of delusive security about to be swept away.[4] In 1630, a courtier poet had celebrated the King's pacific reign:

> *White Peace (the beautifull'st of things)*
> *Seems here her everlasting rest*

[1] Cf. G. Albion, *Charles I and the court of Rome*, L., 1935, ch. VIII and M. J. Havran, *The Catholics in Caroline England*, Stanford, 1962, ch. VIII.
[2] Rubens's ceiling at Whitehall is analysed in P. Palme, *Triumph of peace*. Stockholm, 1962, 230–62.
[3] M. Whinney and O. Millar, *English art 1625–1714*, Oxford, 1957, ch. I.
[4] Cf. *ibid.*, ch. IV.

The Court

To fix, and spreads her downy Wings
Over the nest.[1]

Ten years later England's boasted calm was ready to expire in the heat of public strife. Under a darkening sky the Court advanced towards its defeat and dissolution.

[1] Sir Richard Fanshawe, *An ode, upon occasion of his Majesties proclamation in the year 1630. Commanding the gentry to reside upon their estates in the countrey.*

4

The Country

The Country was the first opposition movement in English history whose character transcended that of a feudal following or a faction. One hundred and fifty years before the seventeenth century, when the kingship itself was at stake in the broken world of the declining Middle Age, the protagonists were a handful of dynasts, their retainers, soldiers, and servants. The mass of Englishmen looked on while the lords of a moribund feudality fought each other to death. During the sixteenth century, after Henry VII established domestic peace, political differences lay centred chiefly about the court. The organic Tudor commonwealth allowed no place for an independent political life. The ruler's will was to be supreme in the determination of policy, the state a unity under its sole head, the prince. No legitimacy or tolerance could be accorded to public argument in which men joined openly to promote a policy contrary to the prince's. When tendencies of this kind appeared, as they did most notably in the Puritan and parliamentary opposition of Queen Elizabeth's reign, they were quashed. Thus, the normal form of political contention was the factional grouping ranged around rival ministers. The latter, competitors for power and favour, held their adherents together by patronage and the prospect of reward. Issues of high policy, inextricably bound up with the differences of factions, were decided in contests waged in court and council to gain the approval of the prince. This was a phenomenon consequent on the nature of personal monarchy, an ineluctable trait of its political system. The rivalry between Essex and the Cecils, the supreme faction struggle of the sixteenth century, was only the last of a number of such quarrels which exercised a deep influence on the internal measures and the course of religion, foreign relations, and war in the Tudor age.

The Country was essentially different from the factional groupings that dominated the Elizabethan scene. Its name, as has been seen, first became current as a political label in the 1620s, and its appearance in this sense signified the formation of a new type of opposition. The Country was not constituted as a system of dependency under the personal authority of great men who aspired to a preponderant share in the prince's favour and the shaping of his policy. Fundamentally, it consisted, rather, of a loose collaboration or alliance of men in the governing class, peers and gentlemen of assured position and often of substantial fortune, alienated for a variety of reasons from the Court. Principles counted for it more than persons. It found its main focus of action in parliament, and to a lesser extent in local government, in both of which it eventually secured an ascendancy beyond the monarch's ability to control.

If faction and party be considered as alternative types of political structure, then the Country approximated more nearly to party, notwithstanding that it was yet far from having evolved into one. It lacked the consciousness of party and possessed none of the formalized mechanisms of leadership, organization, discipline, and propaganda which create such a body and keep it in being. On the other hand, like a party it had some organization, even if informal; it stood for certain policies and opinions which it sought to carry into public life; and it gathered adherents among those persons who concurred with its outlook. It was thus the potential rallying point for a mass disaffection from the King's rule, and this is what it became at the close of the 1630s.

Two conditions made it possible for the Country to take shape as a new kind of opposition movement in the seventeenth century. One was the further growth of parliament under the Tudors, the other the changed circumstances prevailing after the accession of James I.

Parliament's evolution was, together with the progress of monarchical authority and institutions, the most important political fact of the sixteenth century. Fundamentally, both were aspects of the same process. Usually the monarch's cooperative and obedient instrumentality, parliament was employed to effect the greatest acts of state. The reformation under Henry and Edward was its work, as was the Elizabethan settlement of religion. The royal power was buttressed and extended by its enactments. Statute sanctioned the crown's ecclesiastical supremacy, gave it the wealth of the monasteries, authorized some of its new administrative bodies, and erected for its security a formidable barrier of treason legislation. Thus, while representative assemblies elsewhere in Europe were falling into desuetude and decay, or consuming themselves in strife between their constituent orders, parliament went from strength to strength. Statute acquired an immensely broader scope. Procedure and privilege underwent a notable expansion. The size of the House of Commons rose from 298 members in Henry VIII's first parliament to 467 in the first parliament of James I, an increase resulting mainly from the striking extension of borough representation.[1] The calibre of members improved as competition for seats grew and as university and legal education became more common in the governing class.[2] By the end of Queen Elizabeth's reign, parliament occupied a place far greater than ever before. So far as the political nation had a voice, it spoke in the House of Commons.[3]

Opposition to the royal will did not fail, of course, to appear in Tudor parliaments, but its advocates never attained a position of dominance in parliamentary transactions. In Henry VIII's reign, there was outspoken criticism of financial measures and resistance to the passage of the Statutes of Uses and of Proclamations. Under Mary, the government's opponents were sufficiently well-organized in 1555 to defeat a bill in the Commons aimed against the English refugees abroad.[4]

Such intermittent occurrences, rather obscure from paucity of evidence, gave place to repeated and persistent manifestations of opposition in Elizabethan parliaments. Throughout most of her reign, as Professor Neale's masterly researches have shown, the Queen encountered concerted defiance from members in the lower House.[5] These men were the forerunners of the later Country which began to emerge as a proto-party in the 1620s. Like most of the Country leaders of Charles I's time, the Elizabethan oppositionists were Puritan sympathizers, critical of the church establishment and bent on further reformation. They hated Spain, the pope, and Mary Queen of Scots. They judged Elizabeth too *politique* in her policy and blamed her refusal to provide for the succession. Their sort introduced a new figure to the political scene: the man of rigid principles, the idealist with a religious conscience. Of such stuff was the foremost of them, Peter Wentworth, made. The bluntest of the Queen's critics, the most audacious champion of parliamentary privilege, he would have been comfortably at home in the Long Parliament.[6]

Oppositionist activity in the Elizabethan House of Commons was part of an organized campaign of the Puritan clergy and their lay

[1] These figures come from J. R. Tanner, *Tudor constitutional documents*, 2nd ed., Cambridge, 1940, 514–15.

[2] Cf. J. E. Neale, *The Elizabethan House of Commons*, New Haven, 1950, ch. XV.

[3] Cf. *ibid.*, and for a concise survey of parliamentary development in the sixteenth century, G. R. Elton, *The Tudor constitution*, Cambridge, 1962, ch. 8.

[4] Cf. *ibid.*, 22, 305–7; J. E. Neale, *Elizabeth I and her parliaments 1559–81*, L., 1953, 23–6; D. M. Loades, *Two Tudor conspiracies*, Cambridge, 1965, 242–3.

[5] J. E. Neale, *Elizabeth I and her parliaments 1559–81*; *Elizabeth I and her parliaments 1584–1601*, L., 1957.

[6] Cf. J. E. Neale, 'Peter Wentworth,' *E.H.R.*, XXXIX, 2 pts., 153, 154 (1924).

patrons to win parliament's support for church reform. The attention the Puritans gave to petitions and bills was one of their most prominent traits.[1] Theirs was the earliest attempt to create a broad movement agitating openly for its demands in defiance of authority and censorship. The collisions of Puritan members with the government's spokesmen in the Commons, their strainings against the Queen's direction of the House, provided the main impulse in the sixteenth-century parliament's struggle to win a wider liberty. They were the ones who

taught the House of Commons methods of concerted action and propaganda. Indeed, the art of opposition, which might be considered the outstanding contribution of the Elizabethan period to Parliamentary history, was largely learnt from them or inspired by them.[2]

In spite of their challenge, however, the Queen retained control of parliament throughout her long reign. Firmness tempered by occasional concession, and the blandishments, amounting almost to a magical spell, with which she woo'd her subjects' affections, enabled her to keep the House of Commons in tutelage. The oppositionists were only a small number, in any case, and while they sometimes enjoyed the House's sympathy, they could not count on its support. They themselves, moreover, were intensely loyal to Elizabeth. They might chafe at her domination of parliament and press reform upon her, but they well knew that she was the Deborah of their English Israel, the protectress of the Dutch, the enemy of the pope and Spain, the stay of Protestantism in Europe. With her great personal popularity and the successes of her government in diplomacy and the war with Spain, the Queen remained unshakeable. The process which engendered the division between the Court and the Country had not yet begun.

The accession of James I opened a new period in many ways. The Spanish danger had passed and peace was made in the first year of the new reign. With the war's conclusion, a factor promoting the unity of ruler and subject was no longer operative. The King lacked Elizabeth's personal authority and her arts of management. A foreigner, his experience in Scotland did not prepare him for relations with an English parliament. Inflation, heavy debts inherited from the war, and his own extravagance placed his government under continuous financial strain.

[1] Cf. P. Collinson, 'John Field and Elizabethan Puritanism,' *Elizabethan government and society.*
[2] J. E. Neale, *Elizabeth I and her parliaments 1584–1601*, 436; cf. the remarks of A. F. Scott Pearson, *Church & state*, Cambridge, 1928, 95–7.

James therefore found it impossible to exercise the same mastery over parliament as his predecessor. As his reign proceeded, issues of division multiplied. Constitutional disagreements about the limits of the King's prerogative; dislike of the action of the royal supremacy in religion and of the jurisdiction of the ecclesiastical courts; financial grievances; the domination of Buckingham—these were some of the points on which serious differences and political opposition to the crown were gathering.

The place occupied by parliament made it inevitably the focus and *point d'appui* of the movement which then gradually began to take shape as the Country. By the start of James's reign, the corporate consciousness of the House of Commons and traditions favourable to its independence were already well developed. In the King's first parliament, the House ventured boldly on an unprecedented declaration to the monarch in defence of its privileges. These, the members asserted, were no donative from the crown, but belonged to them as a right not to be denied or impaired 'but with apparent wrong to the whole state of the realm.'[1] During the following years the Commons became ever more difficult to manage, so that control slipped from the King's grasp. The crown's financial necessity offered a lever susceptible to pressure. Bacon stated that once parliament

was . . . *in taste with matter of bargain and contribution and retribution and* . . . quid pro quo, *the generous disposition of free giving unto the King, and the politic argument of persuading it upon reason of estate, became dry things, and the endeavour grew* . . . *to draw from the King.* . . .[2]

By the 1620s opposition existed also in the House of Lords, while in the lower House the influence of the privy councillors waned disastrously and leadership of the Commons passed to 'popular men.'[3] The growth of procedure assisted this result. Through the device of the committee of the whole, first used in 1607, the House could turn

[1] *The form of apology and satisfaction of the House of Commons*, 1604, in J. R. Tanner, *Constitutional documents of the reign of James I*, Cambridge, 1930, 221. G. R. Elton has wrongly contended that the *Apology* was never adopted by the House and 'virtually forgotten' afterwards ('A high road to civil war?', *From the Renaissance to the Counter-Reformation. Essays in honor of Garrett Mattingly*, ed. C. H. Carter, N.Y., 1965). In the 1621 parliament, however, when members were discussing the defence of their privileges, the *Apology* of 1604 was frequently cited as a precedent by Coke, Crew, Hakewill, Phelips, and others, and referred to as an act of the House of Commons; cf. *Commons debates 1621*, II, 505, 525, 526, 533, 538, 541, V, 433.
[2] *Works*, XII, 179; cf. an earlier letter on the same theme, *ibid.*, XI, 313.
[3] C. H. Firth, *The House of Lords during the civil war*, ch. II; D. H. Willson, *op. cit.*

itself into a great committee, elect a chairman, and thus evade the rule of the Speaker, who was in effect the crown's nominee. At these occasions members had also the right to speak more than once to a motion. Committees of the whole functioned concurrently for various purposes, employing sub-committees in their work. In 1610, a committee of the whole was first appointed for grievances, thereby giving that irritant subject a sharper emphasis.[1] The consequence of these changes, leading to 'the winning of the initiative by the House of Commons,' was stated tartly by Charles I upon the dissolution of his intractable third parliament in 1629:

We are not ignorant, how much the House hath of late years endeavoured to extend their Privileges, by setting up general Committees for Religion, for Courts of Justice, for Trade, and the like; a course never heard of until of late: So as, where in former times the Knights and Burgesses were wont to communicate to the House, such business, as they brought from Their Countries; now there are so many chairs erected, to make enquiry upon all sorts of men, where complaints of all sorts are entertained, to the unsupportable disturbance and Scandal of Justice and Government, which having been tolerated a while by Our Father, and Our Self, hath daily grown to more height. . . .[2]

Together with procedural developments and the intensification of political conflict, early Stuart parliaments saw an increasing number of opposition sympathizers in the Commons. This was in contrast to the three parliaments of Elizabeth's last decade, in which, according to Professor Neale, opposition diminished considerably due to the passing of earlier militants and the government's suppression of the Puritans' organization.[3] In the parliaments of James I and Charles I, however, a largely new generation of activists became prominent. Although some died before the Long Parliament and others abandoned the Country, their presence ensured an unbroken and strengthening continuity of oppositionist personnel.

Sir Edwin Sandys, Nicholas Fuller, William Hakewill, Edward Alford, and Sir Dudley Digges, for instance, attended all or most of the parliaments convened between 1604 and 1628. Sir Robert Phelips,

---

[1] Cf. W. Notestein, 'The winning of the initiative by the House of Commons,' *loc. cit.* The device of a committee of the whole seems also to have come into use at about the same time in the House of Lords; cf. E. R. Foster, 'Procedure in the House of Lords during the early Stuart period,' *Journal of British studies*, V, 2 (1966), 67–9.

[2] J. Rushworth, I, App., 7.

[3] *Elizabeth I and her parliaments 1584–1601*, 241–2, 325–6, 370–1, 436–7. Neale holds that even in the monopolies dispute in 1601 the royal prerogative was less contested than in the parliaments previous to the 1590s.

Sir John Eliot, Sir Thomas Wentworth, William Mallory, and Sir Walter Erle first entered the House in 1614. Sir Edward Coke, the oracle of the law, returned to the Commons after a long absence in 1621. John Pym, John Hampden, and Sir Francis Seymour were elected the first time in this same year. Denzil Holles and William Strode first sat in 1624, Oliver Cromwell in 1628.

Besides these and other oppositionists of note, repeated contingents of the Country's supporters entered the early Stuart House of Commons. This can be seen clearly from the fact that the Long Parliament contained one hundred and twenty-eight Parliamentarian members who had also sat in parliament prior to 1640. Of this body of royal opponents, ninety-one were members of the Commons in 1628–9.[1] The latter parliament was remarkable for another circumstance as well: with the exception of St. John, Nathaniel Fiennes, and the younger Vane, all the subsequent leaders and managers of the Long Parliament were present in it.

Nothing was more significant in early Stuart parliaments than the Country leaders' efforts to concert their tactics through private consultations. The House of Commons was a body vulnerable to the influence of an organized minority. Since parliaments met irregularly and members came from all parts of the realm, most were strangers to one another. Many, too, having no parliamentary experience, lacked knowledge of procedure and precedents. In the growing state of public differences, therefore, an able group of men who worked together could have an effect in the House out of all proportion to their number.

Signs of oppositionist organization appeared first in the parliament of 1604–10. The presence in the Commons of such vocal critics as Sir Edwin Sandys and Sir Roger Owen was one reason this parliament produced frequent clashes with the King.[2] But there was more to the story than this: for Lord Ellesmere, the Chancellor, touched one of the secrets of the parliament in some 'Special Observations' he wrote about it after its conclusion. In later sessions a group of opposition members 'kept . . . privy conventicles and conferences' to plot 'the carrying of business in the House according to their own humor . . . and . . . in the weightiest and most important causes. . . .' They defeated a subsidy bill by devising that six of them who 'did bear great sway in the House' should speak against it. They talked con-

---

[1] Cf. W. M. Mitchell, *The rise of the revolutionary party in the House of Commons*, N.Y., 1957, 51–4, 122–3; T. L. Moir, *The addled parliament*, Oxford, 1958, 159–60; D. Brunton and D. H. Pennington, *Members of the Long Parliament*, L., 1954, 14–15.

[2] Cf. T. K. Rabb, 'Sir Edwin Sandys and the parliament of 1604,' *American historical review*, LXIX, 3 (1964) and D. H. Willson, *op. cit.*, 120–1.

stantly of grievances and delivered contemptuous speeches against the King's prerogative and regal power. Ellesmere saw a portent in these 'rare and strange proceedings.' Since the beginning of James's reign, he noted,

the popular state . . . hath grown big and audacious, and in every session of parliament swelled more and more. And if way be still given unto it . . . it is to be doubted what the end will be. . . . Great and dangerous inundations happen for the most part by reason that small breaches are neglected and not . . . stopped in the beginning.[1]

In the parliament of 1621, the Country opposition again made use of similar methods. The examination of members whom the King committed for their refractory conduct revealed that they had held private meetings on parliamentary business. Sandys was charged with conspiring to organize a petition against a threatened dissolution. He was further accused of corresponding with Puritan exiles in Amsterdam and was commanded to explain a suspicious writing he had composed on the power of kings. The earl of Southampton, an opposition peer in spite of his being a privy councillor, had taken part in these conferences. He was accused of consulting with members of the lower House at his residence and in the Lord's committee room concerning the passage or defeat of bills. All inflammatory speeches were said to have been delivered by his bosom friends.[2]

These tactics go some way to explain the aggressions which the 1621 parliament committed. Articulating the general sense of grievance, it set out in full cry against the patents of monopoly conferred by the King under his prerogative. The Houses revived impeachment, a procedure in disuse for over one hundred and fifty years, in order to attack dishonest royal officials and patentees.[3] The Commons tried to extend its privilege of free speech to deal with the hitherto forbidden subject of foreign affairs, persisting in its attempt despite the King's prohibitions.[4] The parliament's carriage aroused strong misgivings in James and provoked him to declare: '. . . he that will have all doon by Parliament is an enemie to Monarchie and a traitor to the King of England.'[5]

[1] Printed in *Proceedings in parliament 1610*, ed. E. R. Foster, 2v., New Haven, 1966, I, 276–83.
[2] *Proceedings and debates of the House of Commons in 1620 and 1621*, ed. T. Tyrwhitt, 2v., Oxford, 1766, II, Appendix; Sir Lionel Cranfield to James I, July 1621, *Commons debates 1621*, VII, 615ff.
[3] Cf. C. Roberts, *The growth of responsible government in Stuart England*, Cambridge, 1966, ch. 1. [4] Cf. *infra*, 88.
[5] *Notes of the debates in the House of Lords. A.D. 1621 . . . 1628*, ed. F. Relf, *Camden society*, 3rd ser., XLII, 1929, 14.

There were also indications of oppositionist parliamentary organization in 1624 and 1628–9. The *rapprochement* of 1624 between the Court and the Country could only have been effected by Buckingham's consultations with leading opposition members.[1] In 1628, a group of Country oppositionists met at Sir Robert Cotton's house prior to the opening of parliament. Those present included Pym, Eliot, Wentworth, Phelips, Coke, and Holles. They decided not to renew Buckingham's impeachment from the last parliament, but to concentrate on grievances.[2] When Eliot delivered a bitter attack on the government's misdeeds later in the session, a crown supporter[3] charged that his speech had been planned at 'private counsels and conference. . . .' To this Wentworth replied with a justification of such proceedings:

God forbid but we may speak one with another out of that House concerning those things which concern this House, and yet no confederacy. And this tends much to the disservice of this House not to confer with one another. A man may light his candle at another man's fire.[4]

During the second session in 1629, Eliot, Holles, and several other Country M.P.s conferred at the Three Cranes tavern to decide their course in view of the anticipated adjournment. The result was the unprecedented scene of disorder in the House of Commons on 2 March, when Eliot read out the opposition's resolutions against Arminianism and illegal tonnage and poundage, while his friends forcibly restrained the Speaker from executing the King's command to adjourn.[5] Later that year Eliot was brought to trial for his actions, and his counsel stated in his defence that 'members of the House may advise of matters out of the House, for the House itself is not so much for consultation as for proposition. . . .'[6]

---

[1] Cf. *supra*, 63–5.

[2] J. Forster, *Sir John Eliot*, 2v., L., 1865, II, 114; but cf. the critical remarks on Forster's account by H. Hulme, *The life of Sir John Eliot*, L., 1957, 184.

[3] Sir William Beecher.

[4] H. Hulme, *op. cit.*, 246. As Lord Deputy of Ireland, Wentworth afterwards took a different view of private consultations by M.P.s. He denounced them in a speech to the Irish parliament in 1634, warning that they were punishable, and said, 'I never knew them in all my experience to doe any good, to the publique. . . .', Strafford MSS., v. 21, 119.

[5] Cf. I. H. C. Fraser, 'The agitation in the Commons, 2 March 1629, and the interrogation of the anti-court group,' *Bulletin of the Institute of Historical Research*, XXX, 81 (1957).

[6] *State trials*, ed. T. B. Howell, 21v., L., 1816, III, 298. Eliot was charged with seditious speeches, contempts to the King in resisting the adjournment, and conspiracy with other M.P.s to restrain the Speaker.

Perhaps there were other oppositionist attempts at parliamentary organization in the 1620s; from the exiguous surviving evidence it is impossible to tell. These experiments afterwards bore fruit, however, in the Long Parliament. If Pym and his friends manifested some of the characteristics of a party in the House of Commons in 1640–1, and if by this means they were able to manage the House, it was due in part to opposition members' experience in the organization of their forces in previous parliaments.

2

Although the Country conducted a lengthy resistance to various powers claimed by the crown, its leaders produced no original political doctrine of their own. Moreover, the ends they sought, their conception of their struggle, must be mainly inferred from scattered utterances such as speeches in parliament or the law courts, since they refrained from composing elaborate theoretic justifications. The reason was not that they were intellectually unequipped for such a task. The contrary was rather the case. The opposition movement contained lawyers, learned scholars, gentlemen widely read in the political literature of Europe. That they created little in the way of theory was, in fact, a result of their political mentality and, as such, highly revealing.

The Country was a conservative opposition. Its adherents had no prejudice in favour of change. Certainly, in contesting with James I and Charles I, they did not set out to alter the government. They felt no necessity to rationalize a new version of the state or the English constitution because they conceived themselves defenders of an immemorial legal order of rights and liberties against which the King was the transgressor. He, not his antagonists, was the innovator—so it seemed to the Country.[1]

In 1610, in the great Commons debate over the King's right to impose customs duties of his sole will, Hakewill asserted that such a power in the crown entailed the 'utter dissolution' of the 'politic frame and constitution of this commonwealth. . . .' Pym declared, similarly, in 1629 that the law requiring the subject's consent in parliament to a tax 'was not introduced by any Statute, or by any Charter or Sanction of Princes, but was the antient and fundamental

---

[1] Cf. the full account of the political ideas of the opposition and the King's supporters by M. Judson, *The crisis of the constitution*, New Brunswick, 1949, and the discussion in J. W. Allen, *English political thought*, L., 1938, 3–47; C. H. McIlwain, *Constitutionalism ancient and modern*, rev. ed., Ithaca, 1947, chs. V–VI; G. Mosse, *The struggle for sovereignty in England*, Lansing, 1950, chs. IV–VII; J. W. Gough, *Fundamental law in English history*, Oxford, 1955, chs. IV–V.

83

law issuing from the first frame and constitution of the Kingdom.'[1] This conviction passed with the Country's supporters for an axiom. Thus, they took their stand on the law and the ancient constitution—a position they abandoned only after 1640, when circumstances gradually compelled the leaders of the Long Parliament to embark on a course of revolutionary change.[2]

The Country's supporters fully accepted, of course, the monarchical government inherited from their ancestors and advanced no claim to a sovereignty on parliament's behalf which excluded the King. Indeed, they seem not to have recognized sovereignty anywhere in the state, for they could not believe in a power that gave law to all while legally unlimited itself.[3] They held that the King's authority rested on law and must be exercised legally. The law also, in their view, secured the right of the subject, combining both elements in a well-poised balance. What they conceived themselves as contesting, therefore, were those invasions of power that deranged the equilibrium and violated law. For the King to levy impositions on merchandise; to exact forced loans and benevolences; to commit men to prison without showing lawful cause; to lay a direct charge on his people without their common consent in parliament—these things, done by James I or Charles I, they condemned as altogether illegal.

Against this assertion there was no general claim on the King's part to be exempt from law. The constitutional issue between him and his opponents centred on the nature of his prerogative and his powers under it. The question came before the courts in several great cases of the earlier seventeenth century.[4] In each, the judges, deciding for the King, enunciated a doctrine of the prerogative to justify those exercises of authority which the crown's opponents challenged.

Their opinions freely acknowledged that in many matters respecting

[1] J. R. Tanner, *Constitutional documents . . . James I*, 253; J. Rushworth, I, 596.

[2] Cf. the discussion of the intellectual traits of the 'common-law mind' by J. G. Pocock, *op. cit.*, ch. II.

[3] Whitelocke's argument in the Commons debate on impositions in 1610 was perhaps an exception. He denied the King's right to impose customs duties because the sovereign power in England lay not with the King alone, but with the King-in-parliament. The King therefore required parliament's assent for his action (J. R. Tanner, *Constitutional documents . . . James I*, 260–1). An echo of this idea appeared in the House's petition of grievances, 7 July 1610, in the reference to impositions (G. R. Prothero, *Select statutes and other . . . documents . . . Elizabeth and James I*, 4th ed., Oxford, 1913, 302). The conception of sovereignty remained uncommon, however, and scarcely figured in the armoury of oppositionist argument. Probably not even Whitelocke, moreover, would have allowed that the sovereign power of King-in-parliament was unlimited.

[4] In Bate's case, 1606, the Five Knights' case, 1627, and the Ship-money case, 1637; cf. *State trials*, II, III, for the texts.

private rights the King had to contain himself within the ordinary rules of law. But they declared that his prerogative included a power to act for the general good and safety in which he was not thus limited. This power, the special province of policy and 'matter of state,' they called his 'absolute' prerogative. Further, the King alone was judge of the circumstances in which he might use his 'absolute' prerogative. When he did so, he was to be presumed acting for the welfare of his subjects. Such a power the judges pronounced inherent in his monarchical office.[1]

This doctrine of the prerogative was by no means new. It had respectable mediaeval and Tudor antecedents.[2] Only in the reigns of James and Charles, because of unprecedented parliamentary recalcitrance to the King's will and attacks on his authority, it was magnified to new proportions by elaborate judicial exposition on the royal behalf. Naturally, the Country would have nothing to do with the idea. The crown's opponents admitted that many great powers belonged exclusively to the King under his prerogative, but none to act outside the law. They denied that the ancestral polity allowed him this power. They foresaw the danger that absolute prerogative would eat out liberty and property. Sandys told the House of Commons in 1614 that 'the mayne liberty of the people' was involved in the question of impositions; if the King had power to impose by his sole authority, 'no man Coulde knowe his right and propertye in his owne goodes. . . .'[3] That the judges sanctioned the absolute prerogative did not alter the oppositionists' mind.[4] On the contrary, it caused them increasingly to doubt the integrity and independence of the judiciary. The ship-money decision of 1637, in particular, was popularly regarded as a flagrant example of judicial subservience.

It would be strange, nevertheless, if the Country opposition, for all its professed conservatism, did not somewhere betray the radical implications of its conduct and intimate its gropings towards a new balance of political forces. For there can be no doubt that its adherents, greatly as they respected the *mos maiorum*, were unconsciously shaping a different conception of the polity—one that gave the power

---

[1] Cf. F. Wormuth, *The royal prerogative*, Ithaca, 1939, ch. II; M. Judson, *op. cit.*, ch. IV; P. Zagorin, *A history of political thought in the English revolution*, 192–4.

[2] Cf. C. H. McIlwain, *op. cit.*, 111, 127–9.

[3] *Commons debates 1621*, VII, 653, 654 (from a diary of proceedings in the House of Commons in 1614).

[4] Sandys, for instance, said in 1614: '. . . wheras the kinge dothe alledge that he had a Judgement . . . that he might Laye impositions by his sole Authoritie . . . the Judges had nothing to doe to decide that question, for they are not to meddle with two thinges, viz. the title of the Crowne and Libertie of the kingdome. . . .', *ibid.*, VII, 54.

of decision over policy to parliament, rather than the King. This was especially evident in two particulars: first, in the Country's intense awareness of parliament as the people's representative and trustee; second, in its championship of parliamentary privilege on that account.

That parliament represented the kingdom was no more than a constitutional truism in the sixteenth century: as the first statute of James's reign expressed it, in parliament 'all the whole body of the realm, and every particular member thereof, either in person or by representation ... are by the laws of this realm deemed to be personally present.'[1] The Country, however, gave the notion of representation a new meaning. Its supporters manifested a sort of 'constituency-consciousness' and set themselves against the royal will on the ground of their public trust.[2]

Opposition speakers in parliament repeatedly employed the theme of representation in their arsenal of argument. Coke told the House in 1621: '... when the kinge says he cannot allowe our liberties of right, this strikes at the roote. Wee serve here for thousands and tenn thousands.' William Mallory declared: 'We are entrusted for our country. If we lose our privileges, we betray it.' And Edward Alford: '... lett us remember that England sent us. That must be satisfied.'[3] In 1626 the Commons informed the King that unless members searched into grievances, 'we could neither be faithful to your Majesty, nor to the Countrey that doth trust and employ us. ...'[4] Protesting the imprisonment of men by martial law, Sir Robert Phelips said in 1628: 'The County I serve for were pleased to command me to seek the removal from them of the greatest burthen that ever people suffered. ... it concerns us to preserve the Countrey in freedom. ...' Of the Commons' privileges he asserted, 'If we suffer the liberties of this House ... to be abused, we shall give a wound to the happiness of this Kingdom. ...'[5] Coke laid it down that 'the freedom of this House is the freedom of the whole land. ...'[6] Sir John Eliot solemnly stated,

[1] The Succession Act, 1 Jac. I, c. I, in J. R. Tanner, *Constitutional documents ... James I*, 11; the identical thought in Sir T. Smith, *op. cit.*, 49; R. Hooker, *Laws of ecclesiastical polity*, VIII, c. vi, 11; W. Lambarde, *Archeion*, 1635, written c. 1591, ed. C. H. McIlwain and P. Ward, Cambridge, 1957, 126. Those deemed personally present are the King and the temporal and spiritual peers.
[2] Cf. C. H. McIlwain, *op. cit.*, 115, and A. F. Pollard, *The evolution of parliament*, 2nd ed., L., 1926, for remarks on the changing conception of representation.
[3] *Commons debates 1621*, V, 240, 219, II, 484.
[4] J. Rushworth, I, 401.
[5] J. Rushworth, I, 503; *Commons debates for 1629*, 7. Phelips was knight for Somerset in the 1628–9 parliament.   [6] *Commons debates 1621*, II, 57.

The Country

That which is more than lives . . . than all our goods, all our interests and faculties, [is] the life, the liberty of the Parliament, the privileges and immunities of this House which are the bases and support of all the rest.[1]

In like vein, Pym declared, 'The peace of this kingdom consists in the peace of this House.'[2]

This profound devotion to parliament was gradually replacing the profound devotion the preceding age had accorded the prince. It was a momentous shift of sentiment—from the exaltation of the godly head to the exaltation of the representative body. With such a view, opposition supporters could not but feel anxiety when they considered that the King might succeed in dispensing with parliament altogether. Fears on this score aggravated political differences. '. . . if this power of imposing were quietly settled in our Kings,' Whitelocke said in 1610, 'considering . . . the greatest use they make of assembling of Parliaments, which is the supply of money, I do not see any likelihood to hope for often meetings in that kind.'[3] The Country's leaders did not fail to mark the fate of continental assemblies at the hands of absolute kings. 'Wee are the last monarchy in Christendome,' exclaimed Phelips, 'that retayne our originall rights and constitutions.'[4] Whitelocke noted the decline of the Estates General of France, and Pym the debility of the Estates of Normandy, their privileges devoured by the taxing power conceded the French king.[5] If the House of Commons permitted its privileges to be impaired, Alford warned, it would be 'farewell Parliaments and farewell England.'[6] Charles I stated the danger bluntly when he informed the Houses in 1626 that the existence of parliaments depended entirely on his will: 'therefore as I find the fruits of them good or evil, they are to continue, or not to be. . . .'[7]

The Country's supreme regard for parliament led, logically, to the conclusion that the latter should possess the deciding voice over the King in all matters of public concernment. This outcome, if still not anticipated, was definitely foreshadowed in the efforts of the House

[1] Cited in H. Hulme, *op. cit.*, 190.
[2] *Commons debates 1621*, II, 95.
[3] J. R. Tanner, *Constitutional documents . . . James I*, 262.
[4] *Commons debates in 1625*, 110.
[5] J. R. Tanner, *Constitutional documents . . . James I*, 262; J. Rushworth, I, 601.
[6] *Commons debates 1621*, VI, 155.
[7] J. Rushworth, I, 225. The King's threat was subsequently amplified in a speech by Sir Dudley Carleton, a privy councillor, who, after describing the decline of representative assemblies throughout Christendom, begged the Commons not to trench on the royal prerogative lest parliaments in England be overthrown; *ibid.*, I, 359.

of Commons under oppositionist leadership to intrude into areas of policy hitherto reserved by precedent for the crown alone. When warned off these forbidden topics, the House invoked its privilege of liberty of speech in justification.

As the privilege had grown up in the preceding century, it did not signify the members' right to treat what subjects they pleased. The official position, successfully enforced by Queen Elizabeth, was that they might express their minds freely (though without license) on matters properly within their purview or referred to them by the crown.[1] Numerous questions of high policy were denied them leave to consider. Stuart parliaments, however, abandoned former limits, and the House asserted its privilege of free speech in far more comprehensive terms—to embrace war, peace, foreign relations, and other prerogative matters pertaining to the King's personal decision.

Already in 1610, commanded by James not to discuss the legality of impositions, the members replied with the general claim that everything of concern to the King's subjects lay within the House's 'ancient and undoubted right ... to debate freely. ...'[2] Again in 1621, when defending its right to treat of foreign policy, the House made the blanket avowal, '... we cannot conceive that the honour and safety of your Majesty ... the welfare of religion, and state of your kingdom, are matters at any time unfit for our deepest consideration in ... Parliament.'[3] This contention, submitted in a petition, brought from the exasperated monarch the answer:

... this Plenipotency of yours, invests you in all power upon Earth, lacking nothing but the Popes to have the Keys also both of Heaven and Purgatory. ... For what have you left unattempted in the highest points of Sovereignty, in that Petition of yours, except the striking of Coin? For it contains the violations of Leagues, the particular way how to govern a War, and the marriage of our dearest Son. ... These are unfit

[1] The Lord Keeper's speech in 1593 was the best expression of the official Elizabethan view of the House's privilege of free speech; cf. G. R. Elton, *The Tudor constitution*, 266–7, for the text. Oppositionists like Peter Wentworth championed a far broader interpretation of the privilege. Though not successful under Elizabeth, their position was adopted by the House of Commons in the next reign.

[2] J. R. Tanner, *Constitutional documents ... James I*, 246. In the debate preceding the adoption of this statement, Bacon defended James's command and pointed out to no avail that Queen Elizabeth had frequently inhibited the House from treating of matters within her prerogative; *Parliamentary debates in 1610*, ed. S. R. Gardiner, *Camden society*, LXXXI, 1862, 38–9. One of the extraordinary features of Stuart parliamentary history was the rapidity with which the House of Commons possessed itself of an 'ancient right.'

[3] J. R. Tanner, *Constitutional documents ... James I*, 281.

*King regards as
unfit for discussion*

*things to be handled in Parliament, except your King should require it
of you. . . .*[1]

The Commons nevertheless refused to yield, and adopted a protestation which declared forthrightly that all the arduous affairs of King
and state, the defence of the realm, the church, and the redress of
mischiefs and grievances were proper subjects for counsel and debate
in parliament.[2] Here the elastic privilege of freedom of speech,
stretched to its widest extent thus far, became a claim not much short
of the demand that the King should answer to parliament in every
province of government. No symptom was more revealing of the
challenge parliament and the Country were gradually generating
against the King's supremacy.

The latent possibilities in the House's position, however, were
destined to remain unacted till after 1640. During the 1620s parliament's predominant concern was to contain the King's power within
bounds of law. This in the main determined the opposition movement's perspective. Needless to say, there was as yet no question,
even when relations with Charles I were at their worst, of forcible
resistance or a right of rebellion. Such an idea was far from the
Country's mind, imbued as it was with the long tradition of loyalty to
the monarchy built up in the union of Protestantism and patriotism
from Queen Elizabeth's days.

The Petition of Right in 1628 represented parliament's extreme *Pet of R. 1628*
effort prior to the revolution to fortify the subject's liberty by means
of law. It was called forth by certain arbitrary acts of Charles I—
forced loans, imprisonment of refusers, execution of men by martial
law, billeting of troops on unwilling householders. The Petition
declared these to be grievances contrary to law, and asked the King
to confirm Magna Charta and other good laws which secured his
subjects in their rights and property.[3] That parliamentary and oppositionist pressure compelled Charles to assent was no inconsiderable
achievement. Nevertheless, the Petition had no practical effect at the
time. The conflict between the King and parliament, Court and
Country, was more than legal; it involved serious political and
religious disagreements as well, and to these the Petition was irrele-
vant. Moreover, the Petition provided no means for deciding what
future exercises of power might be illegal, and contained no machinery
of enforcement in case the King should break the law. Control
without accountability remained in the crown, and Charles did not

---

[1] *Ibid.*, 285, 286.
[2] *Ibid.*, 289.
[3] Cf. the text in S. R. Gardiner, *The constitutional documents of the Puritan
revolution*, 3rd ed., Oxford, 1936, 66–70.

deem himself to have parted with any of his prerogative powers by his assent to the Petition.[1]

At such a juncture more was required than a restatement of old law on the subject's behalf. The true situation was that parliament was pulling one way, the crown another. Both were essential elements in the polity, but in the past the King's will, not parliament's, had prevailed. Now the royal will was persistently contested and obstructed. There could be no arbitrator or legal remedy for this division. The character of Charles I's government from 1629 to 1640, when no parliament met, sufficed to show how little the methods of the Petition of Right availed. The King's opponents were to see that political reforms to curb the crown must be effected and guarantees devised. This aim was to be the first preoccupation of the Country politicians when they led the Long Parliament in a wholesale assault on a large part of the monarchy's traditional authority.

3

The outstanding characteristic of the Country from a social-structural standpoint was its uniformity with the governing class. To imagine the Country as 'progressive' in the sense of incarnating, even unwittingly, a new ordering of society, is completely erroneous. Equally so is the supposition that its relation to the Court was the antipathy of 'Outs' to 'Ins'—the social resentment of men denied admission to influence and favour. What made the Country so formidable was that its adherents were pillars of society. They belonged to the elite of Englishmen who owned the soil and administered the law to its inhabitants. They were noblemen, lords of manors, justices, lawyers, members of parliament. Beneficiaries of the society established, they entertained no thought of changing it, much less of overthrowing it. Singular destiny that such men should become revolutionaries! But they were surely the most conservative revolutionists who ever lived. It was not possible that they should foresee the overturnings consequent on the constitutional revolution they accomplished . . .

The Country's social substance and its close integration with the dominant class can best be seen from a review of some of the types drawn into its orbit. First to be noticed must be the peerage: for there was no more sinister omen to the crown than the formation of an alliance of noble oppositionists. They were not a great number, but as the personal embodiment of the regime of privilege which sanctioned their hereditary honours, they brought to the struggle against the King an invaluable prestige. Without their backing, the Country could not have sustained its character as the reaction of the

[1] Cf. F. H. Relf, *The Petition of Right*, Minneapolis, 1917, 56–8.

nation to the dangerously misguided policies of a purblind Court. In the well-founded judgment of Sir Edward Walker, a contemporary chronicler of their order, 'if the Nobility had been unanimous to have defended the just Rights of the King ... it had never been in the power of the Commons to have begun their Rebellion.'[1]

The alienation of part of the peerage began with Buckingham's domination and was soon reflected in parliament and elsewhere. The House of Lords' resumption in 1621 of its power of judicature in cases of impeachment was an effect of it. So also was the Lords' support of the Petition of Right in 1628. Both these notable episodes of cooperation with the House of Commons occurred because of widespread discontent in the upper House and an active oppositionist presence there.[2]

Some seventeenth-century commentators thought political disaffection in the nobility to be the result of the lavish distribution of titles by James I and Charles I. It was a fact that under the early Stuarts the peerage went through one of the most rapid transformations in its history. Queen Elizabeth, as parsimonious with honours as with money, authorized the creation or recognition of only 18 titles. When she died the English nobility stood at 55. James created 65 peers during his reign and Charles did about the same, half of them before the civil war. Between 1615 and 1628, the period of most frequent creations, the peerage grew from 81 to 126, earldoms alone rising from 27 to 65.[3] In addition to English titles, numerous Scotch and Irish peerages were bestowed. Some of these creations were merely the crown's acknowledgment of the claim of distinguished commoner families to be raised to noble rank. Others, however, lacked this justification, being given more in recognition of wealth or to gratify a favourite than as a sign of family distinction and eminent services to the crown. After 1615, moreover, noble titles were frequently sold, a practice never permitted in Elizabeth's time. These mercenary transactions, from which Buckingham and other courtiers profited as intermediaries, ceased only with the favourite's death, and aroused widespread resentment and disapproval.[4]

[1] Sir Edward Walker, *op. cit.*, 304.
[2] Cf. C. H. Firth, *The House of Lords during the civil war*, ch. II; *Notes of the debates in the House of Lords A.D. 1621 ... 1628*, Introduction; J. L. Sanford, *op. cit.*, 109n.
[3] It is not suggested that this increase in earldoms represented new creations. Most were due to promotions of peers to higher rank. A rise of earls by over 100 per cent in such a short time was extraordinary, nevertheless; how much so appears from L. Stone's table of the numbers and composition of the peerage 1487–1641, *The crisis of the aristocracy*, App. VI.
[4] *Ibid.*, ch. III and App. III–VI, a definitive treatment of the inflation of honours and the sale of titles; cf. also C. H. Firth, *The House of Lords during*

The Court and the Country

Sir Edward Walker, who as a herald had a professional interest in the nobility, expatiated at length on the unhappy consequences of its enlargement. He believed that the older aristocracy became antagonized because it felt itself undervalued when it saw men ennobled by the patronage of the favourite or the 'Riches . . . gotten in a Shop. . . .' Most harmful, in his opinion, was the King's inability to reward the entire peerage with offices or gifts, with the result that the noblemen overlooked became envious and factious: 'whereas had the number been smaller, they might every one had opportunity to have tasted of the royal favours.' The same view was expressed by the duke of Newcastle in looking back on the revolution.[1]

Walker's explanation, however, exaggerated the importance of personal motives in the formation of a peerage opposition, and it erred as well in suggesting a connection between these noble oppositionists and antiquity of title that never, in fact, existed. It was, indeed, exactly the sort of opinion to be expected in the Court, where the tendency was to visualize all issues in terms of the manoeuvres for favour so characteristic of the royal milieu. Desire for office and influence was doubtless a strand—but only a strand—in the opposition of the peers. But in that aspect which was politically significant, it was joined with the further aim of effecting a change in policy, to which a change of ministers and the oft-demanded removal of 'evil counsellors' would necessarily be instrumental. This was what made the involvement of certain noblemen with the Country a matter of consequence. So long as the state remained effectively monarchical, so long also did the service of the King present itself as the only means of playing a political role that would be positive and not merely obstructive. In the 1620s and '30s, no other perspective on the exercise of power could be thought of. The partial fulfilment of this point of view, in which a change of men was to confirm a change of measures, occurred in early 1641, when a few of the Country leaders in both Houses received offices of state. By then, however, such reconciling methods had ceased to be effective.[2]

A mixed bag of peers were active in the opposition. One of the most prominent was Robert Rich, earl of Warwick. The Riches were

[1] Sir Edward Walker, *Observations upon the inconveniences that have attended the frequent promotion to titles of honour*, [1653], *op. cit.*, 304–5; S. A. Strong, *A catalogue of documents . . . at Welbeck*, L., 1903, App. I, 215; C. H. Firth, *The House of Lords during the civil war*, 33. Cf. John Selden's remark, 'The making of new lords lessens all the rest.' *Table talk*, L., ed. 1894, 102.
[2] Cf. *infra*, 214–16.

the civil war, ch. II and C. R. Mayes, 'The sale of peerages in early Stuart England,' *Journal of modern history*, XXIX, 1 (1957) and 'The early Stuarts and the Irish peerage,' *E.H.R.*, LXXIII, 287 (1958).

the principal landed family in Essex, and in 1635 the earl owned sixty-five manors in the county. He was a great patron of the Puritans, his house, Lees Priory, being known as 'The common Randezvous of all Schysmaticall Preachers.' The friend of Sir John Eliot and other Country notables, he inspired the resistance in Essex to the King's forced loan and the ship-money tax.[1] Even more conspicuous as an oppositionist was William Fiennes, Viscount Saye and Sele, a Puritan of the Puritans. He was a man of rigid character who unfailingly contradicted every act of state he deemed illegal—forced loans, compulsory billeting of soldiers, ship money. In 1625 Saye was promoted from the degree of baron (he was the fourth of the title) to a viscountcy, an honour which Buckingham secured for him during the Court's brief *rapprochement* with the Country. A story in Saye's family described the favourite's flattering addresses—'that it may be writ upon my Tombe, Here Lies the man who did . . . Lord Say a kindnesse. . . .' But no blandishments could win him over: 'his ambition,' said Clarendon, 'would not be satisfied with offices . . . without some . . . alterations in ecclesiastical matters.' In truth, he wanted nothing less than the removal of bishops. There was not in the 1630s a firmer antagonist of the royal regime than this nobleman.[2]

Robert Greville, Lord Brooke, shared Saye's enmity towards the bishops. His cousin, the poet, Fulke Greville, whom he succeeded in the title, was a courtier and had been Chancellor of the Exchequer under King James. In spite of this, Brooke allied himself with the opposition. He was a youthful idealist of rare intellectual gifts, a Puritan who detested the clerical presumption of the Laudian churchmen and sympathized even with separatists.[3]

William Seymour, earl of Hertford, also adhered to the Country. He was a magnate in Somerset and the west and was esteemed by his contemporaries as a figure of honour. In 1610 he aroused the high displeasure of the King by marrying a royal cousin, Arabella Stuart. Following her death he took as his second wife the sister of the earl of Essex, another noble dissident. His closest associations, wrote Clarendon, were with men who loved the Court least and 'engaged most factiously and furiously against the King.' Nevertheless, he

---

[1] F. Hull, *Agriculture and rural society in Essex 1560–1640*, University of London Ph.D. thesis, 1951; Clarendon, *Rebellion*, III, 27; *A letter from Mercurius Rusticus to Mercurius Civicus*, 1643, 8; *C.S.P.D. 1627–28*, 43, 150; *D.N.B., s.v.*
[2] *C.S.P.D. 1627–28*, 589; *H.M.C. Rutland*, I, 507–8; Clarendon, *Rebellion*, III, 26; Dr. Williams's Library, Morrice MSS., v. G., f. 841; *D.N.B., s.v.*
[3] R. E. Strider, *Robert Greville, Lord Brooke*, Cambridge, 1958; *D.N.B., s.v.* The quality of Brooke's mind and the range of his sympathies are revealed in his published writings, *The nature of truth*, 1640, and *A discourse . . . of . . . episcopacie . . . in England*, 1642.

abandoned his friends after 1640 and supported Charles I, one of the few Country peers to do so. Very likely a strong sentiment of personal loyalty to Charles prompted his reversal.[1]

Edward Montagu, Viscount Mandeville, belonged to the Country as well, although there were a host of Court connections in his background. His uncle was Bishop of Winchester. His father made his career as a lawyer in the royal service, attained the earldom of Manchester, and was Lord Privy Seal from 1628 to his death in 1642. Mandeville began as a courtier and friend of Buckingham, whose patronage obtained him the unusual honour of elevation to a peerage in his father's lifetime. His first wife—he had five—was Buckingham's kinswoman, but after her death in 1625 he married a daughter of the earl of Warwick. Having thus contracted an affinity with a great opposition peer, he detached himself completely from his former associations. He became a Puritan, a resolute opponent of the crown, who believed according to Clarendon, that 'the Court was inclined to hurt and even to destroy the country. . . .'[2]

Another of the Country's noble adherents was Robert Devereux, earl of Essex, son of the unhappy second earl executed for treason in 1601. James I restored Essex in blood and title, only to humiliate him a few years later by aiding his wife to obtain a divorce so that she might marry the earl of Somerset, the King's protégé. Perhaps this and family tradition first led him into the oppositionist camp. He engaged in numerous actions against royal power. For combating Charles I's forced loan he was deprived of his lord lieutenancy of Staffordshire. His friendships were with other opponents of the regime, and he appointed the earl of Warwick, Hampden, and St. John among the executors of his will. A member of his household wrote that he 'ever affected (out of the nobleness of his mind) a naturall & just freedom for the subject.' He enjoyed a reputation for integrity and a personal popularity inherited from his father which made his political support a great resource in the conflict with the crown.[3]

Still another lord in the fraternity of oppositionists was Francis

---

[1] *D.N.B.*, *s.v.*; Clarendon, *Rebellion*, IV, 296, VI, 385.

[2] *D.N.B.*, *s.v.*; Clarendon, *Rebellion*, VI, 407, III, 27.

[3] *D.N.B.*, *s.v.*; Clarendon, *Rebellion*, V, 32; W. B. Devereux, *Lives . . . of the Devereux*, 2v., L., 1853, II, 471n. The quotation is from Arthur Wilson (author of the *History of Great Britain*, 1653), who was first in Essex's service and then became steward to the earl of Warwick; F. Peck, *op. cit.*, pt. II, 470. Cf. also V. Snow, 'Essex and the aristocratic opposition to the early Stuarts,' *Journal of modern history*, XXXII, 3 (1960). B.M. Add. 46188, pt. 7 contains Essex's correspondence relating to his lieutenancy; B.M. Add. 46189, pts. 2, 4, includes correspondence with Warwick, Hertford, and John Selden.

Russell, earl of Bedford. A Puritan magnate, the owner of a great estate, he was an entrepreneur in the development of his London property and the draining of the fens. Among his close associates were Pym and St. John. The former sat in six parliaments for Tavistock, a Devon borough under Russell patronage. The latter was the earl's relation and lawyer and by his interest was elected to parliament in 1640 for Totnes.[1]

These were some of the opposition peers, though by no means all. The earl of Southampton has already been mentioned.[2] His heir, the fourth earl succeeding in 1624, continued to hold to the same position as 'a high assertor of the rights of his country. . . .'[3] Lord Spencer and the earl of Clare, who died before the Long Parliament, were both connected with the Country.[4] Clare's younger son, Denzil Holles, became a noted oppositionist in the House of Commons. The Puritan earl of Lincoln stood out against the forced loan and belonged to the inner circle of the crown's opponents.[5] Other titled dissidents in the 1630s were the earls of Danby, Mulgrave, and Bolingbroke, and lords Paget, Robartes, Savile, Wharton, and Willoughby of Parham.[6] Most of the Country peers—the main exceptions were Hertford, Southampton, and Paget—became Parliamentarians in the civil war, along with a group of noblemen who switched their allegiance from the Court after the assembling of the Long Parliament.

Save for their political and religious position, this gallery of peers differed in no respect from the rest of their order. Some held older, others more recent titles. In fortune they varied from the very rich, such as Warwick, Bedford, and Clare, to those whose estates were moderate or even straitened, such as Saye and Mandeville. What they had in common was precisely their antagonism to the crown's policy and methods, which they expressed sufficiently openly to

---

[1] *D.N.B., s.v.*; G. S. Thomson, *Life in a noble household 1641–1700*, L., 1937, ch. I; L. Stone, *The crisis of the aristocracy*, 355–7, 360–1; Clarendon, *Rebellion*, III, 32; M. Keeler, *op. cit.*, 318, 330.

[2] Cf. *supra*, 81.

[3] *D.N.B., s.v.*, 'Thomas Wriothesley;' H. C. Foxcroft, *op. cit.*, 56.

[4] *D.N.B., s.v.*, 'Robert Spencer;' G. Holles, *Memorials of the Holles family*, ed. A. C. Wood, *Camden society*, 3rd ser., LV, 1937, 106–9; A. Thomson, 'John Holles,' *Journal of modern history*, VIII, 2 (1936). In a letter to Wentworth in January 1628 Clare expressed his fears concerning the operation of regal power, Strafford MSS., v.22 (10).

[5] G. E. Cokayne, *op. cit.*, VII, 696–7; *C.S.P.V. 1626–28*, 126, 160; *C.S.P.D. 1628–29*, 498–9.

[6] Danby: *C.S.P.V. 1636–39*, 110–11; Mulgrave: *D.N.B., s.v.*, 'Edmund Sheffield;' Bolingbroke: *D.N.B., s.v.*, 'Oliver St. John;' Paget: Clarendon, *Rebellion*, III, 339; Robartes: *D.N.B., s.v.*, 'John Robartes;' Savile: *D.N.B., s.v.*, 'Thomas Savile;' Wharton: *D.N.B., s.v.*, 'Philip Wharton;' Willoughby of Parham: *D.N.B., s.v.*, 'Francis Willoughby.'

leave some record of their sentiments. Most also had Puritan sympathies, and there can be no doubt that the Puritanism of the peerage was heavily concentrated among these noblemen.

Another type represented in the Country was the royal official. There were not many such in the 1630s, but enough to illustrate the complete social resemblance of the groupings from whose conflict the revolution arose. Sir Robert Harley, Master of the Mint, may be taken as an instance. He was a prosperous Herefordshire gentleman, prominent in county affairs, and a member of parliament five times before November 1640. In 1623 at the age of forty-five, already twice a widower, he married the daughter of Sir Edward Conway, Secretary of State and Buckingham's dependent. With such a father-in-law he soon tasted favour. In 1626 the office of Master of the Mint was conferred on him for life at a salary of £500.[1] Harley had thus become affiliated with the Court, but he was out of sympathy with it all the same. A story in his family told how Buckingham, inviting him to a private meeting, tried vainly to gain his support.[2] The truth was, he was the friend of oppositionists and a Puritan.[3] Both he and his wife looked sourly on bishops, and in the parliament of 1628-9, in spite of his being elected with his father-in-law's help, he was a vocal assailant of the Arminian clergy who enjoyed the King's protection.[4]

It was his Puritanism that got Sir Robert into difficulty. In 1634, by his own account, 'falling under the disfavour of those ... then powerfull at Court, especially the ... Bishop of Canterbury,' a writ of *scire facias* was brought against his patent of office by Attorney General Noy. His offence was his support and patronage of nonconforming ministers. Since he was appointed for life, it appears that he was not legally deprived of his place. He was not allowed to exercise his function, however, or to receive any income from it. The Long Parliament restored Harley, but he had incurred a loss which he estimated at £3,875 for setting religious principles higher than office.[5]

[1] *D.N.B., s.v.; C.S.P.D. 1625–26*, 573, 577; *H.M.C. Portland*, III, 21.

[2] *The character of Sir Robert Harley*, B.M. Loan 29/124, no. 57. This story was recorded in the early eighteenth century.

[3] Cf. the letter to Sir Robert in February 1637 from Nathaniel Fiennes, Lord Saye's son, which speaks of their frequent meetings, B.M. Loan 29/119, pt. 4.

[4] *Commons debates for 1629*, 116. Harley represented Evesham, to which Conway wrote on his behalf, *C.S.P.D. 1627–28*, 562.

[5] Harley's narrative of his trouble over his office is in B.M. Loan 29/124, no. 65. For his support of nonconformist clergy, cf. *C.S.P.D. 1637–38*, 249, and his correspondence with the Rev. Stanley Gower, the Puritan rector of

Harley's example suggests that oppositionists in office saw nothing questionable about their situation. In any case, not being in the greatest positions, they bore no responsibility for the crown's measures. They were at most administrators, not devisers of policy. So we find Sir Gilbert Gerrard, Bt., an activist in the Country, serving at the close of the '30s as clerk to the Council of the Duchy of Lancaster—a place occupied by his father before him.[1] So, too, John Hutchinson, a Nottinghamshire Puritan hostile to the regime, tried about 1639 to buy an office in the Court of Star Chamber; before his negotiation could bear fruit, wrote his wife ingenuously, 'it pleased God . . . that arbitrary court was, by the parliament then sitting, taken away.'[2] The Suffolk gentleman, John Winthrop, another Puritan, held an attorneyship in the Star Chamber. Assiduously as he had sought the office, he resigned it in the dark year 1629, when the Country's hopes were at a low ebb, in order to emigrate to New England as governor of the Massachusetts Bay Company.[3] The Surveyor of the Court of Wards, Sir Benjamin Rudyard, was associated in the '30s with leading oppositionists.[4] Even John Pym, while not to be classified as an official, was Receiver General of royal revenues for three counties from about 1607 to 1636.[5]

Just as Sir Thomas Wentworth left the Country for office and the Court, so in a corresponding reversal Sir John Eliot left the Court and office for the Country. The latter's was the outstanding case of this kind in the opposition movement. And if Wentworth's change of front gave him power, Eliot's brought him fame as one of the greatest parliamentary champions of his time. Born of a Cornish gentry family, he became attached to the Court in consequence of an early friendship with Buckingham. He was knighted in 1618 through the favourite's influence and four years later Buckingham as Lord Admiral gave him the profitable office of Vice-Admiral of Devon.[6] Here he was shortly in trouble. In 1624, Sir John Coke, the duke's assistant in naval matters, accused him of financial malfeasance in his

[1] M. Keeler, *op. cit.*, 186.
[2] Lucy Hutchinson, *Memoirs of Colonel Hutchinson*, ed. C. H. Firth, 2v., L., 1885, I, 95, 96–7.
[3] R. C. Winthrop, *Life and letters of John Winthrop*, 2v., Boston, 1864, I, 214; C. M. Andrews, *The colonial period of American history*, 4v., New Haven, 1934–8, I, 384–7.
[4] *D.N.B., s.v.*
[5] M. Keeler, *op. cit.*, 318.
[6] H. Hulme, *op. cit.*, 17–19, 26, 30, 32.

his own parish, B.M. Loan 29, *passim*. The account of Harley in the preceding two paragraphs of the text derives from material collected prior to the publication of G. E. Aylmer's *The King's servants*, which also uses him as an illustration. Our discussions differ in a few details.

vice-admiralty. He also quarrelled bitterly with the Vice-Admiral of South Cornwall, Sir James Bagg, who denounced him to Buckingham as obstructive in naval affairs in Devon.[1]

Despite these frictions, Eliot was still loyal to the Court.[2] The duke's help secured his election to parliament in 1624 and 1625; and though in the latter he showed himself somewhat critical of the government, he refrained from joining the attack on the all-powerful minister.[3] The next year, however, with political division hardening and in the background the failure of the English expedition against Cadiz, he broke completely with his patron. Returned to the parliament of 1626 for St. Germans, the borough neighbouring his own estate, he delivered 'the sharpest denunciation of the government . . . ever . . . heard in the House of Commons.' It was a powerful appeal to patriotic feeling in condemnation of the dishonour and loss brought by evil counsellors upon the King and kingdom. A few weeks later he assailed Buckingham as the cause of all the nation's ills. The House chose him, together with Pym, Digges, Erle, Selden, and three others, to manage the duke's impeachment.[4]

Eliot thus renounced the Court to ally himself with the politicians of the Country. His oratorical talents and fearless espousal of the popular cause put him immediately in the front rank of oppositionists in parliament. His conduct did not go unscathed, however. Although never formally removed from his vice-admiralty, in 1626 proceedings were instituted against him for abuses in office and an order of the Privy Council suspended him from his functions.[5] There is scarcely any reason to doubt that his change of front was dictated by political dislike of crown policy and the sincere conviction that Buckingham's domination meant ruin. He was, according to his most painstaking biographer, 'an idealist in government . . . so loyal to his convictions that he was eager to fight and willing to die for them.'[6]

We have mentioned peers and royal officials among the types represented in the Country. There were also citizen and merchant supporters who will be noticed in the following chapter. The predominant element in the opposition movement, however, was the gentry, in particular the upper gentry. The men in the House of

---

[1] *C.S.P.D. Addenda 1625–49*, 203; *H.M.C. Cowper*, I, 177, 190.

[2] Cf. his letter to Buckingham, April 1625, *C.S.P.D. 1625–26*, 5.

[3] H. Hulme, *op. cit.*, 43, 75, 89, 91–3. Eliot represented Newport in these parliaments. He was first elected to the House in 1614; he was not returned in 1621.

[4] *Ibid.*, 104–7, 117–19, 131.

[5] *Ibid.*, 152–4, 165.

[6] *Ibid.*, 13–14.

Commons who led the struggle for parliamentary privilege, liberty of the subject, and security of property; their friends and associates outside parliament; the persons who showed themselves most refractory to forced loans, ship money, and other devices of the regime: they were almost all gentry. Such, to cite a representative sample of families whose members defied the royal power at one time or another in the 1620s and '30s, were Phelips, Seymour, Strangeways, Erle, Ayscough, Armyne, Irby, Wray, Hampden, Luke, Goodwin, Haselrig, Barnardiston, Cheeke, Barrington, Rous, Masham, Buller, Grenville, Stephens, Pelham, Dryden, Knightley, Heyman, Mallory, Belasyse.

Here was a portent. A growing section of the aristocratic order—the privileged elite of landlords and local governors on whose loyalty and obedience the monarchy's stability depended—was hostile to the crown. When a growing body of men in the governing class could be provoked into opposition, a revolutionary situation was in the making. It only remained for Charles I, driving forward on his purblind course in the 1630s, to bring the revolutionary situation to birth.

4

Considered as a whole, the opposition engendered by the rule of Charles I was not an organized affair. If we were to collect from the surviving evidence the name of every one in England and Wales who showed himself in any way recalcitrant towards the royal authority in these years, the result would be a list of hundreds of individuals, most of them personally unknown to each other. There was no coordination, no connection, no design in this large and amorphous mass. Acts of disobedience were frequently spontaneous or due to the force of example, a product of common grievances and sympathies, rather than of planning and calculation.

But at the centre of the Country was something more. Here a definite organization existed: a group united by conviction, linked through family and friendship, meeting to concert the tactics of opposition. In structure an informal alliance of like-minded men, this group was the nucleus of the Country. It was that part of the opposition movement in which the reaction to Stuart rule had produced an organized political force, the embryo of a party. To it belonged the gentlemen with whom the regime had most to reckon, the most resourceful and determined antagonists of the royal power.

A vague but illuminating description of this organization of opposition leaders was set down late in the seventeenth century by the Tory antiquarian, Anthony Wood. According to his account, the

Puritan Lord Saye, godfather of the 'discontented party,' was endeavouring to incite a rebellion and held meetings of his friends at his Oxfordshire house, Broughton Castle,

> *where was a room and passages thereunto, to which his Servants were prohibited to come near: and when they were of a compleat number, there could be great noises and talkings heard among them, to the admiration of those that lived in the House, yet could they never discern their Lord's Companions. At other times he would be present at their meetings in the House of [Richard] Knightley at Fawsley in Northamptonshire; where, as at other places in the Kingdom, they had their Council Chambers and chief Speakers: And what Embryo's were conceived in The Country, were shaped in Greys-Inn-Lane near London, where the Undertakers for the Isle of Providence did meet....[1]*

A pamphlet written forty years earlier, from which Wood drew some of his material, added the detail that John Hampden went annually to Scotland, thereby implying a connection between the Country nucleus and the Scottish rebels. It also reported that John Pym 'rode a Circuite into divers Counties, to promote Elections of men of the Faction' to the Long Parliament.[2]

That a group of the kind pointed at in these statements really existed is beyond question. It is impossible, however, to determine precisely how it came into being or to throw much light on its inner transactions. Opposition was dangerous, meetings were illicit conspiracies, and these Country politicians must surely have been careful to destroy compromising communications and to cover their deliberations with secrecy. Yet despite these difficulties an idea of its nature and activities can be formed.

Probably the group took shape through the cooperation of certain of the principal Country members and their friends in parliament. We have already mentioned some of their private consultations to influence the House of Commons. Then, after the dissolution of 1629 and the cessation of parliaments, they had to establish other means through which to maintain their collaboration. The Country leaders apparently found a solution in several of the companies for colonization. These enterprises, in which the English Puritans took a

[1] Anthony Wood, *Athenae Oxonienses*, 2nd ed., 2v., L., 1721, II, 273–4. The room at Broughton Castle where, according to tradition, these meetings took place, is still shown to visitors.

[2] *Persecutio undecima*, 1648, 55–6. Wood took some of his material from this tract, and both he and it also depended heavily on *A letter from Mercurius Civicus to Mercurius Rusticus*, 1643, which appears to have been their common source. For the latter pamphlet, cf. *infra*, 287.

strong interest, were created to finance and support settlement in the lands across the Atlantic. They were legal incorporations, managing their own affairs under a charter from the crown. In the shelter of their meetings, it was possible to discuss much else besides company business when the occasion warranted. Thus, within some of these bodies, like the Providence Island enterprise founded in 1630, which Wood mentioned, and the Saybrooke patentees of 1632, a virtual interlocking directorate of oppositionists was formed. Its members were the militant Puritan centre of the struggle against Charles I before and after 1640—Pym, Hampden, St. John, Knightley, Sir Thomas Barrington, Sir Gilbert Gerrard, Sir Thomas Cheeke, and a number of others, as well as such noblemen as Warwick, Saye, Brooke, Robartes, and Mandeville.[1] Most likely Eliot would have been associated with them, had he not been put in prison for sedition in 1629, dying there three years later the victim of royal displeasure.

An astonishing number of threads joined these men and led out from them to other enemies of the King's rule. So thick were their ties of family that altogether they resembled a large kith or clan. Thus, both Mandeville and Robartes married daughters of the earl of Warwick. Warwick's sister was married to the Essex oppositionist, Sir Thomas Cheeke. Mandeville's third wife was Cheeke's daughter. Lord Brooke was the son-in-law of the earl of Bedford and his sister married Sir Arthur Haselrig, a Leicestershire adherent of the Country. Of Lord Saye's children, one daughter married the oppositionist earl of Lincoln, another the son of the Dorset oppositionist, Sir Walter Erle. Saye's younger son, Nathaniel Fiennes, was Sir John Eliot's son-in-law. His older son, James Fiennes, and Lord Willoughby of Parham, a Country peer, both married sisters. Richard Knightley and John Hampden were connected by marriage, while the relatives of Sir Thomas Barrington, an Essex member of this inner circle, included Hampden, St. John, Sir Gilbert Gerrard, as well as Oliver Cromwell and such opposition families as Masham in Essex, Luke in Bedfordshire, and Wallop in Hampshire. Warwick and Mandeville were also related to still other supporters of the Country—to the Wrays, the Irbys, and the Ayscoughs in Lincolnshire, who were in turn linked through marriage to each other.[2]

[1] The discovery of the role of the colonizing companies in the organization of opposition to Charles I was due to A. P. Newton, *The colonizing activities of the English Puritans*, New Haven, 1914, a work to which I am indebted.
[2] On these kinship connections, cf. A. P. Newton, *op. cit.*, *passim*; J. H. Hexter, *The reign of King Pym*, Cambridge, 1941, ch. IV; and biographical accounts under the names mentioned in M. Keeler, *op. cit.*, G. E. Cokayne, *op. cit.*, and *D.N.B.* A genealogical chart in J. W. F. Hill, *Tudor and Stuart Lincoln*, Cambridge, 1956, 127, shows the relationships of some of the oppositionist families of Lincolnshire.

Close bonds of friendship, too, held these men together. The correspondence of Sir Thomas Barrington included familiar letters from or allusions to Hampden, St. John, the earl of Warwick, and other political confidants.[1] In 1630 Barrington informed his mother of the possibility that Pym would occupy Barrington Hall 'till winter.'[2] Pym addressed Sir Thomas as 'brother,' the term Puritans often used towards one another in recognition of their spiritual bond.[3] A further impression of these friendships cemented by common convictions comes from the prison correspondence of Sir John Eliot. Warm and sympathetic letters passed between him and Hampden, the earls of Warwick and Lincoln, Denzil Holles, and Sir Oliver Luke. To his great friend, Richard Knightley, a pillar of Northamptonshire Puritanism, he signed himself 'brother'—an expression which, like his account of his spiritual experience as a prisoner, shows that he became a Puritan in the last years of his life.[4]

In spite of the obscurity surrounding the Country nucleus during the 1630s, several important manifestations of its political activity can be traced. One was its role in the resistance to ship money. The King introduced this tax in 1634, giving as ground the necessity to raise a fleet for the security of shipping and the defence of the realm.[5] First imposed only on the port towns, the next year it was made into a general levy. As a device which was in fact, if not in form, a direct impost ordained without assent of parliament, ship money provoked strong protest everywhere. It was seen as a move in Charles I's possible plan to dispense forever with the representative body of the kingdom.

In December 1636 the earl of Danby took the bold step of writing the King to denounce ship money as illegal and ask for the summoning of parliament. The Venetian ambassador, Correr, reported that Danby's letter was the 'long premeditated' result of 'consultation' among leading men. A month later Correr mentioned 'secret meetings' by 'leading men . . . determined to make a final effort to bring the forms of government back to their former state.' He thought they would issue a public call for a parliament and offer the King some

---

[1] B.M. Egerton MSS. 2645, *passim*.

[2] *Ibid.*, f. 184.

[3] B.M. Egerton MSS. 2643, ff. 6, 14. Cf. Wentworth's remark in 1637 about the Puritan Hampden: he 'is a great Brother, and the very Genius of that Nation of People leads them always to oppose . . . Authority. . . .', *The earl of Strafforde's letters*, II, 138.

[4] *The letter-book of Sir John Eliot*, ed. A. Grosart, 2v., p.p., 1882, 52, 55, 63; J. Forster, *op. cit.*, II, 642–5; H. Hulme, *op. cit.*, ch. XV. Eliot seems to have passed through a conversion in prison.

[5] Cf. the text of the writ ordering the levy of ship money in S. R. Gardiner *Constitutional documents of the Puritan revolution*, 105–8.

concessions as an inducement.[1] If such was the oppositionists' purpose, nothing further was heard of it, but meanwhile they were preparing to challenge ship money in the courts. With the aim of laying the basis of a case, both Saye and Hampden had formally refused payment.[2] At the end of February 1637 the directors of the Providence Island Company held several meetings in Northamptonshire at Preston Capes, a house belonging to Richard Knightley not far from his mansion at Fawsley.[3] Pym, Saye, Brooke, Mandeville, Knightley, and doubtless Hampden, too, attended. Probably they discussed the ship-money question, since a declaration by the judges in favour of the King's power to levy the tax had just been made public.[4] At any rate, within two weeks, on 9 March 1637, Hampden's name was certified as a refuser and the legal proceedings thus instituted in which he as defendant and St. John as counsel were soon to win fame for their opposition to taxation without the consent of the subject in parliament.[5]

There is further evidence of the political activity of the inner circle of Country politicians in connection with the Scottish rebellion. They did not fail, of course, to realize the significance of the rising which broke out in the northern kingdom in 1638. The adverse decision of the judges in the ship-money case had made them so despairing of the trend of events that some of them even contemplated emigration across the Atlantic.[6] But then, as if by providence, a storm blew up in Scotland that threatened the carefully erected edifice of arbitrary rule. Sharing the Scots' hatred of Laud, the English oppositionists saw the revolt as the occasion that might reinstate liberty and religion in England: for in the face of danger and possible invasion from the north, the King would have to seek his subjects' aid in parliament. There is no doubt that they sent the rebels secret encouragement. Late in 1639 Lord Saye addressed a message to the earl of Loudoun, one of the Scot leaders. It was carried by Henry Lawrence, a Huntingdon neighbour of Mandeville and Oliver Cromwell, and declared that the English people would oppose a war against the Scots if the latter 'did unanimouslie resolve ... to come in for the publique

[1] *C.S.P.V. 1636–39*, 110–11, 125, 136.
[2] S. R. Gardiner, *History*, VIII, 271.
[3] *Victoria county history, Northamptonshire, Genealogical vols.*, II, 171, 185.
[4] The probable connection between the February meetings of the Providence Island Company and the ship-money struggle is discussed by A. P. Newton, *op. cit.*, 242–3. The judges' declaration justifying ship money was read in the Star Chamber on 14 Feb. 1637, *State trials*, III, 839–44. It was not a judicial decision, but an opinion solicited by the King.
[5] The chronology of the case can be gathered from *State trials*, III, 846. The suit did not come to trial until November.
[6] A. P. Newton, *op. cit.*, 245.

liberties of both kingdomes. ...' Saye's son, Nathaniel Fiennes, subsequently joined Lawrence at Edinburgh in order to represent the state of English affairs to the Scots.[1]

The King, meanwhile, having lost hope of any agreement with his rebellious subjects in Scotland, decided in December 1639 to summon a parliament to assist him against them. The Short Parliament met on 13 April 1640 and lasted only three weeks. It refused to vote a penny to put down the Scots unless English grievances were first redressed. When Charles learned that Pym and a group of fellow M.P.s were about to offer a petition in the House of Commons against a war, he hastily dissolved the parliament.[2] Two months later, as the Scottish army prepared to march south, the rebel leaders communicated with the opposition peers in England to ask assurances of support. The noblemen who replied—Bedford, Essex, Warwick, Brooke, Saye,[3] Mandeville, and Savile—refused to extend an invitation to the Scottish army to enter England, since that would be treason. On the same ground they would make no specific offers of aid. But they pointed out that if the Scots entered England 'in their own just Right ... we are resolv'd to do more, and more effectually, for obtaining their and our honest Ends' than the assistance requested would provide. Between Scotland and England, they said, 'the Enemies are all one, the common Interest one, the End is all one; a free Parliament to try all Offenders, and to settle Religion and Liberty.'[4]

Nothing could have been more clearsighted than this appraisal of the bearing of the Scottish rebellion upon English affairs and the political objectives of the Country. The King's game was now about played out. At the end of August an army of 25,000 Scotsmen crossed the border, occupied Newcastle, and brought most of the north under its power. Disorganized, poorly led, disaffected, the King's forces offered no resistance. The time had come for the opposition leaders to make a last attempt, as they had promised the Scots, to obtain a parliament that would do the work of both. At London

---

[1] The evidence for this episode is an anonymous paper in *The Hamilton papers*, ed. S. R. Gardiner, *Camden society*, n.s., XXVII, 1880, 264–6. It was probably written in 1640, and though mentioning no dates, seems to refer to the later months of 1639. The 'Lawrence' of whom it speaks can be identified by the allusion to his stay in Holland, where he had been a religious exile; cf. *D.N.B.*, *s.v.*, 'Henry Lawrence.'

[2] An account of Pym's consultations with the purpose of laying the case of the Scots before the Commons was given to the Privy Council; cf. *C.S.P.D. 1640*, 144–5.

[3] Not Lord Scrope, given by Gardiner, *History*, IX, 179.

[4] J. Oldmixon, *The history of England during the reigns of the royal house of Stuart*, L., 1730, 142–3. The original of this letter is not extant and is known only from the copy printed by Oldmixon. Its genuineness has been challenged, but is convincingly defended by Gardiner, *History*, IX, 179n.

discussions took place between Essex, Warwick, Saye, Brooke, Bedford, the latter's son, Lord Russell, Pym, Hampden, St. John, and perhaps other participants. The Privy Council, learning of these meetings, feared 'some dangerous practice or intelligence with the Rebels of Scotland.'[1] The outcome of the oppositionists' deliberations was a petition to the King drafted by Pym and St. John in the name of twelve peers. The petitioners recited the evils and dangers threatening church and state by reason of the Scottish war, religious innovations, ship money, and other burdens. They dwelt, too, on the grief caused Charles's subjects by the long intermission and the dissolution of parliaments. To compose the Scottish troubles without bloodshed, to remove the people's grievances and punish those responsible, they asked that a parliament be promptly summoned.[2]

The demand thus voiced was universal—the expression of national feeling too imperious to be withstood. On 24 September at York, where he had summoned a council of the whole nobility, Charles yielded. Devoid of money for war, beset by a Scottish army and the clamour of his discontented people, he announced the convening of a parliament for 3 November.

Although Pym and his friends must have bent all their energies to secure the return to the House of Commons of members favourable to the Country, scarcely any evidence of their election preparations has survived.[3] It is not difficult, however, to imagine the hopes and fears with which they faced the immediate future. Through years past they had done what lay in their power to sustain the political struggle against the crown. The parliament about to meet would present them with the gravest challenge and the greatest opportunity. The prospect existed of enacting measures to put an end to methods of arbitrary rule so productive of animosity and division in the '20s and '30s. For this more than a talent for opposition would be required. Amidst the deepest political crisis in more than a century members from all parts of the kingdom were assembling to take their seats at Westminster. It remained to be seen whether the Country leaders could maintain their unity and apply the lessons of their collaboration to guide parliament in achieving a great work of constructive reform.

[1] Secretary Windebanke to the King, 31 Aug. 1640, *Clarendon state papers*, ed. R. Scrope and T. Monkhouse, 3v., Oxford, 1767–86, II, 94–5.
[2] Printed in S. R. Gardiner, *The constitutional documents of the Puritan revolution*, 134–6. Pym's and St. John's authorship of the petition was attested by Lord Savile, who had joined in the previous message to the Scots and was in a position to know; cf. Savile to Lady Temple, November 1642, *Camden miscellany*, VIII, 1883, 2.
[3] A few scanty indications of the Country group's electioneering activity preliminary to the Long Parliament are mentioned by M. Keeler, *op. cit.*, 9 68, 166.

The period that witnessed the generation of the Country's conflict with the Court also saw a great awakening of political awareness in society at large. There was a heightened interest everywhere in public questions, along with growing hostility to the Court and royal government. Beneath the surface of events, profound tremors of popular discontent made themselves felt. Sectional grievances resulting from one or another aspect of the crown's policy were merging behind the spokesmen of the Country in a broad front of opposition. Sullen and resentful, the offended hosts of sufferers from the prerogative and prerogative courts, financial exactions, monopolies, and religious repression were drawing together in one swelling mass of enmity, their hope of redress and a day of reckoning centred on the opposition movement. A formidable insurgent temper was taking possession of the English people which in the end endowed the Country leaders with power to impose their will on Charles I.

The awakened political consciousness of the 1620s had its origin in the attention with which the public mind followed the fortunes of continental Protestantism and the progress of controversies in parliament. A decade of defeat for the Protestant forces in central Europe, Germany, and France made it appear that the princes and peoples adhering to the Reformation might be overwhelmed by a rising tide of Catholic conquest. The failures of Stuart foreign policy and the reverses which Charles I encountered against Spain and France became matters for general comment and criticism. Together with angry disputes in parliament and dislike of Buckingham and royal financial pressures, they raised the political temperature to fever height.

Under these circumstances, a rapid evolution of public opinion occurred. The Venetian ambassador told his government at the end of 1620: '... this kingdom has never had its eyes so wide open ... and it has never been so teeming and pregnant with ideas and grievances as now.'[1] Preoccupation with governmental affairs was widespread. '... now-a-days,' said Bacon, 'there is no vulgar, but all statesmen.'[2] On the eve of the parliament of 1621, King James found it necessary to issue a proclamation against 'excesse of lavish Speech of Matters of State.' It declared that 'there is at this tyme a more licentious Passage of lavish Discourse and bould Censure in matters of State than hath been heretofore or is fitt to be suffered.' James commanded his presumptuous people not to meddle with 'Causes of

[1] *C.S.P.V. 1619–21*, 490.
[2] *Works*, XIV, 129.

State and Secretes of Empire either at Home or abroade, but containe themselves within that modest and Reverend Regard of Matter above the Reach and Calling that to good and dutiful Subjects appertaineth.'[1] This royal attempt to silence public discussion was fatuous, however, in the face of powerful domestic and international forces whose effect everyone could feel or see.

Just at this time, appropriately enough, in December 1620, the first English newspaper or coranto saw the light. Printed at Amsterdam and translated from Dutch, it was imported into England to supply the demand for information about the European war. Some of the corantoes published the next year were printed in London, but bore a fictitious Dutch imprint to defeat government attempts at suppression.[2] A second proclamation issued in July 1621 against the 'inordinate libertie of unreverent Speech touching Matters of high Nature unfit for vulgar Discourse,' was probably aimed partly at them.[3] From the middle of 1622, however, weekly news sheets began to be printed in England by rival writers with the consent of authority.[4] These confined themselves to dry accounts of foreign occurrences, leaving domestic topics alone. The government allowed them because the appetite for such news was too keen to be stifled by prohibition.

In general, anything of immediate political relevance was seized on avidly by a growing public. *Vox Populi*, a tract published in 1620 against a Spanish marriage alliance, won instant notoriety and its Puritan author, the Rev. Thomas Scott, had to flee the kingdom.[5] Three years later, Thomas Middleton's play, *A Game At Chesse*, a sharp-witted satire that took off the Spanish ambassador, Gondomar, to the life, became a nine-day-wonder—the longest run of any play to that time. It 'hath ben followed'—so wrote the best of all Jacobean news correspondents—'with extraordinarie concourse, and frequented by all sorts of people old and younge, rich and poor, masters and servants, papists and puritans ... churchmen and statesmen. ...'[6]

But the chief focus of political attention in the 1620s was parliament. Concentration on its proceedings produced an extraordinary

---

[1] T. Rymer, *Foedera*, ed. 1742, VII, pt. 3, 187. The proclamation was dated 24 Dec. 1620.

[2] Cf. L. Hanson, 'English newsbooks, 1620–1641,' *The library*, 4th ser., XVIII, 4 (1938) and J. Frank, *The beginnings of the English newspaper*, Cambridge, 1961, ch. I.

[3] T. Rymer, *op. cit.*, VII, pt. 3, 207.   [4] L. Hanson, *op. cit.*

[5] *Letters of John Chamberlain*, II, 339; *D.N.B.*, *s.v.*, 'Thomas Scott.' *Vox populi* went through four editions in 1620. Scott's writings as an anti-Spanish publicist are discussed by L. B. Wright, 'Propaganda against James I's "Appeasement" of Spain,' *Huntington Library quarterly*, VI, 2 (1943).

[6] *Letters of John Chamberlain*, II, 578.

increase in the dissemination of parliamentary news and speeches, so that the import of the conflict at Westminster between the Court and the Country was communicated to every quarter. Debate, of course, was supposed to be secret and members' revelation of parliamentary business a breach of privilege. The tendency, however, of the oppositionists to carry their fight in an appeal beyond the walls of parliament caused the restraints against disclosure to be seriously undermined. Manuscript copies of speeches, petitions, and declarations circulated far and wide. Such 'separates' of parliamentary utterances began first to appear in small numbers in the middle of Elizabeth's reign. Gradually increasing in volume, their quantity reached new proportions amidst the bitter arguments of the 1620s. From this time, parliamentary affairs were conducted in an unprecedented glare of publicity, while the words of Pym, Eliot, Coke and other oppositionist orators were studied and preserved in scores of country houses. Members themselves passed around manuscripts of their own and other men's speeches to the end, said an unfriendly critic, 'That all the people might take notice of the zeal they had to the common liberty of the nation.'[1] Private intelligencers, procuring copies, sold them to subscribers; writers of news letters summarized them in accounts of parliamentary transactions. These expanding facilities for learning of what passed in parliament developed in almost direct relation to the progress of political opposition. They were at one and the same time both a consequence of enlarged public awareness and a further means of stimulating its growth.[2]

Revolution is never a sudden birth. It must ripen through a considerable period of gestation. Before the decisive battle is joined, there are preliminary skirmishes and engagements. Usually the men in power repel the first challenges. The attacking forces fall back momentarily, fatigued and defeated, while the disturbed political atmosphere settles down for a little. But soon a new crisis erupts creating fresh difficulties for the regime. Opposition revives with resurgent energy, the struggle against the government attains greater dimensions than before, and this time its enemies are victorious. Such was the phasing of the course of events between the inception of Charles I's rule and the meeting of the Long Parliament. From 1625 to 1629 the deterioration of relations between the King and his subjects brought England close to rebellion. The period ended with the temporary defeat of the Country, and an interval of quiescence ensued. Then after 1635 occurred the growing reaction against ship

---

[1] P. Heylyn, *Examen historicum*, 1656, pt. 2, 74, cited in *Commons debates for 1629*, xxviii.
[2] Cf. *ibid.*, Intro., chs. III–IV, for an account of the circulation of parliamentary news and separates.

money, the renewal of open conflict in the wake of the disturbances in Scotland, and the generalization of disaffection throughout the kingdom. When revolution came, it was because an invincible body of support had gathered about the opposition leaders which the King was powerless to resist.

The first outbreak of large-scale disobedience to the royal government occurred in 1626-7 in consequence of the forced loan. Repulsed in his attempt to obtain a money grant from the parliament of 1626 for the Spanish war, Charles resorted to a device the Tudor rulers occasionally employed and commanded the levying of a loan. It was to be demanded from everyone liable to the payment of parliamentary subsidies. In palliation of the measure, the King published a proclamation promising that it would not be made a precedent nor used to evade the future summoning of parliament.[1] These professions had no effect, and during the next months a spirit of insubordination burst forth throughout the kingdom. Frequently, men appointed as commissioners for the loan would neither perform their duty nor lend themselves. In some counties the principal gentry refused to lend and also influenced the freeholders to follow their example. The Privy Council was kept busy summoning recalcitrants before it to warn them of the penalties of their defiance. In Northamptonshire the Council learned that twenty-two gentlemen had drawn half the county into opposition and threatened to infect the neighbouring shires by their conduct. Two hundred and five freeholders there were reported as refusers.[2] Sizeable opposition manifested itself in Somerset and Gloucestershire; in the latter, twelve of the twenty-five loan commissioners would give no money for reasons of conscience.[3]

Many refusers also appeared in Yorkshire: one landlord was haled to the Council board for saying that no one who lent should hold land of him.[4] In Cornwall three justices were ordered removed from the commission of the peace for their opposition while in Norfolk some of the loan commissioners went on a sort of strike, declining to attend meetings of their body.[5] A numerous group of refusers gave

---

[1] S. R. Gardiner, *History*, VI, 143; R. Steele, *op. cit.*, I, 1494.
[2] *C.S.P.D. 1627–28*, 15; *The court and times of Charles I*, I, 184. Several striking instances of defiance by Northamptonshire gentlemen summoned before the Privy Council appear in *Acts of the Privy Council, Jan.-Aug. 1627*, 42, 62.
[3] *C.S.P.D. 1627–28*, 58–9, 76; W. B. Willcox, *op. cit.*, 117–20; T. G. Barnes, *op. cit.*, 165–7.
[4] *C.S.P.D. 1627–28*, 32, 194; *Fairfax correspondence*, ed. G. W. Johnson, 2v., L., 1848, I, 73–4; *Acts of the Privy Council Jan.-Aug. 1627*, 54, 67.
[5] *C.S.P.D. 1627–28*, 231; *State papers relating to musters, beacons, ship money in Norfolk*, ed. W. B. Rye, Norwich, 1907, 83–4.

the Council trouble in Lincolnshire, Essex, and Warwickshire.[1] In several London parishes the loan provoked riots. The refusers were many and the constables would not distrain upon their goods as ordered.[2] Six hundred persons in Hertfordshire subscribed a letter to their lord lieutenant, the earl of Salisbury, protesting the loan.[3] Some of the nobility were adamant in their refusal of money. A servant of the earl of Lincoln was apprehended for dispersing letters against the loan among freeholders inscribed, 'To all true-hearted Englishmen.' '. . . this scattering of letters,' reported a news writer, 'is grown rife in divers parts, and they are but ill symptoms.'[4] At the beginning of 1628, according to the Privy Council's records, seventy-eight men were still in prison or under some form of restraint for their disobedience. The list included twenty-six knights, fifteen esquires, three gentlemen, and twenty-three described as Londoners.[5]

Although only a small minority stood forth openly against the loan, they expressed the sentiment of multitudes. The angry kingdom stirred with unrest. A hard will against giving to the King in any but a parliamentary way had been revealed. Furthermore, with all the pressures the crown could apply, fourteen months after the loan was undertaken it was still over £55,000 short of its estimated total of £300,000. The balance was never obtained.[6]

During 1628 and 1629, the political mood worsened. While the resentments of the forced loan lingered, abuses from the billeting of soldiers and the operation of martial law added to the general sense of grievance.[7] At the ports, the customs officials extracted tonnage and poundage duties from unwilling merchants without a grant from parliament for the purpose. Buckingham was universally execrated. In June 1628 a London mob lynched Dr. Lambe, a quack astrologer reputed to have some shady connection with the duke. The city officials did nothing to suppress this outbreak of violence.[8] Two months later Buckingham himself was murdered by an assassin who said he acted solely for patriotic and public reasons.[9] The elections to

---

[1] *C.S.P.D. 1627–28*, 81; *The court and times of Charles I*, I, 207; P.R.O. S.P. 16/56, no. 70.

[2] *The court and times of Charles I*, I, 154, 157.

[3] *Ibid.*, I, 176.

[4] *Ibid.*, I, 172, 177, 202, 207; *C.S.P.D. 1627–28*, 43.

[5] *Acts of the Privy Council Sept. 1627–June 1628*, 217–18.

[6] W. R. Scott, *The constitution and finance of English . . . joint-stock companies*, 3v., Cambridge, 1910–12, I, 190. I have preferred these figures to those given by S. R. Gardiner, *History*, VI, 219–20.

[7] Cf. the Privy Council's letter of June 1628 about the opposition to billeting, *Acts of the Privy Council Sept. 1627–June 1628*, 490, and L. Boynton, 'Martial law and the Petition of Right,' *E.H.R.*, LXXIX, 311 (1964).

[8] *Acts of the Privy Council Sept. 1627–June 1628*, 492.

[9] *The court and times of Charles I*, I, 387.

the parliament of 1628, which were held in February and early March, provoked more excitement than any since the Stuart accession. 'All the counties,' the Venetian ambassador reported, 'have uniformly rejected candidates who had even a shadow of dependence upon the Court, electing members who refused the late subsidies ... now everywhere called good patriots.'[1] Loan refusers and oppositionists were returned as knights of the shire in Kent, Essex, Dorset, Northampton, Yorkshire, Norfolk, Cornwall, Gloucester, Lincoln, and elsewhere.[2] The first session saw the passage of the Petition of Right after a hard fight; but in the second, rancorous quarrels ensued because of the King's collection of tonnage and poundage and his patronage of well-known Arminian divines. The resolutions condemning these royal acts which Eliot and his friends forced through the Commons on the eve of dissolution raised passions to white heat. Not all the Country's sympathizers approved of their conduct. Some, like the Puritan Sir Simonds D'Ewes, blamed it as imprudent and extremist—the work of 'fiery spirits.'[3] Their unprecedented defiance of the Speaker, however, backed by the House, was a sign that confidence in the King had sunk nearly to the vanishing point.

It was in these months that the likelihood of rebellion was spoken of here and there for the first time. The Venetian ambassador had been expecting an outbreak all along. In September 1626 he considered one to be imminent because of the intense popular dissatisfaction.[4] At the end of 1627 a Suffolk clergyman confided a similar belief to his diary, the result of political discussions with his acquaintances. In June 1628 he mentioned rumours of a secret intent to depose Charles in favour of his sister, Queen Elizabeth of Bohemia. 'Our King's proceedings,' he wrote, 'have caused mens mindes to be incensed, to rove, and projecte. ...'[5] From 1626 onward, Salvetti, the agent of the Grand Duke of Tuscany, also repeatedly reported to his government on the prospects of a rising. In May 1628 he held it certain that serious disorders would occur. At the end of the year, he reiterated his prediction, in view of the 'growing and daring opposition of the people.'[6]

Perhaps if the Country leaders had believed in the right of forcible

---

[1] *C.S.P.V. 1628–29*, 21.

[2] Cf. on the elections to the parliament of 1628 H. Hulme, *op. cit.*, 173–6 and W. M. Mitchell, *op. cit.*, 114–16. The list of M.P.s is printed in *Members of Parliament. Return of the names of every member ... to the present*, 1878, pt. 1, 474–9.

[3] *The autobiography and correspondence of Sir Simonds D'Ewes*, I, 402.

[4] *C.S.P.V. 1625–26*, 548, 511–12.

[5] *Diary of John Rous ... 1625 to 1642*, ed. M. A. E. Green, *Camden society* LXVI, 1856, 11–12, 19.

[6] *H.M.C. Skrine*, 44, 48, 150, 172.

resistance, there really would have been a rebellion. But their legalist, constitutionalist convictions precluded such a course. Non-violent, civil disobedience was still as far as they were prepared to go. Their influence in this direction, however, made itself strongly felt even after parliament's dissolution in March 1629 and the arrest of Eliot and eight other M.P.s. The Commons' resolutions had denounced anyone who voluntarily paid tonnage and poundage as an enemy to the liberties of the kingdom. In consequence, a stoppage of foreign trade occurred for some weeks, the merchants preferring to suspend business rather than pay the duties. The Merchant Adventurers Company ceased to ship cloth and the foreign commerce of London came nearly to a halt. In April it was reported that the King, 'who usually obtained 500 l. sterling a day from the duties, has not obtained 30 l. in the last three weeks.'[1] At the port of Colchester the merchants refused to pay duties, but offered to enter bond for such customs as the next parliament should establish.[2] When April ended there was still only a trickle of duties coming into the custom house in London. The Council was told that many are 'terrified at Sir John Eliot's *brutum fulmen*. . . . The ill spirit of obstinacy lies . . . in the merchants' breasts. . . .'[3] In May, Richard Chambers, a London merchant, was fined £2,000 in the Star Chamber for seditious words spoken in condemnation of the duties, and sentenced to prison till he acknowledged his offence.[4] This example and economic necessity broke the mercantile boycott. Later in the month the Merchant Adventurers agreed to resume trading and others followed suit.[5] For the time being the government had won.

Besides political and religious differences, hard times aggravated the mood of resentment. Between 1620 and 1624 a severe trade depression occurred from which the recovery was only partial. The end of the '20s and most of the '30s were again a period of slump and stagnation due to foreign competition, the contraction of established markets, and currency manipulations abroad. The textile industry, the most important non-agricultural occupation in the national economy, was particularly affected. The hard-hit clothing districts in East Anglia, Yorkshire, and the counties of the west and southwest experienced widespread unemployment and wage-cuts. Misery and unrest were rife. In 1630–1 the position was worsened by poor harvests, which raised the price of grain to famine levels.[6]

---

[1] *C.S.P.V. 1629–32*, 7–8, 19, 29.
[2] *Acts of the Privy Council July 1628–April 1629*, 378–9.
[3] *C.S.P.D. 1628–29*, 524.
[4] Cf. his trial, *State trials*, III, 373ff.   [5] *C.S.P.D. 1628–29*, 550.
[6] W. R. Scott, *op. cit.*, I; B. Supple, *Commercial crisis and change in England 1600–1642*, Cambridge, 1959, chs. III, V–VII; C. Wilson, *England's apprenticeship 1603–1763*, L., 1965, 52–7; instances of distress and unrest in the

While the Privy Council exerted itself vigorously to enforce the poor laws and control the price of grain, other aspects of royal intervention in the economic field during the '30s increased hardship and discontent so much that, on balance, the antagonism the crown created far outweighed any gratitude it may have derived from its efforts to mitigate the effects of depression. The most conspicuous grievances were the monopolies granted by Charles I for mainly fiscal reasons, which not only injured existing trading and industrial interests but also raised prices—and this in a time of slump. Rights to the manufacture or sale of salt, glass, coal, and wine, for instance, were all vested or reinforced in monopolist companies in return for a revenue promised the crown. Since in addition to domestic use soap was required in the textile industry, salt in fishing, and coal for diverse industrial purposes, the injurious effects were broadly felt. A further factor was the bad feeling and resistance, occasionally breaking out in violence, of the sellers and producers whom the royal patentees either excluded or subjugated.[1]

The government's agrarian policy also provoked serious repercussions during these depressed years. Its disafforesting and enclosure of royal forests in Wiltshire, Dorset, and Gloucester, undertaken between 1628 and 1631 for revenue purposes, led to some of the largest disturbances before the civil war. In the forests of Braydon, Gillingham, and Dean, hundreds of armed commoners rioted in defence of their customary rights threatened by enclosures.[2] Such men of little means were extremely vulnerable to the effect of short-term economic fluctuations, and a royal measure so plainly detrimental to their interests inevitably produced a violent reaction. Compared with such enclosures effected on royal initiative, the results obtained by the government's Depopulation Commission, created in 1633 to protect small tenants against enclosing landlords, were

---

[1] W. R. Scott, *op. cit.*, I, 216–17: W. H. Price, *The English patents of monopoly*, Cambridge, 1906, chs. III, VI, X, XI; E. Lipson, *The economic history of England*, 3v. (v. II–III, 7th ed.), L., 1943, III, 362–72; *Extracts from the records of the Company of Hostmen of Newcastle . . .*, ed. F. W. Dendy, *Surtees society*, CV, 1901, xxxiii, 78n.; J. U. Nef, *Industry and government in France and England 1540–1640*, Philadelphia, 1940, 113–17. For examples of the independent producers' defiance of the soap monopoly, cf. *C.S.P.D. 1634–35*, 218, 358, 393 and R. Steele, *op. cit.*, I, 1680.

[2] Cf. instances of these outbreaks in *C.S.P.D. 1631–33*, 67, 74, 87, 88, 90, 178, 182, 190–1 and *Acts of the Privy Council June 1630–June 1631*, 284, 352–3, 390–1; an account of the whole episode is given by D. G. C. Allan, 'The rising in the west 1628–1631,' *Economic history review*, 2nd ser., V, 1 (1952).

---

clothing districts appear in *C.S.P.D. 1628–29*, 521, 554, *ibid. 1629–31*, 8, 20 391, 419, *ibid. 1631–33*, 14, 37.

negligible.[1] In Wiltshire, for instance, the thousands of acres enclosed at the King's command overshadowed all the enclosures of the preceding century. Because of them, many of the inhabitants of the affected areas must have come to regard Charles I as an implacable foe.[2]

Although the symptoms foreshadowing the breakdown of the King's authority were gradually maturing, the government weathered its difficulties for the present. Once parliament ended, it was free to deal with its enemies in church and state without hindrance. In the next few years, while Laud ascended to Canterbury and Wentworth was at Dublin, the King ruled without concession. Opposition fell to its lowest ebb. A reflection of the gloomy mood among the Country's close adherents was contained in a paper distributed in Puritan circles in the summer of 1629 to justify the intended migration to New England. With one eye on the evil auguries to religion from the condition of English politics, and the other on the recent disasters of continental Protestantism, the paper declared:

All other churches of Europe are brought to desolation ... & whoe knowes, but that God hath provided this place to be a refuge for many whome he meanes to save out of the general cu..amity ... seeing the Church hath no place lefte to flie into but the wildernesse. ...[3]

No doubt, to many of the regime's Puritan opponents it must have seemed in the early '30s that prayer or flight were the sole recourses left them.

Not until after ship money was made a general tax in 1635, with the manifest likelihood that it would become a permanent impost, did the national movement against the crown revive. Then, aided by the pressure of the Scottish rebellion, the flood of opposition rose until it overwhelmed the King's authority. Most pronounced was the resistance in the governing class: the 'knowing gentry,' commented a contemporary, 'expressed great discontent at this new ... burden as an imposition against law and the rights of the subject.'[4] The scope of ship money, reaching to both real and personal property and falling with annual regularity upon thousands of small owners and

[1] The commission was issued to inquire into depopulation and the conversion of arable to pasture since the tenth year of Queen Elizabeth; J. Rushworth, II, 333. Cf. the summary of government measures in the '30s regarding enclosures in E. Lipson, *op. cit.*, II, 404–6.

[2] E. Kerridge, 'The revolts in Wiltshire against Charles I,' *Wiltshire archaeological and natural history magazine*, CCVI, 1958.

[3] *Reasons to be considered for iustifeinge the undertakers of the intended plantation in New England, Life and letters of John Winthrop*, I, 309.

[4] B. Whitelocke, *Memorials*, 4v., Oxford, 1853, I, 69–70.

householders, also contributed to the popular reaction against it. The entire responsibility for the collection lay with the sheriffs in the counties, who were to be assisted by the justices, the deputy lieutenants, and the constables of the hundreds. Some showed their antagonism by openly condemning the tax, others by the sluggishness with which they performed their duty. Many of the previous opponents of the forced loan renewed their disobedience. Considerable remissness appeared among the high and petty constables ordered to distrain on the goods of non-payers. Complaints about inequities in assessing the tax on the different parts of the counties repeatedly became a pretext for default and obstruction. To try to cope with the insubordination of the magisterial order, the Privy Council commanded in November 1636 that lords lieutenants, deputy lieutenants, and justices who refused or forbore to pay ship money should be discharged from their offices.[1]

Through 1638 and 1639 opposition mounted. From all parts of the realm accounts came in of refractoriness. Men chosen as sheriffs and deputy lieutenants did everything in their power to evade office.[2] The sheriff of Norfolk declared that he had become odious by carrying out his duties.[3] From Gloucestershire it was reported that if all the refusers were committed there would not be jails enough to receive them.[4] A general backwardness showed itself in Huntingdon, Surrey, Bedfordshire, Buckinghamshire, Oxfordshire, and Northamptonshire.[5] The Somerset grand jury in the summer of 1638 blamed the high price of grain on 'the great and heavy taxations by new invented ways. . . .'[6] In Derbyshire hundreds of defaulters let their goods be distrained rather than pay.[7] During the summer and fall of 1639 the Privy Council wrote the sheriffs admonishing them for lack of affection and diligence in the work of collection.[8]

One more prophecies of revolt appeared, together with strong expressions of support for the Scots. The Venetian ambassador again looked for an outbreak.[9] Most Englishmen were so discontented, said the earl of Northumberland, that they 'will be readier to join with the Scots than to draw their swords in the King's service.'[10]

---

[1] *C.S.P.D. 1636–37*, 181; cf. the excellent account of the operation of ship money in Somerset and the progressive resistance to it in T. G. Barnes, *op. cit.*, ch. VIII. Documents illustrating the sheriff's difficulties in Buckingham are printed in *Ship money papers and Richard Grenville's note-book*, ed. C. G. Bonsey and J. G. Jenkins, *Buckinghamshire record society*, XIII, 1965. The Gloucestershire opposition is described by W. B. Willcox, *op. cit.*, 124–33.
[2] A. H. Dodd, *Studies in Stuart Wales*, Cardiff, 1952, 63.
[3] *C.S.P.D. 1638–39*, 48–9, 61.   [4] *Ibid. 1637–38*, 337.
[5] *Ibid.*, 420, 432, 337.   [6] *Ibid.*, 551.
[7] *Ibid. 1638–39*, 29.   [8] *Ibid. 1639, passim.*
[9] *C.S.P.V. 1636–39*, 273, 297, 429–30.
[10] *The earl of Strafforde's letters*, II, 186.

Laud began to read the writing on the wall. 'The minds of men are mightily alienated,' he told Wentworth at the end of 1638: '. . . I fear you will see the King brought upon his knees to a parliament. And then farewell church and ship monye.'[1] In gentry houses in the south-west an anonymous paper circulated which said that if the King put down the Scots, England would be reduced to slavery.[2]

By the middle of 1640 Charles's power was visibly disintegrating. The nation was on a tax strike and the latest levy of ship money far in arrears. In May the Privy Council issued an order against 'the great and supine negligence of the high sheriffs of divers counties in executing the last writs for ship money.' It required the attendance of the sheriffs of London and Middlesex, Yorkshire, Berkshire, Surrey, Leicester, Essex, and Northamptonshire, and threatened them with trial in the Star Chamber for their contempt and neglect.[3] All was to no avail. Local government was ceasing to respond to royal command. Strong in their sense of grievance, the worshipful gentlemen who controlled its machinery had fallen under the Country's political influence. The complete defeat of ship money was attested by the collection figures for 1640. The King demanded for this year a total of £214,400; of that amount, only £43,417 was paid.[4] The remainder was never obtained.

On the eve of the Long Parliament, the structure of royal sovereignty had virtually crumbled. Although not a single hand had risen against it in England, in the face of universal insubordination and disaffection Charles and his Council were powerless to rule. What occurred was possible only because the King had no independent force at his disposal with which to scourge and chastise his refractory subjects. Totally dependent on the support of the aristocratic order to carry out his mandates, he was helpless the moment it ceased to obey. By its folly and blindness, the royal government had enabled the Country to attain political ascendancy over a great part of the dominant class and the kingdom as a whole. It was to the men prominent in opposition that the King's subjects now looked to direct them on the road to redress. While the governing class stood largely united around the Country, royal authority would remain in eclipse.

The elections to the Long Parliament, held in October, completed the rout of the Court. The issue lay between the Court and the Country—between those who, in the common belief, bore respon-

[1] *Works*, VII, 502.
[2] *The Buller papers*, ed. R. N. Worth, p.p., 1895, 27.
[3] *C.S.P.D. 1640*, 126.
[4] M. D. Gordon, 'The collection of ship money in the reign of Charles I,' *Transactions of the Royal Historical Society*, 3rd ser., IV, 1910, 144.

sibility for the discredited policies of the King's government, and those determined on redress and reform. As yet Royalist and Parliamentarian, the parties that formed in 1642 as civil war loomed up, had no being in either name or fact. Electoral contests took place in about seventy of the existing two hundred and fifty-nine constituencies. They were fought most hotly in the shire elections, at which the freeholders voted in thousands.[1] Sometimes keen personal rivalry between candidates from leading county families figured as much or more than politics in these contests.[2] As in the past, too, the majority of members were elected unopposed and frequently as a result of personal or official influence on their behalf.

The fundamental point about the elections, nevertheless, was that they occurred on a flood-tide of animosity against the regime which had no parallel in living memory. In whatever circumstances members reached the House of Commons, most were imbued with the prevailing sentiment when the Long Parliament began. Thus the political composition was strongly adverse to the King. Charles's most resolute and active opponents were returned to the House. Of the original 547 members elected,[3] nearly 60 had resisted his demand for loans; 18 of these had been imprisoned for their refusal to lend; an additional 20, not part of the former, had been imprisoned for other expressions of opposition; 50 members had stood out in some way against ship money; 14 others had been sheriffs who incurred the Privy Council's displeasure for their failures in the administration of ship money. Altogether, the known number of members who had demonstrated their antagonism to the crown, or whose close relatives had done so, was 143, more than one out of four.[4]

The decay of the crown's electoral influence was noticeable.[5] 'The court laboured to bring in their friends,' wrote Bulstrode Whitelocke, a Country M.P., 'but those who were most favoured at court had least respect in the country . . . so that very few of that party had the favour to be chosen members of this parliament.'[6] The Duchy of

[1] M. Keeler, *op. cit.*, 7.
[2] This was apparently the case in the Somerset election, *ibid.*, 61. T. G. Barnes, *op. cit.*, has stressed the importance of the rivalry of eminent families in Somerset affairs. By contrast, in Suffolk political issues were uppermost. Over two thousand freeholders voted for the two victorious Puritan gentlemen as knights of the shire. The loser by about seven hundred votes was a Court sympathizer; cf. M. Keeler, *op. cit.*, 64.
[3] Cf. M. Keeler, *op. cit.*, 6. By her tabulation the 547 members consisted of 493 elected before 3 November 1640 when the Long Parliament met; 14 elected for boroughs which were given representation soon after 1640; 40 who replaced others or were replaced themselves before January 1642.
[4] Cf. the discussion in M. Keeler, *ibid.*, 13–15.
[5] This has been remarked on by D. Brunton and D. H. Pennington, *op. cit.*, 8–9.
[6] *Op. cit.*, I, 107.

Cornwall failed to elect a single one of eight nominees whom it recommended to the Cornish boroughs under its jurisdiction.[1] In the Cinque Ports, where royal patronage operating through the Lord Warden, was usually decisive, nine of the fourteen members elected were supporters of the Country. Of twelve men, ten of them law officers of the crown, for whom the Secretary of State was instructed to find seats, only three were returned.[2] What was said about the county election in Kent was quite generally the case: '. . . the common people had been so bytten with shippe money they were very averse from a courtyer.'[3]

Even though it was true that by no means all the Country's sympathizers were passionately committed to struggle against the King, that many were moderates and others lukewarm or opportunists, the victory of Charles's opponents was a great one. In an election in which issues of policy predominated as never before, the political nation had spoken unequivocally. It had voiced its confidence in the cause of the Country's leaders, who now held the initiative in their hands.

[1] D. Brunton and D. H. Pennington, *op. cit.*, 134; M. Keeler, *op. cit.*, 37; M. Coate, 'The Duchy of Cornwall: its history and administration 1640–1660,' *Transactions of the Royal Historical Society*, 4th ser., X, 1927, 156.
[2] R. N. Kershaw, 'The elections for the Long Parliament, 1640,' *E.H.R.*, XXXVIII, 152 (1923), 497, 499. Cf. M. Keeler's account of the election of the Puritan Edward Partridge as M.P. for Sandwich as an instance of what happened in the Cinque Ports.
[3] *Proceedings . . . in . . . Kent*, ed. L. B. Larking, *Camden society*, LXXXI, 1862, 6. The remark was Sir Roger Twysden's.

The Citizen Element

Below the aristocratic and elite groups in the social order that formed the substance of the Court and the Country lay the broadly extended intermediate strata in which the nation's citizen and commercial elements were comprised. By seventeenth-century observers searching the causes of the revolution, the spread of the insurrectionary contagion to these strata was remarked as one of the most unfortunate fatalities in the overthrow of the King's power. There was a note both of snobbery and of the immemorial suspicion of the country-bred man for the town dweller in the acid comments in which the friends of royal authority summed up the apostasy of their fellow-subjects in the towns. '. . . 'tis notorious,' said a writer after the Restoration, 'that there is not any sort of people so inclineable to seditious practices as the trading part of a nation. . . . And, if we reflect upon our late miserable distractions, 'tis easy to observe how the quarrel was chiefly hatched in the shops of tradesmen. . . .'[1] It was considered almost a truism that in 'Market-Towns . . . the People . . . were more apt to Faction and Innovation than in other places. . . .'[2] James Howell, the epistolarian, fancied he saw an anti-monarchical tendency in the members of parliament who sat for towns: they 'are the for the most part all tradesmen, and being bred in corporations . . . are more inclining to popular government and democracy.'[3] Hobbes, with his eye fixed on London, asserted that 'those great capital Cities, when Rebellion is entered—into upon Pretence of Grievances, must needs be of the Rebel Party: because the Grievances are but Taxes, to which Citizens, that is Merchants (whose Profession is their private Gain), are naturally mortal Enemies.'[4] Clarendon, speaking of Manchester, referred to the 'factious humour which possessed most corporations, and the pride of their wealth'; while

[1] S. Parker, *Discourse of ecclesiastical politie*, 1671, cited in C. Hill and E. Dell, *op. cit.*, 238.
[2] P. Heylyn, *Cyprianus Anglicanus*, 1671, 198.
[3] James Howell, *Some sober inspections*, 1655, 36–7, cited in C. Hill and E. Dell, *op. cit.*, 239.
[4] T. Hobbes, *Behemoth*, *loc. cit.*, II, 576.

London he described, *tout court*, as 'the sink of all the ill humour of the kingdom. . . .'[1]

These statements provide an interesting revelation of Royalist opinion, but they certainly cannot qualify as an adequate description of the role of the citizen element in the genesis of the revolution. The political stand of the urban segment of the society was, in fact, by no means uniform. To say that most of its members had become, like other Englishmen, estranged from the crown by 1640 would probably be true, but insufficient as a rendering of the complex reality. A diversity of circumstances governed the outlook of the citizen and trading part of the kingdom, and it is only in the light of them that its political posture amidst the deepening conflict of the Court and the Country can be understood.

If the revolution begun in 1640 may be regarded as 'bourgeois' in the very general meaning which this expression has come to possess in historical discourse, it was not one in the strict and etymologically precise sense of 'bourgeois'—*burgenses*, the descendants in status of the inhabitants of the *burgi* of the Middle Ages in whom the awakening commercial life of Europe was first incarnated. When we consider the English burghers of the sixteenth and seventeenth century, we have to observe that they had no living traditions of political struggle for liberty like those that once animated the citizens of the great towns of Italy and Flanders. Their predecessors had lived for the most part in faithful obedience to kings; they had not risen in rebellion against emperor or count to win a jealousy-guarded self-government or independence for their communities. They had not taken a leading part in the trade and diplomacy of Europe, as had the Venetians and Florentines, or parleyed on terms of relative equality with popes and secular princes. Nor had these predecessors, not even those of London, belonged to world-cities whose merchant statesmen watched with an imperial eye for every shift of the political weather and its effect on the destinies of their commerce. Up through the sixteenth century, the story of the English towns is mainly a tale of provincial occurrences, hardly a record of events of wider European significance such as occur in the Florentine histories of Compagni, Villani, and Machiavelli.

English towns in the earlier seventeenth century, except for London, were small and could not compare in population or economic importance with many continental cities. London's population about 1640 has been estimated at 350,000,[2] but the capital towered as far

---

[1] *Rebellion*, VI, 271, III, 57.

[2] W. K. Jordan, *The charities of London*, L., 1960, 16. At the beginning of the century the capital's population has been estimated at 250,000 and 300,000; cf. C. Wilson, *op. cit.*, 45 and G. N. Clark, *The wealth of England*

over other urban centres as Everest over its foothills. Not a single provincial town important to the national economy—not Bristol or Norwich, for example, which came next after London—had more than 15,000 inhabitants.[1] So far, therefore, as urban wealth and economic power might be a force to reckon with politically, only London possessed sufficient leverage to make its resources and sentiments count for something truly formidable in the constitutional conflict. But apart from this, there were other factors which made it impossible that citizen wealth and opinion should play an initiating or dominant part on the political scene. These had to do with the inferior position in the social structure of the *bourgeoisie* as a whole, with the internal differentiation of the strata belonging to it, and with the sectional and protectionist spirit that still widely prevailed in urban life and economy.

We have previously emphasized the persisting significance of status in the society of the earlier seventeenth century. Within the hierarchy of orders in which every rank was assigned its place, the *bourgeoisie* was lumped together as a single entity occupying a middle position respectable but nevertheless distinctly subordinate. Sir Thomas Smith classified townsmen as 'citizens' or 'burgesses,' Dr. Wilson similarly as '*cives*'; and both expressed contemporary opinion in setting them firmly below the gentlemen, the *nobiles* greater and lesser, to whom the highest honour and authority were due.[2] It is possible that in wealth the greatest merchants in the citizen body exceeded every other order in England, except the very richest of the nobility.[3] But if this was so, it did not suffice to remove the stigma of inferiority from men whose fortunes were acquired by trade and finance and in daily resort to a warehouse or a shop. The burgher style of life left no place for the prestigeful pursuits of aristocratic existence. '. . . when we do not hunt we hawk. . . .'—so wrote a carefree peer before the civil war—'the rest of the time is spent in tennis, chess, and dice, and in a word we eat and drink and rise up to play; and this is to live like

[1] Bristol's population at the beginning of the seventeenth century has been estimated at 12,000 and Norwich's at 15,000; J. Latimer, *The annals of Bristol in the seventeenth century*, Bristol, 1900, 34, and *The records of the city of Norwich*, ed. W. Hudson and J. C. Tingey, 2v., Norwich, 1906–10, II, cxxviii. Cf. also on the population of London and provincial towns the figures given by J. N. L. Baker in *An historical geography of England before A.D. 1800*, ed. H. C. Darby, Cambridge, 1936, 441–2.

[2] Cf. *supra*, 27.

[3] The size of mercantile wealth, especially London's, in the earlier seventeenth century, has been emphasized by W. K. Jordan in his monumental study of wills, *Philanthropy in England*, 335–6.

from 1496 to 1760, Oxford, 1946, 93. In 1636, according to James Howell, the lord mayor made an informal census and estimated London's population at 700,000 (*Londinopolis*, 1657, 403). This figure is incredible.

a gentleman, for what is a gentleman but his pleasure.'[1] It was not by such recreations nor in such leisure that burgher fortunes were gained and preserved.

In the urban community itself, the highest status belonged to the merchant, a designation which, in the parlance of the time, referred not to any mere retailer, but, more particularly, to the minority of men engaged in wholesale trade or foreign commerce.[2] Yet however secure and authoritative the merchant's position was among his fellow townsmen—and it was such as he who almost invariably formed the magistracy of the urban corporations—his status in the general body politic was much lower and even somewhat contemptible to those above him. A scattering of merchants might achieve knighthood as the reward of valuable financial services rendered the crown or in recognition of their business eminence; a tiny few, such as Cranfield, Robartes, Hicks, or Bayning, might move from the highest regions of commerce and money lending into the peerage, as all of them did in the 1620s, and then hope in a generation or so to leave the aroma of the counting-house behind. But the majority of merchants had no such opportunity; and these, according to the aristocratic standard of the time, were disqualified by their vocation from any claim to real gentility.

Ample testimony bears witness to the defensive and self-justifying attitude which the merchant and his advocates adopted in the face of this upper-class prejudice.[3] '... I cannot wonder,' wrote the antiquarian, Gervase Holles, a kinsman of the earl of Clare, whose family was established on the land by the wealth of a London lord mayor of Henry VIII's reign, 'at the vanity and folly of many of our English gentry who, in the sickness of their understanding, apprehend this worthy calling of a merchant to be but ignoble and derogatory to the honour of a gentleman. All ... are not of this opinion, but the generality are.'[4] Bishop Goodman, of mercantile stock himself, defended the honour of the merchant against the complaints of the base origin of Sir Lionel Cranfield, who began his career in the City.[5] Another exponent of the merchant's worth denied that sons of gentlemen apprenticed in trade lost their status. '... such Gentlemen

---

[1] Viscount Conway's words, cited in W. Woodfill, *Musicians in English society from Elizabeth to Charles I*, Princeton, 1953, 221. It should be noted that these sentiments would not have been endorsed by noblemen and gentlemen of Puritan or other serious religious persuasion.
[2] Cf. J. Stow, *A survay of London*, ed. C. Kingsford, 2v., Oxford, 1908, II, 207. This was first published in 1598.
[3] A good survey of contemporary writings on the citizen's status is given in L. B. Wright, *Middle class culture in Elizabethan England*, Ithaca, 1958, ch. II.
[4] G. Holles, *Memorials of the Holles family*, 18. This was written in the 1650s.   [5] G. Goodman, *op. cit.*, I, 297–8.

are much deceived,' he asserted, 'which no sooner heare one named to be of this, or that Societie, or Colledge of trade in London, as of Grocers, Haberdashers, Fishmongers ... but they forthwith entertaine a low conceit of the parties quality, as too much beneath their owne ranck, and order. ...'[1]

The playwrights of the age were wont to underscore the prejudice against trade by depicting its practitioners more often than not as cheats, usurers, and social climbers.[2] Ben Jonson's goldsmith, Guilt-Head, declares:

> *We live, by finding fooles out, to be trusted.*
> *Our shop-bookes are our pastures, our corngroundes,*
>
> . . . .
>
> *Wee Citizens never trust, but wee doe coozen. ...*[3]

Quomodo, the woollen draper in Middleton's *Michaelmas Term*, orders his accomplice:

> *Go, make my coarse commodities look sleek;*
> *With subtle art beguile the honest eye.*

When by deceit he has the land of Easy, an Essex gentleman, within his grasp, he exults:

The land's mine ... now shall I be divulged a landed man throughout the livery. ... Now come my golden days in. Whither is worshipful Master Quomodo ... rid forth? To his land in Essex. Whence come those goodly loads of logs? From his land in Essex. Where grows this pleasant fruit, says one citizen's wife in the row? At Master Quomodo's orchard in Essex. O, O, does it so? I thank you for that good news, i' faith.[4]

The rule by which the Court of Wards guided itself, a good index to social custom, also assumed the inferiority of the merchant. The court was required not to give a ward in marriage to his disparagement, and even in the seventeenth century, it seems, this was held to mean that one of gentle rank should not be wed to a burgher. Sir Edward Coke, as well, listed marriage with a *burgensis* as a disparagement to a ward.[5] A parallel instance of the grudging conception taken

---

[1] [E. Bolton], *The cities advocate, in this ... question ... whether apprenticeship extinguisheth gentry*, 1628, 45, 46–7.
[2] Cf. L. C. Knights, *Drama & society in the age of Jonson*, L., 1936, chs. VII, IX.
[3] *The divell is an asse*, III, 1, ll. 16–17, 22.
[4] Cited in C. W. Camp, *The artisan in Elizabethan literature*, N.Y., 1924, 95–7.   [5] Cf. J. Hurstfield, *op. cit.*, 139–40.

of the merchant was the case of Humphrey Chetham, a great Lancashire business man and money lender. Appointed sheriff of his county in 1634, he undertook to display armorial bearings as part of the pomp appropriate to his office. This was regarded by his social superiors as an act of rash presumption, and he was informed that 'some malicious knaves have endeavoured to disgrace you about your Coate of Armes' and that 'Gentlemen in the Countie are aggrieved and will have the truth tryed. . . .' Through the influence of friends, however, and a payment to Sir Henry St. George, Norroy herald, Chetham succeeded in having his arms confirmed.[1]

Of course, in point of fact the interrelations between trade and aristocracy were much closer than the status ideology and its attendant snobbery made out. That had always been the case to a certain extent, and was doubtless far more so in the economic conditions of the sixteenth and seventeenth centuries. A thin top layer of merchants was continuously abandoning trade for the land and entrance to the lower levels of county society;[2] marriage between the ranks was an old story, more than one nobleman matching with the heiress to a commercial fortune;[3] and sons of gentlemen were regularly apprenticed in mercantile pursuits.[4] But so long as distinction of degree

[1] F. R. Raines and C. W. Sutton, *Life of Humphrey Chetham, Chetham society*, n.s., 2v., XLIX, L, 1903, I, 102, 104.

[2] The recruitment of landed society from merchant families at this period has not been systematically studied. The impression derived from recent research is that it was not a sizeable phenomenon. Of Exeter, for instance, it has been said that while 'most . . . merchants put some money into land . . . very few had purchased enough to secure independence from mercantile pursuits.' (W. T. MacCaffrey, *Exeter 1540–1640*, Cambridge, 1958, 260–1, 266). Similar observations have been made about London and Bristol merchants; cf. T. W. Willan, *The Muscovy merchants of 1555*, Manchester, 1953, 73, and P. McGrath, *Merchants and merchandise in seventeenth century Bristol, Bristol record society*, XIX, 1955, xxiv. The gentry of Kent, near as the county lay to London, were largely indigenous and descended from the pre-Tudor gentry; few came of transplanted London stock; cf. C. W. Chalklin, *Seventeenth-century Kent*, L., 1965, 192–4. A historian of Norwich merchants, however, has seen a steady movement of its ruling families on to the land; cf. Bruce Allen, *The social and administrative structure of the Norwich merchant class*, Harvard Ph.D. thesis, 1951, 355–6, 368–9.

[3] Instances in L. Stone, *The crisis of the aristocracy*, 628–32. The proportion of intermarriage between peers and merchants was small, however. Stone's figures on the status of the wives of 465 noblemen married between 1540–1659 shows only 17 or 4 per cent to have been of merchant stock. Only 5 marriages of 129 noblemen between 1600–29 were to wives of merchant rank. Most noblemen married within their own order or the gentry.

[4] Some indication of the social origin of merchants can be obtained from apprenticeship records. Between January 1600 and May 1660, the Newcastle Merchant Adventurers Company admitted 749 apprentices. The status of their fathers was as follows: gentleman, including 24 clergy, 324;

retained its hold on contemporary attitudes and behaviour, the political influence of the *bourgeoisie* on the national scene was bound to be limited and its role one of follower, not leader.

As a consequence, it was extremely rare for a merchant to rise to high ministerial office, and this continued to be equally the case under the revolutionary governments of the 1640s and '50s. The career of Sir Lionel Cranfield, Buckingham's client, who became Master of the Wards, Treasurer, and earl of Middlesex, was most exceptional. Cranfield, indeed, was elevated by James I because of his financial expertise and in the hope that his administration would effect much-needed economies in crown expenditure. He strove vigorously, but when Buckingham abandoned him and he was impeached by the Commons, there is no doubt that the prejudice of members against the insolence of a *parvenu* aggravated his faults and contributed to his downfall.[1] On the whole, it is unlikely that even the greatest merchants entertained high political ambitions or aims. Their interest was mainly in business, and the rewards they sought were usually of the tangible pecuniary sort.[2]

Although the citizen element formed a middle order in the body politic, it was itself differentiated internally by profound inequalities of status and wealth which had considerable bearing on the outlook of its component strata. Stow, the memorialist and historian of London, anatomized the city's population on lines broadly applicable to the urban structure as a whole at this period. Its four main divisions, according to him, were the merchants, the retailers, the handicraftsmen, and the hired labourers. The merchants, though least in number, were first in wealth, together with some principal retailers. The next place pertained to the other retailers, who with the craftsmen also made up the larger part of the inhabitants. Economically, the craftsmen came after the retailers and 'have not much to

---

[1] Cf. R. H. Tawney, *Business and politics under James I*, Cambridge, 1958.
[2] Miss Thrupp's remarks on this point in connection with the mediaeval merchant are applicable also to his sixteenth- and early seventeenth-century successor; S. Thrupp, *The merchant class of medieval London*, Chicago, 1948, 55. Cf. also A. H. Dodd, 'Mr. Myddelton the merchant of Tower Street,' in *Elizabethan government and society*, 266. Dodd remarks what was probably true of the great majority of merchants: 'Business, religion, family: these were Myddelton's three dominant interests . . .' (*ibid.*, 277).

---

yeoman, 188; merchant or craftsman, 169; other or status undetermined, 68; figures from *Records of the Merchant Adventurers of Newcastle*, 2v., ed. J. R. Boyle and F. W. Dendy, *Surtees society*, 93, 101, 1895–9, II, *ad finem*. At Bristol, merchants admitted 377 apprentices between 1600–30. Their fathers' status or occupation was: gentleman, 88; merchant, 70; yeoman, 37; husbandman, 24; mariner, 11; vintner, 11; mercer, 10; clerk, 2; bishop, 1; miscellaneous trades and crafts, 123; P. McGrath, *op. cit.*, App. B.

spare,' while the labourers, who were in the lowest position, 'have neede that it were given unto them.'[1] A considerable proletariat existed in London and the same class was present as well in smaller numbers in the main provincial towns. Composed of porters, car men, floating labourers, wage earners in the textile industry, the tailoring trades, brewing, dyeing, wire and pin manufacture, this portion of the population lived in grinding poverty and hardship.[2] Several evidences from Professor Jordan's study of the charitable donors of the sixteenth and seventeenth centuries show how pronounced was the disparity of wealth in the urban sector of society. In London, for instance, 7,391 charitable benefactors have been traced over the period 1480–1660. Four hundred and thirty-eight merchants of this number—less than 6 per cent of the entire body of givers— contributed nearly 50 per cent of all the city's gifts, a total amounting to the huge sum of more than £907,000. The scale of mercantile riches in the years preceding the revolution is suggested by the fact that 40 per cent of this total was provided by merchants between 1611 and 1630.[3] At Bristol as well, the same overwhelming pre-eminence of mercantile wealth can be inferred from the philanthropy of its inhabitants.[4]

As we might expect in a privilege-ridden age, the minority of citizens distinguished for their money and success in commerce dominated all aspects of municipal life. Every important town without exception was ruled by a small and virtually self-perpetuating body of such men, for the urban constitutions were invariably oligarchical, vesting the substance of power in organs little subject to popular check or dismissal. The gilds and companies, in which the urban division of labour was broadly organized, were equally controlled by the few who were masters, wardens, assistants, and members of the livery. The journeymen and yeomanry of these associations, though comprising the majority, had scarcely any voice in their affairs.[5] It was characteristic of this oligarchic pattern that when King James gave new charters to nine of London's twelve great livery companies, he confined their narrow structure of rule still further. Their govern-

---

[1] J. Stow, *op. cit.*, II, 207–9.
[2] J. L. Archer, *The industrial history of London 1603–1640*, London M.A. thesis, 1934, 140–3; W. K. Jordan, *Philanthropy in England*, 329. W. G. Hoskins has stressed the number and poverty of town wage-earners in Tudor times; cf. 'English provincial towns in the early sixteenth century,' *Provincial England*, L., 1963.
[3] W. K. Jordan, *The charities of London*, 50–1, 64–5, 71, 321n.
[4] W. K. Jordan, *The forming of the charitable institutions in the west of England*, Philadelphia, 1960.
[5] G. Unwin, *Industrial organization in the sixteenth and seventeenth centuries*, Oxford, 1904, and the same writer's *The gilds and companies of London*, L., 1909, ch. XIV.

ing bodies were given life-tenure, made self-elective, and authorized as well to enact ordinances for the whole membership.[1]

Nowhere was the prevalence of status and privilege in the distribution of power within the municipalities more strikingly evident than in the capital. Here, both the restrictions on the popular element and the narrow composition of even the latter relative to the inhabitants as a whole were equally pronounced.[2]

London's government rested on three main institutions: the lord mayor and court of aldermen, the court of common council, and the court of common hall. Far the most powerful of these was the first, since the mayor and the twenty-six aldermen possessed the entire executive authority. The aldermen, who were required to have a £10,000 property qualification for their office, held their places for life. Such was their wealth that Sir Ralph Freeman, mayor in 1633, boasted that he and his aldermanic brethren could buy out a hundred burgomasters of Amsterdam.[3] They co-opted their members from the nominees presented to them by the wards, and the lord mayor was customarily chosen each year from the senior among them.

The court of common council was the city's legislative body with a membership of about two hundred and fifty.[4] Contemporary writers likened it and the court of aldermen to parliament, the former resembling the lower House, the latter the upper one.[5] In theory the choice of councilmen belonged to the freemen—citizens—i.e., to all persons free of any of the city companies and hence possessed of the right to trade—who constituted the wardmote for this purpose. Practice, however, had come to limit the election of councilmen to a minority of well-to-do residents who had usurped the wardmote's power. In much the same way, the nomination of aldermen was made not by the freemen, but only by those citizens who were either councilmen or members of the livery of their companies.[6] John

---

[1] W. Herbert, *History of the twelve great livery companies of London*, 2v., L., 1836-7, I, 186-7.

[2] G. A. Williams, *Medieval London. From commune to capital*, L., 1963, describes the earlier history of London's governmental structure. For the sixteenth and early seventeenth century, a definitive account is given by V. Pearl, *London and the outbreak of the Puritan revolution*, Oxford, 1961, ch. II. I have drawn for the following paragraphs on the latter and also on J. Strype's ed. of J. Stow, *Survey of London*, 2v., L., 1720, II, ch. V. Useful also is *The corporation of London. Its origin, constitution, powers and duties*, Oxford, 1950.

[3] J. Howell, *op. cit.*, 389.

[4] This was the figure given by John Bellamie, *A plea for the commonalty of London*, 1645, 15. J. Strype (ed.), *op. cit.*, II, 375, gives the number of councilmen as two hundred and thirty-four.

[5] *Ibid.*, II, 375; J. Howell, *op. cit.*, 38.

[6] J. Strype (ed.), *op. cit.*, II, 157.

Strype, the learned eighteenth-century editor of Stow's *Survey of London*, declared that the common council was 'in Representation many Thousands.'[1] While that may have been so, it nevertheless exercised its functions in strict subordination to the mayor and court of aldermen. Convened only a few times a year, its summons and dissolution, its agenda and proceedings, were controlled by the mayor and his colleagues, who met with it and had a veto on its deliberations.

Lastly, the court of common hall was the assembly that elected the four city M.P.s and submitted nominations for mayor and certain other officers to the court of aldermen from which the latter made choice. Only the liverymen of the companies had the right to vote in it, and these were said to number about four thousand in the middle of the century. The common hall was the most broadly constituted of London's organs of government, yet the small proportion of liverymen to unenfranchised freemen-citizens merely emphasized how tightly power was concentrated in the great and populous capital. In 1646 it was stated that the ratio of liverymen to freemen was one to three hundred.[2] While this estimate was certainly too high, company records confirm that the difference was substantial. In the Drapers Company, for instance, one of the twelve great companies of the city, the masters, wardens, assistants, and liverymen never exceeded 136 during the reign of James I, while the highest number of freemen was 2,106.[3] In the Goldsmiths, another of the twelve great companies, there were 90 wardens, ex-wardens, and liverymen in 1641, and 373 freemen.[4] Many of these freemen without voice in the common hall were also of low economic condition, as appears from the poll tax levied by the Long Parliament in 1641. Of the 1,427 freemen of the Drapers Company assessed £2 or less, only 835 could pay, and a considerable number were too poor even to pay their quarterly fees to the gild.[5] In the Goldsmiths Company, most of the freemen were able to pay only one shilling.[6]

The government of the principal provincial towns resembled London's in being similarly constituted by a small minority of rich citizens who dominated affairs.[7] At Norwich, it was the mayor and

[1] *Ibid.*, II, 375.

[2] J. Lilburne, *Londons liberty in chains discovered*, 1646, 52.

[3] A. H. Johnson, *The history of the worshipful Company of Drapers of London*, 4v., Oxford, 1914–22, III, 87–8.

[4] *Memorials of the Goldsmiths Company*, ed. W. S. Prideaux, 2v., L., n.d., I, App.

[5] A. H. Johnson, *op. cit.*, III, 194.

[6] *Memorials of the Goldsmiths Company*, I, App.

[7] Historical accounts of the government of the English towns containing material applicable to the earlier seventeenth century are to be found in

Same sort of system at other towns

twenty-four aldermen who possessed the preponderant authority with broad civil and judicial powers.[1] At Bristol, the twelve aldermen recruited their own body and also had the dominant share in choosing the common council. The affairs of the city, probably the second in commercial importance after London, 'were in the hands of about forty-five individuals who elected themselves and were . . . answerable only to themselves.'[2] At Exeter, the government was closely concentrated in a self-perpetuating chamber of twenty-four.[3] At Newcastle, power over the municipality was confined to a couple of dozen men who elected and co-opted each other.[4]

The men of this kind in the more important towns formed an urban sector of the governing class. Mayors and aldermen, sheriffs and justices of the peace within their municipalities, they ruled their fellow citizens in the same way that the gentry ruled the countryside and county communities. Although socially below the aristocratic order and certainly less weighty in the kingdom's political affairs, they bore an equal responsibility in their own jurisdiction for the execution of the crown's mandates. As a dominant minority, they were very conscious of their position and strongly apprehensive of every sign of disturbance or unrest among the citizenry or the poor. Perhaps one-half the urban population lived near or below the subsistence level, vulnerable in the extreme to any adverse movement of prices and the trade cycle.[5] The spectre of riot and anarchy breaking out in this poverty-stricken mass haunted the town rulers, causing them to show a compulsive concern with the poor rate and the maintenance of civic order and discipline. Police forces were non-existent, and other resources available for the preservation of the peace slender and inadequate. The urban magistrates practised a ceaseless vigilance and refused to tolerate the slightest gesture of disrespect for their persons or dignity. Not infrequently they had to invoke the support of the

[1] Cf. *Minutes of the Norwich court of mayoralty 1630–31*, ed. W. L. Sachse, *Norfolk record society*, XV, 1942, Introduction.

[2] *Bristol charters 1509–1899*, ed. R. C. Latham, *Bristol record society*, XII, 1946, 17.

[3] W. T. MacCaffrey, *Exeter 1540–1640*, 29–30; cf. also W. G. Hoskins, 'The Elizabethan merchants of Exeter,' *Elizabethan government and society*, 165.

[4] Cf. the Newcastle charter of 1600 in J. Brand, *The history and antiquities . . . of Newcastle*, 2v., L., 1789, II.

[5] Cf. the remarks of W. G. Hoskins, 'An Elizabethan provincial town: Leicester,' *Studies in social history*, ed. J. H. Plumb, L., 1955, 45, W. T. MacCaffrey, *Exeter 1540–1640*, 249, and W. K. Jordan, *Philanthropy in England*, 66–72.

First report on municipal corporations, Parliamentary papers, vols. XXIII–XXVI, 1835, and S. and B. Webb, *English local government . . . the manor and the borough*, 2v., L., 1908.

Privy Council to render their action more effective or to assist them in coping with local difficulties of scarcity, high food prices, and unemployment. They were also continually appealing to the royal government for measures to strengthen the town's economy against competitors.

These circumstances naturally influenced the political conduct of the municipal elite. The masters of the towns looked to the King to support their privileges and were imbued by their responsibilities of rule with a conservative bent. They shared Charles I's solicitude, communicated on one occasion to the magistrates of Norwich, 'that the orderly gouvernment of cittie and corporacions should be maynteined, and that popular and factious humours that trouble the same should be supprest and punisht.'[1] Hence, in spite of antagonism among them to the Court, they were not of one political mind nor disposed to make forthright commitments. Surveying their position, a variety of responses appeared as the conflict grew between the King and his opponents. Many inclined to hedge, restrained by their care for civic stability and the perpetuation of their own authority. Others sided with the King. A greater militancy, on the other hand, was likely to exist in the outer edge of the urban governing class, in men of substance who were not, however, at the pinnacle of civic wealth and power. Situated on the fringe of the ruling oligarchy, these obtained an opportunity in the conflict to enlarge their importance in their communities' affairs. As for the citizens of lesser status, such of them as were sensible of their slight or non-existent voice in the civic order also frequently showed themselves favourable to the Country's cause. Finally, the effects of Puritanism at all levels of the urban social structure must be taken into account.[2] All susceptible to its influence—and the citizen element was markedly so—were likely to develop a distrust and hostility towards the Court which figured significantly in turning many townsmen against Charles I's regime during the '30s.

A last factor affecting the political position of the citizen element was the predominance of sectional and protectionist concerns in the urban economies. The English *bourgeoisie* was not yet a national *bourgeoisie*. Merchants and retailers tended to be particularist in their aims, while the towns were divided by keen commercial rivalry and by the exclusiveness which they all showed to outsiders. To prevent strangers from acquiring any share in the town's trade; to uphold the regulatory power of its companies and gilds and confine commerce and crafts solely to their members; to secure, if possible, a privileged or monopoly position for its merchants in their trading

---

[1] *Acts of the Privy Council Sept. 1627–June 1628*, 141.
[2] Cf. *infra*, ch. VI.

area;—such were the ends at which municipal policy commonly aimed. The outports resented the supremacy of London, through which the largest part of the kingdom's foreign trade passed, and endeavoured to preserve their own markets and commerce against the competitive pressure of the Londoners. The pursuit of similar objectives appeared in the relations between the municipalities and the royal government. The businessmen who directed urban affairs were not champions of economic freedom or opposed on principle to the controls which the crown laid on commercial and industrial enterprise. Every town and every association liked controls beneficial to itself and protested against others not to its advantage. In consequence of the persistence of the protectionist spirit, the economic interest of the trading part of the nation was fixed first and foremost in its own communities. When merchants and retailers appraised national developments, appreciation of the impact of events and policies on their town was always an important and sometimes a decisive consideration. Their civic allegiance conditioned their political consciousness more decidedly than any general interests they may have shared as an order. With such parochialism of outlook, the citizen element was incapable of leadership in the kingdom's affairs. The wealth of the towns might be an invaluable asset to the side that could gain their support, but they were too intent on their single advancement, too unaccustomed to cooperation, to assume an independent or initiating part in matters of general political import.

2

As the supreme patron in a patronage-ridden society, the crown naturally distributed some of its favours in the urban section of the population—not, of course, gratuitously, but in return for the advantages thereby to be obtained for royal finance. The men who were thus drawn into the Court were not the common-garden variety of merchants. They were the magnates of the financial world, a handful of outstandingly successful London businessmen, customs farmers, and revenue officials of the crown; in fact, the germ of what subsequently came to be designated in its financial connotation as the City. The nature of this important minority has been admirably described by Professor Tawney. Entrepreneurs on a great scale, their activity transcended the conventional boundaries between the different lines of business activity that prevailed lower in the economic hierarchy of the municipalities. Having accumulated large capitals in commerce, they moved from one venture to another, ready to exploit an opportunity as it arose even while they continued to carry on their regular trade. Heavy lenders to the crown both for themselves and on behalf of others with whose money they were entrusted, established in the royal financial administration, they were indispensable instruments of government finance. Promoters as well as merchants, their forte was the 'deal,' that typical progeny of the union of political connections and business acumen. 'With a footing in more than one world and fingers, if they please, in every pie . . . so closely interlocked that the ledger of an important figure can contain a substantial assortment of them; propitiating, when expedient, ministers and courtiers with tips as to possibilities in the wind, and sometimes . . . with more material rewards,' these men, the tycoons of commerce, were of all the citizen element the closest to the crown.[1]

The favoured position enjoyed by these capitalists was due to the effectiveness with which they mobilized the resources of private enterprise to provide for the revenue needs of the King's government. The activity of the customs farmers was the prime example of this function.[2] From the middle years of Elizabeth's reign, the crown adopted the practice of leasing the collection of its customs to businessmen who, in return, paid a lump sum for the contract and an annual rent. After 1604, the scale of this operation became larger as most species of duties were consolidated in a single great farm which was then let competitively to the syndicate that offered the best bargain. The magnitude of the transaction appears from the annual rent which the farmers of the great customs undertook to pay: £112,400 in 1604–5, rising steadily to reach £160,000 from 1621 to 1625; then, after a drop to £150,000 during the depressed years of the later 1620s and earlier '30s, rising once more to £172,500 in 1638–9.[3] The reasons that the crown preferred to lease the customs to private concessionaires instead of directly administering them with its own servants had to do with the urgency of its fiscal requirements. It was prepared to forego the gain which direct administration might have yielded for the sake of rendering its customs revenue certain year by year and, perhaps even more important, because the financial ability of the customs farmers made them a major source of government loans. The arrangement was founded on a *quid pro quo*: in return for its profits, the syndicate used its immense resources to enable the King to anticipate his revenue by allowing advances on its rent for

---

[1] R. H. Tawney, *Business and politics under James I*, 79–81.
[2] The following remarks on the customs farmers are based on W. P. Harper, 'The significance of the farmers of the customs in public finance in the middle of the seventeenth century,' *Economica*, X, 25 (1929) and especially on the penetrating account by R. Ashton, *The crown and the money market 1603–1640*, Oxford, 1960, ch. IV and 'Revenue farming under the early Stuarts,' *Economic history review*, 2nd ser., VIII, 3 (1956).
[3] Cf. the tables in R. Ashton, *The crown and the money market*, ch. IV.

current and future years and by outright loans—both, naturally, bearing interest.[1]

The farmers' efficiency in supplying the royal demand for funds was based on their own large fortunes and on their credit and reputation in the business world. Those of Charles I's reign included some of the foremost figures in London commerce. Sir Paul Pindar, Sir John Wolstenholme senior, Sir Nicholas Crispe, Sir John Harrison, Sir Job Harby, Sir Abraham Dawes, and Sir John Jacob were prominent merchants, speculators, and financial experts who, beside their share in the customs farm, were active in the East India, the Levant, and other companies and were repeatedly called on by the royal government for advice in questions of economic and trade policy.[2] The function of these men was to serve as intermediaries through whom the profits of trade found an investment outlet in government borrowing; and through their instrumentality, in turn, the revenue needs of the crown promoted the growth of financial capitalism. A major source of their loanable funds was the mercantile community as a whole, since numerous persons lent them as if they were bankers the money which they in turn advanced to the King.[3] Thus, while the customs farmers themselves were few and exceptional in their privileges, a good many others had a stake in their favoured position and stood to lose if they failed to meet their obligations.

The farmers of the customs were not the only business men who enjoyed a profitable relation to the Court. Others willing to assist the regime in providing for its financial requirements obtained similar advantages. Sir William Russell, a great merchant and one of the directors of the East India Company, acquired the treasurership of the navy under Charles I, in which place he became a substantial

[1] The farmers' profits arose from the surplus over their rent in the proceeds of the customs; from the interest they received on their loans and advances; and from the large cash balances which they had on hand for considerable periods and could invest on their own account. Their reputation also made it possible for them to borrow money from others at a lesser rate of interest than the crown paid them. According to Ashton, the profits of the farmers cannot be accurately estimated; 'Revenue farming under the early Stuarts,' *loc. cit.*, 319n. A report made on 22 May 1641 by a House of Commons committee on the customs farmers contains information concerning their various gains; cf. D'Ewes, Journal, B.M. Harl. 163, ff. 219–22.

[2] Most of these men are listed in the *D.N.B.* Their participation in the customs is described by R. Ashton, *The crown and the money market, passim.* Their names occur frequently in the state papers of James's and Charles's reigns in connection with service on government commissions and with topics of economic significance on which they were consulted.

[3] The dependence of the farmers on loans from others has been stressed by W. P. Harper, *op. cit.*, 69, who describes them as resembling bankers or financial agents, and by R. Ashton, 'Revenue farming under the early Stuarts,' *loc. cit.*, 320.

lender to the crown, recouping himself by means of the opportunities his office put in his way.[1] The viscountcies given in 1628 to the merchants, Sir Baptist Hicks and Sir Paul Bayning, were also probably a reward for the large sums these money lenders had advanced the King.[2]

Apart from the matter of loans, the government's impact on the contemporary economy was so extensive, the details of its regulation so complex, that, inevitably, some business groups benefited considerably from its policies.[3] The Statute of Monopolies of 1624, the culmination of thirty years of complaint in parliament, had excepted incorporated companies from its provisions. In consequence, the monopolies of Charles I's reign differed from their predecessors in being granted, not to a limited number of private persons, but to corporations in order to evade the statute.[4] The practice of conferring monopoly rights over a particular trade upon companies in return for a revenue to the crown reached a height in the '30s. Due to the corporate character of these enterprises, they created a net of business interests closely dependent on the crown. These, at any rate, had little to complain of from royal economic intervention, however outraged were the protests against monopolies in other quarters.

Involved so deeply in the royal revenue system, the magnates of the customs farm probably had a greater stake in the survival of Charles I's rule than any other business group. Their economic well-being was based on the King's ability to meet his obligations and to enforce the powers he claimed under his prerogative. There was nothing surprising, therefore, in the fact that the farmers supported the crown in its conflict with the Country opposition. During the first fifteen years of the reign, they continued to collect the tonnage and poundage duties declared unlawful by parliament and which the Commons' resolutions of 1629 had condemned. Nor did they fail to come to the King's assistance when the outbreak of the Scottish rebellion put a new strain on royal finances. While the Privy Council was meeting the severest difficulty in raising money elsewhere because of the political isolation of the Court and the decline in the King's credit, the farmers utilized their own great resources on the crown's behalf.

[1] Cf. *D.N.B.*, *s.v.* and R. Ashton, 'The disbursing official under the early Stuarts: the cases of Sir William Russell and Philip Burlamachi,' *Bulletin of the Institute of Historical Research*, XXX, 82 (1957).
[2] Cf. L. Stone, *The crisis of the aristocracy*, 534–5. Hicks became viscount Campden, Bayning viscount Bayning. Their loans to the King are mentioned by R. Ashton, *The crown and the money market, passim.*
[3] Cf. R. Ashton, 'Charles I and the City,' *Essays in the economic & social history of Tudor & Stuart England.*
[4] W. H. Price, *op. cit.*, ch. III; C. T. Carr (ed.), *Select charters of trading companies A.D. 1530–1707, Selden society*, XXVIII, 1913, lxxii.

Sir Paul Pindar personally advanced £85,000 in 1638–9, while the syndicate formed in 1640 through a merger of two previous groups of farmers provided well over £100,000 and perhaps as much as a quarter of a million.[1]

Faithful to Charles I in the period of parliament's eclipse, they thereby incurred the ruin which the wrath of the Long Parliament brought on them. In 1641 they were declared delinquents and guilty of heinous crimes for their unlawful collection of customs duties. Besides the loss of the huge sums they lent the King, the farmers were fined £150,000 and left to confront the claims of the creditors on whom they had now defaulted.[2] The greatest capitalists in the kingdom, their estates were wrecked in the collapse of the King's power.

3

The one municipality whose magnitude made its political sympathies a factor of crucial importance was London. The residence of the King and royal family, the seat of the central government and the law courts, the resort of the wealthier gentry who came to further their litigious concerns, to take part in the season that was just then starting to be a feature of the city's social life, and to patronize the shops where European luxuries might be obtained, the capital was already a great metropolis. Two-thirds or more of England's foreign trade was exported there. It was equally preeminent industrially and as a centre of consumption whose economic impact was felt throughout the kingdom and whose expanding demand provided the chief stimulus to its own industrial development.[3]

The extraordinary growth of London was a phenomenon that staggered and dismayed contemporaries. The thousands of workmen who lived in the city and its suburbs made industrial regulation exceedingly difficult and created serious problems of government and public order.[4] Administratively, the municipality was encumbered by anomalies inherited from the past. Within and about it were liberties and franchises, once the property of religious houses, that had passed to new lay and clerical owners after the dissolution of the monasteries and were exempt in whole or part from the jurisdiction of the lord

---

[1] R. Ashton, *The crown and the money market*, 175, 110–11.

[2] *Ibid.*, 111–12; Notestein, *D'Ewes*, 197–200; *C.J.*, II, 157, 163–4.

[3] Cf. F. J. Fisher, 'London's export trade in the early seventeenth century,' *Economic history review*, 2nd ser., III, 2 (1950) and 'The development of London as a center of conspicuous consumption in the sixteenth and seventeenth centuries,' *Transactions of the Royal Historical Society*, 4th ser., XXX, 1948; J. L. Archer, *op. cit.*, 47–54.

[4] Cf. V. Pearl, *op. cit.*, ch. I.

mayor and aldermen. Here dense populations resided, including many aliens, who, as Stow said, enjoyed the *quondam* clerical immunities now 'wrested to artificers, buyers and sellars. . . .'[1] The suburbs also, though integral to the city's economy and peace, were only partially subject to its authority. To accommodate London's increasing numbers, cheap dwellings were erected and large houses, formerly monastic or noble establishments, subdivided by landlords into 'small tenements, letten out to strangers, and other meane people.'[2] In such slums a large miscellaneous population swarmed, complicating the task of the municipal magistrates. As an instance of the resultant crowding, in 1607 the recorder of London described four large buildings which housed eight thousand inhabitants, of whom eight hundred had died in the last plague visitation: '. . . if it be not reformed,' he stated, 'the people cannot have food nor can they be governed.'[3]

Alarmed by the capital's growth, Elizabeth, James, and Charles all tried to control it by publishing proclamations against new buildings and sub-division. The Privy Council in 1613 referred to the 'inconveniences which cannot be avoyded by the swelling multitudes of people . . . drawne hether from all partes of the Kingdome, and that as well in regard of the price of victuall . . . as also in respect of government and order.'[4] Prohibition was ineffectual, however, and new construction continued to go up in hundreds during the earlier years of the century. 'The desire of Profitte greatly increaseth Buyldinges,' wrote a Jacobean pamphleteer,

and so much the more for that this great Concourse of all sortes of people drawing nere unto this Cittie, everie man seeketh out places, highewayes, lanes and coverte corners to buylde upon, yf it be but sheddes, cottages, and small tenements for people to lodge inn which have not any meanes either to live or to imploye themselves. . . . This sorte of covetous Buylders exacte greater renttes, and daiely doe increase them, in so much that a poore handiecraftsman is not able by his paynefull laboure to paye the rentte of a small tenement.[5]

When Stow published his *Survey of London* in 1598, he took note of the apprehension which the city's disproportionate size and wealth had already created. At the end of his work he appended a discourse on the advantages of cities, 'Written by way of an Apologie (or

---

[1] J. Stow, *op. cit.*, I, 309.
[2] *Ibid.*, I, 163.
[3] Cited in N. G. Brett-James, *The growth of Stuart London*, L., 1935, 83–4.
[4] Cited in *ibid.*, 87–8.
[5] Cited in *ibid.*, 98–9.

defence) against the opinion ... that the greatnes of [London] standeth not with the profit and securitie of this Realme.' As well as stressing the close connection between cities and a civilized, religious life, he took pains to emphasize that great towns, if rightly ordered, are a bulwark of aristocracy and just kingship. Rebellions, he pointed out, are the offspring of ambition or covetousness. Hence they are likely to be incited either by high and noble personages or by unthrifts and needy men who may be numerous in the city but have no part of its rule. Although the capital had supported some rebellions, it had opposed others and was never the author of any; nor could it be so long as it continued to be well governed. But he had to confess that 'London is a mighty arme and instrument to bring any great desire to effect, if it may be woon to a man's devotion; whereof ... there want not examples in the English Historie.'[1]

This was a lesson Charles I failed to learn. The citizens' deep-rooted feeling for property and their hard religious sensibilities were, indeed, dangerous to offend. The mass of apprentices, workmen, and shopkeepers who inhabited the city's parishes and suburbs could not be controlled when they assembled in angry multitudes to shout their will. If the Londoners withdrew their allegiance, the King would suffer a calamitous reverse. Yet with the shortsightedness that marked so much of his rule, his treatment of the capital produced exactly this result.

In the relations between Charles I and London, the financial aspect was inevitably uppermost. The King's treatment of his capital was aptly described by Clarendon: 'The City of London,' he wrote, 'was looked upon too much of late time as a common stock not easy to be exhausted, and as a body not to be grieved by ordinary acts of injustice.'[2] It is impossible to pinpoint any one particular act of state which focused all the resentment provoked by the crown's projects to exploit the wealth of London. But in the twenty years or so before the revolution, there was not a single financial transaction between the crown and the city of London as a corporate body in which the royal government behaved toward its municipal creditor with the probity essential in maintaining its respect and credit within the business community. In 1617, the Corporation of London stood guarantor for a loan to the King of nearly £100,000 which was raised among the wealthier citizens with repayment promised in a year at ten per cent interest. The royal pledge was not kept, and for over a decade there were repeated prolongations of the debt, while most of the interest due remained unpaid. In the meantime, the crown obtained what was in effect a conversion of the terms of its loan, when an act of 1624 fixed eight per cent as the statutory maximum

[1] J. Stow, *op. cit.*, II, 196ff.   [2] *Rebellion*, IV, 179.

that could be charged for interest. While repayment of the loan of 1617 hung fire, Charles I soon after his accession borrowed another £60,000 also underwritten by the Corporation of London. He undertook to repay both this and the earlier debt within a year. Once more, however, the crown defaulted on its obligation. In 1628, an expedient was agreed upon to satisfy the citizen creditors to whom the Corporation of London stood bound. The latter advanced another £120,000 to the King, much of it raised by assessments which the city authorities levied on the livery companies; in return, crown lands were conveyed to the Corporation which it was to sell, the proceeds being applied to the repayment of the several loans. The scheme went into operation, but four years later, the government accused the city of misconduct in its role as contractor of royal lands. There was in fact some profiteering by land purchasers; yet it was scarcely the part of the crown to reproach the Corporation of London for its management of an arrangement it had been persuaded to accept as the only means of recovering debts legally due it and long outstanding. Although the city finally decided to compound for its alleged offence, the dispute retarded the further disposal of royal lands, and during the 1630s the loans of 1617, 1625, and 1628 were still being repaid. Even in the '40s not all the creditors had yet received their principal and accumulated interest.[1]

Another notable instance in which London discovered the baneful effects of royal bad faith was the Star Chamber prosecution against the city in connection with the Londonderry plantation. Like the royal loans, the plantation in Ireland was a project undertaken by the Corporation of London at the crown's behest and in which some of the money raised was lent with considerable unwillingness. The task of assisting to colonize and anglicize Ulster was first laid upon London by King James in 1610, the necessary capital being advanced at the Corporation's call by the livery companies, who assessed their members for the purpose. The enterprise in the end yielded no profit: in fact, the contributing companies incurred a net loss of more than £50,000. However, in 1631 the Attorney General entered a bill against the Corporation in the Star Chamber, charging it with fraud and excessive profit in its administration of the Londonderry plantation. The political significance of the case was perhaps as great as the financial. The prosecution was instituted after Charles had resolved to summon parliament no more and his subjects had shown strong signs

[1] Cf. for the details of these transactions the account by R. Ashton, 'Deficit finance in the reign of James I,' *Economic history review*, 2nd ser., X, 1 (1957) and *The crown and the money market*, chs. V–VI. The mode of raising these loans in the city is described in R. Sharpe, *London and the kingdom*, 3v., L., 1894–5, II, 70, 104–5.

of disaffection. According to Secretary of State Coke, if the King won the suit, 'Hee may breake the confidence of the times that have encroached uppon him and increase his royalties and revenue in an ample and faire manner.'[1] The trial took place in 1635 and lasted over the unprecedented time of thirteen days. Its conclusion was probably predictable. The Corporation was sentenced to a fine of £70,000 and the forfeiture of its Irish lands. Although the fine was subsequently mitigated to £12,000, the city's loss was nonetheless substantial. Their treatment must have left a sour taste in many citizens' mouths and could only have contributed to bring both the Court of Star Chamber and the royal government into discredit. Even Wentworth was of the opinion that the Londoners, 'out great Sums upon the Plantation,' had been dealt with too severely.[2]

In spite of the royal exactions to which the city was subjected, its government was too closely connected with the crown to become a sounding board for the swelling animosity of the citizens. The lord mayor and aldermen did try to defend the corporate interests of the municipality, as in 1626, when they demurred to the King's demand for twenty ships from the city, and in 1634, when they with the common council petitioned that London by reason of its privileges should be exempt from ship money.[3] But they invariably yielded in these instances under the slightest pressure from the crown; and equally important, they carefully avoided taking up the larger political issue implicit in the King's attempt by his fiscal measures to gain a revenue independent of parliamentary assent. Neither to the forced loan of 1627 nor to ship money, the supreme national grievance of the 1630s, did the city of London express any official opposition. The municipal authorities were even fortified in their adherence to the King when he permitted the city to compound in 1638 for various offences of which it stood accused and granted it a new charter amplifying some of its privileges.[4]

The crown's laxity in paying its debts had so seriously impaired its credit in the capital that from 1628 to the outbreak of the Scottish rebellion it made no further attempt to raise any loans through the Corporation of London. Its borrowing needs in these years were mainly met by the customs farmers supplemented by a number of individual lenders and companies to whom it had granted monopoly

[1] Sir John Coke to Viscount Dorchester, August 1630, cited in T. W. Moody, *The Londonderry plantation 1609–41*, Belfast, 1939, 259. The account in the above paragraph is based on this excellent work.
[2] *The earl of Strafforde's letters*, II, 25.
[3] R. Sharpe, *op. cit.*, II, 98–9, 113–14; M. Wren, 'London and the twenty ships, 1626–27,' *American historical review*, LV, 2 (1950).
[4] Cf. V. Pearl, *op. cit.*, 82–7, for an account of the negotiations that led to the 1638 charter.

privileges.[1] The Scottish crisis, however, forced the King to turn to the city once more, and in June 1639 the Corporation was asked for a loan of £100,000. The consequences of the crown's former bad faith to its creditors now declared themselves. The lord mayor and aldermen denied the request, though as a sop they offered a free gift of £10,000. Their refusal was based primarily on financial grounds, but must have been reinforced by their awareness that the unpopularity of the Scottish war in the capital would have created serious difficulties in persuading citizens to lend.[2]

In the spring of 1640, they were once more approached for a large loan. The crown's credit was worse than ever and they again refused. By now the King's insistent pressure on them for money provoked a small reaction even in the aldermanic bench. When the aldermen were commanded to submit lists of the richest citizens in their wards from whom contributions could be demanded, four declined to do so, and were jailed by the Council for a few days.[3] This was the limit of opposition to the King in the governing body of London. Sir Henry Garway, mayor in 1639–40, had close financial ties with the crown, and he and most of the aldermen were well disposed towards Charles, as they were to show at a heavy cost to themselves in the months to come.[4] They were all accustomed to serve the royal power both as magistrates and as business men frequently summoned to advise on trade matters. But their unwillingness at such a time to open the city's purse without good security was disastrous for the King. It made his financial plight so desperate that no recourse was left him but to throw himself upon parliament. And, in fact, not until October, after the summons of parliament had been announced and ten peers had given their personal security in anticipation of a parliamentary grant, did the capital's authorities become cooperative and agree to assess the livery companies for an advance of £50,000.[5] No doubt, London lenders and moneyed men believed that parliament's recall after its long intermission promised the end of extraordinary fiscal exactions and the regularization of the entire financial position of the crown.

In contrast to the attitude of the official municipality, there was an

---

[1] Cf. R. Ashton, *The crown and the money market*, ch. VII.

[2] R. Sharpe, *op. cit.*, II, 120–1.

[3] *Ibid.*, II, 122–4, 125. The four aldermen were Rainton, Gayer, Soame, and Atkins.

[4] The Garways were one of the wealthiest merchant families in London and participated as principals or under-sharers in some of the syndicates that farmed the customs under James and Charles; cf. the references to them in R. Ashton, *The crown and the money market*, *passim*, and the account of Sir Henry in V. Pearl, *op. cit.*, and *D.N.B.*, *s.v.*, 'Sir Henry Garraway.'

[5] R. Sharpe, *op. cit.*, II, 128–30; R. Ashton, *The crown and the money market*, 181–2.

organized opposition to the royal government within the citizen body. Its core was a group of merchants who were allies of the Country leaders and united through their Puritan convictions and support for the claims of parliament. Their political activity is shrouded in obscurity, but they probably were behind some of the attempts in London to challenge the King's power. Their chief bond of association was the Massachusetts Bay Company, which paralleled the Providence Island Company as a centre for the London elements of the anti-Court party that was taking shape before 1640. In May 1628, when certain adventurers received a grant from the Council for New England, an earlier colonizing enterprise, for settlement in Massachusetts, twenty-two of the original forty-three participants were London merchants. These included Mathew Cradock and John Venn, both of whom represented London in the Long Parliament as adherents of the Country leaders. A few months later, Samuel Vassall, another future London M.P. of identical sympathies, became an adventurer.[1] We can well believe that the hearts of these men must have been deeply committed to this enterprise, under whose auspices the great Puritan migration to Massachusetts began. When, as the sequel to this undertaking, the Massachusetts Bay Company was formed in the following year, its charter appointed Cradock as governor and mentioned Venn and Vassall as founder members. Vassall had already suffered imprisonment for refusing to pay tonnage and poundage, and a few years afterwards the Privy Council noted him as friendly to the Scottish rebels. Some of the other men among the company's first investors—Thomas Andrewes, William Perkins, Owen Rowe, Nathaniel Wright, and William Spurstowe—became well known in London after 1640 as enemies of the Court. Spurstowe, who resisted the forced loan in 1627, possessed family and trading connections with Shrewsbury and was elected one of its M.P.s in the Long Parliament, where he showed himself keen for political and religious reform. The others in 1641–2 were active in the struggle to align the government of the capital behind Pym, Hampden, and their party in parliament.

With the probable exception of Cradock and Spurstowe, none of these London supporters of the Country was in the first rank of citizen wealth; but almost all were men of substance—rich or prosperous merchants, exporters with interests in several trading companies, members of the urban governing class well qualified to take a prominent share in the political life of the city.[2]

[1] Cf. F. Rose-Troup, *John White, the patriarch of Dorchester*, N.Y., 1930, 111–12, 122, and the same writer's *The Massachusetts Bay Company and its predecessors*, N.Y., 1930, 19–21.
[2] Cf. *Records of the governor and company of ... Massachusetts Bay*, ed.

A direct connection existed between the London oppositionists and the men involved in another enterprise dear to the heart of Puritan England. This was the Feoffees for Impropriations, a body of trustees formed in 1625 to finance the purchase of places in the church for Puritan clergy.[1] John White, the Massachusetts Bay Company's counsel, was one of these feoffees. He represented Southwark in the Long Parliament and was a supporter of the Country. Another lawyer in the Bay company, also a feoffee, was Samuel Browne, first cousin to Oliver St. John and future M.P. for Dartmouth. Three other feoffees in the Bay company—George Harwood, Francis Bridges and Richard Davis—were all London merchants. John Davenport, the Puritan vicar of St. Stephen's Coleman Street in London until his emigration to New England in 1633, was likewise both a feoffee and a charter member of the Massachusetts Bay Company.[2]

Besides the feoffees, there were looser associations through the Bay company between the Londoners and some of the Country peers and gentry. Two of the subscribers to the company's capital were brothers-in-law of the opposition nobleman, the earl of Lincoln.[3] Another subscriber was a son of Lord Saye.[4] Sir William Brereton, an oppositionist who subsequently represented Cheshire in the Long Parliament, and Henry Darley, whom the Country leaders later sent as their intermediary to the Scots, also a future M.P., were both stockholders in the Bay company.[5] As president of the Council for New England, the earl of Warwick gave substantial support to the promoters of the Massachusetts enterprise.[6] Thus, the merchant group, while not of the inner circle of the opposition movement, was related in various ways to its leaders. Once again, in these multi-

[1] On the Feoffees for Impropriations, cf. *infra*, 179–82.

[2] The feoffees' names are listed in I. Calder, *Activities of the Puritan faction of the Church of England*, L., 1957, x–xi. Those mentioned in the text are included in the list of adventurers in the Bay company in F. Rose-Troup, *The Massachusetts Bay Company and its predecessors*, ch. XVI.

[3] These were John Humphrey and Isaac Johnson; cf. C. M. Andrews, *op. cit.*, I, 355, 360.

[4] Charles Fiennes.

[5] M. Keeler, *op. cit., s.v.*

[6] F. Rose-Troup, *The Massachusetts Bay Company and its predecessors*, 45; C. M. Andrews, *op. cit.*, I, 366–7.

N. B. Shurtleff, 5v., Boston, 1853, I, 11, and the list of adventurers in F. Rose-Troup, *The Massachusetts Bay Company and its predecessors*, ch. XVI. Biographical references to, or accounts of, the names mentioned in the text may be found in M. Keeler, *op. cit., D.N.B.*, and V. Pearl, *op. cit., passim.* Cf. also the cordial letter sent by Cradock and Owen Rowe to John Winthrop on the transfer of the company's government to New England, *Winthrop papers*, III, 226, 377.

farious connections, we have a sight of the uncanny ability of the Puritan oppositionists to devise methods of organization and common action, even at the time the King's power seemed at its highest. In London as elsewhere, the forces were forming whom Pym and his collaborators could mobilize when the hour came.

While the city's governing body consistently refrained from taking a stand in the political conflict, the temper of its citizens was increasingly hostile toward the crown. Considerable resistance appeared to the forced loan, and in 1629 the King's collection of tonnage and poundage provoked a trade stoppage for several weeks by the protesting merchants.[1] Political sentiment in London found an opportunity to manifest itself unmistakably in the election to the parliament of 1628. The choice of London's members lay with the liverymen assembled in the court of common hall. What occurred may well have been planned in advance by opposition elements in the city. The recorder, customarily always returned as one of London's members, was ignominiously rejected. Instead, the electors named as two of their four representatives Alderman Bunce and Henry Waller, both known to be opponents of the Court. Bunce had stood out against the forced loan; Waller was a good friend of Sir John Eliot and subsequently a subscriber to the Massachusetts Bay Company.[2] During the later '30s, the levying of ship money was also met by the Londoners with a recalcitrance and dislike that no threats from the Privy Council could subdue.[3] A pointed symptom of London's discontent was the unwillingness of qualified citizens to accept municipal office, particularly the place of sheriff, on which the burden of the ship-money collection lay. At the end of 1639, an act of the common council was constrained to take notice of this state of affairs. Remarking on 'the greate number of Commoners men of good worth and ability ... elected to the place of Sherivalty ... refusing the same,' it removed the disabilities which an act of common council a century before had imposed on such refusers.[4]

During 1640, as the unpopularity of the royal government reached an extreme, signs of a revolutionary situation began to appear in the great city. The spring election to the Short Parliament went strongly against the Court. Besides Cradock and Vassall, who belonged to the group of city oppositionists, two junior aldermen, Thomas Soame and Isaac Penington, were returned. Neither had taken part in previous

[1] Cf. *supra*, 110, 112.
[2] Cf. the account of the London election in a news letter to Lord Fairfax, February 1628, *Fairfax correspondence*, I, 89; J. Forster, *op. cit.*, II, 100, 592, 596; F. Rose-Troup, *The Massachusetts Bay Company and its predecessors*, 91, 157; P.R.O. S.P. 16/89 no. 2.
[3] Cf. V. Pearl, *op. cit.*, 89–91.
[4] Journal, 39, f. 36.

manifestations of resistance to the King, but Penington, who became an alderman early in 1639, was a prominent Puritan and proved himself an uncompromising enemy of the royal power.[1] In May, dislike of the Scottish war broke out in rioting in Lambeth and Southwark against Archbishop Laud. An angry mob of hundreds attacked the archiepiscopal residence, forcing Laud to flee across the river to Whitehall for safety. Insulting placards were posted denouncing the Queen and popery. A royal proclamation ordering the repression of these 'late Rebellious and Traiterous assemblies' gave some indication of the social status of the rioters. It commanded the arrest for treason of John Archer, glover, George Seares, poulterer, and William Seltrum, shoemaker. Archer and several others were executed for their share in the outbreak.[2] Clearly, a spirit of rebellion was springing to dangerous life among the heaving mass of apprentices, artificers, and tradesmen in the capital. The fears of wealthy citizens were aggravated by the spectre of violence from below, while they worriedly watched the King's desperate efforts to find money for the war against the Scots. Having failed to obtain a loan from the city government, in July Charles seized the bullion deposited by merchants and goldsmiths at the royal mint and threatened to debase the coinage unless financial help from London were forthcoming. This last scheme, commented a privy councillor, 'is conceived the most mischievous thing that could be thought on, and would be the destruction of all trade if it should go on. All the merchants and monied men in the citty are much troubled at this project. . . .'[3]

At the beginning of September, with the Scottish Covenanters already in occupation in the north, London heard the first justification of forcible resistance against the King to issue from an English pulpit. The Puritan preacher was Dr. Calybute Downing, his auditors the members of the Artillery Company of London. Other than the trained bands, the Artillery Company was the only organization in the capital exercised to the use of arms. Vassall, Venn, Rowe, and other militant oppositionists belonged to it; Henry Waller, the London M.P. in 1628, had once been its commander. Evidently it had become notorious as a centre for anti-Court citizens.[4] It could hardly have been by chance that Downing addressed his insurrectionary

---

[1] Cf. on Penington the account in M. Keeler, *op. cit.*, *s.v.*, and V. Pearl, *op. cit.*, 176–84.

[2] R. Steele, *op. cit.*, I, 1817; S. R. Gardiner, *History*, IX, 132–3, 141.

[3] The earl of Northumberland's statement; *H.M.C. Third report*, 82. Cf. the petitions of the merchants, goldsmiths, and Merchant Adventurers Company against the seizure of their bullion, *C.S.P.D. 1640*, 543–4.

[4] Cf. *A letter from Mercurius Civicus to Mercurius Rusticus*, 8–9, and V. Pearl, *op. cit.*, 170–2. Waller died in 1631.

sermon to this body. Taking his text from Deuteronomy, the preacher declared that the injurious treatment of the people of Israel by their ungodly enemies gave an example of 'all the justifiable causes of a legall warre. . . .' '. . . for the safety of the Body of the State,' he said, 'there are . . . Latitudes allowed. . . .' The application to the Scots in arms could not have been more clear. But the preacher left the 'chief Legionaries of this royall City' in no doubt about their own duty. There is in England, he told his congregation, a 'Jesuited faction' which must be destroyed as the Israelites of old righteously destroyed their persecutors, the Amalekites. 'Be wise, be resolute,' was his conclusion, 'you have Amalekites amongst you.'[1] After this discourse, Downing, no longer able to remain safely in London, went for refuge to the earl of Warwick's house in Essex.[2]

As pressure on the King intensified to force the summoning of another parliament, many Londoners threw their weight into the effort. In September, just after the petition of the twelve peers for a parliament,[3] a petition to the same effect was circulated among the citizens. This was an organized campaign to back up the demand of the opposition noblemen with London's numbers. The government received information that nearly three hundred persons had consulted about the petition and that a secret press existed in the city to print seditious literature. Despite the Privy Council's attempt to stop the proceedings and the petition's disavowal by the aldermanic bench, it was delivered to the King at York with ten thousand signatures.[4] A hard indictment of royal misrule, it complained of unlawful taxation, monopolies, religious innovations, and the spread of popery. The petitioners asserted that they could obtain no redress through ordinary justice and demanded that a parliament be called.[5]

Tension in London ran high and the annual election of lord mayor to succeed Sir Henry Garway took place at the end of the month in a disturbed and tempestuous atmosphere. A disorderly crowd assembled in a common hall, with many 'young mechanics' present who had no right to vote. Altogether, about fifteen hundred votes were cast. In a violation of long established usage, the electors passed over the senior alderman, Sir William Acton, whose loyalty to the Court was well known, and nominated two other aldermen for mayor instead, Edmund Wright and Thomas Soame. Wright's choice had

---

[1] C. Downing, *A sermon preached to the renowned Company of the Artillery,* 1641, 10, 11, 37, 39. The sermon, delivered on 1 September 1640, was published by Downing the following year in response to widespread demand.
[2] *A letter from Mercurius Civicus to Mercurius Rusticus,* 8–9.
[3] Cf. *supra,* 105.
[4] *C.S.P.D. 1640–41,* 67, 72, 84; Repertories, 54, f. 307b.
[5] Cf. the text of the citizens' petition in *C.S.P.D. 1640–41,* viii.

no political import, but Soame had recently become popular for disregarding the Privy Council's order to the aldermen to give in lists of the rich men in their wards. The Council was gravely concerned about the result of common hall's departure from tradition. If it were not reversed, wrote Secretary of State Windebank to the King, 'the government of the City is utterly lost.' In the end, after consultation with the Council, the court of aldermen selected Wright, the next in seniority to Acton, as mayor, and he proved to be a dependable friend of royal authority.[1]

Although the Court thus retained its hold on London's government, the citizenry had turned against the crown. At the October election to the Long Parliament, the recorder, Thomas Gardiner, on whose return the Privy Council counted, was rejected. The members of the previous spring—Cradock, Vassall, Soame, and Penington— were again chosen to represent the capital.[2] All four took their stand in the House of Commons with the Country leaders. A contemporary tract stated the reasons for their election:

> ... *Alderman Soame for his imprisonment in denying ship-money, Vassall for his obstinacy against Customes, Craddock for the Cause of New-England, Alderman Pennington for his knowne zeale by his keeping a fasting Sabboth throughout his Shirifalty.* ...[3]

There remained, nevertheless, a formidable obstacle to the supremacy of the oppositionists in London. So long as the mayor and majority of aldermen favoured the King, they would stand in the way of every effort to throw London's voice and resources behind the leaders of opposition in parliament. London's M.P.s might represent the political feeling of the citizens, but they could not speak for the aldermanic bench which dominated the official municipality. The anomalous situation that existed was clearly revealed when the mayor and aldermen on 1 December 1640 named a committee of twenty-three persons to consult on matters to be propounded to parliament on the city's behalf. Not one of London's representatives in the House of Commons was appointed.[4] Evidently the London magistracy had no confidence in its own M.P.s. Thus, if the Country's London sympathizers were to be free to work their will in the capital, they would either have to circumvent the mayor and aldermen

[1] *C.S.P.D. 1640–41*, 115; *Clarendon state papers*, II, 124–5, 128. A detailed account of the mayoralty election is contained in V. Pearl, *op. cit.*, 110–12. Biographical notices of Acton, Wright, and Soame are in *ibid.*, App. J and M. Keeler, *op. cit.*, 345–6 (Soame).

[2] M. Keeler, *op. cit.*, 55; Gardiner, *History*, IX, 220.

[3] *Persecutio undecima*, 57. Penington was sheriff in 1638.

[4] Cf. V. Pearl, *op. cit.*, 195–6.

or annul their power under the civic constitution. This was the task the fraternity of London oppositionists confronted in the months ahead. The struggle against Charles I had acquired a momentum that was to subvert the traditional structure of rule in the capital.

4

The reaction of the towns of provincial England to the crisis of 1640 is much less documented than London's. The impact of national events and the state of local opinion are often impossible to ascertain. All municipal authorities preferred to maintain the fiction of a harmonious community. Their practice, therefore, was to exclude from official records as much as possible any traces of dissension in the urban corporation or the citizenry. In the case of London, the limitations of the official evidence can be somewhat overcome by means of the considerable information to be derived from state papers, letters, and pamphlets. Such supplementary sources of know-ledge are far fewer for other towns, and the history of their relation to the developing revolution is accordingly more obscure. Despite the paucity of evidence, however, there is no reason to doubt that factors similar to those in the capital were operative in the political stand of the provincial *bourgeoisie*. Again there was a deep and widespread dissatisfaction with the crown among the citizens. Again the urban governing bodies usually hesitated or evinced a conservative ten-dency, notwithstanding the grievances royal policy and financial exactions had inflicted on their communities. Bristol, Newcastle, and Norwich, three leading provincial towns, may serve as illustrations. Here lived business men inferior only to the Londoners in wealth. The cross-currents and play of forces in these lesser centres throw a further light on the posture of the citizen element as revolution approached and the Court's power disintegrated.

Bristol, the metropolis of its region and the second trading city in the kingdom, had suffered numerous difficulties from the royal government. Its merchants, carrying on a large commerce with France and the Iberian peninsula, complained frequently of the duties levied on their wine imports by the customs farmers. There were city petitions to parliament against these duties in the 1620s; and after the first session of the 1628 parliament, the Bristol members, we are told, 'laid before the common council six books concerning the liberty of the subject.'[1] These probably related to the Petition of Right. In 1631 the prohibition of tobacco importation through any port but London adversely affected an important Bristol trade, while

[1] J. Latimer, *op. cit.*, 84, 89, 101.

the monopolies which the crown granted to the London companies of soap makers and vintners also did injury to the city's economy.[1] Leading merchants suffered harassment from royal agents and were even prosecuted in the Star Chamber for illegal trade in prohibited goods.[2]

As against these grievances, on the other hand, there were royal measures calculated to gain the city's favour. The municipal corporation realized a long-standing desire when the King gave it sole jurisdiction over Bristol castle and precincts, till then part of Gloucestershire. The limitation of tobacco imports to London was lifted in 1639, and the Merchant Venturers Society, the dominant factor in the city's political and economic life, received an ample confirmation of its privileges from the crown.[3] Moreover, the peace made with France and Spain at the end of the '20s led to a period of expanding trade and prosperity in Bristol. Its substantial commerce with Ireland also benefited by royal action to suppress piracy in the Irish channel.[4]

In 1640 Bristol appointed a deputation to represent its mistreatment to the Short Parliament.[5] Yet however much their grievances aroused the rancour of the citizens, they did not suffice to turn the leading men of the municipality against the crown. This was made clear in the election to the Long Parliament. The parliamentary franchise was confined to the officers of the urban corporation and the resident freeholders. Mere citizen-freemen had no vote and vainly protested their exclusion in a petition to the city government. Even if their request had prevailed, however, the enlargement of the electorate would have been negligible, since it appears that from 1619 to 1699 only five hundred and fifty persons were admitted to the freedom of the city.[6] The members elected were two aldermen, Humphrey Hooke and Richard Long, each in the top rank of Bristol's mercantile elite. Although both had tried to defend the city's interests in their dealings with the royal government, neither was in the least disaffected to the crown or the church. In May 1642 the House of Commons expelled them as monopolists, in spite of their contention that they had cooperated in the wine monopoly of the London

[1] *Ibid.*, 116, 121–2; *Proceedings . . . of the Company of Soapmakers 1562–1642*, ed. H. E. Matthews, *Bristol record society*, X, 1940, 3; *Records relating to the Society of Merchant Venturers of . . . Bristol*, ed. P. McGrath, *Bristol record society*, XVII, 1951, 223–5.

[2] *C.S.P.D. 1634–35*, 177; *ibid. 1637–38*, 168–9; *ibid. 1639–40*, 39–40.

[3] J. Latimer, *op. cit.*, 90–1, 144; J. Latimer, *The history of the Society o Merchant Venturers of Bristol*, Bristol, 1903, 87–8.

[4] P. McGrath, *op. cit.*, xix.

[5] J. Latimer, *The annals of Bristol in the seventeenth century*, 147.

[6] *Ibid.*, 147–8; P. McGrath, *op. cit.*, ix, n.

Vintners only to avoid exclusion from the trade entirely. Both became Royalists in the civil war.[1]

Other Bristol notables, indistinguishable from Hooke and Long in social or economic terms, supported the Country, judging by some of the aldermen who later appeared as active partisans on the Parliamentarian side in the civil war.[2] In 1640, however, the aldermanic body as a whole was either too cautious to commit itself against the King or averse from doing do. Apparently, the political alignment in Bristol at the convening of the Long Parliament was not very different from what it was to be two years later, when a native stated, '. . . here are many malignants of the great ones amongst us . . . yet I conceive that the Major part of this City . . . stand firm for the Parliament.'[3]

Newcastle, the centre of the English coal industry, supplied London with all its mineral fuel. A great provincial town, it was described by a traveller in the 1630s as 'inferior for wealth and building to no city save London and Bristow. . . .'[4] Here the 'lords of coal' resided. These colliery owners and merchants maintained a monopoly through the Hostmen's Company of Newcastle, whose members, in return for a shilling duty to the crown on every chaldron shipped, possessed the sole right to buy and sell coal on the Tyne. It was a token of the dominance of this association of coal traders in Newcastle that the same royal charter of 1600 which completed the town's oligarchical constitution also established the privileges of the Hostmen.[5] So close was the relation between the Hostmen and Newcastle's government that every mayor in the earlier seventeenth century was a leading figure in the company.[6]

Charles I's undeviating support of the political and commercial privileges of Newcastle's ruling minority caused most of its members to favour the Court. A few signs of opposition to the oligarchy's dominance, nevertheless, appeared in the town. In 1633, the freemen petitioned the Privy Council against the misgovernment of the mayor

---

[1] Biographical notices of Hooke and Long are contained in M. Keeler, *op. cit., s.v.* The former also represented Bristol in the Short Parliament. The Bristol merchants' defence of their collaboration in the wine monopoly is printed in *Records relating to the Society of Merchant Venturers of . . . Bristol*, 223–5. When the House expelled Hooke and Long, it declared that they were beneficiaries of the wine monopoly, but not its projectors, *C.J.*, II, 567.

[2] Cf. *infra*, 339–70.

[3] *A declaration from the city of Bristol . . . sent from M. John Bell*, 1642, 1–3.

[4] Sir W. Brereton, *Travels*, ed. E. Hawkins, *Chetham society*, I, 1844, 85.

[5] For the history and privileges of the Newcastle Hostmen, cf. *Extracts from the records of the Company of Hostmen.*

[6] Cf. J. U. Nef, *The rise of the British coal industry*, 2v., L., 1932, II, 126.

and aldermen. They complained of corruption in the disposal of town revenues and leases and asked for an addition to Newcastle's charter to curb the excessive power of the mayor and his brethren. Their petition was referred to the Council of the North at York which, as might have been expected, upheld the magistrates in their powers. The Council's report on the case expressed a keen awareness of the need for subordination in a centre so important to the King's service. Newcastle, it stated,

is now growne to be very populous . . . the farr greater parte of the Com'ons consisting . . . of Mariners . . . Watermen, Colliers, Keelmen and other people of mean condition, who are apt to turne every pretence and color of grievance into uproare and seditious mutinye. . . .

Again in 1638 the freemen made a similar protest against the civic government, but with no greater effect than before.[1]

The chief threat of political disaffection in Newcastle came not from the commonalty, but from a few influential citizens—a threat the more serious because of the town's strategic importance in the defence of the north against the Scottish Covenanters. There was a small Puritan group in Newcastle; and at the autumn mayoralty election in 1639, Robert Bewick, who belonged to it and was believed sympathetic to the Scots, was chosen mayor. The Privy Council, although warned of the danger of his election, was unable to prevent it.[2] A prominent Hostman, son of a former mayor and already once mayor himself as well as sheriff of Northumberland, Bewick's status fully qualified him for his position. No accusation was made of any irregularity in his election. But in spite of his being one of the oligarchy, his reputation as a Puritan made him deeply suspect to his fellows in the town elite.[3] During his mayoralty, Newcastle manifested dislike of ship money, and the Privy Council was told that some of the magistrates refused to be assessed, 'pretending the tax . . . an unjust pressure on them.'[4] Moreover, on the eve of the Short Parliament, several merchants organized a petition instructing

[1] R. Welford, *History of Newcastle and Gateshead*, 3v., L., 1884–7, III, 315–16, 359–62. The report of the Council of the North and other documents relating to the free burgesses' protest are printed in C. S. Terry, 'The visits of Charles I to Newcastle,' *Archaeologia Aeliana*, n.s., XXI, 1891, 91–5.
[2] *C.S.P.D. 1639*, 450–1, 480.
[3] Cf. *The mayors and sheriffs of Newcastle*, ed. C. H. Hunter Blair, *Archaeologia Aeliana*, 4th ser., XVIII, 1940, 53. Bewick participated in the cartel agreement of the Hostmen to limit the sale of coal in order to maintain the price; cf. *Extracts from the records of the Company of Hostmen*, 66, 69, 73. His Puritan sympathies are mentioned in *C.S.P.D. 1639–40*, 346, 402.
[4] *C.S.P.D. 1639–40*, 460.

the municipal M.P.s to oppose Laud's religious innovations and preserve the liberty of the subject. The ringleader in this move was Anthony Errington, the warden of the Newcastle Merchant Adventurers Company. The organizers were denounced to the Privy Council by a number of aldermen, who called the petition 'as ill as the covenant of Scotland.'[1]

The dissatisfaction in the town towards Charles I's regime was registered at the election to the Long Parliament. What the parliamentary franchise was is uncertain, but probably it was broader than the franchise in civic elections. Perhaps the presence of the Scots, who were already at Newcastle, also had some effect on the outcome. At any rate, both the members chosen were supporters of the Country. Sir Henry Anderson, scion of a family prominent in public affairs and the coal trade, was one of the representatives.[2] The other was John Blakiston, not one of the inner circle of Newcastle wealth or power, but a prosperous merchant who had recently been in trouble with the Court of High Commission for religious nonconformity.[3] His return, in particular, must have reflected the oppositionist sentiments of the electors.

There can be no doubt that the election result was decidedly unwelcome to almost all Newcastle's notables. These—Marlays, Davisons, Carrs, Coles, Liddells, Riddells, and their like—adhered from first to last to the King, the buttress of their privileges. One of them, Sir Nicholas Cole, succeeded Bewick as mayor, an indication of their determination to keep the town in line with their own position. They afterwards swelled the roll of Royalists in the civil war, while even Sir Henry Anderson in a couple of years went over to the King's party.[4] In 1640-1, with some of the freemen aroused against the Court and a few of the elite estranged, the town government's power may have been momentarily impaired. This is particularly suggested by an order of December 1641 giving the common council a voice in the disposition of the corporation's revenues and leases.[5] Eight years previously the freemen had petitioned in vain for such an arrangement. But if the oligarchy's position was indeed shaken, the situation

[1] *Ibid.*, 600–4; *Memoirs of Ambrose Barnes*, ed. W. H. D. Longstaffe, *Surtees society*, L, 1867, App., 329–30.
[2] Cf. M. Keeler, *op. cit.*, *s.v.*
[3] *Ibid.*, *s.v.* and *Acts of the High Commission Court ... of Durham*, ed. W. H. D. Longstaffe, *Surtees society*, XXXIV, 1858, 157–8. Blakiston was named in a disputed return with Sir John Melton, Secretary of the Council of the North. Melton's death a few weeks after parliament's opening enabled Blakiston to take his seat without further difficulty; cf. M. Keeler, *op. cit.*, 59.
[4] Cf. *infra*, 339, and M. Keeler, *op. cit.*, 59, 87.
[5] *Extracts from the Newcastle ... council minute book 1639-1650*, ed. M. H. Dodds, *Newcastle upon Tyne records committee*, I, 1920, 7–10.

did not last. For it was not many months until the coal masters of Newcastle turned their town into a royal stronghold completely subservient to their will.

Norwich, the third city in the kingdom, owed its importance to its position in the East Anglian textile industry. Long a centre of the worsted manufacture, in the reign of Queen Elizabeth several thousand Protestant refugees from the Low Countries were permitted to settle there, and they introduced to Norwich the making of the 'new draperies,' the lighter woollens on which its prosperity in the earlier seventeenth century was principally based.[1] As elsewhere, so at Norwich the governing court of mayoralty was composed of merchants and well-to-do retailers in the textile and a few other trades vital to the urban economy.[2]

The civic rulers were indebted to the crown in more than one respect for its favour to themselves and the cloth manufacture. Under its fifteenth-century charters, power in the municipality was centred in the mayor and twenty-four aldermen, the latter of whom possessed life tenure. Some scope still remained for the popular element, nevertheless, since the general body of citizens had the right to nominate the mayor and his brethren, while the choice of common councillors lay with the resident householders in the four wards. In 1619, after a disputed mayoralty election, a royal order curtailed the citizens' privileges. To quash 'factious opposition,' it was decreed that henceforth the office of mayor should be annually filled by the senior alderman who had not yet served. Another alteration in 1621 confined aldermanic office to men who had previously been sheriffs, and also transferred the nomination of aldermen from the citizens to the mayor and his sitting colleagues. In this way, the participation of the citizen-freemen was all but eliminated and the control of the oligarchy fixed more firmly than ever. The crown showed its determination to preserve this state of affairs when it upheld the mayor and aldermen in a disputed shrievalty election in 1627 that had caused disturbance in the city.[3]

[1] Cf. E. Lipson, *The history of the woollen and worsted industries,* L., 1921, 21–4. A document of 1575 attests the benefits the Dutch and Walloon refugees brought Norwich; cf. R. H. Tawney and E. Power (eds.), *Tudor economic documents,* 3v., L., 1924, I, 315–16.

[2] Cf. *Minutes of the Norwich court of mayoralty 1630–1631,* 21–3. Of the mayors and aldermen in the earlier seventeenth century, merchants, grocers, mercers, and drapers exceeded all other occupations.

[3] A full account of the evolution of Norwich's government is contained in *The records of the city of Norwich,* I, Introduction; a shorter sketch is given in *Minutes of the court of mayoralty 1630–1631,* Introduction. For crown

To Norwich's textile industry the crown also extended its support. In 1610, for instance, the Privy Council helped the mayor to suppress a strike of journeymen and apprentices directed against the employment of weavers who had not passed their apprenticeship in the trade. The strikers' complaint was justifiable under the Statute of Artificers of 1563, yet such was the magistrates' fear of insubordination that the ringleaders were brought to trial for conspiracy and sedition by the Council's intervention.[1] Again, in 1638 when a royal proclamation ordered that all cloth shipped to London for sale should be inspected in the capital, Norwich woollens were exempted on the mayor's petition. Thus the magistrates retained the authority to supervise the quality of the stuffs manufactured in their city.[2] In general, it was only because the King sustained their privileges that the civic rulers were able to exercise a comprehensive regulation of the cloth industry.

Despite these benefits, there was much enmity to the Court both among the citizens and the governing elite. The chief reason for this was Charles I's religious policy. Puritanism had struck deep roots in Norwich, and Archbishop Laud's rule of the church helped to alienate people in every stratum of the community.[3] The threat of action by the ecclesiastical authorities made the inhabitants circumspect, yet signs of religious disaffection were apparent. In 1627 and 1636 a number of citizens petitioned for liberty of preaching and for lectures.[4] Four aldermen belonged to a group of trustees who, like the London Feoffees for Impropriations, were engaged in securing places for Puritan ministers in Norwich and Norfolk.[5] One of them was Alderman Thomas Atkins, a cloth merchant who left Norwich in 1637 owing to Bishop Wren's prosecution of citizens for nonconformity. Settling in London where he had business connections, he became an alderman there and won renown in 1640 for resisting the King's financial demands upon the capital.[6]

Bishop Wren's pressures in the diocese of Norwich from 1635 to 1638 aroused particular antagonism. As the collaborator of Laud, he did everything in his power to carry the archbishop's programme into effect. He imposed the Anglo-Catholic ritualistic innovations on the

---

[1] J. U. Nef, *Industry and government in France and England 1540–1640*, 40–1.
[2] *Records of the city of Norwich*, II, 259–66.
[3] The extent of Puritanism in Norwich is stressed by Bruce Allen, *op. cit.*
[4] F. Blomefield, *An essay towards a . . . history of . . . Norfolk*, 2nd ed., 11v., L., 1805–10, III, 374, 379.
[5] P.R.O. S.P. 16/531 no. 134.
[6] *C.S.P.D. 1637*, 219 and *supra*, 170.

---

action in behalf of the civic oligarchy, cf. *Acts of the Privy Council Jan. 1618–June 1619*, 484, *ibid. Sept. 1627–June 1628*, 75, 114. 140–1; *C.S.P.D. 1627–28*, 348.

churches and purged the city's pulpits of their Puritan incumbents and lecturers. Eight ministers in Norwich were thus deprived for non-conformity in 1636.[1] Besides the rigour of his visitations, he touched Norwich's inhabitants in a sore place when he forced them to increase their tithes to the parish clergy. To consolidate this achievement, he procured a royal order commanding all disputes on tithes to be heard in Chancery or his own episcopal court, to the exclusion of common law jurisdiction.[2]

These proceedings turned Norwich against the crown. The sequel was seen in 1640. To the Short Parliament the city elected its ex-alderman, Thomas Atkins, and Alderman John Tooley, another Puritan and one of the Norfolk feoffees.[3] The franchise must have been open to all freemen, since more than a thousand citizens voted in the fall election of the Long Parliament.[4] Again two M.P.s opposed to the Court were returned. They were Alderman Richard Harman, mayor in the previous year, and Richard Catelyn, who did not reside in the city but possessed long-standing family connections with it. In due course, Catelyn became a Royalist; his membership in the Norfolk feoffees, however, indicates that he supported the Country when elected.[5] A minority of the ruling oligarchy took a different stand, to judge from the Norwich merchants who later became notorious Royalists in the civil war.[6] But in 1640 most of the court of mayoralty undoubtedly favoured the opponents of Charles I. Strong oppositionist sentiment also probably accounted for the citizens' resumption in 1641 of their privilege of nominating the mayor, which they had lost twenty-two years before. They used their newly regained power to nominate a mayor whose political sympathies accorded with their own.[7]

---

[1] *H.M.C. Gawdy*, 158. One of the deprived was William Bridge, later a well-known Independent, on whose behalf a committee of aldermen petitioned in 1634. He had been rector of St. Peter's Hungate and curate of St. George's in Norwich; *Minutes of the Norwich court of mayoralty 1630–1631*, 49–50 and J. Browne, *History of Congregationalism in Norfolk and Suffolk*, L., 1887, 105, 107.

[2] *State trials*, IV, 35; cf. Norwich's petition to parliament in December 1640 against Bishop Wren and his tithe exactions, *C.J.*, II, 56.

[3] *Members of parliament*, 491; P.R.O. S.P. 16/531, no. 134 lists Tooley's name among the Norfolk feoffees.

[4] M. Keeler, *op. cit.*, 57n.

[5] On the Norwich members, cf. M. Keeler, *op. cit.*, *s.v.* Catelyn is mentioned as a feoffee in P.R.O. S.P. 16/531 no. 134.

[6] Cf. *infra*, 339.

[7] F. Blomefield, *op. cit.*, III, 381. The citizens first nominated Alderman Thomas Carver, and after he died they named Adrian Parmenter, sheriff in 1632, who was to become a strong Parliamentarian (*ibid.*, III, 383–4, 388, 398).

5

The outstanding conclusion to emerge from this survey of the citizen element before and during the crisis of 1640 is the absence of any simple uniformity in its political stand. Like the aristocratic order it was divided. But this division, of course, was far from equal. Even as in 1640 the greater part of the nobility and gentry stood with the leaders of the Country and endorsed their insistence on redress of grievances and reform, so did the greater part of the *bourgeoisie*. That was the meaning of the Court's deep isolation at the moment when the Long Parliament assembled.

Yet, as has been seen, important sections of the mercantile elite either continued to support the King or at any rate failed to take a public position against his government. In the case of the customs farmers the reason was obvious: so involved were their pecuniary interests with crown finance that they necessarily stood and fell with the regime. In other instances, however, *bourgeois* dependence on the crown was less close. Had the coal capitalists of Newcastle not shown themselves hostile to the partisans of the opposition movement in their town, they might have retained their privileges with the Long Parliament's sanction, instead of incurring its enmity as they soon did. The mayor and aldermen of London supported the crown partly because they were accustomed to do so, partly because they knew that the struggle against Charles I would provoke unrest in the capital and place their own authority in question. Even so, their refusal to lend to the King in his time of need spelled ruin for the Court. As for other town corporations, many, we may be sure, harboured a hostility to the crown which they refrained from expressing. If they failed to pronounce an official condemnation of ship money or to make a public demand for a parliament, it was because they were too cautious to do so. It was not in their power to give a political lead, and they did not care to jeopardize their civic interests by risking royal displeasure. They chose the unheroic course and awaited the initiative of the peers and gentlemen who were the natural and inevitable spokesmen of the kingdom's grievances.

Puritanism

Puritanism first became a force on the political scene in the reign of Queen Elizabeth. Its early adherents by their pressure helped shape the religious settlement of 1559; and soon after, they turned towards parliament to obtain its support in imposing their design of reformation upon an unwilling Church of England. Between the coming forth in 1572 of the famous Puritan manifesto, *An Admonition To The Parliament*, and the prospect of reform that opened at last with the Long Parliament's assembly, more than three generations elapsed: long years during which the Puritans wandered in the wilderness, far from the Canaan for which their souls thirsted. Suppressed by the Queen and Archbishop Whitgift, the organized Puritan movement broke up and its inspirers, Cartwright, Field, Travers, together with their great lay patrons of the Elizabethan age, passed from the scene.[1] The successors of these militants preserved the hope of reformation, but with a more temperate zeal. Kept down, like their predecessors, by the crown and the ecclesiastical authorities, they found an outlet for their energies in preaching and writing. From pulpit and press they unceasingly propagated the Puritan scheme of life and way of salvation. And thus in the first two Stuart reigns there grew up an active clergy and a numerous laity whose moral ideals and spiritual temper were deeply stamped by Puritan teaching.[2] Here began the incorporation of Puritanism as a formative element in English civilization and character, which was to be its enduring legacy after the revolutionary gales of the seventeenth century had blown themselves out. But before the long post-revolutionary epilogue set in, the tale of Puritanism militant and Puritanism suffering was to culminate in a third act of Puritanism triumphant: a triumph prepared by the reaction of hatred to the rule of Archbishop Laud, and achieved in the alliance of Puritanism with the Country opposition.

The singular fact about Puritanism was that it survived and

[1] Cartwright died in 1603, his last years having been spent relatively remote from former controversies; Field died in 1588; Travers lived until 1635, but remained in obscurity during the Stuart reigns.

[2] Cf. the account of Puritan preaching and writing by W. Haller, *The rise of Puritanism*, N.Y. 1938.

tenaciously preserved its identity in the Church of England through seven decades of repression and postponed hopes. Never extirpated and never assimilated, it never ceased to manifest its powerful energies in the cultivation of its own religious ethos and the defiance of ecclesiastical authority. So prolific was it that the era of its predominance after 1640 became the climax of the English reformation. We can think of no other instance in the history of revolutions of a movement that maintained itself in the abundance of its creative strength for so long a period.

We have already referred frequently to Puritanism in preceding chapters. We must now take a closer view of it: our purpose will be to ascertain its relation to the revolution that was in the making prior to 1640. Much confusion will be avoided if we state at the outset what is to be understood by 'Puritan.' First used in the mid-1560s, the name, like that of all broad movements which attract many and diverse supporters to their cause, quickly acquired an overlay of various meanings.[1] The commonest was an abusive one designating the censorious rigorist who professed to take his moral and religious duties with greater earnestness than other men. 'Who are so much branded with vile terms of Puritans and Precisians,' asked the famous Puritan divine, William Perkins, 'as those, that most endeavour to get and keepe the puritie of heart in good conscience?'[2] 'To bewail the distresses of God's children,' said a Puritan member of parliament in 1587,

it is puritanism. To reprove a man for swearing, it is puritanism. To banish an adulterer out of the house, it is puritanism. . . . I fear me we shall shortly come to this, that to do God and her Majesty good service shall be counted puritanism. . . .[3]

Praising the Puritan clergy, another lay favourer in 1576 referred to them as 'those faithfull ministers whom none can justly reprove . . . in doctrine or life, and yet of the wicked worldlings and vaine courtiers falsly termed Puritanes. . . .'[4]

[1] Thomas Fuller placed the origin of 'Puritan' in 1564, *The church history of Britain*, 1651, 3rd ed., ed. J. Nichols, 3v., L., 1842, II, 474; A. F. Scott Pearson assigns the term to 1564 or 1566, *Thomas Cartwright and Elizabethan Puritanism*, Cambridge, 1925, 18 and n.; M. Knappen, in his account of the history of the name, traces it to 1567–8, *Tudor Puritanism*, Chicago, 1939, 488–91. Many illustrations of the word are given by C. Hill, *Society and Puritanism in pre-revolutionary England*, L., 1964, ch. I.

[2] William Perkins, *An exposition upon Christs sermon on the mount, Works*, 3v., 1626–31, III, 15.

[3] Job Throckmorton, cited by J. E. Neale, *Elizabeth I and her parliaments 1584–1601*, 151.

[4] *Letters of Thomas Wood, Puritan, 1566–1577*, ed. P. Collinson, *Bulletin of the Institute of Historical Research supplement*, 5 (1960), 16.

Undoubtedly this description, though the Puritans repudiated it, closely approximated the traits of character and behaviour they tended to display. However, it provides no criterion by which to identify Puritanism as a factor in the ecclesiastical and political conflicts of the age. For this purpose another usage of contemporaries affords a guide. From the time it first became current, 'Puritan' retained one indisputable sense with considerable consistency whatever other meanings of a more ambiguous kind were added to it. It regularly signified those members of the Church of England who opposed its hierarchy and many of its ceremonies, while rejecting on principle any separation from it. People who adopted this position in the established church were known as *non-conformists*; and thus, following the practice of the church historian, Fuller, and many other writers and controversialists of the time, Puritanism may be regarded as synonomous with non-conformity and with sympathy for nonconformity, in any of the latter's numerous manifestations.[1]

It is undeniable, of course, that those who separated from the Church of England were offshoots of Puritanism, with which they shared some important characteristics. But in the context of ecclesiastical and political controversy, Puritanism and the varieties of separatism were distinct phenomena and were so conceived by their respective adherents. A Puritan confession of faith of 1572, in stigmatizing withdrawal from the public assemblies of the church, declared, 'we thincke it not meete for private persons of their own auctoritie . . . to establish churches. . . .'[2] The Puritan author of the Marprelate tracts pointed out that he 'doth account no Brownist [separatist] to be a Puritan. . . .'[3] Thomas Cartwright, the foremost Elizabethan champion of Puritan reform, maintained throughout his career a consistent stand against separatism.[4] A Puritan clergyman, the Rev. John White of Dorchester, remarked, 'we doe and ought to put a great difference between Separation and Non-conformity.'[5] Such statements, which could be added to indefinitely, expressed the general Puritan attitude towards separation right down to the era of the revolution. On the other hand, the animosity of the separatists against the Puritan 'reformists' was scarcely less bitter than their

---

[1] *The church history of Britain*, II, 474–5. Fuller declared that when referring to the Puritans, 'The reader knoweth that only nonconformists are thereby intended.'

[2] Drawn up by John Field and Thomas Wilcox, *The seconde parte of a register*, ed. A. Peel, 2v., Cambridge, 1915, I, 86.

[3] *Hay any worke for a cooper*, 1589, cited in F. J. Powicke, *Henry Barrow separatist*, L., 1900, 83.

[4] Cf. A. F. Scott Pearson, *op. cit.*, for numerous illustrations of Cartwright's opinion.

[5] Cited in P. Miller, *Orthodoxy in Massachusetts*, Cambridge, 1933, 141.

feeling towards the bishops and 'pontifical clergy.' Henry Barrow assailed the Puritans as 'enemies of Christ's kingdome, the pharisees of these times . . . great learned preachers . . . that sigh and grone for reformation, but their hands with the sluggard denie to worke. . . .'[1] Henry Ainsworth voiced the common separatist attitude when he said of the Puritans, 'all that know the truth of God . . . aright have just cause to blame them for their long halting and dissembling.'[2]

Our concern in the following pages is with Puritanism alone, since its role in the genesis of the revolution was incomparably greater than that of any other species of religious dissent. This was so precisely because of its refusal to abandon the Church of England. Had it done so, Puritanism would have been reduced to impotence. Separation would have cut it off from almost all its patrons in the governing class who, as pillars of society, were hardly likely to jeopardize their social dominion, renounce their public privileges, and expose themselves to the penalties of the law—all of which would have certainly been the consequence of secession from the national church. Correspondent to this, it was revelatory of the political potentialities of the Puritan movement that it never merely sought toleration for itself in a community estranged from its beliefs. Its outlook was imperial: determinedly clinging to its lodgment in the church, it aimed at mastery, the power to impose its system on the whole of religious life. There was here an affinity with the mentality of its aristocratic lay sympathizers. Such men, landlords, magistrates, law-makers, statesmen, were accustomed to rule. They could far more easily understand and support the Puritan attempt to transform and dominate the national church than they could those who by their withdrawal appeared to generate an anarchy of sects. And in point of fact, while Puritanism attracted adherents of high rank and influence, the disciples of separatism before the revolution belonged almost exclusively to the inferior and labouring orders of the society.

In the largest sense, Puritanism was a reaction not merely against the survival of Catholic practices in the established church, but even more, against the plight of religion rendered subservient to the political expediencies of the crown and placed at the mercy of a rapacious and unscrupulous laity. Already in a decadent condition at the end of the Middle Ages, the church was further weakened by the Henrician reformation and the vicissitudes of the reigns of Edward and Mary. The spoliations committed on its wealth by Henry VIII

[1] Henry Barrow, *A brief discoverie of the false church*, 1590, *The writings of Henry Barrow, 1587–1590*, ed. L. Carlson, L., 1962, 556–7.
[2] Henry Ainsworth, *Counterpoyson*, 1608, cited in B. Hanbury, *Historical memorials relating to the Independents or Congregationalists*, 3v., L., 1839, I, 171.

and his successors, and by the officials and nobility whom they allowed to share in the plunder, did it grave damage. With the loss of corporate autonomy went the church's ability to enforce its will on those who defied it. It became completely dependent on the secular power. The clergy were notoriously poor. Their educational qualifications were grossly inadequate and few could preach. Pastoral efficacy fell to a low ebb. In the later sixteenth century, therefore, the restoration of the church's institutional life, its spiritual strength, and its material resources became for many conscientious men a matter of urgent necessity. Puritanism was one form of response addressing itself to this extraordinarily difficult task. The means which it chose, however, placed it in antagonism to both royal and episcopal authority and thus set it on a course of opposition for decades to come.[1]

The palpable presence of a dissident Puritan party first became evident in the 1560s, when a number of clergy demonstrated their dissatisfaction with certain externals of church worship and the vestments prescribed for ministers. Denouncing both as Romish and unfit for a reformed church, they conducted an agitation that gave serious trouble to Archbishop Parker of Canterbury. Here already, in their disobedience to their ecclesiastical superiors, the Puritans showed how stiff they could be in non-conformity. Although they were unsuccessful in this campaign and had to submit, they did not resign themselves to its outcome. It was, in fact, only the first engagement in a prolonged struggle.[2]

As the Puritan movement evolved in the next years, it advanced well beyond the ground on which its early encounters were fought. This Puritanism was more radical than its predecessor of the '60s. Its leaders were new and younger men, exponents of a programme which became the standard of a rebellious generation.[3] The intellec-

---

[1] On the condition and difficulties of the established church in the later sixteenth century, cf. W. H. Frere, *The English church in the reigns of Elizabeth and James I*, L., 1904, R. G. Usher, *The reconstruction of the English church*, 2v., N.Y., 1910, and C. Hill, *Economic problems of the church from Whitgift to the Long Parliament*, Oxford, 1956.

[2] Cf. M. Knappen, *op. cit.*, for a general account of this and the subsequent stages in the history of sixteenth-century Puritanism. P. Collinson's *The Elizabethan Puritan movement*, L., 1967, which is now the best and fullest treatment of the subject, appeared too late for use by the present writer.

[3] The age of the Puritan leaders in 1572, when the *Admonition* appeared, is suggestive. Cartwright, the oldest, was 37; Walter Travers (whose birthdate has been settled by S. J. Knox, *Walter Travers: paragon of Elizabethan Puritanism*, L., 1962, 14) was 24; John Field and Thomas Wilcox, the *Admonition's* authors, were respectively 27 and 23. In 1583, Archbishop Whitgift told some Puritan ministers: 'You are . . . but boyes in comparison of us, who have studied divinity before you for the most part were borne'

tual inspirer of this fresh phase was Thomas Cartwright, chief
theorist of the Puritan party, who held a divinity professorship at
Cambridge until ousted by the authorities in 1570. As their central
tenet, the Puritans now demanded the abolition of the ecclesiastical
hierarchy and its replacement by a presbyterian polity in the national
church. The *Admonition to the parliament* of 1572 declared their
position with unsurpassed trenchancy; while two years later, Walter
Travers's *Ecclesiasticae Disciplinae ... Explicatio* (for which Cartwright provided the preface) expounded it more fully and systematically.[1]

'... we in England are so fare of, from having a church rightly
reformed,' said the *Admonition*, '... that as yet we are not come to
the outward face of the same.'[2] It went on to present a formidable
indictment of the state of the church, noting unsparingly the incapa-
city of the clergy, the transgressions of the bishops, and the prevalence
of popish abuses contrary to God's word in the service and prayer
book. Here for the first time the Puritans adopted the doctrine that
'ecclesiastical discipline' is one of the essential marks of a true
Christian church.[3] This the *Admonition* concisely explained as church
government by ministers, elders, and deacons, the 'order left by
God ... wherby men learne to frame their wylles and doyngs
accordyng to the law of God. ...' It offered parliament a scheme of
reform which touched every aspect of the ecclesiastical system. The
proposals included election of ministers by their congregations and
elimination of impropriations, patronage, and advowsons. The
spiritual rulers of the church, the ministers and elders, were to
exercise the power of excommunication against the carnal and unre-
pentant in independence of the secular authority. The unscriptural
superiority of bishops was to give place to the equality of the clergy.
Parliament, the *Admonition* concluded, must 'go foreward to a thorow
and a speedy reformation.' The task was no longer to 'patch and
peece,' but to 'remove ... Antichrist, both head body and branch,
and perfectly plant that puritie of the word, that simplicitie of the

---

[1] Cf. S. J. Knox, *op. cit.*, ch. II and F. Paget, *An introduction to the fifth book
of Hooker's ... Laws of ecclesiastical polity*, Oxford, 1899, 52–63, for an
analysis of Travers's work.
[2] I cite the text of the *Admonition* from *Puritan manifestoes*, ed. W. H. Frere
and C. E. Douglas, L., repr. 1954.
[3] The two other marks of a true church were the 'preaching of the worde
purely' and the 'ministring of the sacraments sincerely.'

(Cited in A. F. Scott Pearson, *op. cit.*, 242). Both Gordon Donaldson, *The
Scottish reformation*, Cambridge, 1960, 187–90 and P. Collinson, *op. cit.*,
136–7, have rightly stressed that it was a Puritan party under new leaders
that opened the attack on episcopacy.

sacraments, and severitie of discipline, which Christ hath commanded. . . .'

Voice and temper in this manifesto were nearly as significant as its substance. The reproving sharpness, the peremptory dismissal of all that hindered reformation, the religious superiority assumed by the sponsors—these notes of a self-accrediting intransigent righteousness were to characterize the Puritan movement during its heroic age. As for the revolutionary essence of the *Admonition*, that lay in ecclesiastical discipline—the presbyterian system of church government and censure derived from the influence and practice of Beza and Calvin in Geneva. Since the Discipline, as it became known, would have not only abolished bishops, but would also have established the church's independence from the civil magistrate, it was no way compatible with the ecclesiastical supremacy of the crown.[1] No wonder that the Queen felt compelled to proceed severely against a movement so corrosive of royal power in a vital department of state.

Much of the subsequent activity of Elizabethan Puritanism aimed at putting the presbyterian church order into effect in despite of the crown. In localities where their influence predominated, the Puritan clergy introduced instalments of the Discipline on their own initiative and altered the liturgy and service to accord with their views.[2] Essex, Northamptonshire, Warwickshire, and London were the main scenes of this attempt, which was well organized and hard to check. After 1583, however, when John Whitgift became Archbishop of Canterbury, the government took vigorous measures to deal with nonconformity. The archbishop insisted on strict obedience to the ordinances of the church and, with the backing of the Queen, brought the repressive machinery of the High Commission and the Star Chamber to bear against the Puritan ministers. By the end of the reign the firmness of the ecclesiastical authorities had attained success. The movement for the Discipline was shattered and its promoters driven into silence or submission. Cartwright, its leading ideologue, withdrew himself from the struggle under the government's pressure. Retreat and tribulation were the lot of Puritanism in the setting years of Elizabeth's reign.

While Puritanism continued to be a significant factor in the national church, its presbyterian phase was over for the time. It was to reappear forty years afterward, fanned into life by the revolution, when the Long Parliament began to canvass models for a reformed

---

[1] On the political bearings of the Discipline, cf. A. F. Scott Pearson, *Church & state*.

[2] Cf. the texts and introduction in *The presbyterian movement in the reign of Queen Elizabeth*, ed. R. G. Usher, *Camden society*, 3rd ser., VIII, 1905.

church.[1] The demand to abolish bishops now receded into the background. At James I's accession, it was not mentioned in the proposals for reformation which the Puritan clergy gave the new ruler in their Millenary Petition of 1603.[2] Neither did their spokesmen talk of eliminating episcopal church government at the Hampton Court conference, which the King held the next year to discuss the Puritans' desires. The subject was too inflammatory to be touched. Henceforth Puritan non-conformity expressed its persistent defiance of ecclesiastical authority in other ways. There was even perhaps a possibility that, having laid aside the Discipline, the Puritans could have been brought gradually to live at peace in the church by moderate concessions from the crown. But if such a chance did exist in the earlier seventeenth century, it was never taken. James yielded little to Puritan wishes,[3] while its harsh treatment by Charles and Laud made it intractable.

2

The impact of Puritanism, as we have already suggested, depended on the retention of its hold in the established church; and that, in turn, required the presence of a clergy able to sustain it through all its trials by their teaching and example. From the outset of the movement Puritan ministers confronted some painful dilemmas of conscience: how to justify remaining in the church in view of the blemishes which disfigured it; and how far to persist in non-conformity if threatened with suspension or deprivation (expulsion) from their spiritual functions. These questions, canvassed in the heyday of the movement's Disciplinarian phase, continued to be equally pressing in the earlier seventeenth century. The problem of conscience was aggravated after 1583, as a result of the oath of three articles imposed on the clergy by Archbishop Whitgift, which was later incorporated in the canons of 1604 and thus made the law of the church. Under its provisions every ecclesiastical person had to subscribe on oath *ex animo* acknowledging the royal supremacy in religion and declaring that the prayer book, the ordination service, and the thirty-nine articles of religion contained nothing contrary to

---

[1] Cf. W. Shaw, *A history of the English church . . . 1640–1660*, 2v., L., 1900, I, 5–6 and C. Hill, *Society and Puritanism in pre-revolutionary England*, 502.
[2] Cf. the text of the petition in J. R. Tanner, *Constitutional documents . . . James I*, 56–60. The Oxford vice-chancellor and heads of houses, indeed, denounced the petition, contending that the framers really aimed at the Discipline, though not daring to avow it. The Puritans replied repudiating the accusation; cf. S. B. Babbage, *Puritanism and Richard Bancroft*, L., 1962, 54.
[3] On the King's concessions, cf. M. Curtis, 'The Hampton Court conference and its aftermath,' *History*, XLVI, 156 (1961).

the word of God.[1] This subscription, of course, was devised to coerce the Puritans. The latter, however, were neither hypocrites nor cowards. They remained fast in their hope of a national church that would yet be rightly reformed; and while a few were deprived of their clerical office, most demonstrated remarkable ingenuity in avoiding this fate. In consequence, the Puritans succeeded in preserving a considerable place for themselves in the ministry right down to the meeting of the Long Parliament.

The premiss of their conduct was relatively simple. They believed that it was right and lawful to remain in communion with the Church of England, which possessed the *esse* of a church, if not yet the *bene esse*;[2] and they attached such value to the work of the ministry that they held it justifiable to bear with the church's shortcomings if loss of their vocation should ensue from refusal. There may be added the more mundane consideration that the average clergyman, entirely dependent on his small professional income to support himself and his family, had a strong inducement against quitting his place. Since the Puritans, however, displayed a more than ordinary readiness for self-sacrifice, the influence of conscientious motives upon their actions must be fully acknowledged.

The view we have described was strongly stated by Thomas Cartwright in the Puritan argument with separatism. On this ground, in a 'Resolution of Doubts touching a mans entrie into ye Ministrye,' he defended the church against its separatist critics and vindicated the assumption of the ministerial function within it.[3] When consulted, he advised Puritan clergymen to bear with popish cermonies if necessary rather than renounce their calling.[4] Most non-conformists held this opinion. In 1578, for instance, seven suspended ministers of Norwich made their submission in order to be restored to preaching. The ceremonies and government of the church, they declared, 'are so farre tolerable that for the same no man ought to withdrawe himselfe . . . neither ought any minister for these to refuse to preche the Worde of God and to administer the Sacraments.'[5] The position was most clearly formulated nearly forty years later in an admirable work

---

[1] Whitgift's oath became, with slight changes, canon XXXVI in the canons of 1604. The texts of both, together with earlier precedents for subscription, are printed in R. G. Usher, *op. cit.*, II, 293–310.

[2] So Cartwright argued; cf. A. F. Scott Pearson, *Church and state*, 57–8, who ascribes Cartwright's opinion to the influence of the Aristotelian doctrine of the gradations of reality.

[3] Printed in *Cartwrightiana*, ed. A. Peel and L. Carlson, L., 1951. Cf. also his defence of remaining in the national church in *An answere unto a letter of Master Harrisons*, in *ibid*.

[4] *The seconde parte of a register*, I, 137–43.

[5] *Ibid.*, I, 146.

written by the Rev. John Sprint, a Gloucestershire Puritan. He contended that deprivation for non-conformity did more harm to religion than conforming, and that the good received from the preaching of ministers outweighed the inconvenience of objectionable ceremonies. A reply to his tract pointed out that though many clergy were ready to conform, they could not subscribe the oaths ordained by the canon of 1604. To this Sprint returned the revealing answer, 'it is well knowen, that for these later 5. or 6. yeares, subscription hath not been urged to Incumbents or settled Ministers, but meere conformity. ....' Thus, as he saw it, the choice was conformity vs. deprivation, not subscription vs. deprivation, and he was convinced that conformity ought to be preferred.[1]

Undoubtedly subscription was the chief stumbling block to the Puritan non-conformists. Of the oaths required of them, their reservations were not directed against the acknowledgment of the crown's religious supremacy. Well before the canons of 1604 and Whitgift's three articles, the Supremacy Act of 1559 had exacted a similar oath from the clergy. Even the presbyterian proponents of the Discipline could and did subscribe to the supremacy, despite its apparent contradiction to their conception of an autonomous church order of which Christ alone, not the Queen, was head. They were able to do so because the explanation of the nature of the royal supremacy contained in the thirty-nine articles was such as to allay their scruples.[2] The real difficulty lay in subscribing that the prayer book and articles of religion were throughout agreeable to the word of God. At the Hampton Court conference, a Puritan spokesman told King James what a heavy burden this was and entreated that it should not be imposed.[3] In 1607 some Puritan clergy issued a declaration that they desired the continuance of their ministry 'above all earthly things,' but could not subscribe to the whole of the prayer book.[4] On the other hand, as Sprint pointed out, if a man conformed, subscription was sometimes waived.

This stemmed from the policy of Archbishop Bancroft, Whitgift's successor, in administering the 1604 canons. Though a notorious opponent of the Puritans, he instructed his episcopal colleagues to distinguish between two sorts of 'Revolters' among the clergy: the

---

[1] *Cassander Anglicus, showing the necessitie of conformitie to the prescribed ceremonies of our church, in case of deprivation*, 1618, 211–12, 237. Sprint was vicar of Thornbury in Gloucestershire; he is noticed in *D.N.B.*, *s.v.*

[2] Article XXXVII, 'Of the civil magistrate.' Cf. the valuable account of the grounds on which the Puritans acknowledged the crown's ecclesiastical supremacy in A. F. Scott Pearson, *Church and state*, 54–7.

[3] T. Fuller, *The church history of Britain*, III, 206.

[4] *The ministers reasons for refusal of subscription to the Book of Common Prayer*, 1607, cited in B. Hanbury, *op. cit.*, I, 128–9.

one 'promiseth conformitie, but is as yet unwilling to subscribe;' the other 'in his obstinacie will be induced to yield to neither.' Bancroft directed that subscription should be respited the former sort in the hope that they would eventually change their minds.[1] Accordingly, the canons did not lead to a grand purge of Puritan churchmen. Altogether, the number actually deprived in their aftermath was between eighty and ninety. These were the most inflexible who refused both conformity and subscription.[2] Most Puritan ministers— they must have amounted to some hundreds—survived.[3]

At a pinch even subscription could be swallowed. The authors of the Millenary Petition told King James,

> ... *divers of us that sue for reformation have formerly, in respect of the times, subscribed to the Book [of Common Prayer], some upon protestation, some upon exposition given them, some with conditions, rather than the Church should have been deprived of their labour and ministry. ...*[4]

After the enactment of the canons, some ministers found it possible to subscribe with explicit provisos that satisfied conscience. 'I doe ... willingly subscribe,' wrote one, 'soe as I may be allowed to interpret the things in the fayrest sense which the words of subscription ... may beare. ...'[5]

In fact, then, several alternatives were open to the Puritan clergy. They might subscribe, perhaps with conditions or qualifications; or they might submit to a merely partial and occasional conformity just sufficient to retain their place. If they cooperated thus far, they gained the inestimable consolation of being able to continue their spiritual calling. This, as Laud sardonically pointed out, was on the whole the policy of the Puritan clergy of his time. Ever since the Hampton Court conference, he said,

> *they have put in practice, and have yeilded a kind of Conformity; not that they thought any whit better of the things, but for that they held*

[1] Cf. the text of Bancroft's letter to the bishops, December 1604, in S. Babbage, *op. cit.*, 110–12.

[2] Historians have variously estimated the number of ministers deprived by the enforcement of the canons. The subject has been carefully investigated afresh by S. Babbage, *op. cit.*, ch. 6, whose conclusions I have adopted.

[3] All figures as to the number of Puritans in 1605 are mere guesswork. R. G. Usher's total of 281 is incredibly low; by another computation which he cites, it would be 746 (*op. cit.*, I, 249–51). According to a report of the bishops, there were in 1603 about 10,000 clergy in England altogether (*ibid.*, I, 207).

[4] J. R. Tanner, *Constitutional documents ... James I*, 58.

[5] S. Babbage, *op. cit.*, 227–9.

*them (though in themselves unlawfull) not to be such as for which a man
ought to hazard (not his lyving, that might savour of covetousnes, but)
his Mynisterie, and the good which gods people might by that meanes
receave.*[1]

An incident from Laud's visitation of his London diocese in 1631
was characteristic of the situation. At Braintree, the Rev. Stephen
Marshall, one of the foremost Puritans of Essex, came before him
together with other ministers accused of non-conformity. They
denied the charge and Marshall told the bishop he was misinformed.
'Ay,' declared Laud,

*but do you conforme always? He answered he did some times but not
always. . . . The Bishop answered, your preaching I like wel and your
Catechising wondrous wel but I mislike your answers . . . you wear the
Surpless sometimes, and then you lay it aside from you for a long
time. . . .*

The narrator of this scene commented:

*these good men cannot abide these ceremonies, and if they might they
would never use them: But to avoid the Persecution of these Bishops
that would fetch them up to the High Commission . . . these good men
are fain to stoop to them sometimes.*[2]

Undoubtedly, this story was many times paralleled. A Puritan thus
described the years of his ministry in London up to 1640:

*I never had a canonical coat . . . took not the canonical oath, declined
subscription for many years . . . (though I practised the old conformity,)*[3] *would not give ne obolum quidem against the Scots, but
dissuaded other ministers; much less did I yield to bow to the altar, and
at the name of Jesus, or administer the Lord's supper at a table turned
altarwise, or bring the people up to the rails, or read the Book of
Sports. . . .*[4]

[1] Cited in S. Babbage, *op. cit.*, 225.
[2] *Winthrop papers*, III, 59.
[3] The 'old conformity': acceptance of the form of church services before the
Laudian innovations.
[4] Thomas Edwards, *Gangraena*, pt. I, 1646, cited in D. Williams, 'London
Puritanism: the parish of St. Botolph without Aldgate,' *Guildhall miscellany*,
II, 1 (1960). In 1629, Edwards, then lecturer at St. Botolph without Aldgate,
was in trouble for non-conformity and had to promise to conform and to
preach a sermon on obedience to superiors, *C.S.P.D. 1628–29*, 543, 593,
ibid. 1629–31, 1.

The Rev. John Carter, a Suffolk minister for over fifty years, 'was always a Non-conformist, one of the good old Puritans of England. He never swallowed any of the Prelatical Ceremonies against his Conscience.'[1] The Rev. Richard Mather, minister of Toxteth in Lancashire, confessed that he did not wear the canonical surplice once in fifteen years.[2] The Rev. Thomas Toller, vicar of Sheffield for nearly forty years until finally suspended for non-conformity in 1635, used almost none of the services prescribed in the prayer book, and neither he nor his assistant ever wore a surplice or a hood.[3]

There were other ways by which the Puritans could indulge their scruples. John Cotton, later famous in the New England ministry, was a non-conformist when vicar of St. Botolph's in Boston, Lincolnshire; by arrangement a fellow clergyman performed those ceremonies Cotton refused to practise.[4] The non-conformist could seek shelter in a lectureship, where his main business was preaching and he was only required by canon law to read divine service twice a year. Arthur Hildersam, a patriarch of Stuart Puritanism, having been deprived in 1605 as vicar of Ashby-de-la-Zouch, became lecturer there four years later, and engaged a curate to perform the services.[5] This harbour was only temporary, however, for he was suspended in 1613 and was afterwards often in trouble.[6]

If the Puritan had the luck to live under a lenient or moderate bishop, he might remain unmolested in his non-conformity. A speaker in the parliament of 1625 pointed out that 'moderate Bishopps' did not demand subscription, a statement that was certainly correct.[7] This, of course, was before the severe rule of Archbishop Laud and his brethren turned the Puritans into unforgiving enemies. While Archbishop Mathew, for instance, governed the diocese of York between 1606 and 1628, numerous clergy refusing conformity on conscientious grounds were allowed to go their way.[8] The administration of the Laudian Archbishop Neile (1632–40), one of Mathew's successors, was quite a different story. Bishop Bayley of Bangor ordained the Rev. John Angier in 1629 without subscription

---

[1] Carter died in 1634; cf. his life in S. Clarke, *A collection of the lives of ten eminent divines*, 1662.

[2] S. Clarke, *The lives of sundry eminent persons*, 1683, pt. 1, 130. Mather went to New England after suspension in 1634; cf. *D.N.B.*, *s.v.*

[3] R. H. Marchant, *Puritanism and the church courts in the diocese of York*, Cambridge, 1960, 68–73.

[4] L. Ziff, *The career of John Cotton*, Princeton, 1962, 50–6.

[5] S. Babbage, *op. cit.*, 229.

[6] *D.N.B.*, *s.v.* Hildersam died in 1632.

[7] *Commons debates in 1625*, 26. The speaker was Sir Benjamin Rudyard.

[8] R. H. Marchant, *op. cit.*, 166.

and was believed partial to non-conformists.[1] Bishop Williams of Lincoln, while trying to persuade John Cotton to use the ceremonies, took no measures against him for non-conformity.[2] Bishop Hall of Norwich instituted the Rev. Samuel Fairclough to a Suffolk living without subscription.[3] There were frequent examples of this kind in the annals of Puritan biography.

In the last resort, the Puritan minister might simply conform, resolved to possess his soul in patience until the day of reformation. When Richard Baxter was ordained in 1638, he carefully studied the case for non-conformity, and then decided to conform despite his dislike of certain ceremonies.[4] The Rev. John Davenport, vicar of St. Stephen's Coleman Street in London, left his living in 1633 because of the

alteracion of my iudgment in matters of conformity to the ceremonies whereby I cannot practise them as formerly I have done. Wherein I doe not censure those that doe conforme (nay I account many of them faithfull, and worthy instruments of Gods glory, and I know that I did conforme with as much inward peace, as now I doe forbeare, in both my uprightness was the same, but my light different).[5]

Such a 'faithfull and worthy instrument' was Robert More, the Puritan rector of Guiseley in Yorkshire, who left in his will an illuminating explanation of his conformity. '. . . though many learned and good men,' he said,

have always holden and doe still hold, and that with great reason that needles Ceremonyes . . . remaneing still in our Church are very inconvenient and daingerous. . . . for my selfe, I doe confesse that as I could never take upon me to bee a resolute Patron of such humane ordinances, soe could I never find iust cause of sufficient waight to warrant my selfe or any other to oppose or renounce them being commanded by lawfull Authority; but rather regardinge the peace of our Church, the liberty of the Gospell and obedience to Authoritie; I have held it to bee fitt . . . to submitt my selfe to a wise and discreete Tolleratinge and using of them till the tyme of reformacion. . . .[6]

[1] O. Heywood, *The life of John Angier*, ed. E. Axon, *Chetham society*, n.s., XCVII, 1937, 56–7.   [2] L. Ziff, *op. cit.*, 55–7.
[3] S. Clarke, *The lives of sundry eminent persons*, pt. 1, 163.
[4] F. J. Powicke, *A life of the Reverend Richard Baxter*, 2v., L., 1924–7, I, 22–3.
[5] John Davenport to Lady Vere, *Letters of John Davenport*, ed. I. Calder, New Haven, 1937, 39.
[6] Quoted in R. H. Marchant, *op. cit.*, 213–14. More, rector of Guiseley since 1587, died in 1642.

These various practices go far to explain the impossibility of rooting Puritanism out of the church. Through difficult times the Puritan clergy held their ground, while by their ministrations they fortified the consciences of a laity who with hard assurance would tread the government of Charles I under foot.

3

If the clergy were the teachers and ideologues of Puritanism, the laity were its patrons who provided it with an indispensable assistance. Without lay backing, the Puritan movement would have remained an exclusively clerical tendency and could never have acquired the power to shake church and state. The Puritan ministers realized fully, of course, the necessity of support from persons of substance. 'The countenance,' wrote one of them, '. . . which a man of great Estate and Power doth give to a Minister is of great import and influence unto his Ministry.'[1] Enemies saw the ties between the non-conformist clergy and their patrons in the governing class as the fruit of deliberate policy. According to Richard Bancroft, the Puritans 'will have the chiefest and the richest, to be their Elders.' They

doe practize daylie how they may not onlye creep into noble & gentlemens bosomes in the Contrye . . . but also thrust themselves forward by all the power of their frendes, to be . . . Readers, but I feare Seducers in the Innes of Courte. . . . Verye manye gentlemen . . . and some others of greater callinge (as it is thought) have ioyned themselves in this faction, and are become great favourers and maynteyners thereof, who beinge manye of them Iustices of peace &c, doe not only countenance theire leaders, but discourage with all theire might the rest of [the] ministerie.[2]

Nor did Bancroft feel any doubt concerning the motives of these lay protectors of the Puritan movement:

Certaine hypocriticall Brethren of the Laytie have clapped [the clergy] uppon the shoulders, followed their sermons, set them at the upper ende of their tables, and sought by all their strength to procure them credit & favour with the people: not that they cared either for them, or for Religion . . . but hopinge that by the violent course, which they saw these men run into, the Bishops, & the rest of the Cleargie, would growe . . . to be so odious: as it would be a very small matter, to disposses

[1] S. Clarke, *The lives of sundry eminent persons*, pt. 1, 169.
[2] *A survay of the pretended holy discipline*, 1593, 154; *Tracts ascribed to Richard Bancroft*, ed. A. Peel, Cambridge, 1953, 57, 71.

Puritanism

them of all their livings, whereof some portion might come to their shares.[1]

Perhaps Bancroft's explanation of the laity's attitude applied in a few instances; but, in general, it was a prejudiced description from one of the Puritans' bitterest enemies. Writing under Elizabeth, he must have been referring to someone like the earl of Leicester, the Queen's favourite, whose unscrupulous ambition and help to non-conformists were both equally well known. Leicester, however, was hardly representative of the Puritan laity. While sharing the Puritan hatred of the pope and Spain, he knew little or nothing of the spiritual side of religion. His interventions on behalf of Cartwright and other ministers were probably less the result of zeal than strata-gems in the factional manoeuvres which formed the substance of Elizabethan politics and at which he was a master.[2] In any event, he contained his support of the movement within prudent limits. Once when reproved for lukewarmness by a friend of the Discipline, his answer was, 'I am so resolved to the defence of that ... already established, as I mean not to be a mayntaynor or allower of any that wold troble or disturbe the quiett proceeding thereof.'[3] Even finan-cially, his interests were better served by the continuance of the existing church establishment than by the Puritan programme. His great position at court allowed him to enrich himself at the church's expense without the disendowment of the bishops; whereas if the Puritans had been able to effect their reformation, they would have stopped the depredation of ecclesiastical property and would have used episcopal revenues to improve the lot of the parish clergy.[4]

Thus it was not of such as Leicester that the Puritan laity were formed. First and foremost, they were men of firm religious convic-tions, diligent attenders at sermons, sharp reprovers of swearing, drunkenness, and sexual transgressions. Often they had undergone a spiritual conversion. Psychologically speaking, conversion was the core of Puritan experience and from it arose the unwavering faith and sense of righteousness (and frequently of self-righteousness) so prominent in the Puritan temper.[5] Filled with the awareness of a new birth, having won through to the knowledge that God, in spite of their transgressions, had predestined them among the elect, they could never imagine they were wrong. Men like these were dedicated to

[1] *A survay of the pretended holy discipline*, 246.
[2] The famous libel against the earl, *Leycesters commonwealth*, 1584, con-nected his patronage of the Puritans with his factional purpose of building up a structure of clientage.
[3] Leicester to Thomas Wood, August 1576, *Letters of Thomas Wood*, 13–15.
[4] Cf. the editor's remarks, *ibid.*, xix, xxiii.
[5] Cf. A. Simpson, *Puritanism in old and New England*, Chicago, 1955, 2.

warfare against sin. They sustained and protected the non-conformist clergy and collaborated in the opposition to Charles I's methods of government. Once their loyalty turned to disaffection, nothing could gain on their intransigence. The King's worst blunder was that he alienated them irrevocably.

Puritan biographies and letters offer lively revelations of these laymen and the sources of their moral and spiritual strength. 'I remember,' wrote one, a Yorkshire gentleman connected with the Barringtons of Essex and other notable Puritan families in the Country opposition,

in the beginninge of my conversion my soule was so abundantlie ravished with the beautie of the lambe, that trulie I was scarce wel when my toungue was not speakinge of the infinitenes of that mercie to me so unworthye a wretche. . . .[1]

Oliver Cromwell described his spiritual experience to his cousin, the wife of Oliver St. John, so as

to honour my God by declaring what He hath done for my soul, in this I am confident, and I will be so. . . . Oh, I lived in and loved darkness, and hated the light. I was . . . the chief of sinners. . . . yet God had mercy on me. O the riches of his mercy! Praise Him for me, pray for me, that He who hath begun a good work would perfect it to the day of Christ.[2]

John Winthrop, the leader of the Puritan migration to New England, gave a similar account of his religious travail. At the age of eighteen,

I married into a family under Mr. Culverwell his ministry in Essex; and living there sometimes I first found the ministry of the word to come to my heart with power.

He wrestled stubbornly with his carnality and so arrived 'to some peace and comfort in God.'

I honoured a faithful minister in my heart and could have kissed his feet. . . . I had an unsatiable thirst after the word of God and could not misse a good sermon, though many miles off, especially of such as did search deep into the conscience.

[1] Thomas Bourchier to Lady Joan Barrington, undated, but probably written at the end of the 1620s, B. M. Egerton MSS. 2650, f. 205.
[2] Written October 1638, W. C. Abbott, *Writings and speeches of Oliver Cromwell*, 4v., Cambridge, 1937–47, I, 96–7.

Finally, after many sore afflictions, Christ was revealed to him when he was thirty years old, and he saw clearly 'into the covenant of free grace.'[1]

Sir Nathaniel Barnardiston, Bt., of whom a pious biographer left an edifying narrative, belonged to this type of Puritan layman in the aristocratic order. Born in 1588 of a distinguished family, he was the 'Top-Branch of the Suffolk Cedars,' the twenty-third knight in lineal descent. In his youth he passed through a religious conversion: this was the 'second Birth' which confirmed his faith in his salvation. He prayed daily, read the Scripture much, and was always careful to sanctify the Sabbath, while 'his preparation for the Sacrament of the Lord's Supper was transcendent.' Few could outdo him in his 'constant attendance upon the Ministration of the Word, publickly dispensed. . . .' A warm friend of the Puritan clergy, he was of the mind that 'he had rather fall with the Ministry of England, than stand in greatest power with their enemies.' He sat in all the parliaments of Charles I. As a public man, 'none could put on a braver obstinacy, or more peremptory refusal . . . to the most lofty Commands, or most zealous Importunities, even of the greatest Man, if what was urged was unjust, or against his happy Rule of Life, the Word of God.' Thus he exposed himself 'to a Gulph of Hazards' in defence of the liberties of his country because he resisted the forced loan and ship money. It was a note of Sir Nathaniel's patriotism that he annually celebrated Queen Elizabeth's accession day. When he went as Suffolk's senior knight to the Short Parliament, he declared that God's 'covenant and call is the only supporter of my faith. . . .' Barnardiston was one of many like-minded religious gentlemen whose wrath the King and Archbishop Laud had to face in 1640.[2]

Ignatius Jurdain, merchant, alderman, and mayor of Exeter, was another of this sort of layman whose stiff rectitude presented a front of iron to the pressures of Charles I. Converted at fifteen, according to his biographer, he continued in the life and power of religion until his death at the age of seventy-nine in 1640. He was a great reader of the Bible, of books of practical divinity, and had gone through Foxe's *Martyrs* seven times. Sermons were a strong interest. He took notes regularly in church, 'not for his own benefit alone, but for the good of his Family to whom he did constantly repeat the Sermons.' As a magistrate, 'the Stocks and Whipping-post could testifie what

[1] *Winthrop papers*, I, 155–6, 158–9. Winthrop wrote this history of his progress in religion when he was forty-nine. Cf. also E. S. Morgan, *The Puritan dilemma. The story of John Winthrop*, Boston, 1958, ch. I.

[2] S. Clarke, *The lives of sundry eminent persons*, pt. 2; *Winthrop papers*, IV, 218. The local importance of Sir Nathaniel and his family is noticed in *Suffolk and the great rebellion*, ed. A. Everitt, *Suffolk records society*, 3, 1960.

swearers, drunkards, unclean persons ... were punished by his indifferent execution of justice.' At one time he accepted usury for loans; but some ministers having convinced him this was wrong, he made restitution of his gains and thereafter took no more for a loan than the borrower would freely give. Twice he represented his city in parliament where he 'was a great stickler to have the Bill passed for the punishment of Adultery with death. . . .' This became known as 'Mr. Jurdains Bill.' It failed because 'those times would not bear it.' He interceded for non-conformist clergy and did not fear to write Charles I protesting the profanation of the Sabbath by the King's encouragement of Sunday sports. It was of Alderman Jurdain that the satiric Bishop Corbett spoke in his poem on the parliament of 1628, joining him with Pym and William Prynne:

> *A sad presage of dainger to this land*
> *When lower strive to gett the upper hand:*
> *When Prince and Peeres to Peysants must obey,*
> *When Lay-men must their Teachers teach the way:*
> *When Pym and Prinn and Jourdain must define*
> *What Lords are het'rodox and what divine*
>
> *. . .*
> *It is a Paritie must sett all right:*
> *Then shall the Gospell shine like Phoebus bright.*[1]

There were many men of this pious kind in the civic oligarchies and landed society. On them the interest of religion as they conceived it exercised a profound influence. Knowing their importance, the Puritan clergy laboured painfully to shape their faith from earliest youth. The Rev. John Preston, referred to previously in another connection,[2] while a teacher at Cambridge was the 'greatest pupil-monger in England . . . having sixteen fellow commoners (most heirs to fair estates) admitted in one year.' Among his pupils he counted such offspring of opposition families as the earl of Lincoln and sons of Lord Saye and the earl of Warwick.[3]

The same devout laity figured among the benefactors of non-conformity whom Puritan hagiography delighted to honour. There was, for instance, Mr. Taylor, the recorder of Richmond in Yorkshire, 'a very Gaius or Onesiphorus to the silenced ministers of

---

[1] S. Clarke, *A collection of the lives of ten eminent divines . . . and of some other eminent Christians*, 1662; 'Against the opposing the duke in parliament, 1628,' *The poems of Richard Corbett*, ed. J. A. W. Bennett and H. R. Trevor-Roper, Oxford, 1955.
[2] Cf. *supra*, 63, 65–6.
[3] T. Fuller, *The worthies of England*, ed. P. A. Nuttall, 3v., L., 1840, II, 1517; I. Morgan, *op. cit.*, 28–31.

England;' the 'honourable and Elect Lady, the Lady Bowes,' who gave £1,000 a year to maintain preachers in the north and Derbyshire, all of them formerly 'silenced men by reason of Non-conformity;' Lady Margaret Bromley in Shropshire, 'a constant and unparallel'd favourer of all good Ministers . . . who suffered under Prelaticall pressures. . . .'[1] Of a slightly earlier generation was the zealous Sir Francis Hastings, brother of the third earl of Huntingdon, whose incessant efforts in behalf of non-conformist clergy provoked James I to remove him from the commission of the peace and the deputy lieutenancy.[2] Equally representative of the type were the Hereford-shire gentleman, Sir Robert Harley, and his wife, both strict Sab-batarians, observers of fast days, and stout friends of the Puritan ministry. To her son of fourteen at Oxford, Lady Brilliana Harley wrote urging him on in his reading of Calvin. The Scottish rebellion naturally claimed all her sympathy, so that she thought 1639 'the yeere in which . . . Antichrist must beginne to falle.' Soon after the Long Parliament's assembling, where her husband represented his county, Lady Brilliana was saying that the church hierarchy 'must downe, and I hope now.'[3]

Moral narrowness and intolerant incomprehension of other forms of religion than their own were a common characteristic of these Puritan laymen. Perhaps without such qualities they might not have been so inflexibly resolute in withstanding the frowns and distaste of royal authority. Yet to this type there were striking exceptions. In a Cromwell or a Milton, for instance, austerity mingled with an idealist passion and heroic spirituality that raised them far above the average Puritan. Such men were destined to a pilgrimage of conquests and chastenings that opened their field of vision to truths altogether beyond the ken of the Barnardistons and Jurdains. Theirs were natures no orthodoxy could confine.

Moreover, as the mention of Milton should suggest, there was no hostility towards culture in these Puritan adherents. While the revolu-tion was in embryo, the youthful Milton dedicatedly pursued his studies, fitting himself for his high vocation as a poet who would teach virtue to nations, fusing in his artist's imagination the didactic aims of the Puritan with the idealism of Plato.[4] The Country noble-man, Lord Brooke, was another inspired by Platonist influence. Revealed in his work, *The Nature of Truth* (1640), was a mind seeking a harmony between Puritan moralism and the humanist exaltation of

---

[1] S. Clarke, *A generall martyrologie*, 2nd ed., 1660, pt. 2, 88, 157, 195.
[2] C. Cross, *The Puritan earl*, N.Y., 1966, 49–51. Sir Francis died in 1610. The third earl, who died in 1595, was also a great Puritan patron.
[3] *Letters of the Lady Brilliana Harley*, ed. T. Lewis, *Camden society*, LVIII, 1854, 20, 41, 111.   [4] Cf. W. Haller, *op. cit.*, ch. VIII.

175

reason as the divine faculty in man. Sir Robert Harley, though disliking the bishops, was the friend of John Donne, of George Herbert, and of the latter's philosophic brother, Lord Herbert of Cherbury. With Lord Herbert he exchanged letters on deism; and such was his affection for George Herbert's piety that he was solicited to assist in the posthumous publication of *The Country Parson*.[1] Further indicative of the cultural range of an ordinary Puritan gentleman is the list of books bought between 1635–9 by the Essex oppositionist, Sir Thomas Barrington. The one hundred and six titles included not only legal texts, biblical commentaries, Catholic and Protestant controversy, and popular Puritan treatises, but also the poems of George Herbert, writings by Erasmus and Raleigh, and the works of Shakespeare.[2]

It was the constant support of such well-disposed persons in the governing class that more than anything else insured the survival of Puritanism. The Puritan ministers recognized the debt and expressed their gratitude in the writings they dedicated to their aristocratic patrons. Leading oppositionists were among the recipients of these tributes. Cornelius Burges dedicated *Baptismall Regeneration* (1629) to the earl of Bedford in thanks to 'that Ancient, Noble, and much honoured Family, to which I was, and ever will be a faithfull & humble servant.' Jeremiah Burroughs's *The Excellency of A Gracious Spirit* (1638) and Richard Sibbes's *Bowels Opened . . . The Love Betwixt Christ And The Church* (1639) were dedicated to Lord Mandeville. One of the most popular Puritan devotional works, John Preston's *The New Covenant* (1629), was published with dedications to Lord Saye and the earl of Lincoln. Several other writings of Preston, *The Breast-Plate of Faith And Love* (1630) and *The Golden Sceptre* (1638), were dedicated respectively to the earl of Warwick and Richard Knightley. Warwick also received the dedication of Thomas Stoughton's *The Christians Sacrifice* (1622). '. . . God himselfe,' wrote the author,

hath now honored your Noble house, and made it renowned in the

[1] *H.M.C. Portland*, III, *passim*, contains Harley's correspondence with Donne, Herbert, and Herbert of Cherbury. A letter to him from Robert Cooke in 1641, asking his aid on behalf of Herbert's *The Country Parson*, begins, 'Mr. George Herbert (whose memory I love as well as you did his person) . . .', B.M. Loan 29, 119, pt. 3. The work was not published until 1652 in *Herbert's remains*. A point of affinity between Herbert and Harley is suggested by the former's well-known line referring to the Puritan migration, in which religion stands 'on tip-toe in our land, Readie to passe to the American Strand.'

[2] M. E. Bohannon, 'A London bookseller's bill: 1635–1639,' *The library*, 4th ser., XVIII, 4 (1938). Barrington owned Shakespeare's second folio of 1632, bought for 18s. 6d.

*Church, both by the profession of the Gospell, and also by the protection
of the possessors thereof, even now to the third generation of your
name. . . .*

To Richard Knightley, the venerable John Dod dedicated *A plaine
. . . . exposition on the lords prayer* (1635), a 'testimony . . . of mine
unfeined and hearty thankfulnesse, for all your favours and good-
nesse to mee and mine.'[1]

In view of the close connections between the Puritan clergy and
their protectors in the governing class, descriptions of the former as
'alienated intellectuals' and as an 'intelligentsia' cut off from tradition
and seeking a new order have an altogether anachronistic ring.[2] It is
doubtful that the ministers were intellectuals at all in the modern
sense. At any rate, they contributed virtually nothing to the work of
universal desacralization and de-mystification of society and nature
which has probably been the foremost function of the intellectual in
recent times. Certainly, they were not alienated from traditional
society. Whatever their religious discontents, they accepted unques-
tioningly the inherited status order in which their own calling held an
acknowledged place. Their preaching was all of social subordination
to superiors; for they knew, as one of the most admired of them
wrote, that

*God hath appointed . . . in every society one person should bee above or
under another; not making all equall, as though the bodie should bee
all head and nothing else: but even in degree and order, hee hath set a
distinction, that one should be above another.*[3]

It was with a grateful unction that the Puritan ministers invoked
God's blessing on the citizen worthies and well-descended gentlemen
who were their supporters and defenders.

No contribution of these same laymen to the cause was more
important than their use of ecclesiastical patronage. By installing
Puritan ministers in church livings, lectureships, and chaplaincies,
they secured them both a haven and a fruitful field of activity as

---

[1] I have found these dedications by means of F. B. Williams (ed.), *Index of
dedications and commendatory verses in English books before 1641*, L., 1962.
Several of the works cited were published posthumously with dedications by
their editors, Puritan clergymen of note.
[2] Cf. M. Curtis, 'The alienated intellectuals of early Stuart England,' *Past
and present*, 23 (1962) and M. Walzer, *The revolution of the saints*, Cambridge, 1965, 121, 124–7.
[3] William Perkins, 'A treatise of callings,' *Works*, I, 755. The conservative
nature of Puritan social attitudes is well brought out by C. and K. George
The Protestant mind of the English reformation, Princeton, 1961.

pastors and preachers. In Lincolnshire before 1640, for instance, a group of Puritan adherents of the Country—Sir William Wray, Sir George St. Paul, Sir William Armyne, Sir Thomas Grantham, and the earl of Lincoln—held twenty-seven advowsons between them which were available to clergy of their own persuasion.[1] In 1628, with the help of the earl of Warwick, the Puritan Samuel Clarke obtained a lectureship in the town of Warwick. When he was forced out five years later for non-conformity, Lord Brooke gave him a rectory in Warwickshire. There he also received the protection of Richard Knightley.[2] The Essex oppositionist, Sir William Masham, known to Laud as 'a very factious Puritan,' had the ministers, John Norton and the famous Roger Williams, as chaplains before their emigration to New England.[3] Sir Nathaniel Barnardiston, we are told, always took care to present the church livings in his possession to 'eminent and worthy Divines. . . .' Most of the other leading families of Suffolk, like the Heveninghams, Parkers, Bacons, Gurdons, and Playters, were also Puritan and bestowed their patronage in the same way.[4]

Where Puritan influence could exert itself in corporate bodies, these, too, assisted non-conformists with their patronage. In the 1630s, the Haberdashers and Mercers companies of London appointed Puritans to curacies and lectureships in their gift in Cheshire, Gloucestershire, and Durham.[5] The English churches in the Dutch republic belonging to the Merchant Adventurers Company were notorious havens not only for non-conformists but even for dissenters of a more extreme kind. An official account drawn up in 1632 described them as 'Seminaries of disorderly preachers' who hold 'continuall Correspondence with the Refractories in England.'[6] The vestrymen of the London parish of St. Stephen's Coleman Street, one

<hr />

[1] J. W. F. Hill, *op. cit.*, 112–15.

[2] S. Clarke, *The lives of sundry eminent persons*, Preface.

[3] H. Smith, *The ecclesiastical history of Essex under the Long Parliament and Commonwealth*, Chelmsford, 1933, 26–7, 51.

[4] S. Clarke, *The lives of sundry eminent persons*, pt. 2, 112; *Suffolk and the Great Rebellion*, 18.

[5] *C.S.P.D. 1631–33*, 36; *ibid. 1633–34*, 444; *ibid. 1636–37*, 549–50; *ibid. 1639–40*, 104–5.

[6] *C.S.P.D. 1631–33*, 432; P.R.O. S.P. 16/224 no. 57. Cf. R. P. Stearns, *Congregationalism in the Dutch Netherlands*, Chicago, 1940; A. C. Carter, 'The ministry to the English churches in the Netherlands in the seventeenth century,' *Bulletin of the Institute of Historical Research*, XXXIII, 88 (1960); and documents printed in C. Burrage, *The early English dissenters*, 2v., Cambridge, 1912, II, App. XVII. The Merchant Adventurers churches in the Low Countries had conformed to the Dutch church with its presbyterian discipline since 1579 by agreement between the English government and the Dutch authorities.

of the few parishes in the capital that owned the presentation to its church, showed their Puritan sympathies under Charles I by appointing John Davenport and John Goodwin as vicars.[1] In York, the mayor, John Vaux, obtained the appointment in 1637 of a non-conformist, John Shaw, as lecturer of the church of All Saints. Shaw was summoned before Archbishop Neile, who declared, '. . . you are brought in by the lord mayor . . . to head the Puritan party against me, but . . . I will break Vaux and the Puritan party.'[2] The York church of St. Martin's Micklegate, whose advowson was in the hands of citizen trustees, had Puritan vicars during most of the earlier seventeenth century.[3] Several York aldermen during the '30s were Puritans, including Thomas Hoyle and Sir William Allanson, the city's future representatives in the Long Parliament. In consequence, the corporation encouraged non-conformity under Laud and petitioned against episcopacy in 1641.[4]

But all these efforts to entrench the Puritan clergy in the church through patronage were overshadowed by the ambitious scheme undertaken by the Feoffees for Impropriations. Their project gave further proof of the immense resourcefulness the Puritan movement displayed in promoting its aims despite royal and ecclesiastical disfavour. Founded in 1625 as a group of twelve unincorporated trustees, the Feoffees' object was to raise money for the purchase of impropriated tithes and other church revenue and appointments, which were to be used in the maintenance of a preaching ministry. The members, all well-known London Puritans, consisted of four clergymen, four lawyers, and four, later five, merchants. Such a venture could only have taken shape as a result of extensive consultation and planning by important laymen and ministers. There was thus good reason for the hostile contemporary judgment which traced the scheme to 'a secret combination of the brotherhood, to advance their projects;' not one man amongst them, the same writer added, 'wished well to the present government.'[5]

One of the Feoffees' rules specified that they should assist none but conformable men. This may have been a blind, however, for some whom they helped were non-conformists. Perhaps they even adopted

[1] E. Freshfield, 'Some remarks upon the . . . parish of St. Stephen Coleman Street . . . ,' *Archaeologia*, L (1887) and D. A. Williams, 'London Puritanism: the parish of St. Stephen Coleman Street,' *Church quarterly review*, CLX, 337 (1959).
[2] *The life of Master John Shaw*, ed. C. Jackson, *Yorkshire diaries, Surtees society*, LXV, 1877, 129.
[3] R. H. Marchant, *op. cit.*, 75–6.
[4] *Victoria county history. City of York*, 201–2.
[5] P. Heylyn, *Examen historicum*, 1659, 208–9, cited in C. Hill, *Economic problems of the church*, 255.

it for the record in the event of future legal trouble.[1] As their trans-actions required the avoidance of publicity, they refrained from incorporating themselves. This was cited against them by Attorney General Noy in 1633, when they were dissolved as unlawful, in proof of their policy of secrecy.[2] Their method was to retain ownership of the tithes, revenues, and appointments they acquired, and to grant them only conditionally to such clerical beneficiaries as they approved. They thus had complete discretion in selecting the recipients of their help, who in turn were wholly dependent on the Feoffees' bounty. They extended their patronage chiefly to curates and lec-turers, since these, unlike beneficed men, could be appointed and removed without episcopal permission. By this expedient they were able to function with almost complete freedom from interference by the church officials.[3]

In their eight years of existence, the Feoffees' achievement was an impressive one. According to their accounts, they received more than £6,300, almost all of it in contributions from sympathizers. The smallest individual gift was six shillings, the largest £500, some hundreds of men and women having provided donations and legacies to further their work. With this money, the Feoffees bought impro-priations, advowsons, and nominations of curacies, lectureships, and school masters in numerous counties. Their greatest acquisition was the nomination of the six lecturers of St. Antholin's London, an old and famous lectureship, which they obtained from the vestry of the parish in 1628. The fact that the rector of the church, Charles Offspring, was a Feoffee, no doubt facilitated this notable transac-tion. Another piece of patronage was the impropriation of the vicarage of Presteigne in Herefordshire, which they bought from Sir Robert Harley for £1,400 at ten years purchase. Sir Robert added the advowson gratis.[4]

That a group of Puritans should dispose of patronage on such a scale was manifestly dangerous to the crown and the ecclesiastical order alike. Accordingly, in 1632 the government, spurred on by Laud, proceeded against the Feoffees in the Court of Exchequer,

---

[1] *Activities of the Puritan faction of the Church of England 1625–33*, ed. I. Calder, L., 1957, 55–6, 82. This book prints the documents in the Exchequer case against the Feoffees, from which almost all that is known of them has to be derived. Cf. also the accounts by E. Kirby, 'The lay feoffees: a study in militant Puritanism,' *Journal of modern history*, XIV, 1 (1942), I. Calder, 'A seventeenth century attempt to purify the Anglican church,' *American historical review*, LIII, 4 (1948), and C. Hill, *Economic problems of the church*, ch. XI.
[2] *Activities of the Puritan faction of the Church of England*, 54, 78.
[3] *Ibid.*, 50, 52.
[4] *Ibid.*, 28–36, 37–42, 85.

charging them with acting illegally as a corporation and usurping on the King's regality. Policy rather than law was the real issue and Attorney General Noy drew forcible attention to the implications of the Feoffees' aims. '. . . to what end tendeth this?', he asked.

If they goe this way to buy up all impropriations, They may get almost halfe the Churches in England. . . . They might come to be supreme Patrons. . . . And to make great a number of Clergy men dependant on them to follow their wills. . . . They place men in eminent places, meane places they doe not ayme at, But London, Hertford, Cirencester, Shrewsburye, Dunwich, and good Borough townes.

Moreover, as he showed with examples, 'their eyes are upon factious men . . . such they deall with, and labor to uphold.'[1]

The Exchequer judges reinforced Noy's argument in rendering judgment against the Feoffees. '. . . for a Corporation,' declared Baron Trevor,

or theis men that are like a Corporation, to ioyne together to get into their hands a multitude of Church livings to dispose as they please, this is to beare a great stroak in the Comonwealth, and it tendeth to make a new Church, A Church in a Church. It is so great a matter as it toucheth the Kings aucthority.[2]

A vigilant government thus frustrated the scheme the Feoffees had at heart. To their Puritan contributors and well-wishers the Feoffees' dissolution with the loss of all the patronage they had acquired must have come as a heavy blow. It taught the lesson that methods of private enterprise and unofficial initiative must fail against the hostility of the regime. Viewing the destruction of their pious work, politically conscious men could only have concluded that the power of the state itself must be in friendly hands if the cause of religion were to be made secure and flourishing.

4

It is much harder to form a conception of the Puritan laity outside the privileged elite of wealth and status. We can sometimes see as individual beings the gentlemen and prosperous citizens who left some record of their spiritual journey; whereas the poor and inferior we have perforce to look at mostly in the mass, though now and again the darkness that encircles them is lighted up by a surviving bit of evidence. These largely unknown men and women were 'the Religious

[1] *Ibid.*, 51, 53, 61, 82. [2] *Ibid.*, 113.

serious People' whom Richard Baxter knew from his own experience of ministering to them, who had

a suspicion of all that is Ceremonious in Gods Service, and of all which they find not warrant for in Scripture, and a greater inclination to a rational convincing earnest way of Preaching and Prayers, than to the written Forms of Words, which are to be read in Churches. And they are greatly taken with a Preacher that speaketh to them in a familiar natural Language and exhorteth them as if it were for their Lives. . . .[1]

In short, they were Puritans, with a spiritual outlook probably no way different from the Puritan laity superior to them in worldly station or riches. We discover such men in the two hundred yeomen of Essex parishes who petitioned King James in behalf of the non-conformist clergy.[2] We meet them in a minister's description of the Puritan people that 'do heare sermons, talke of the scriptures, singe Psalmes together in private houses. . . .'[3] We see them in Baxter's industrious flock of weavers at Kidderminster who 'as they stand in their Loom . . . can set a Book before them, or edifie one another.'[4] We notice their zeal in religious exercises in an account composed by the Rev. Samuel Clarke of his ministry in the late 1620s in a part of Cheshire where he was almost the only preacher. Lacking a regular benefice, he was maintained by voluntary offerings, and Sunday by Sunday the people came to hear him in all weathers. Every three weeks he held a day of conference for Scripture discussion and prayer, 'unto which repaired all the Professors, both Men and Women, out of all the Country.' 'I was never acquainted,' Clarke recorded, 'with more understanding Christians in all my Life, though the best of them went but in Russet Coats, and followed Husbandry.'[5]

The sermon had far the strongest effect in forming the religious personality of the Puritan people. On Sundays Englishmen were at church, and many attended at least once more in the week as well if there were a lecture to supplement the work of the Sabbath. In that plain, practical preaching which was a calculated point of style with Puritan clergymen, their congregations had set before them the great epic of the spirit—the radical depravity of man, free grace and the election of the saints, God's covenant with the chosen ones, their perseverance, sanctification, and glory. Sermons of this kind, diversi-

---

[1] R. Baxter, *Reliquiae Baxterianae*, 1696, pt. I, 32.
[2] H. Smith, *op. cit.*, 19–20.
[3] Josias Nichols, *The plea of the innocent*, 1602, 12.
[4] R. Baxter, *op. cit.*, pt. I, 89.
[5] S. Clarke, *The lives of sundry eminent persons*, Preface, which contains a narrative of the author's life.

fied by forceful disquisitions on moral duties, displaying frequently a strong common sense and a keen perception into the psychological condition of the soul fearful and uncertain of its salvation—these were the staple of the Puritan pulpit. Never was there a more vertebrate faith, a tougher moral and social discipline, than that which the Puritan preachers inculcated in their auditories.[1] It could act on the souls of common men with consoling assurance, fortifying their self-respect according to a divine standard above the judgments of the world.

An indication of its educative power may be gathered from a memoir by William Kiffin, who experienced it fully as a young apprentice. In 1629 at the age of thirteen, Kiffin, later to become a wealthy merchant, was bound in London to a 'mean calling.' Two years after he began to consider his spiritual state and fell into a deep melancholy. It was the Puritan preachers who sustained and helped him in his depression. At St. Antholin's, where there was a lecture six mornings a week, he heard Thomas Foxley and John Norton. At St. Stephen's Coleman Street he drew comfort from the sermons of John Davenport and John Goodwin. All these lights of the Puritan ministry were to feel the persecution of Archbishop Laud. Several apprentice friends shared Kiffin's religious concerns, and 'our constant practice,' he said, was

to attend the morning lecture, which began at six o'clock. We also appointed to meet together an hour before service, to spend it in praying, and in communicating to each other what experience we had received from the Lord; or else to repeat some sermon which we had heard before.[2]

So did the clergy effect the youth's conversion to the narrow way of faith. Kiffin's history belonged to the authentic milieu of the Puritanism of the inferior order: the life of hard work, the bareness and discipline, and the relief which the consolations of spiritual achievement gave to straitened circumstances.

It would be easier to judge the impact of Puritanism within the humbler strata of society if it were possible to estimate the extent of literacy at this period. For second only to the pulpit as a factor in the spread of Puritan sympathies were the scores of books of practical

---

[1] Cf. the account of the Puritan preachers and their work in W. Haller, *op. cit.* Useful observations are also contained in W. F. Mitchell, *English pulpit oratory from Andrewes to Tillotson*, L., 1932.

[2] *Remarkable passages in the life of William Kiffin*, ed. W. Orme, L., 1823, 4–12. An account of the St. Antholin's sermons which Kiffin attended is given by I. Calder, 'The St. Antholin lectures,' *Church quarterly review*, **CLX**, 334 (1959).

divinity and of religious and moral exhortation written by the clergy, as well as the Bible itself viewed through the glass of Puritan interpretation. The works of divines like William Perkins, Richard Sibbes, and John Preston, were widely read and offered both instruction and comfort to people of every condition. They did not, of course, touch the controversies that were dividing the body politic, but their temper and teachings were infinitely remote from the theology and ritualism of the Laudian church and from the religious sensibility prevalent around Charles I and Henrietta Maria. The men and women nursed at the breasts of the Puritan writers could have felt only hostility at the course of religion and politics under the first two Stuart kings.

Possibly the literacy of the humbler laity, and hence its access to such books, was more widespread than might be supposed in a society where inequality was so pronounced.[1] In quantitative terms, benefactions for education rose enormously during the earlier seventeenth century, a goodly proportion of the donors being merchants of Puritan persuasion. One consequence was the endowment of many new grammar schools.[2] These, of course, taught Latin and Greek, not English; but their growth may also have reflected an increased opportunity of other kind for poor and middle people to acquire a degree of literacy. Nehemiah Wallington, an anti-prelatical London craftsman, studied Richard Sibbes's The *bruised reed*, Thomas Beard's *Theatre of God's judgements*, and the Geneva translation of the Bible.[3] Kiffin, the young apprentice, drew strength from reading Thomas Goodwin's *Childe of light* and Thomas Hooker's *The souls preparation for Christ*; and it must be assumed that boys like him put into trade could read and write, however they learned to do so. Moreover, the torrential output of pamphlets during the revolution would be inexplicable without the existence of a substantial readership among the great London populace.

Literacy, however, was not essential to holding strong views on religion. In 1641, when many parishes were petitioning a sympathetic parliament against Laud's ceremonial innovations, some of the protesters could not write their names. From Kent came denunciation of clergymen who required the people to 'cringe and bowe' at the name of Jesus, who introduced 'superstitious ceremonyes,' and who abused their opposers as 'itching Puritans.' The authors of these

---

[1] This has been suggested for the fifteenth and sixteenth centuries by J. W. Adamson, 'The extent of literacy in England in the fifteenth and sixteenth centuries: notes and conjectures,' *The library*, 4th ser., X, 2 (1929).
[2] Cf. W. K. Jordan, *Philanthropy in England*, 281–91.
[3] N. Wallington, *Historical notices*, ed. R. Webb, 2v., L., 1869, I, xxv. Wallington, a turner, kept a shop in Eastcheap.

complaints, obscure church wardens, parish constables, and over-seers, being illiterate, had to make their mark.[1]

Had Puritanism a determinate basis in the social structure? Was it bound up with a particular kind of economic existence? Were sympathy for the non-conforming clergy, dislike of ceremonies and bishops, responsiveness to Puritan moral preachment determined by social situation? It must be answered at once that any connections of this sort except of the most general and tenuous kind would be extremely difficult to prove; while to demonstrate a causal relation between Puritanism and status or class would be even harder.

What seems least disputable concerning the social incidence of Puritanism is that it was greatest in the towns and trading part of the nation. On this the judgment of both contemporaries and most modern historians concur. The Arminian Richard Montague, for instance, called Coventry 'a second Geneva,' and an associate of Laud characteristically remarked, '. . . where are all these pestilent nests of Puritans hatched, but in corporations, where they swarm and breed like hornets in a [dead] horse's head.'[2] Similarly, A. F. Scott Pearson expressed the common opinion of modern scholars in stating that the majority of Puritan adherents were to be found in the towns.[3] It has further been noted that Puritanism flourished especially in the textile districts—in places such as Essex, Suffolk, Norfolk, Warwick, the West Riding of Yorkshire, and parts of Somerset, Wiltshire, and Lancashire: so much so that one writer has even asked, 'why was industrial England Puritan England.'[4] To this may be added that some of these Puritan areas also had a long history of receptiveness to heresy. The parts of Essex about Colchester and Dedham where Puritanism took root were formerly centres of Lollardy and early Lutheranism. Moreover, most of the county's victims in the Marian persecutions derived from there.[5] This was true as well of the textile communities in the West Riding, which having previously shown

---

[1] *Proceedings in Kent*, ed. L. B. Larking, *Camden society*, LXXX, 1861, 102ff., *passim*.

[2] *The correspondence of John Cosin*, 66; *C.S.P.D. 1639–40*, 515–20.

[3] A. F. Scott Pearson, *Church & state*, 104–5; cf. C. Hill, *Society and Puritanism in pre-revolutionary England*, 235–6, for the same view that the Puritan appeal was especially to the urban middle class and 'industrious' people.

[4] G. C. Homans, 'The Puritans and the clothing industry in England,' *New England quarterly*, XVI, 3 (1940). The Puritanism of the Lancashire textile towns has been stressed by F. Walker, *Historical geography of Southwest Lancashire*, Chetham society, n.s., CIII, 1939, 76–7. On Yorkshire, cf. R. H. Marchant, *op. cit.*, 51 and M. E. François, 'The social and economic development of Halifax 1558–1640,' *Proceedings of the Leeds philosophical and literary society. Literary and historical section*, XI, pt. VIII (1966), 271–7.

[5] H. Smith, *op. cit.*, 6.

themselves hospitable to Lollard and Protestant beliefs, then became strongly Puritan under Elizabeth and the early Stuarts.[1]

That Puritanism exercised a strong appeal to the citizen element is explicable both on social and psychological grounds. Its members, even the wealthy who enjoyed the privileges of town rule, held an inferior position by the aristocratic standards of the society. To them the doctrines of election and the covenant, a religion of personal experience sealed by conversion, must have given a powerful access of esteem and consciousness of worth. The moral code taught by the Puritan ministers would have had the same effect. That code was not one, as has sometimes been thought, which sanctioned capitalist acquisitiveness. It stressed, rather, the religious and ethical value of work in one's calling, and exalted habits of sobriety, decorum, and self-discipline in all stations of life.[2] It rigorously subjected worldly activity to religious ends, thereby investing such activity, when conducted under proper restraints, with genuine spiritual signifi-cance.[3] Possibly it also provided the middle people with a subjectively secure ground from which to direct their moral opprobrium and indignation at the Court way of life so alien to their own.[4]

However, the tendency of Puritanism to take root in the town was no more than that. Certainly, not all citizens were Puritans, and there is no way of knowing whether even most were. Moreover, the Puritan laity included, as has been seen, numerous persons belonging to the aristocratic order as well as others of inferior status who lived by husbandry. As to the dissemination of Puritanism in the textile districts, this was probably due to causes not directly related to the social structure. The East Anglian and Yorkshire areas which became successively centres of Lollard, Protestant, and Puritan sympathies were particularly susceptible by geographic situation and commercial intercourse to continental influence. They were thus easily accessible

---

[1] A. G. Dickens, *Lollards and Protestants in the diocese of York*, L., 1959 247–8.

[2] Cf. the account of Calvinist Puritanism as a work ethic, rather than a capitalist ethic, by C. H. George, 'English Calvinist opinion on usury, 1600–1640,' *Journal of the history of ideas*, XVIII, 4 (1959) and the discussion of the calling in C. H. and K. George, *The Protestant mind of the English reformation*, 169–72.

[3] The affinity between Puritanism and burgher values appears clearly in William Scott's *An essay of drapery, or the compleate citizen*, 1635, ed. S. Thrupp, Cambridge, 1953. Described as 'the first substantial ... writing known in English that exalts business as a career' (*ibid.*, 1), Scott's tract gives emphatic expression to the conception of trade as a calling and discip-line in the world, while also advocating cultural pursuits as both profitable and pleasant to the merchant.

[4] Cf. S. Ranulf, *Moral indignation and middle class psychology*, Copenhagen, 1938.

to the heresies appearing on the continent, especially those coming out of the Low Countries and Germany. Lollardy was largely indigenous; but Lutheranism and Calvinism found their earliest hospitality in England among the eastern communities and ports in closest contact with the Netherlands and the lower Rhine. Religious influences from the continent became even stronger in the later sixteenth century, as refugee industrial groups in flight from the Catholic repression in France and the Netherlands arrived in England. The Fleming and Walloon craftsmen who brought the manufacture of the New Draperies to Essex, Suffolk, and Norfolk also carried with them their Calvinist church polity and worship which they continued to practise with the permission of Queen Elizabeth and James I. Residing for decades in those counties, they must certainly have promoted the spread of extreme Protestant beliefs. It was no wonder that Archbishop Laud, seeing a cause of infection in the foreign congregations, determined to break them up and make their members attend the parish churches under episcopal jurisdiction.

In truth, whatever its particular appeals, the sway of Puritanism extended over a broad social spectrum of the laity. Though it doubtless flourished more in the urban, citizen environment, it was by no means limited to the latter. This constituted a fundamental feature of its political significance. Religion here became the bond uniting a large, composite mass of the laity in common sympathies and antagonisms. It cut across diversities of status and neighbourhood to form a movement of high and low that was potentially revolutionary if once roused to wrathful resistance. Puritanism thus resembled the part played previously by Calvinism in engendering the revolutionary parties of France and the Netherlands in the sixteenth century.[1] But while in the Netherlands rebellion and the French wars of religion Protestantism had been fighting a life-and-death struggle for survival, there was no such issue at stake in England, where a Protestant state church had existed since Elizabeth's time. It should have been one of the foremost tasks of Stuart rule to deal cautiously and moderately with the Puritans in the established church. Instead, by his support of Laud's severity against them, Charles I drove the Puritans to revolt. In this way the opposition to his policies became for many people a holy war involving not only the liberty of the subject and the future of parliament, but even the fate of religion itself.

---

[1] Cf. H. Koenigsberger, 'The organization of revolutionary parties in France and the Netherlands during the sixteenth century,' *loc. cit.* and R. M. Kingdon, 'The political resistance of the Calvinists in France and the Low Countries,' *loc. cit.*

If not for Archbishop Laud's administration, Puritanism might have continued to live in its restless and uneasy peace within the Church of England. Troublesome as the ecclesiastical authorities found non-conformity to be, it was nevertheless a long-established trend in religious life which they might have contained and controlled as they had done in the past. Certainly, Puritanism was too rooted and widespread for any policy to succeed that aimed at extirpating or silencing it. Just this, however, is what Laud, with the crown's endorsement, set out to do.

The nature of the Laudian rule must be correctly stated, for it was not its intolerance as such that made it hateful. The Puritans were themselves intolerant; had they possessed the power, most would not have hesitated to silence their opponents. But Laud's programme signified in certain respects an abandonment of the Protestant foundations of the national church as fixed in the Elizabethan settlement now three generations old. Hence it awoke the fears not only of the Puritans, but of all those Anglicans—and they were the majority—who could not share the archbishop's prepossessions, driving the two into a common front. Indeed, it permitted the Puritans to stand forth as the champions-in-chief of English Protestantism threatened by what appeared an attempt to subvert it from within.

The Laudians constituted an Anglo-Catholic or High Church party in the Anglican establishment.[1] Because they repudiated the doctrine of predestination, they were known to their enemies as Arminians, after the theologian, Jacobus Arminius and his disciples, the intellectual critics of Calvinist orthodoxy in the Dutch Republic during the early seventeenth century. The Laudians, however, were not influenced by Arminius, nor was the religious latitudinarianism and rationalism which animated Dutch Arminianism characteristic of their outlook. 'Anglo-Catholic' and 'High Church,' accordingly, describe their position much more appropriately.[2]

[1] 'Anglo-Catholic' is used by A. W. Harrison, *Arminianism*, L., 1937, 132 and W. K. Jordan, *The development of religious toleration in England*, II, 115–16, 'High Church' by W. R. Fryer, 'The High Churchmen of the earlier seventeenth century,' *Renaissance and modern studies*, V (1961). In calling the Laudians Anglo-Catholics, I am mindful of their differences from the Anglo-Catholic tractarians of the nineteenth century, which are well brought out in *ibid.*, 115–16.

[2] Both W. K. Jordan, *The development of religious toleration in England*, II, 115 and W. R. Fryer, *op. cit.*, App. A, recognize the inapplicability of the term 'Arminian' to the Laudians. It is worth noting as an instance that Richard Montague, one of the best known Arminian churchmen, said in

Puritanism

The Anglo-Catholicism of the Laudians represented a high clericalist reaction in the church and a reaching out towards a conception of catholicity in which Rome and Canterbury could both share. The jettisoning of Calvinist theology was a necessary phase of the movement. For of all the creeds to emerge from the Reformation, Calvinism alone appeared as a comprehensive and systematized structure standing in uncompromising antithesis at every point to the teachings of Rome. Owing to this immense achievement, Calvinism became the greatest intellectual influence in European Protestantism, its sway extending beyond as well as within the Reformed churches. On the theological side, and apart from issues of ecclesiastical polity, the Church of England itself was largely Calvinistic. Most Elizabethan divines regarded predestination and election as points of orthodoxy, interpreting the Thirty-Nine Articles in that sense; and though these doctrines never became canonical, they received a quasi-authoritative expression in the Lambeth Articles of 1595.[1] The prevalence of Calvinistic theology persisted into the seventeenth century. The religious controversies of the Dutch republic were observed from England with close interest, and the churchmen whom King James sent to the Synod of Dort in 1618 took part with the majority in condemning the Arminians.[2] Predestination was commonly thought fundamental to Protestant belief. By denying free-will in man to obtain merit before God, it humbled the sinful pride of human nature and exalted God's incomprehensible power and mercy. It left no slightest room for the apparatus of priestly intercession and sacramentalism which the Roman church provided to help believers to salvation. Thus when Anglo-Catholics rejected predestination, they rejected a tenet long received in the Anglican church and supposed to be essential in differentiating Protestant from Catholic principles. It was from this standpoint that in 1629 a sub-committee on religion of the House of Commons condemned Arminianism as contrary to the doctrine publicly professed in the Church of England and all reformed churches.[3]

Their enemies grossly libelled and gravely misinterpreted the Anglo-Catholics when they called them papists. Yet Laud, Richard

[1] Cf. the excellent account of the Elizabethan controversy over predestination and assurance of election by H. C. Porter, *Reformation and reaction in Tudor Cambridge*, Cambridge, 1958, chs. 13–16.
[2] The disputes within Dutch Calvinism are described by D. Nobbs, *Theocracy and toleration*, Cambridge, 1938.
[3] Printed in S. R. Gardiner, *Constitutional documents of the Puritan revolution*, 80–1.

1626 that he had only just read Arminius for the first time. He added: 'The man had more in him than all the Netherlands.' (*Correspondence of John Cosin*, I, 90.)

Montague, John Cosin, and other doctors of the school felt a nostalgia for the ancient catholicity of an undivided church which the militant, embattled Protestantism of their time did not share and could not fail to misunderstand. They held that Rome for all its errors was a true church in which salvation was possible; and they showed a warmer interest in the practices of Roman Catholic worship than for the other Protestant communions of Europe. Devoted to ritual, they imitated Rome by introducing ceremonies emblematic of the believers' adoration of the holy mysteries of religion. They liked crossings and bowings, candles and incense; they cared much more for liturgy and sacrament than for edification through preaching; and they turned the communion table into an altar surrounded by a rail, at which they required communicants to kneel. These ceremonial innovations ran counter to Anglican tradition and gave great offence. The Anglo-Catholics called them decency and order; their enemies, idolatry, superstition, and popery.

Finally, the Anglo-Catholics took a different view of episcopacy from that prevailing earlier in the Anglican church. They did not merely justify the episcopate as an institution sanctioned by historic tradition and expedient to the monarchical regime. They exalted it as a divinely commissioned order appointed by God to be the stay of religion and the church. His external legal jurisdiction, said Laud, he and all bishops derive from the King; 'but my order, my calling, my jurisdiction *in foro conscientiae*, that is from God and from Christ, and by divine and apostolical right.'[1] It was for the bishops and their clergy to proclaim religious truth and what was to be publicly professed; it was for the laity to hearken and obey. Nothing was better calculated to release the spring of anti-clericalism in Puritan and non-Puritan alike. In fact, by these pretensions the Anglo-Catholics brought obloquy and ruin upon the episcopacy they wished most dearly to uphold.

The Anglo-Catholics, though a minority, were able to enforce their dictates because they possessed Charles I's support. Laud's highest goal was an outward uniformity and order, and he imagined that severity could establish the peace of the church. He set out to suppress the Puritans as disturbers of religion and enemies to monarchy. It was only natural that the Anglo-Catholic divines should exalt the crown's powers to the fullest. '. . . defend thou me with the sword,' Richard Montague addressed the King in *Apello Caesarem* (1625), 'and I will defend thee with the pen.' Other clergy of the party preached compliance with forced loans and royal exactions as a religious duty.[2] If their doctrines were true,

[1] Cited in W. R. Fryer, *op. cit.*, 135–6.
[2] Cf. Robert Sibthorpe, *Apostolike obedience*, 1627; Roger Manwaring,

said the oppositionist, John Selden, 'there is no *meum* or *tuum* in England.'[1]

Inevitably, Puritan and moderate Anglican opposition to the Anglo-Catholics merged with the Country's political opposition to Charles I. Their coalescence occurred as the direct consequence of the alliance between the crown and Anglo-Catholics. In the first three parliaments of the reign Country supporters led the House of Commons in a repeated hue-and-cry against the High Churchmen.[2] Not the least of the causes inflaming hostility was the favour Charles showed them. He protected them from parliament's anger and gave them preferment. In 1628, Montague received the bishopric of Chichester; the Anglo-Catholic Neile was translated from Durham to Winchester and thence to York in 1632; Laud, already the governing influence in the church, went to London in 1629 and four years later to Canterbury; Roger Manwaring, a notorious object of parliament's displeasure, became bishop of St. David's in 1635; Matthew Wren was appointed to Hereford in 1635 and next year to Norwich.

In full control during the '30s, the Laudians crowned their dominance by the canons which the clerical convocation passed in the spring of 1640. These enacted their programme into ecclesiastical law binding clergy and laity alike. They prescribed the ceremonial practices the archbishop favoured, and they imposed an oath on ministers and various classes of laymen promising never 'to alter the government of this Church by archbishops, bishops, deans, and archdeacons, &c. as it stands now ... and as by right it ought to stand. . . .'[3] The canons were the Laudians' last act before the rage of the Long Parliament drove them from power.

Because of Charles's patronage of the Anglo-Catholics, 'Puritan' turned into a catchword covering every form of opposition to the regime. This only confused its meaning further, but was nevertheless a clear indication that the religious and political struggles had become completely identified with one another. Oppositionists charged in parliament that the Arminians 'under the name of Puritanes ... collecteth the greatest parte of the King's true subjects. . . .'; and that 'to be an honest man is now to be a Puritan. . . .'[4]

---

[1] *D.N.B.*, *s.v.* 'Robert Sibthorp.'
[2] Cf. the account of parliamentary attacks on the Anglo-Catholic clergy in W. K. Jordan, *The development of religious toleration in England*, II, 117–29.
[3] H. Gee and W. J. Hardy, *Documents illustrative of English church history* L., ed. 1921, 535–6.
[4] *Commons debates in 1625*, App., 180–4; *Commons debates, 1629*, 178.

Religion and allegiance, 1627; cf. the discussion of the political opinions of the Anglo-Catholic clergy in J. W. Allen, *op. cit.*, pt. II, ch. IX and M. Judson, *op. cit.*, ch. V.

On the other hand, the Laudian view held that 'Puritanism is the root of all rebellious and disobedient intractableness in Parliament . . . and all schism and sauciness in the country. . . .'[1]

In 1641, with revolution under way, the consequences of labelling all opposition as Puritanism were astutely described by Henry Parker, one of the keenest writers of the time. 'Puritans,' he pointed out, '. . . were at first Ecclesiasticall only . . . but now it is come about, that by a new enlargement of the name, the world is full of nothing else but Puritans. . . .' Thus,

whole Kingdoms are familiarly upbrayded with this sinne of Puritanisme: As for example, All in Scotland, who wish well to the Covenant, though some Papists, some Courtiers, and almost all the whole body without exception have now declared themselves for it, yet all these are manifest Puritans. So also in England, all the Commons in Parliament, and almost all the ancient impartiall temporall Nobility, and all such as favour . . . the late proceedings of both the houses, which is the mayne body of the Realme . . . all these are Puritans. They which deprave this great Councell of the Kingdome, suggest to the King that the major part is gull'd . . . by the Puritan party. . . .

In fact, Parker suggested, the Scottish rebellion, the eleven-year cessation of parliaments in England, and the King's estrangement from his subjects were 'all caused by the abusive mistake and injurious misapplication of this word *Puritan*.'[2] His analysis attested that hostility to the government, become well-nigh universal, extended far beyond the Puritans. It attested, too, that Charles's policies had forced every sort of antagonism into a united front of disaffection.

6

Religious controversy in the pre-revolutionary years took on an almost unprecedented bitterness. Puritan rancour towards the church hierarchy found vent in incendiary writings by men willing and eager to undergo martyrdom for their beliefs. The anti-prelatical pamphlets of William Prynne, Alexander Leighton, John Bastwick, and Henry Burton expressed an implacable hatred, testifying that a spirit of unrelenting fanaticism was loose in the land.[3] Councillors might

---

[1] *C.S.P.D. 1629–31*, 411.

[2] [Henry Parker], *A discourse concerning Puritans*, [January] 1641, 10–11, 41–2.

[3] Cf. the account of these writings by W. Haller, *op. cit.*, ch. VII. The nature of Prynne's attitude toward the Laudian clergy is discussed by W. M. Lamont, *Marginal Prynne*, L., 1963, ch. I.

well have reminded themselves of Bacon's warning that religious innovation was a main cause of disturbance in states. Despite their execrations on 'Popish Arminians,' these works steadfastly, and doubtless sincerely, avowed their authors' loyalty to the King. Yet they could only have had the effect upon sympathetic readers of discrediting the crown for its support of the Anglo-Catholic party in the church.

The government found it impossible to stop such writings. The Court of High Commission, charged with enforcement of the crown's ecclesiastical supremacy, dealt with religious dissent; while the Court of Star Chamber had jurisdiction over the press and could punish the publication of unlicensed works.[1] The boldness of authors and printers, however, defeated censorship and attempts at suppression. Produced secretly at home, or else smuggled into England from Dutch presses abroad, anti-Laudian propaganda circulated along a transmission belt of Puritan sympathizers in London and other towns. In 1637, for instance, a wax chandler of St. Clement Danes parish in the capital was brought before the High Commission for selling prohibited books by Bastwick and others, and a Gloucester clothier was accused of receiving a hundred copies of Prynne's *News From Ipswich* to dispose in the neighbourhood at eighteenpence apiece.[2] A Norwich citizen was examined on suspicion of distributing *News From Ipswich* and *The Divine Tragedie*, another of Prynne's tracts. It appeared that he got fifty copies of both in London from one, Stephen Moor, 'a packer of stuffs in Philpot Lane.'[3] John Lilburne, then a London apprentice and soon to emerge as the greatest agitator of the revolution, first tasted persecution in 1637 when the Star Chamber sentenced him to prison, whipping, and the pillory for importing seditious books from Holland.[4]

Since the government could not suppress anti-prelatical pamphlets, it retaliated by punishing the authors. Bastwick, Burton, and Prynne became the most notorious victims of the repression of Puritanism by the King's prerogative tribunals, the High Commission and the Star Chamber. Of the three, only Burton was a clergyman; Bastwick was a physician, Prynne a lawyer. All, however, had attacked the Arminian clergy and bishops with envenomed pens. After several less grave encounters with the law, they were brought into the Star Chamber in 1637 charged with seditious libel. They were convicted,

---

[1] Cf. F. S. Siebert, *Freedom of the press in England 1476–1776*, Urbana, 1952, chs. 5–7.

[2] *C.S.P.D. 1636–37*, 546; *The court and times of Charles I*, II, 273–4.

[3] *C.S.P.D. 1636–37*, 427.

[4] Lilburne arranged to print Bastwick's *The letany of John Bastwick* in Holland and then brought it into England.

sentenced to have their ears cut off and ordered committed to distant prisons. Such were their provocations that they must have expected severe punishment and even desired it in order to bear witness to their faith. When it came upon them, they embraced it with the zeal of martyrs. Their bearing turned the scene into a demonstration of their own righteousness before the unchristian cruelty of their judges. A wave of sympathy went out to them from the spectators, and later from the crowds who gathered to see them on their way to prison. When Prynne passed Chester, his well-wishers were so many that the ecclesiastical authorities threatened some with punishment. At Coventry, the citizens' warm reception of Burton caused a *quo warranto* proceeding to be instituted against the town's charter.[1] It was said that the brand of S.L. for *Seditious Libeller* burned on Prynne's cheek really stood for *Sion's Lawyer*. 'You may say what you wil,' wrote one of his sympathizers in Essex, 'the King hath a wife, and he loves her wel, and she is a papist and we must al be of her Religion, and thats the thing the Bishops aime at. . . .'[2]

The harsh treatment of dissent by the Star Chamber and High Commission brought both tribunals into discredit. Such cases were merely a small fraction of their judicial business, but they left a strong impression on the public mind. The Star Chamber, in particular, long considered by English legal opinion as a court of the highest dignity in Christendom, declined in reputation. Its identification with the policy of Laud, who sat as a judge with the other privy councillors and did not hesitate to shed blood, helped make it unpopular.[3] The High Commission, on the other hand, had always possessed a questionable reputation. Under Elizabeth and James, Puritan clergymen and common lawyers denied its legality and attacked its procedures and jurisdiction. These assaults were repelled, so that the court was never busier than in Charles's reign. Moral delinquencies and Catholic recusancy occupied far more of its time than non-conformity. Yet its role in the religious repression and its power to fine and imprison even laymen without appeal reinforced its image as the epitome of clerical injustice and arrogance.[4] No institution was more detested in the '30s. Probably many would have echoed the sentiments of a

[1] Edward Burghall, *Providence improved*, ed. J. Hall, *Lancashire and Cheshire record society*, XIX, 1889, 13; *C.S.P.D. 1638–39*, 142; *H.M.C. House of Lords, XI, Addenda 1514–1714*, 380.

[2] *Winthrop papers*, III, 486.

[3] Cf. H. E. I. Phillips, 'The last years of the Court of Star Chamber 1630–41,' *Transactions of the Royal Historical Society*, 4th ser., XXI, 1939.

[4] R. G. Usher, *The rise and fall of the High Commission*, Oxford, 1913. Usher greatly underestimates the extent of opposition to the court over the years preceding its abolition.

prominent Northumberland gentleman haled before it in 1633 who hoped that

if ever a parliament came . . . it would pull downe and abate the pride of the usurping bishops. . . . for these courtes . . . are but bawdy courtes, and merely to oppresse people and get monie for themselves.[1]

Ever since Queen Elizabeth's time, the Puritans' enemies had warned that their attacks on the church would lead to revolution. Whitgift, Bancroft, and Laud all considered them potential rebels who, as Laud said about Prynne and his fellows, 'do but begin with the Church, that they might after have freer access to the State. . . .'[2] This was a plausible opinion in the sixteenth century because of the affinity between Elizabethan Puritanism and the beleaguered Calvinist parties in Scotland, France, and the Netherlands. The theorists of these parties expounded a right of resistance to princes; and since Calvinism was an international movement, Bancroft attributed the same doctrine to the English Puritans. He taxed them with taking over the 'most strange and rebellious propositions' of Buchanan's *De jure regni apud Scotos*, Beza's *De jure magistratuum in subditos*, and the *Vindiciae contra tyrannos*. '. . . your drift,' he charged Cartwright on trial before the High Commission in 1591, '. . . is to bring in the further reformacion against the Princes will by force and armes.'[3]

It was indeed true that two of Calvin's English disciples, Christopher Goodman and John Ponet, had written boldly in justification of rebellion against ungodly rulers. That, however, was in relation to the Catholic reign of Elizabeth's sister, Mary, and her husband, Philip II of Spain.[4] After Elizabeth's accession no such doctrine was ever maintained by any Puritan advocate, and for more than seventy-five years the non-conformists remained at one with English Protestantism in upholding the duty of obedience and non-resistance to princes. Even under the tribulations of the Laudian rule they continued to adhere to this position.

---

[1] This was the case of Robert Brandling, previously sheriff of the county, who was cited before the High Commission at Durham for adultery and other misdemeanours; *The acts of the High Commission Court within the diocese of Durham*, 64.

[2] *The earl of Strafforde's letters*, II, 101.

[3] A. F. Scott Pearson, *Thomas Cartwright and Elizabethan Puritanism*, 462; *Church & state*, 89–90.

[4] Christopher Goodman, *How superior powers ought to be obeyed*, 1558 (published in Geneva); John Ponet, *A short treatise of politike power*, 1556; cf. the discussion of these writings by J. W. Allen, *Political thought in the sixteenth century*, 116–20.

The views of the London minister, Henry Burton, one of Laud's victims, were typical of the Puritan attitude. Intemperately as he condemned the prelates, his political professions were of quite another character. The little liberalism they possessed appeared only incidentally. In a writing addressed to the parliament of 1628, for instance, he warned 'The Lay Elders of Israel' against the 'Arminian Papists' who 'daily creep into high favour in Court,' telling the King he is omnipotent and not bound by laws.[1] Or again, in 1636 he referred to 'the mutual stipulation in covenant which the King and his subjects make at his coronation,' and called the Petition of Right a 'solemn covenant.'[2] Such assertions that the King was under law were political commonplaces and not in the least novel. Moreover, Burton joined them to emphatic declarations of the duty of subjection and non-resistance. Even commands contrary to God's law, though they ought to be disobeyed, were no justification for rebellion. 'It is one thing,' he said,

not to obey; and another to be rebellious: Superiors ought not to be obeyed, if they command against God. Yet this is no rebellion—where men are ready to yield passive obedience to their unjust cruelty, by not resisting it; though they detest, and deny active obedience, to their unjust commands. . . . Thus all God's true-bred children have, and will do.[3]

John Lilburne held the same position. Writing in 1639 as a martyr to the prelates' rage, he declared that the King's authority is from God, so that to disobey it is to disobey God. If the King commands something against God's work, he would refuse obedience and submit his body for punishment: 'for I doe hold it unlawfull for any of Gods people, in their greatest Oppression by the Majestrate, to rebell or take up any Temporall armes. . . .'[4]

Burton and Lilburne were only restating the traditional doctrine of English Protestantism respecting the limits of obedience. It could provide a religious rationale for defiance of the Laudian hierarchy. Politically, however, it was at most a basis for obstruction, never for revolution.

Yet just as in the sixteenth century the restraints which European Calvinism maintained against resistance gave way under the sword of Catholic persecution, so was the same pattern soon to repeat itself

[1] Henry Burton, *Israel's fast*, 1628, Prefatory epistle, cited in B. Hanbury, *op. cit.*, I, 481–3.
[2] Henry Burton, *For God and the King*, 1636, cited in *ibid.*, I, 549–51.
[3] Henry Burton, *The law and the gospel reconciled*, 1631, cited in *ibid.*, I, 507.
[4] John Lilburne, *Come out of her my people*, 1639, 14.

with English Puritanism. Calvin had forcibly enjoined the duty of non-resistance to superiors, leaving, however, one loophole: in kingdoms where inferior magistrates, such as the estates of the realm [*in singulis regnis tres ordines*] were ordained *ad moderandam regum libidinem*, they had the right to oppose tyrants with force.[1] Out of this and a motley assortment of other conceptions, John Knox, Beza, Hotman, and the whole company of European Monarchomachs forged a justification for rebellion in Scotland, France, and the Netherlands. Incited by Laud's ecclesiastical government, moved, too, by an almost hysterical fear of popery, Puritanism was at length to react in an analogous way.

The Scots gave the signal earliest, when they began their revolt in 1638 against the new liturgy the King and archbishop commanded to be used in the Scottish church. In England, nevertheless, despite widespread sympathy with the Scots, two years elapsed before any public justification of resistance appeared. It came in September 1640 in the Rev. Calybute Downing's sermon to the London Artillery Company.[2] Delivered even before the Long Parliament met, the sermon was a straw in the wind. The Puritan clergyman was no daring speculator. On the contrary, his ideas were familiar and unoriginal. Precisely this gave his sermon its significance. He was as far as known the first preacher to express openly the momentous reversal that was occurring in Puritan opinion. Drawing on the Old Testament and 'Rationall Grotius' to justify the Scottish rebellion, he merely stated what many Englishmen had become ripe to consider: that resistance to the King might be a religious duty as well as a political necessity. Evidently the belief in subjection and non-resistance, entrenched and reiterated for decades, was starting to crumble. With the meeting of the Long Parliament before it, Puritanism was about to set forth on a revolutionary path whose consequences it was far from perceiving.

[1] J. Calvin, *Institutio religionis Christiani*, IV, xx, 31.
[2] Cf. *supra*, 144–5.

The Country and the
Constitutional Revolution

It is a universal characteristic of revolutions that their course can neither be predicted nor controlled. Their occurrence brings with it such a multiplication and acceleration of political forces that every stage of their progress forms an equation of unknown quantity. The agitation during the period of preparation has already undermined the habitual obedience and unreflecting loyalty which ensure the equilibrium of states. When the revolutionary gale then breaks upon the body politic, it shatters them completely. The men who lead the movement in the beginning must necessarily sharpen and inflame the popular temper in order to use it for their ends. Thereby they call up a spirit from the vasty deep that once having learned its strength will not be so easily commanded. Criticism and propaganda expose the *arcana imperii* to the light of common day. Subjects ask if they should obey, and whom, and why. Authority is constrained to plead its case with reasons or impose itself by violence. In either instance it has lost its virtue: for while authority remains itself, it neither argues nor coerces, but merely speaks and is accepted. Upon the complex scene already charged with tense uncertainties, unexpected fresh initiatives supervene. Negotiations and threats are followed by civil war. And while the original parties are locked in their angry struggle, they find themselves joined by other combatants. Limited aims in time give way to more extended ones. With an unlooked-for dynamism the movement advances, generating utopian passions and idealistic rage. Partisan love and hate fashion objects for themselves equal to their own ample dimensions. Thus public and private life become thoroughly deranged. Driven by incalculable combinations of force and intrigue, of heroism and vileness, of principled action and unscrupulous manoeuvre, the revolution proceeds through its successive stages to its conclusion and liquidation.

The men who assembled at Westminster on 3 November 1640 could not know that this was the earthquake history about to be enacted in their land. The meeting of the Long Parliament, however, marked the beginning of the revolution in England as definitely as the convening of the Estates General in the next century dated the commencement of the revolution in France. The parliament set out to obtain redress and reform. But before its unprecedented thirteen-year life was done, it stayed to wage a war against the King and to raise the whirlwind that destroyed the monarchy. It outlived its first great leaders, and many of its members fell away in enmity or disillusion. At last a military dictatorship by the general of its own creation put an end to it.[1] Such was the unimagined journey, carrying the kingdom far from its old moorings, on which a revolutionary parliament launched England in 1640.

From the day it opened the parliament met continuously to 9 September 1641, when the Houses, exercising a newly acquired power, voted to adjourn for six weeks to 20 October.[2] The first sitting, therefore, occupied ten months: a period forming a definite epoch in the revolution's progress. The alliance that had taken shape in support of the Country then accomplished its main work. While the ranks behind them were still more or less united, the Country leaders effected a constitutional or legal revolution, shearing away by statute a century and a half's accretion of royal power. In this interval of relative consensus, the last that revolutionary England was to know for many a year, the heritage of the Tudor monarchy was taken to pieces. But this achievement, instead of producing a settlement, left a void. Fixed in a posture of extreme distrust, the King and his opponents could not collaborate to work the new arrangements. The need for security and guarantees gave rise to fresh demands; the fresh demands only widened the gulf. Reform, accordingly, did not beget a new political equilibrium. It brought on, rather, a violent struggle for sovereignty.

When parliament met, the auspices strongly favoured the Country leaders. The King's government was completely discredited and the ministers feared the wrath of the Houses. In the north, the intimidating presence of the Scottish rebel army enforced the pressure at Westminster for reform. A cessation of arms made with the Scots in October left them in occupation of Durham and Northumberland until the conclusion of a peace treaty, which was to be negotiated at London with their commissioners. In the meantime the King was obliged to maintain them at a cost of £850 a day. Facing the Scots

---

[1] Even Cromwell's expulsion of the Long Parliament in 1653 was not its final demise. It went through two resurrections, another expulsion, and a last dissolution by its own vote during the political unsettlement of 1659–60.

[2] *C.J.*, II, 289; *L.J.*, IV, 396. The act against dissolving the present parliament without its consent (16 Car. I, c. 7, *Statutes of the realm*, V, 103–4) provided also that neither of the Houses should be adjourned except by its own order.

lay the King's army, which was also to remain in being pending a treaty. Parliament alone could provide the great sums needed to support the two armies: Charles would have to pay the price in concessions.

What was to be hinged largely on the oppositionist leaders' strategy and their ability to sway the parliament. Here their informal organization of recent years stood them in good stead. Accustomed to consultation and common action, they were able by these means to govern the proceedings of the House of Commons. No body of men brought together as were its members could possibly achieve any constructive result without direction from one quarter or another. Even with direction the task was sufficiently formidable. The odium of the privy councillors was such that they could not exert the least influence upon the House. The Country with its numerous supporters supplied the control and cohesion that could come from nowhere else. In the prevailing temper the renown of its leaders as defenders of the kingdom's rights gave them an immediate authority. Pym, Hampden, St. John, Holles, Nathaniel Fiennes, and others of their political circle therefore took the management of the Commons into their hands from the very outset.

For them to retain their ascendancy, however, was no easy matter. Theirs was only an embryo or proto-party, and they wielded neither the powers of discipline nor the blandishments of patronage by which modern politicians secure their rule. Lacking these resources, the heads of the Country had to exercise control in other ways. The basis of their strength was superiority of organization and adeptness in the methods always indispensable to the government of great assemblies. As most of them were veterans of earlier parliaments, they possessed a solid acquaintance with the details of procedure. They were knowledgeable about precedents and privilege, never failing to appear as the most conspicuous champions of the House's liberties. They understood the necessity of making their presence felt in important committees. They gave themselves up to a multitude of parliamentary labours with incessant energy. By their denunciations of grievances and continued warnings of plots and dangers, they roused the members' passions and never allowed them to flag. Such a mastery of tactics reaped its reward. Aided by the general animosity against the Court, it gained the party managers a dominion from which they could not be deposed.

Of the Country leaders, none acquired so commanding an authority as did Pym. To him both the opposition movement and the House of Commons owed an incalculable debt. He was a man who lived wholly for the public cause and whose being became merged in it. His private personality was thus so much obscured by the events in which he took part that he remains least known among the prominent figures who most influenced the revolution's course. But while the depths of his character and the circumstances of his intimate life are closed to us, it is possible to discern the nature of his leadership. Pym possessed in a supreme degree the art of parliamentary management. Of tireless industry and great practical sense, he was a committee-man of genius. He knew how to make men work together and how to promote his party's enterprises among them without noise or vanity. Although he had firmness and strong principles, he was neither a doctrinaire nor a radical. He always tried to moderate differences on his own side, and whenever it was compatible with the safety of his cause he was ready for conciliation. To these qualities as a politician he united the gifts of an orator who could address his fellow members in memorable words. Nowhere did the faith and fears of the parliamentary leaders attain more eloquent expression than in his speeches. But the final secret of his power was that while his abilities were superior to most in the Commons, his ideas were not. With all his militancy against the Court, he was conservative and old-fashioned. He believed himself a preserver of old ways, not a shaper of new ones. He harboured the same convictions and prejudices, the same hopes and anxieties as the majority of members. That was why they trusted him and permitted him to achieve a position among them rarely equalled in parliamentary annals.

By comparison with the House of Commons, the House of Lords was much less susceptible to control. When parliament began it consisted of one hundred and twenty-four lay and twenty-six spiritual peers.[1] It prided itself on its greatness and did not intend to be a subordinate partner of the lower House. The basis of its corporate consciousness was the conviction that its role ought to be one of mediator between the King and the Commons. This was the position the peers strove to occupy in the constitutional disputes preceding the Petition of Right and towards which most of them probably aspired in 1640. It was notable that in the abortive Short Parliament the Lords had dissented from the Commons, a majority voting that supply should come before grievances.[2] Haughtiness of rank, ancestry, and wealth made many noblemen moderate by every inclination. When that posture eventually became untenable, honour or interest drove them towards royalism or withdrawal from public life. Nonetheless, within the upper House the Commons managers also possessed some firm allies. Bedford, Warwick, Essex, Saye, and Mandeville belonged to the Country's innermost counsels, while a number of others shared

---

[1] C. H. Firth, *The House of Lords during the civil war*, 74 and n.
[2] *Ibid.*, 66–7.

their political sympathies. Noble defectors in Court offices, like the earls of Northumberland, Pembroke, and Holland, Warwick's brother, could also be counted as friends of the opposition. There was in consequence an active sentiment among the peers favourable to close cooperation with the lower House.

The Country had a considerable organization in the House of Commons, though its detailed workings cannot be traced precisely. The leaders of course consulted frequently. Pym was known to hold meetings with political associates and friends at his lodgings in a house behind Westminster Hall.[1] The parliamentary diarist, Sir Simonds D'Ewes, M.P. for Sudbury and our incomparable informant about the transactions of the Commons, gives us a rare and tantalizing glimpse of a private conference on the night of 10 June 1641, where Pym, Hampden, Sir Robert Harley, the Rev. Stephen Marshall, and some others decided that the bill against episcopacy should be moved next day in the House: 'for Mr Hampden out of his serpentine subtletie did still putt others to move those businesses that he contrived.'[2] This was undoubtedly how the party chiefs directed affairs from behind the scenes. In one such earlier meeting, to be noticed presently, the leaders in both Houses worked out their strategy at the opening of the parliament.[3]

The machinery of the Commons was subjected to the Country through the prevalence of its supporters on committees.[4] In grand committees of the whole House, which any member could attend, men became prominent by diligent participation and by exploiting the general animosity against the Court. When we find, for instance, John White, M.P. for Southwark, reporting to the House for the grand committee on religion in the early days of the parliament, and George Peard, M.P. for Barnstaple, reporting for the grand committee on courts of justice, it is likely that oppositionist influence in these committees was pretty considerable.[5] White, a Puritan lawyer, was one of the old Feoffees for Impropriations and connected also with the Massachusetts Bay Company. Peard had spoken strongly against ship money in the Short Parliament of the preceding spring.[6]

Oppositionist ascendancy was equally pronounced in select com-

[1] Clarendon, *Life*, 936.
[2] D'Ewes, Journal, B.M. Harl. 163, f. 306b. Gardiner's statement (*History*, X, 77n.) that D'Ewes's reference to Hampden was inserted long after the date in which it is placed in the Journal is not borne out by the manuscript.
[3] Cf. *infra*, 207.
[4] Cf. M. Keeler, ' "There are no remedies for many things but by a parliament." Some opposition committees, 1640,' *Conflict in Stuart England*, ed. W. A. Aiken and B. Henning, L., 1960.
[5] Cf., e.g., *C.J.*, II, 35, 70, 72.
[6] M. Keeler, *The Long Parliament*, 299, 390.

mittees. This was especially true of the small committee which bore
responsibility for the most crucial of all the Commons' early enterprises, the preparation of the case against Strafford. The eight
members appointed on 11 and 12 November included the opposition
chiefs and trusted associates: Pym, Hampden, St. John, Holles,
William Strode, Sir John Clotworthy, and Sir Walter Erle. Only Lord
George Digby, the earl of Bristol's son, had no connection with the
party: he was probably chosen because of his and his father's known
zeal against the Court.[1] The large committee on privileges, established on 6 November to report on disputed elections, was another
instrument of the Country's purpose. Its supporters, who were
heavily represented, used the committee to strengthen the party's hold
by deciding contested returns against opponents. Sir Edward Osborne, for instance, Strafford's friend and Vice-President of the
Council of the North, was returned in a disputed election at Berwick.
The committee recommended that his return should be void.
Osborne was thus kept out of parliament, where he might have been
able to help Strafford.[2] John Hampden was also named in a disputed
return for Buckinghamshire. The esteem the House felt for him was
shown by its vote when appointing the committee on privileges that
his election for the county should not be questioned.[3]

A major factor contributing to the Country's ascendancy was the
intensification of political consciousness in the kingdom at large. The
crisis at the close of the '30s infused a fresh vigour into public discussion, which developed after November 1640 with extraordinary
rapidity. The result was a veritable transformation of the political
scene. For the first time, decisions affecting the common lot had to be
taken amidst incessant popular argument and scrutiny. Greater
numbers than ever before—people on the margins of the political
nation, even elements within the traditionally mute and inarticulate
mass—concerned themselves with questions of the day. Aroused by
hatred of Laud and Strafford, this powerful upsurge of popular
awareness ranged itself almost entirely behind the opposition party, a
force to be reckoned with and appeased.

The press, no longer controllable by the palsied hand of the regime,
poured forth a torrent of publication to sustain the general interest in

---

[1] *C.J.*, II, 26, 27; *D.N.B.*, *s.v.*, 'George Digby, second earl of Bristol,' 'John
Digby, first earl of Bristol.' On the 12th Holles asked to be excused, doubt-
less because Strafford was his brother-in-law. He was replaced by Harbottle
Grimston, recorder and M.P. for Colchester, one of the most Puritan towns
in the most Puritan county in England. On 23 January 1641, the lawyers,
Selden, Whitelocke, Palmer, and Maynard were added to the committee,
C.J., II, 72.
[2] *C.J.*, II, 20–1, 47; Clarendon, *Rebellion*, III, 12; M. Keeler, *The Long
Parliament*, 10 and n.   [3] Notestein, *D'Ewes*, 3n.

public affairs. The most impressive evidence of its output during the revolutionary years is the British Museum's great Thomason collection—the collection of books, pamphlets, and newspapers formed by the London bookseller, George Thomason, between 1640–61. Amounting to nearly 30,000 titles, the writings Thomason gathered by unsparing effort and expense equal or perhaps exceed the sum of works printed in all languages in the British Isles and in the English language abroad during the whole period 1475 to 1640.[1] The entire mind of the revolution survives in this collection; and though it contains titles of the utmost diversity, from *belles lettres* to joke books, its greater part relates directly to political, religious, and economic controversies. According to a tabulation of its contents, 721 publications appeared in 1641, 2,134 in 1642, the latter the highest total in any year up to the Restoration: a fact that sufficiently demonstrates the accelerated preoccupation with political-ecclesiastical issues in the first stages of the revolution's progress.[2]

But Thomason's collection should not be regarded only as an endlessly rich hunting ground for subsequent generations of historians. For his undertaking it was in itself a sign of the growth of contemporary consciousness under the influence of the opposition movement's struggle. Thomason, strongly sympathetic to the Country in the early '40s, realized from the beginning that the Long Parliament's meeting was a great historic event. He therefore resolved, he said, to make 'an Exact Collection' of everything published from November 1640 onwards, in the conviction that it would be both useful for his own age and 'of great Advantage to Posterity.' He found the amassing of his collection a 'chargeable and heavy . . . Burthen. . . .'; but the prescience that led him to attempt it has attached his name permanently to the greatest of all sources of knowledge of the revolutionary epoch.[3]

Nothing attracted more public attention than occurrences in parlia-

---

[1] *A short-title catalogue . . . 1475–1640*, ed. A. W. Pollard and G. R. Redgrave, L., ed. 1946, lists 26,143 publications from 1475–1640. More will be added in a second ed. now in progress. This number, however, includes hundreds of royal proclamations, statutes, and different editions of the same work. In comparison, Thomason estimated his collection at nearly 30,000 items, while modern writers using other modes of computation have counted the total as 26,000 and 22,255; cf. L. Spencer, 'The professional and literary connexions of George Thomason,' *The library*, 5th ser., XIII, 2 (1958). G. K. Fortescue, editor of the Thomason catalogue, believed the collection was nearly complete for the years it covered; cf. *Catalogue of the pamphlets . . . George Thomason*, 2v., L., 1908, I, xxii.

[2] *Ibid.*, I, xxi.

[3] Cf. Thomason's statement of his purpose and methods in L. Spencer, *loc. cit.*, 114–15. The fullest account of Thomason is in *ibid.* and the same author's 'The politics of George Thomason,' *The library*, 5th ser., XIV, 1

ment. The stationers catered to this interest by printing speeches in large numbers. The spread of political division had already undermined the restraints on the disclosure of proceedings in the earlier parliaments of Charles I, and after 1640 all barriers were down. Although the House of Commons made occasional gestures to suppress the 'License of Printing,' they were quite ineffectual.[1] Frequently members themselves gave the stationers the text of their remarks or connived in some other way at publication. More commonly stationers obtained a copy from a scrivener working from second-hand reports and hence likely to make errors or even to resort to wholesale fabrication where knowledge failed him.[2]

The circulation of speeches probably helped considerably to advance members' reputations as well as to form opinion. Every major speech by Pym and St. John, for instance, got into print, thus reinforcing their authority as leaders. Numerous speeches on grievances, on Strafford's misrule, and on church government, replete with citations of legal precedent, political writers, and scriptural texts, opened every issue of controversy to ordinary readers. The great majority of printed speeches embodied the oppositionist standpoint and were highly critical of royal policies and ministers. When members published unpopular views, they ran the risk of retaliation by the Commons. Lord Digby learned this to his cost after he put into circulation the speech he delivered in April 1641 denouncing the legality of Strafford's attainder. He gave the text to one, Moore, 'a common writer,' to make twenty copies. Through the latter it came to Parslow, a stationer, who printed an edition of five hundred which was then distributed with the help of Digby's relative, Sir Lewis Dyve. The lower House was so provoked that it authorized a committee to investigate the circumstances of publication. On receiving the committee's report, the members voted that the speech was false and its appearance in print defamatory to the House. Moore, Parslow, and Dyve were declared delinquents and the speech was ordered burned by the common hangman. As for Digby, who had recently been summoned by the King to the House of Lords, they resolved on a petition requesting Charles to refrain from conferring any honour or employment upon him.[3]

[1] Cf. *C.J.*, II, 168, 5 June 1641, an order of the House to the Master and Wardens of the Company of Stationers to take measures against the licence of printing speeches and other pamphlets.
[2] For an account of the publication and circulation of parliamentary speeches, cf. *Commons debates for 1629*, Introduction, and Coates, *D'Ewes*, xx–xxiii.   [3] D'Ewes, Journal, B.M. Harl. 163, f. 396b; *C.J.*, II, 208–9.

(1959), and cf. also the introduction to the *Catalogue of the pamphlets . . . George Thomason*, I.

Together with speeches a great spate of pamphlets poured from the press to gratify an increasing demand. The minds of Englishmen were in a ferment. Political and religious argument became the daily diet of people who read, and the appetite for information and controversy grew by what it fed on. It was in this setting that the first weekly newspapers reporting parliamentary and national affairs appeared in London. There had been nothing of their kind before in England, since their predecessors, the corantoes of the '20s, limited themselves strictly to continental news.[1] The earliest, *The heads of several proceedings in this present parliament*, came out in the week of 22–29 November 1641. The work of an enterprising publisher, it was soon followed by competitors, two in December, still others in 1642. These newspapers of 1641 were cheaply printed in eight pages, badly written, and devoid of personality. They sold in the capital for a penny. Their publication day was Monday, in time for the mail which left London for the north on Tuesday mornings. Primitive though they were, they were the forerunners of a journalistic phenomenon that was to propagate itself during the following years with astonishing fecundity. The issues of newspapers acquired by Thomason from 1641 to 1660 fill sixty-eight pages in the catalogue of his collection. '. . . when these diurnalls were first printed,' said a parliamentary speaker in March 1642,

ther came out but one each weeke, & then ther was some moderate truth in them. But now ther are sometimes printed twelve or fourteene in a week, & they commonlie labour in that worke all the Lords day, to gett them readie by monday morning.[2]

This was already the power of the press on an unexampled scale. And it was to continue to grow, so that in the civil war and after, newspapers became regular party organs and propaganda instruments written by men of real literary ability.[3] The appearance of the newspaper in 1641 was an indication of how far political life had broken through its former limits. Opposition to the regime had engendered a broad public which wished both to participate and to be informed. To mobilize popular support and stiffen conviction, the press was indispensable. The systematized provision of news, the presence of the journalist and publicist, were the necessary adjuncts of an energized politics.

[1] Cf. *supra*, 107.
[2] From a speech by D'Ewes, Journal, B.M. Harl. 163, f. 52b.
[3] Cf. J. Frank, *op. cit.*

2

Immediately after the opening of parliament, the chief oppositionists met to work out their strategy. Viscount Mandeville, one of those present, later described their deliberations in his memoirs. '. . . some of the members of both houses,' he recorded, 'had private meetings and consultacons how to direct their parliamentary resolutions in order to a present redresse and future security. . . .' They concluded that 'the most certaine way, and most consistent with the duty and allegiance of Subjects' was 'to fix their complaints and accusations upon evill Councellors, as the imediate actors in the tragicall miseries of the Kingdome, rather then upon the personall faileings and male administrations in the King.' In particular, they decided to aim their attack at the judges, the bishops, and the privy councillors, and especially against Laud, Strafford, Cottington, and the marquis of Hamilton, the King's representative to the rebellious Scots.[1] Hamilton's inclusion with the other malefactors was significant: the English and Scottish oppositions were clearly working together and intended to coordinate their blows against the ministers.

The assault began on 7 November—perhaps therefore even before the party leaders' meeting—in a powerful speech delivered by Pym.[2] In it he called for a reformation and for the discovery and punishment of the authors of the kingdom's ills. Surveying in detail the recent misrule in church and state, he linked it with the malignity of the Arminian clergy and the secret influence of papists on the King's affairs. In all that had occurred he saw evidence of a sinister design. And he gave the first intimation of what was to form the foundation of the House of Commons' charge against Strafford: that an attempt of the highest treason was under way to change the form of government to a despotism, for which purpose it had been planned to bring an Irish army into England.[3]

Pym's address, together with the decisions he and his friends had made, marked out the line on which they tried to lead parliament during the following months. Their strategy was eminently sound. In refraining from a direct attack on the King, these conservative

[1] B.M. Add. 15,567, f. 30. This anonymous manuscript is easily identifiable from internal evidence as a fragment of Mandeville's memoirs. Passages from it have been printed in J. Nalson, *An impartial collection*, 2v., 1682-3, II, 689, and J. L. Sanford, *op. cit.*, 307ff. I am indebted to Dr. De Lloyd Guth and Mrs. Susan Guralnik for making a transcript of this manuscript for me.

[2] Mandeville mentions no dates, but says the oppositionists' consultations occurred after the kingdom's grievances had been declared in the House; Pym's speech was such a declaration.

[3] Notestein, *D'Ewes*, 7-11.

revolutionists acted in keeping with the strongest instincts of constitutional propriety. They left inviolate the profession of loyalty to the monarch's crown and person which was a primary article in the creed of the governing class. The rank-and-file member could support them in good conscience, his sentiments of respect for the King unimpaired. Pym's accusation of an Arminian-popish conspiracy was false, but it reflected a rooted popular prejudice that could be used against the Court with deadly effect. Finally, the determination to fix responsibility on ministers carried far-reaching implications. If the parliamentary leaders succeeded, Charles would be forced to take new councillors.[1] He would have to receive men into his service who could reconcile King and parliament, Court and Country, because their presence would be the sign and guarantee of a change of policy. Only those who possessed parliament's confidence could undertake the task. The perspective of the oppositionists therefore envisaged the assumption of ministerial offices by some of themselves as an indispensable step towards the goal of reform. Had they attained their aim of entering the King's service as effective agents of a parliamentary and popular will, there would have been no civil war. Their failure inevitably advanced the revolution to a further stage that required more drastic solutions.

Parliament pressed its offensive with unremitting vigour over the next months. Needing no prodding, the members loosed a storm of anger on the ministers and servants of royal misgovernment. The first and greatest victim was Strafford, whom the party leaders needed to immobilize to succeed in their attack against the Court. They intended to impeach him and had made careful preparations to this end. A key role was assigned to Sir John Clotworthy, an Irish landowner elected to the Commons for the town of Maldon through the influence of the earl of Warwick. Clotworthy was a Puritan, a friend of John Winthrop and Pym, who possessed family and business connections with Strafford's greatest enemies in Ireland. His return to the House had been contrived so that he could expose the record of the Lord Lieutenant's Irish administration and its dangerous implications for the liberty of England.[2] Pym had also secretly obtained vital evidence against Strafford through his friendship with

---

[1] In this connection, a comment made in December 1640 by Robert Baillie, one of the Scottish commissioners in London, is significant. Among the aims he ascribed to the parliamentary leaders was 'the displanting of the Court' and 'the planting the Court'; *The letters and journals of Robert Baillie*, I, 285.

[2] M. Keeler, *The Long Parliament*, s.v.; H. F. Kearney, *op. cit.*, 199–200; *Winthrop papers*, III, 190. Clotworthy was also returned to parliament for Bosinney, probably by the patronage of the earl of Pembroke, Lord Warden of the Stannaries. This suggests that Pembroke's assistance was available to the party leaders; cf. V. Rowe, *loc. cit.*, 253.

The Country and the Constitutional Revolution

Sir Henry Vane junior, son of the King's co-Secretary of State. Notwithstanding his father's position, the younger Vane's religious and political sympathies lay altogether with the Country. In October he had shown Pym without his father's knowledge a copy of notes of a Council meeting held the previous 5 May after the Short Parliament's refusal to grant the King money against the Scots. According to these notes, Strafford advised Charles that he was now absolved from law and spoke words that could be construed as urging the introduction of an Irish army to compel England to obedience. The army referred to was one Strafford had raised in 1640 to assist the King to crush the Scottish rebellion, but which had not got into action and remained on foot in Ireland. Secretary Vane destroyed his original notes at the King's order before the Long Parliament opened. Pym, however, had made a copy of his own. The damning statements confirmed his worst fears and were to form the substance of the gravest charge in the Lord Lieutenant's impeachment.[1]

Strafford was too bold and resourceful merely to await his enemies' onslaught. He arrived in London from Yorkshire on 9 November planning to accuse the opposition leaders in both Houses of high treason for complicity with the Scots. Learning of his purpose from connections at the Court, Pym acted hastily to forestall its execution.[2] Clotworthy had already denounced Strafford's oppressions in Ireland in a long speech on the 7th.[3] Four days later the blow against him fell. On the 11th the House was tense with wild rumours of Strafford's intentions and reports of a far-reaching Catholic plot. Clotworthy related a story from Ireland that Strafford had promised the King he should be able to do as he pleased in England with the help of the Irish army. Thoroughly worked up, the members appointed a committee to frame a charge against the earl.[4] That same day Pym took the charge to the House of Lords and there in the Commons' name impeached Strafford of high treason. The Lord Lieutenant was not permitted to make a reply. In response to Pym's request, the peers sequestered him from his seat in their House and committed him to custody.

The party leaders thus removed the most dangerous of the King's ministers from the political scene. Although they still had to make good their case in Strafford's trial, they were meanwhile free to press

[1] On 10 April 1641, during the proceedings against Strafford, the younger Vane told the lower House how he had obtained his father's notes and shown a copy to Pym, D'Ewes, Journal, B.M. Harl. 164, ff. 162a–b, 163a.
[2] Mandeville relates in his memoirs the story of Strafford's reported intention and the oppositionists hastening their impeachment, B.M. Add. 15,567, f. 31.
[3] Notestein, *D'Ewes*, 13–14.
[4] *Ibid.*, 24–9; *C.J.*, II, 26–7.

the House's assault on the Court with increased momentum. On 18 December Laud was impeached and sent to the Tower. Sir Francis Windebank, the other Secretary of State, had already taken flight to France rather than face the members' accusations of favouring Catholic recusants. He was joined there by the Lord Keeper, Lord Finch, charged with treason on 21 December for his earlier conduct as a judge in the ship-money case. The other six judges who had upheld the legality of ship money were also accused in the House, and on 12 February Sir Robert Berkeley, justice of the King's Bench, was impeached.[1]

The first rule of revolutionaries is to preserve the initiative and to advance more boldly with each success. Within a couple of months, the parliamentary attack on ministers had done the Country's work. Too weak to resist, the Court disintegrated as a political force. The King was powerless. His councillors could neither help him nor find safety in his protection. Their only hope was to seek their preservation from the favour of parliament. Cottington, Master of the Wards and Chancellor of the Exchequer, saved himself by pledging to give up his offices so that they would be available to the parliamentary leaders. The marquis of Hamilton averted the storm by a promise to promote the aims of the oppositionists and their Scottish allies.[2]

Along with ministers, lesser officials and beneficiaries of royal favour who sat in parliament joined the general defection. Fear or opportunism, sympathy with the Country, hatred of Strafford and Laud, were amongst the several motives determining their conduct. Sir Miles Fleetwood and Sir Benjamin Rudyard, occupants of important places in the Court of Wards; Sir Robert Pye, Auditor of the Exchequer; Sir Henry Mildmay, Master of the Jewel House; Sir Arthur Ingram, Sir John Hippesley, Cornelius Holland, and Lawrence Whitaker, all monopolists and profiteers through Court patronage; every one of them attached himself to the opposition party.[3] Although the lower House voted to expel monopolists, Mildmay, Whitaker, and their like retained their seats as a result of their zealous cooperation with the party managers.[4]

With the Court routed, it became likely that a redistribution of offices would occur. At this stage, however, the question of office appeared under a double aspect. To the parliamentary leaders, office was not the goal of a merely personal policy inspired by the desire for

---

[1] *C.J.*, II, 44, 54, 55, 56, 83; Notestein, *D'Ewes*, 103, 175–6.

[2] Mandeville mentions these bargains in his memoirs, B.M. Add. 15,567, ff. 30–1.

[3] Cf. the biographies of these officials in M. Keeler, *The Long Parliament*, and the account of Sir Arthur Ingram's political stand by A. F. Upton, *op. cit.*, ch. X.

[4] *C.J.*, II, 24; Clarendon, *Rebellion*, III, 13.

emoluments and honour. It was, on the contrary, a serious political objective. Assuming the continuance of the monarchical regime— and of course they did not consider any other possibility—ministerial office was essential to the realization of their aims. But they had not risked royal disfavour for so many years only to abandon their principles at this juncture. If they entered Charles's service, it would be for a public purpose: to resolve the crisis and reconcile the King to parliament by carrying out a new policy in his name.

On the other hand, the Court's disruption and the expectation of changes naturally introduced an element of opportunism into the situation as well. Its centre was the Queen, whose influence on her husband was a factor that could affect the choice of ministers. Henrietta Maria did not understand the depth of political and religious differences from which the quarrel in the state arose. To her the dispute was predominantly a contest for places and honours, and from this frivolous premiss all her interventions proceeded. It was her intent to become the channel through which promotion flowed and thus to fix the dependence of all men on herself. She imagined that in this way, by bargaining with offices, she would gain the leading politicians for the King.[1] The opposition leaders, of course, were hardly likely to tolerate the Queen in such a mischievous role. For a moment, however, while she tried to play it, aspirants eager for promotion on any terms had a keen incentive to enlist her support on their behalf.

This opportunist aspect of the pursuit of office was most markedly exemplified by the earl of Leicester, the King's ambassador in France. Through his marriage to Lady Dorothy Percy, the nobleman belonged to an aristocratic Court circle. His brothers-in-law were the earl of Northumberland, Lord Admiral, and Henry Percy, a favourite courtier in the Queen's household. His sister-in-law was the dowager countess of Carlisle, an intimate of the Queen and of Strafford, one of those *grandes dames* who aspire to affect the course of affairs behind the scenes by their friendship with the great. Although Leicester possessed no special fitness to be a minister, he was nevertheless strongly ambitious for higher office, and at the end of the '30s had hoped to become Secretary of State or to replace Wentworth in Ireland.[2] The King's dislike of him, however, and Laud's enmity disappointed these designs.[3] At the same time, while cultivating his

---

[1] Cf. Clarendon's description, *Rebellion*, II, 130.

[2] Leicester became ambassador to France in 1636. For his earlier attempts at promotion, cf. *H.M.C. De L'Isle and Dudley*, VI, 77, 182, 192, 203–4, 211; A. Collins, *op. cit.*, II, 604, 618, 631, 634.

[3] Laud suspected Leicester's opinions and spoke of him as 'a most dangerous practicing Puritan. . . .' (*Works*, VII, 568). He was certainly wrong in this belief, since the earl's chaplain and occupant of the living at Penshurst was

Court connections for all they were worth, he did not fail to keep up friendly relations with the oppositionist, Lord Mandeville, to whom he professed his warm sympathies for the Puritans.[1]

Neither Leicester nor Northumberland agreed with the policies that brought disaster on the King in 1640. But in their frigid, self-centred world, political judgments were invariably dominated by hard material calculations as to the effect of events on their own personal position. Feeling little loyalty to their royal master, they viewed his plight without commiseration and prepared to exploit his weakness to the best advantage. Thus less than three weeks after parliament began, Northumberland found himself able to write Leicester in France of the splendid prospects now opening:

Both howses understand one an other so well, and are so fully resolved upon a reformation of all things that I do verily beleeve we shall see many persons questioned that within these 6 months thought themselves in great securitie, and such are the Kings necessities that he will not be any way able either to defend those men or to helpe himselfe, be their proceedings never so distastefull to him. . . . I should be glad to know which . . . offices . . . [Leicester] doth most affect. . . . if [Treasurer] can not be had [Northumberland] may use his best endevors to gett some of the others for him.[2]

In truth, what Leicester wanted was nothing less than the lord lieutenancy of Ireland as Strafford's successor. Accordingly, while Northumberland undertook to see that his nomination should be acceptable to the party managers in parliament,[3] Leicester himself began an intrigue to secure the Queen's support of his appointment. In this his intermediary was his old family friend, Sir John Temple, whose letters to the earl, chafing with impatience in Paris, described the labyrinthine progress of the negotiation.[4] On the Queen's side, the agent with whom Temple conducted most of his dealings was

[1] P.R.O. Manchester MSS. 30/15/466.

[2] *H.M.C. De L'Isle and Dudley*, VI, 343, some words in cipher. In a previous letter, Northumberland had suggested the posts of Treasurer, Irish Deputy, or Secretary of State; A. Collins, *op. cit.*, II, 663.

[3] Northumberland's good relations with the opposition leaders had lost him the King's favour, but he thought he could get parliament to recommend Leicester for the Irish office; A. Collins, *op. cit.*, II, 665, 666.

[4] On Temple, cf. *D.N.B.*, *s.v.* He was born and educated in Ireland and had Irish interests. Early in 1641, contemporaneously with his efforts on Leicester's behalf, he was made Master of the Rolls in Ireland in succession to Strafford's kinsman, Sir Christopher Wandesford.

Henry Hammond, a clergyman firmly attached to the Anglican establishment; cf. on the latter *D.N.B.*, *s.v.*

her Vice-Chamberlain, Henry Jermyn, who enjoyed her full confidence.[1]

Having begun his approach early in January 1641, Temple soon reported that while the King was averse to Leicester, the Queen was well-disposed; Jermyn, however, would do nothing without money.[2] He therefore took the liberty of offering Jermyn £4,000 on his principal's behalf. He justified this on the ground that the Queen's power 'will not long continew in this heigth' and that once the opposition leaders were settled in office, as he expected, they would 'find a way to cutt short Jermyn so as he will not have power to doe . . . that service he now desires.'[3] Leicester was prepared for a bribe, but not so large a one, and on learning the amount, he angrily disavowed it as excessive.[4] Jermyn nevertheless professed himself still willing to continue his efforts and wait for his recompense; but Temple attributed some of the subsequent delay in the business to the earl's reluctance to provide Jermyn with an incentive to make him prompt and stirring.[5]

As the transaction dragged on, Temple's letters alternated between gloom and optimism. At the end of January he wrote that the Queen still could not overcome the King's dislike of Leicester's appointment.[6] In February, Jermyn secured from Strafford in the Tower a letter expressing readiness to resign his office in Leicester's favour. This letter was made known to Charles by the Queen, who now promised to press hard to obtain the settlement of Ireland on the earl.[7] Still no result ensued, and in March Temple thought the Irish appointment would be held up until the outcome of Strafford's trial should become clear. He also reported that he had sounded Sir John Clotworthy, who declared that Leicester was not '[Puritan] enough.'[8] The earl had already tried to correct this impression by writing early in February to Lord Mandeville to express his good will and desire 'to live in the good opinion of the brethren. . . .'[9] But Temple now took the further precaution of sending Leicester's son, Lord Lisle, down to the family residence at Penshurst to remove some incriminating pictures from the chapel, lest the earl's lapse towards ceremonialism become known and arouse the animosity of parliament.[10]

In spite of these actions, Leicester's suit still continued without

---

[1] On Jermyn, cf. *D.N.B.*, *s.v.* Temple did some of his business with Jermyn through Robert Long, Surveyor of the Queen's lands, *H.M.C. De L'Isle and Dudley*, VI, 360, 362–3. [2] *Ibid.*, VI, 362–3. [3] *Ibid.*, VI, 366–7.
[4] *Ibid.*, VI, 369, 375–6. Leicester's replies to Temple are not extant and have to be inferred from Temple's letters.
[5] *Ibid.*, VI, 379, 391. [6] *Ibid.*, VI, 369. [7] *Ibid.*, VI. 379, 382.
[8] *Ibid.*, VI, 288, bracketed word in cipher.
[9] P.R.O. Manchester MSS. 30/15/488.
[10] *H.M.C. De L'Isle and Dudley*, VI, 388–9.

issue, and in April Temple indicated that the managers in the House of Commons felt some suspicion of him as having formerly been a friend of Strafford. He urged the nobleman in the strongest terms to come at once to England, as nothing but his own presence could rectify him.[1] After some hesitation, Leicester accepted this advice and left unannounced for home near the end of the month.

With his departure from Paris, Temple's letters to him ceased so that it becomes impossible to follow the intrigue to its conclusion. His return, however, accomplished its purpose, and on 14 June 1641, a month after Strafford's execution, he was finally created Lord Lieutenant of Ireland. By this time the Queen was thoroughly discredited and under fierce attack for complicity in a plot to use elements of the King's northern army against parliament, while Jermyn, who was also involved, had fled to France. All this was a matter of complete indifference to Leicester, now that he had attained his goal. By his wife the news of his promotion was received with appropriately pious gratitude. 'God has been mercifull to us in a great preportion,' she wrote, 'and I doe beseche him to give us such a thankefulnes as may be acceptable to him.'[2] Unfortunately, Lady Leicester's acknowledgment of divine favours was premature: for the Irish rebellion, breaking out in the following autumn, ruined her husband's prospects, and he never arrived in Ireland to exercise his office.

Leicester's sordid intrigue represented the quest for office in its most unscrupulous form. Meanwhile, however, the momentous question of office for the opposition leaders was also under consideration. The earliest intimation of its possibility came at the end of December 1640 in reports that the 'ruling partie in ... parliament' expected the earl of Bedford to be made Treasurer. A month later rumour added that Pym would become Chancellor of the Exchequer and Lord Saye Master of the Wards. Sir John Temple thought that the 'new men' would take office 'to make up an entire union betweene the Kinge and his people. ...'[3] The first honours bestowed on the party chiefs were nevertheless of a more modest character than the current gossip predicted. At the end of January St. John was named Solicitor, a legal post devoid of political significance, and three weeks later the King created Bedford, Essex, Saye, Mandeville, and Hertford privy councillors. The latter appointments were procured by the marquis of Hamilton as one of his services to his new-found Country

[1] *Ibid.*, VI, 399.

[2] P.R.O. De L'Isle and Dudley MSS., XIII, 214. This passage is omitted from the published calendar.

[3] A. Collins, *op. cit.*, II, 666; *C.S.P.D. 1640–41*, 439; *H.M.C. Cowper*, II, 272; *H.M.C. De L'Isle and Dudley*, VI, 367–8.

allies.[1] Although the King's promotion of these noblemen looked like a concession, it was in reality only a gesture, since the new councillors held a merely honorary position and their advice counted no more after their elevation than before.

In fact, behind the scenes the Queen was endeavouring with the bait of office to win concessions from the parliamentary managers. Prior to Strafford's trial, which began on 22 March, and while it was in progress, she talked secretly with Pym, Bedford, and Saye to offer them advancement in return for Strafford's life.[2] In April the King gave audience to Pym with the same object.[3] But no inducement could move Pym and his collaborators from their determination to pursue Strafford to the death.[4]

It was indeed the King's unhappiness that while he could be driven so far in his adversity as to confer a few offices on the opposition leaders, he never made these grants the foundation of a fresh orientation of his government. Because he gave the shadow and withheld the substance, his appointments effected nothing. In the middle of May Saye was created Master of the Wards in Cottington's stead.[5] Bedford would probably have been named Treasurer if not for his unexpected death about the same time.[6] Bishop Juxon in any case ceased to be Treasurer in May and the office was at once put in commission of which Saye was made a member.[7] In May also the earl of Essex was appointed lord lieutenant of Yorkshire and two

[1] S. R. Gardiner, *History*, IX, 264, 292. On 27 April the earl of Warwick was also made a privy councillor, *H.M.C. Cowper*, II, 280. Hamilton's role in the oppositionists' promotions was noted by the Scotsman, Baillie (*op. cit.*, I, 305) and by Sir John Temple (*H.M.C. De L'Isle and Dudley*, VI, 367).
[2] *H.M.C. Cowper*, II, 272; B. Whitelocke, *op. cit.*, I, 120. In the account she gave Mme. De Motteville, Henrietta Maria said she held interviews with the 'most wicked.' She obviously thought the parliamentary managers were animated solely by personal and factious motives (*Memoires de Mme. De Motteville*, ed. Petitot, Paris, 1824, 98–9).
[3] *C.S.P.D. 1640–41*, 560.
[4] According to the story told by Clarendon, Bedford complained of parliament's passion against Strafford and tried to persuade his friends to concur with the King in sparing the earl's life on condition of his exclusion from all employment and banishment or prison (*Rebellion*, III, 161–2). It is impossible to believe, however, that Bedford could have been divided from Pym and St. John on so crucial a point. Firth expressed the opinion that Clarendon's story contained 'manifest impossibilities.' (*D.N.B.*, *s.v.*, 'Edward Hyde').
[5] S. R. Gardiner, *History*, IX, 374.
[6] That Bedford's appointment was probably intended appears from the detailed memorandum on the King's revenue which was prepared for him in April, *C.S.P.D. 1640–41*, 565–7.
[7] *D.N.B.*, *s.v.*, 'William Juxon'; *H.M.C. Cowper*, II, 284. The treasury commission was established on 18 May with Lord Keeper Littleton as its head, *D.N.B.*, *s.v.*, 'Edward Littleton.'

months later he succeeded the earl of Pembroke as Lord Chamberlain.[1] During the summer of 1641 there were rumours of further appointments, as that Hampden or Holles would become Secretary of State, Saye Treasurer, and Lord Brooke a privy councillor; but nothing came of these.[2]

The sum of places conferred by Charles on the opposition leaders therefore did not amount to very much in political terms. It was further noticeable that Pym and Hampden, in spite of their great authority in the House of Commons, were overlooked. Most important, perhaps, the recipients well understood that they derived their advancement only from their reputation in parliament, not from the King's esteem or desire to receive their advice. Lacking any testimonial of his confidence and intention to rely on them, they resolved, as Clarendon pointed out, 'to keep up principally the greatness of that place to which they thought they owed their greatness.'[3]

The King's refusal to make effective use of a policy of 'bridge appointments'[4] was a great error that brought many subsequent evils upon him. Had he been willing to take the Country leaders unreservedly into his service and cooperate fully with their counsels, the political crisis might have been overcome before it became intractable. No doubt this step would have entailed some painful consequences: disavowal of the measures of the previous years, abandonment of old servants, acceptance of permanent restrictions on his prerogative powers. Yet in the long run he would have served his crown better if he had given his countenance to the parliamentary managers. Once in office as ministers on whose advice the King was seen to depend, Pym and his associates could have closed up the schism in the body politic. Their parliamentary ascendancy would have secured the penurious crown a revenue. Charles, devoid of reliable advice because of the attack on the Court, would have gained the aid of a council composed of some of the ablest and most popular men in the kingdom.

Because the opportunity was let slip to build on office a bridge to draw King and people, Court and Country, together, parliament's attitude inevitably hardened. If the King would not of his own will confide the management of affairs to men parliament trusted, he must be forced to do so: the revolutionary consequence could not be avoided. Thus it soon came about that the parliamentary choice and

---

[1] J. Nalson, *op. cit.*, II, 247; *C.S.P.D. 1641–43*, 59. In July, prior to the King's departure for Scotland, Essex was also made lieutenant-general south of Trent (Clarendon, *Rebellion*, III, 248).
[2] *C.S.P.D. 1641–43*, 53, 63.
[3] *Rebellion*, III, 54.
[4] This excellent phrase is B. H. G. Wormald's, *Clarendon*, Cambridge, 1951.

control of councillors—a new fetter forged to bind the royal power—
began to be considered an indispensable ingredient of any secure
settlement.

4

Str. Trial

On 22 March in Westminster Hall the peers took their place as judges
and Strafford appeared at the bar to answer his accuser, the House
of Commons, for life or death. Here in this grim prosecution the
contending parties of a divided state met face to face in fear and
hatred. If Strafford stood at his life's turning point, the opposition
leaders confronted their severest test. In bringing the Lord Lieutenant
to trial, they intended to pass judgment on a system of government as
well as a man. For them Strafford personified more than any other
the injustice and misrule they meant to end. He was the minister at
York and Dublin who in the long intermission of parliaments trod
down with brutal severity the rights and property of the King's
subjects. He was the dark councillor conspiring to erect an absolutist
tyranny on the ruins of English freedom. The party managers knew
they must affix these stigmata on Strafford and impose exemplary
punishment or suffer an irreparable reverse. Failure would undermine
their sway in parliament and prepare the ground for a reaction. They
could never consider themselves or their cause secure while Strafford
lived. His trial represented a crisis in their personal and political
fortunes alike.[1]

In formulating the grounds of the impeachment, the legally-
minded managers of the prosecution showed how far they could
depart from law in almost complete unconsciousness of where they
were tending. No one professed a profounder reverence for the law
than Pym and his colleagues: the law was not only a religion to them,
but a superstition. With praiseworthy effort they excavated the mines
of precedent to the depths to prepare their case. Yet that case rested
on a principle really revolutionary in its nature. The illegal actions
laid to Strafford's charge were declared to constitute treason in that
they expressed a fixed determination to subvert the fundamental laws
of the realm and therefore the existing form of government as well.
This was the gravamen to which all twenty-eight articles of the impeachment were tied. But to conceive treason thus was to base it on
the norms of revolutionary justice, not on law. Treason hitherto had
been acts against the King's person and authority as defined by

[1] The proceedings in Strafford's trial are printed in J. Rushworth, III. Cf.
also the account by C. V. Wedgwood, *op. cit.*, which contains references to
other sources as well.

statute and by judicial interpretation.[1] Now it was acts against the commonwealth rather than the King, as defined by the House of Commons: including even actions done, as Strafford's were, with the King's command or authorization. On such a view of treason, the King ceased to be the head and protector of the body politic. Not he, but parliament, became the guardian of the law. The supreme crime was not one that struck at the King's person or power, but that undermined the immemorial constitution of the kingdom by attacking its free institutions.[2]

A month before the trial began, Lord Digby, conscious of the legal flaw in the impeachment, urged the House to proceed by bill of attainder instead: this would be the best way, he believed, to remove the scruples the peers might feel as judges that Strafford's offences, however heinous, were not treason.[3] The managers and members rejected his advice. They did not doubt the justice of the accusation, and they desired the solemnity of a judicial condemnation from the upper House that would permit Strafford to be punished without need to have the King's assent, as a bill of attainder required.

But as Digby foresaw, their conception of treason was vulnerable to arguments that Strafford used during his trial with powerful effect. It was hard, the earl pointed out, that a man should be called a traitor for an offence unknown to any statute and now invoked for the first time. His prosecutors could not show a single action of his that was treasonable in itself according to the law. They posed as the law's defenders, but to make out their case, they resorted to an arbitrary construction that placed his treason in the sum and tenor of his deeds rather than in any definite transgression.

The course of Strafford's trial, however, was overshadowed by political exigencies which made even-handed justice impossible. An extremist mood dominated its atmosphere, such as arises when the

---

[1] Cf. G. R. Elton, *The Tudor constitution*, 59–61, for an account of the earlier law of treason.

[2] Precedents for the treason charge against Strafford have been carefully discussed by C. Russell, 'The theory of treason in the trial of Strafford,' *E.H.R.*, LXXX, 314 (1965). Although such precedents existed, the present writer remains convinced that the impeachment involved an appeal to an essentially revolutionary principle. Suggestive observations on the case will also be found in Clayton Roberts, *op. cit.*, ch. 3.

[3] Notestein, *D'Ewes*, 410n., 415–16. Digby was not the only member who saw difficulties. Somewhat earlier, Geoffrey Palmer, one of the lawyers who appeared for the Commons against Strafford, said in reference to the impeachment of Judge Berkeley that the justice's 'offence was not Treason within the 25 Ed. 3 butt whether it was Parliamentary Treason or nott, hee left.' (*ibid.*, 354n.). The phrase is highly significant and illustrates how the parliamentary leaders were asserting a revolutionary doctrine under the guise of law.

opponents of a regime believe that everything they contend for is at stake. Increasingly, a sense of impending violence hovered over the proceedings. Outside parliament the capital's populace stirred with hatred of the Lord Lieutenant. Within, the Commons' members met in daily dread of some intended treachery against them. The Irish army raised by Strafford, of such import in his trial, was still in being: nine thousand men, papists in arms, whom Charles refused to disband despite the House's request.[1] Who knew for what sinister purpose it was reserved? There were fears of Strafford's escape, fears too of intervention from the King's northern army which lay inactive and discontented for want of pay. Suspicions on the latter score were well-founded, for at the beginning of April Pym learned the first details of a plot to march the army to London to overawe the parliament. Its organizers, a group of courtiers and M.P.s holding military commands, undertook their scheme with the King's knowledge and the Queen's encouragement.[2] The party leaders harboured profound distrust of Charles which he did nothing to dissipate. Beset on every side by apprehension, they considered Strafford not only a criminal, but a public enemy whose annihilation was essential to the safety of the state.

Yet with each day the impeachment went on, its outcome seemed more uncertain. The peers did their duty in a judicial spirit, not as partisans, and the Commons' anger rose against them for the latitude —in truth, it was little enough—they allowed Strafford in his defence. The relations between the Houses became badly strained as the trial ran its unprecedented length. The peers, determined to maintain their dignity, would not be the Commons' tool, while the Commons treated their impartiality as an inexcusable indulgence to a traitor.

Strafford behaved under his ordeal with dauntless composure. His mien and reasoning gained palpably upon his judges. The most damaging article was the twenty-third, which charged him with advising the use of the Irish army 'to reduce this kingdom'—a phrase, according to the impeachment, that referred to England. The source of this accusation was the testimony of Secretary Vane, whom the prosecution managers had questioned with other privy councillors in a pre-trial examination. On 5 April Vane was called to give his evidence on Strafford's words in open court. In reply, the earl denied

---

[1] Notestein, *D'Ewes*, 213. On 14 April the King replied to a request for the Irish army's disbanding with what in effect was a denial, *L.J.*, IV, 216. It was not until the summer of 1641 that he ordered the demobilization of this army; cf. Clarendon, *Rebellion*, III, 252 and *infra*, 257.

[2] Cf. S. R. Gardiner, *History*, IX, 308–18, for an account of the army plot. On 6 April, the House of Commons, fearing danger from the northern army, voted that anyone who ordered it to advance without the consent of both Houses should be accounted an enemy of the state, *C.J.*, II, 116.

ever speaking them or proposing such a thing. The Irish Army, he said, was intended against Scotland, not England. When other councillors were called, none, not even the earl of Northumberland, corroborated Vane's recollection on the crucial point. Thus, as Strafford emphasized, there was but the memory of a single witness to the charge. He countered further with a strong appeal to the sensibility of his judges. They were born, he told them, to great employments. If every opinion a councillor delivered were to be raked over by enemies seeking a treasonous intent, then no noble person of fortune could ever be safe in serving the King.

As the day's proceedings ended, it might well seem that the case against Strafford was in heavy trouble. Yet at this juncture, the opposition leaders became divided themselves on the tactics to be pursued. Despite all difficulties, Pym still hoped for a favourable verdict from the Lords. To protect the younger Vane, he had so far kept secret that he himself had seen and copied the notes of the Council meeting where Strafford was accused of giving his treasonable advice. He now resolved to make public this additional evidence in support of Secretary Vane's testimony. On 10 April he and Sir Henry Vane junior told the House of Commons of their transaction the previous October and Pym read from his own copy the passages relating to the charge in the twenty-third article.[1] Other members, however, weary of the obstacles encountered in the case, probably despairing of the result as well, were already planning to abandon the impeachment for another way. Thus, on the same day that Pym made his sensational disclosure, the oppositionist Sir Arthur Haselrig introduced a bill of attainder against Strafford.[2] After some discussion in which most speakers advocated attainder rather than impeachment, the bill received a first reading.[3]

This was the first political difference to arise among the opposition leaders since the beginning of parliament. To drop the impeachment amounted to a declaration of non-confidence in the peers. It would insult them and impair further the unity of the Houses so necessary to the achievement of reform. These considerations did not weigh with the attainder's proponents. They had seen enough of the Commons' spokesmen appearing before the Lords as pleaders. A legislative declaration of treason would put both Houses on an equal footing; moreover, it would not need to be so strictly subject to the rule of law behind which the traitor sheltered.

---

[1] *C.J.*, II, 118.

[2] Clarendon, *Rebellion*, III, 128, gives Haselrig as the proposer, though he confuses the chronology. It is most unlikely that Halserig would have acted without the support of other oppositionists of like mind.

[3] D'Ewes, Journal, B.M. Harl. 164, f. 163b.

Pym ag.

Att

It was thoroughly characteristic of Pym's leadership that he was unwilling to endorse a course of action calculated to offend the Lords if he could possibly avoid it.[1] On the 12th, he spoke against a second reading of the attainder bill, urging the House 'to goe the other way because this is the safer to shew that wee & the Lords are reconciled & not severed. . . .' For the moment the House heeded his words; but on the 14th the bill was read a second time.[2] Next day St. John and others vehemently opposed any further pleading before the Lords as prejudicial to the attainder. Both Pym and Hampden, however, as well as Strode and Sir Walter Erle, declared that the House would dishonour itself if it withdrew from the proceedings. The result of the disagreement was a compromise of sorts on the 16th. The members *Comp.* consented to be present in Westminster Hall as a committee of the whole to hear Strafford's counsel argue the issues of law arising from the evidence; nevertheless, they would not permit the managers of the prosecution to reply. If the Lords desired satisfaction on any point, it should be given in a conference of committees of the two Houses.[3] The peers had to acquiesce in this arrangement. In fact, it signified that notwithstanding Pym's and Hampden's persuasions, the House of Commons had definitely abandoned the impeachment.

The attainder was debated in the Commons from the 14th to the 21st. Once the question of procedure was settled, all the party leaders threw themselves into the effort to pass the bill. Everything possible was done to give it the semblance of a judicial verdict whose form alone was altered. The charges in the impeachment were discussed one-by-one in a committee of the whole House which voted them to have been proved and to constitute high treason. Debate revealed that Strafford had made converts. Some members doubted if his acts were treason or tended to subvert the fundamental laws. Others demanded to know what the fundamental laws were. 'I was much amazed,' recorded the indignant D'Ewes, 'to see soe many . . . speak on . . . Straffords side.'[4] The most conspicuous defector was Lord Digby, a manager of the prosecution, who denounced the attainder, even though he had been the first to suggest it. He professed to hate Strafford's tyranny as much as ever, yet he could not in conscience, he declared, vote a death sentence 'upon a Law made a Posteriori.'[5]

[1] Miss Wedgwood (*op. cit.*, 357–9) takes no account of the fact that Pym did not favour proceeding by attainder and erroneously supposes that the bill was his idea.   [2] D'Ewes, Journal, B.M. Harl. 164, f. 165a; *C.J.*, II, 120.
[3] D'Ewes, Journal, B.M. Harl. 163, ff. 47a–48a; *Notes of the proceedings in the Long Parliament . . . by Sir Ralph Verney*, ed. J. Bruce, *Camden society*, XXXI, 1845, 49–50; *C.J.*, II, 122, *L.J.*, IV, 220.
[4] D'Ewes, Journal, B.M. Harl. 163, f. 45a.
[5] Digby's speech, an eloquent utterance, is printed in J. Nalson, *op. cit.*, II, 157–60.

Selden, a long-standing adherent of the Country, also opposed the
bill on legal grounds.[1] On 21 April, it passed the Commons in a vote
of 204 to 59. Pym was immediately delegated to take it to the Lords.
In spite of the large majority, many members deliberately refrained
from voting: 'a symptom,' said one of these absentees, 'of no great
satisfaction.'[2]

The House of Lords' assent to the attainder was obtained only
with the very greatest difficulty. The majority, deeply annoyed by the
Commons' refusal to go on with the impeachment, showed its
resentment by opposition and delay. Although the peers received the
bill on the 21st with a message stressing its urgency, they did not even
give it a first reading till the 26th. Three days later both Houses met
in Westminster Hall as committees of the whole to hear the Commons
justify the legality of the attainder.[3] It was no accident that St. John,
the principal advocate of the bill, spoke for the lower House on this
occasion. Despite its thick larding of lawyer's citations, his argument
stretched the law to make room for its antithesis, reason of state. In a
bitter passage, he likened Strafford to a beast of prey, no more
entitled to law than foxes or wolves who are killed as they are
found.[4] The iron doctrine of a necessity higher than the law was thus
publicly enunciated in the most solemn way by a leader of the Long
Parliament.[5] It was to reappear in time to haunt its promulgator and
to be repeatedly invoked as a justification for every political overturn
of the next twenty years.

The advance of a revolution steadily destroys the ground on which
moderates try to keep a stand between contending extremes. This was
the lot of the peers, who would probably have asserted their independence by rejecting the bill if not for the intensifying pressures on them.
Two great fears beset them which all moderates feel in revolutionary
times: fear of a 'rightist' reaction, fear of the mutinous people. While
they debated the attainder, the air was thick with rumours predicting
Strafford's escape and a *coup* against parliament.[6] The Country
leaders were convinced that a calamity impended which only Strafford's immediate condemnation could avert. In its agitation, the

[1] *Verney notes*, 54.

[2] *C.J.*, II, 125; Sir John Coke, M.P. for Derbyshire, to his father, *H.M.C.
Cowper*, II, 279, 283.

[3] *L.J.*, IV, 227.   [4] J. Rushworth, III, 702–3.

[5] This was not the first time, however, that an oppositionist used the plea of
necessity. On 20 February Pym invoked the same idea in a debate concerning
the raising of money to pay the Scots. He declared that the Londoners could
be compelled to lend in case of public necessity and that parliament could
assume a legislative power to this end. One parliamentary diarist noted that
Pym's words were more dangerous to liberty and property than Strafford's;
Notestein, *D'Ewes*, 382 and n.

[6] *C.J.*, II, 130; *L.J.*, IV, 230.

House of Commons on 3 May sounded an alarm akin to the famous *la patrie en danger* proclaimed at the end of the next century in revolutionary France. On a proposal from Pym, the members adopted a Protestation vowing to each other before God to defend liberty and religion, the King and the law, against conspiracy and violence.[1] In the next two days the Lords also accepted the Protestation and its circulation was permitted throughout the kingdom. At the same time Pym told the lower House of the plot to disaffect the northern army.[2] His account gave the menacing shapes of the public fever a habitation and a name. Indirectly, it implicated the King and Queen in a conspiracy by some of their own attendants to bring down the army with the aim of intimidating the Houses and liberating Strafford. Under the impression of these developments, the Commons took an extraordinary step. Fearful lest the King dissolve parliament and render it powerless to defend the kingdom, the House ordered a bill drawn up to prohibit the present parliament from being dissolved, adjourned, or prorogued without its own consent. The bill was passed on the 7th and transmitted immediately to the Lords.[3]

No doubt the threat of violence on the King's behalf convinced some of the peers of the necessity to preserve unity with the Commons by passing the attainder. If that were insufficient to persuade them, there was the London populace to reckon with. Thus far the main scene of the revolution had been parliament, but now it poured out on to the streets to incarnate itself for the first time in armed and angry masses. Reports of plots had roused the Londoners to a pitch of excitement and they seethed with impatience at the Lords' recalcitrance. On 3 and 4 May thousands of them carrying swords and staves thronged down to Westminster to demand Strafford's condemnation. Most probably this demonstration was organized by Venn and other citizen oppositionists.[4] Pressing thickly around the arriving noblemen, the crowds clamoured for the earl's execution. Inside the House of Lords the members had to deliberate with the outcries of riotous citizens ringing at the doors.[5]

[1] *C.J.*, II, 132; *Verney notes*, 66–71.
[2] *L.J.*, IV, 234; *C.J.*, II, 134, 135; J. Rushworth, IV, 240. Rushworth dates Pym's report on 3 May, but it was most likely delivered on the 5th; cf. S. R. Gardiner, *History*, IX, 351n. For the army plot, cf. *supra*, 219.
[3] *C.J.*, II, 136, 137.
[4] This may be surmised from Venn's prominence in the presentation of a citizen petition to parliament on 24 April which called for Strafford's punishment. The crowd that assembled on 3 May professed to be seeking an answer to the earlier petition; *C.J.*, II, 125; *L.J.*, IV, 232.
[5] C. H. Firth, *The House of Lords during the civil war*, 86–7; R. Sharpe, *op. cit.*, II, 138–9. The crowds were estimated at five or six to ten thousand. They consisted of shopkeepers, craftsmen, apprentices, and many citizens 'of very good account. . . .'

Before the spectres of reaction and mob violence the peers gave in. On the 4th they intimated to the Commons that they would expedite the attainder if the crowds departed. Four days later, in a House of many absentees, they passed the bill.[1] Because the entries in the Lords' Journal pertaining to the attainder were expunged after the Restoration, the exact vote remains uncertain. Contemporary estimates reckoned it variously as 26 to 19, 35 to 11, and 51 to 9.[2] What is clear is that many noblemen who lacked courage to vote against the attainder still had courage enough not to vote for it. The same day that the upper House condemned Strafford, it also passed the bill against the sitting parliament's dissolution without its own consent.[3] The party leaders in the Commons, aided by the London crowd, thus secured the Lords' assent to the two measures they deemed indispensable to the safety of parliament and their own cause.

Strafford's tragedy was nearly done. Day and night on 8 and 9 May, while threatening multitudes surged around Whitehall, the King in an agony of conscience considered whether to consent to the bill of attainder. Prior to the opening of parliament he had promised to preserve the earl's life and fortune; moreover, honour and gratitude alike bound him to the minister. Yet on the 4th Strafford wrote Charles from the Tower, magnanimously absolving him from all obligation and beseeching the passage of the attainder for the peace of the kingdom.[4] And, in fact, no other course was possible if the King did not wish to provoke civil war.[5] The capital was clearly out of control, even the royal family itself in danger. On the 10th he ratified both Strafford's condemnation and the bill against parliament's dissolution without its own consent. Two days afterward on Tower Hill, before an immense mass of onlookers, the axe prepared by the opposition leaders struck off Strafford's head.

In the momentous confrontation between Strafford and his accusers, it was he rather than they who stood out larger to absorbed contemporaries, as he does still to posterity. He was the greatest tragic figure among the revolution's victims. A man of many flaws, brought low from the summit of power by his arrogance and injustice, he proved himself at the close the equal in spirit of the forces that destroyed him. Yet his triumph in adversity was a purely personal one. Politically, his work was sterile and ended in complete

[1] *L.J.*, IV, 233, 240.

[2] Cf. Clarendon, *Rebellion*, III, 196 and n.; C. Russell, *loc. cit.*, 48–50, prints thirteen propositions respecting Strafford's guilt on which the Lords voted affirmatively on 5, 6, and 7 May.   [3] *L.J.*, IV, 241.

[4] Cf. the letter in J. Rushworth, III, 743–4.

[5] Cf. the description in Clarendon, *Rebellion*, III, 197, 202, of 'The rage and fury of the people.'

failure. 'Holder of one position, wrong for years,' he had no legacy to bequeath a revolutionary generation. The men who interposed their will against King Charles I and his two royal sons could receive nothing from Strafford.

The course of Strafford's trial revealed the explosive potencies beneath the surface of the Country's revolution. The germs of a civil war were already present, only held in check for the time by the King's weakness and capitulation. Raging political passions, the intervention of turbulent crowds, a trend towards violence—all ominous pointers that the conflict might easily assume another form. In an ordeal that tried their mettle to the limit, the parliamentary leaders neither wavered nor compromised. They demonstrated that they were no triflers playing at opposition, but shrewd, determined politicians who would have their way.

Nevertheless, to attain their end they subjected the Houses to such pressure that they strained the unity of their parliamentary support. Of the fifty-nine in the House of Commons who voted against the attainder, only four were on parliament's side fifteen months later when the civil war began.[1] It must be assumed that for most of the others, if not all, Strafford's trial was a milestone in their progress towards the King. In the House of Lords, the earl of Southampton, known previously like his father as an adherent of the popular party, dissociated himself from the attack on Strafford, refused to take the Protestation, and thenceforth supported the King. The oppositionist earl of Hertford followed a similar path.[2]

Despite some defections, however, the alliance around the Country in the House of Commons was still intact. Men like Edward Hyde and Lord Falkland, afterwards prominent Royalists, voted for the attainder.[3] The task of reform was only begun, and if members resented the way the parliamentary leaders drove the House, this feeling was offset by their fears of violence from the King. Before this threat they drew together, judging Strafford's death necessary to parliament's safety.

It was on the King that the proceedings against Strafford bore hardest. Pym's party forced from Charles concessions scarcely compatible with his conception of what it meant to rule. His assent to the

[1] Cf. D. Brunton and D. H. Pennington, *op. cit.*, App. VI. The four Parliamentarians who voted against the attainder were John Alford, Robert Scawen, Selden, and Sir Richard Wynn.

[2] *D.N.B.*, *s.v.*, 'Thomas Wriothesley, fourth earl of Southampton;' Clarendon, *Rebellion*, IV, 294, VI, 385.

[3] Hyde's silence on the matter in both the *Rebellion* and the *Life* gives convincing ground to conclude that he voted for the attainder. Firth also thought he did so; cf. *D.N.B.*, *s.v.* On Falkland's vote, cf. *D.N.B.*, *s.v.*, 'Lucius Cary, second viscount Falkland.'

attainder was extorted, not given. The act against parliament's dissolution without its consent was not the redress of a grievance but an aggression upon a long consecrated attribute of regal authority. Faced with the possibility of a *coup*, the Houses ventured to possess themselves of a power never previously claimed by their predecessors. On the other hand, the party managers could declare with reason that they acted from self-defence. Charles obstinately protected the minister whom they branded traitor, while he showed by his encouragement of the army plot that he was ready to sanction the use of force against parliament. Whatever trust they had in his intentions suffered a profound deterioration. Trust, without which reconciliation was impossible and even constitutional reform ineffectual, was the greatest casualty of Strafford's attainder. The earl had laid his head on the block as a peace-offering, but his death made the split between the King and his opponents wider than ever.

5

The storm that struck the King's regime also broke down the barriers to religious innovation. With the meeting of the Long Parliament the Laudian rule collapsed. Its fall put an end to the further possibility of any effective control over the religious life of the people. All at once the rebellious spiritual forces which crown and church had kept in check for many decades found an outlet. Against the desire of parliament itself, England entered an era of religious experimentation unparalleled in its history.

The one point on which nearly all men agreed in 1640 was that the bishops must be paid out for their delinquencies. On 7 November, the speakers who rose for the first time in the Commons to recite the kingdom's woes dwelt with indignation on episcopal usurpations.[1] Not a voice was raised in the prelates' defence. These men found themselves dangerously isolated because of the Anglo-Catholic predominance of recent years. They were pursued in the next months with stinging obloquy, while all about them a clamour of voices proclaimed the hour of emancipation from clerical tyranny.

Among the Commons' earliest actions was to order the release from prison of Prynne and other victims of Laudian persecution.[2] On 28 November thousands of Londoners greeted Prynne and Burton as they arrived in the capital. It was akin, wrote a Puritan witness of the scene, to 'the returne of the captivity from Babilon.'[3] In December

[1] Cf. the speeches in J. Rushworth, IV, 21–37. Several are dated the 9th, but D'Ewes's *Journal* makes clear that they were delivered on the 7th.
[2] *C.J.*, II, 22, 24.
[3] From the diary of Robert Woodford, steward of Northampton, *H.M.C. Ninth report*, pt. II, 499.

226

the House loosed its thunderbolt against convocation, which had
deeply offended because of the canons and oath enacted earlier that
year.[1] Resolutions of the 15th and 16th stated that convocation had
no power to bind either clergy or laity without assent of parliament
and that the canons of 1640 were contrary to law.[2] This declaration,
founded on a claim expressed unavailingly in former parliaments,
was of far-reaching importance.[3] It extended the principle of lay
representation to ecclesiastical legislation; and it tore a gaping breach
in the crown's religious supremacy, since hitherto canons had been
made with the royal assent alone.[4]

The denunciation of the canons mentioned Laud as 'an Actor in
the great Design of the Subversion of the Laws of the Realm, and of
the Religion,' i.e., of the Calvinist-Protestant foundation of the
national church. This laid the basis for his impeachment on 18
December. The Lords immediately ordered him into custody.[5] He
was to remain in prison till his trial and execution four years later.
This was still not the end of the canons, however. In April 1641 the
lower House was considering a bill to fine the members of convocation of both ecclesiastical provinces, and in August it impeached
thirteen bishops for high crimes and misdemeanours in making
canons and constitutions ecclesiastical.[6]

Beyond the culpability of individual bishops and the presumption
of convocation lay the question of episcopacy itself—whether to try
to reform the institution or to abolish it entirely. When parliament
opened, London Puritans were already busy circulating a petition in
favour of the more radical solution. By mid-November, many names
had been secured, but the promoters, on the advice of friendly
M.P.s, decided to postpone the petition's delivery until the attack
against the bishops had gained momentum.[7] On 11 December it was

[1] Cf. *supra*, 191.
[2] *C.J.*, II, 51, 52; cf. the debate on the powers of convocation in Notestein, *D'Ewes*, 152–7, 160–2.
[3] Cf. J. E. Neale, *Elizabeth I and her parliaments, 1584–1601*, 67, and R. G. Usher, *The reconstruction of the English church*, I, 363–4, II, 116–17. In 1607, the House of Commons passed a bill, subsequently rejected by the Lords, 'to restrain the execution of canons ecclesiastical not confirmed by Parlia-ment'; cf. J. R. Tanner, *Constitutional documents . . . James I*, 230–1.
[4] The House of Lords concurred in these resolutions in June 1641, *L.J.*, IV, 273.
[5] *C.J.*, II, 54.
[6] *Ibid.*, II, 129, 235. J. Rushworth, IV, 235–8, prints some particulars of the bill to fine the members of convocation. It imposed very stiff sums, but seems to have been laid aside.
[7] Edward Bagshawe, the anti-clerical M.P. for Southwark, was shown the petition immediately after his election to the House of Commons. Baillie, one of the Scottish commissioners, saw it in mid-November; B. Hanbury, *op. cit.*, II, 141; R. Baillie, *op. cit.*, I, 274, 275.

brought to the House of Commons. Printed, with a roll of fifteen thousand signatures attached, and accompanied by a crowd of fifteen hundred people, it was presented to the House by the city's oppositionist M.P., Alderman Penington. Only a well-organized group of activists could have planned a demonstration of such size[1].

The petition of the London citizens was the fiercest denunciation of episcopacy to be heard in England since the days of the Disciplinarian movement. Its bold language and comprehensive indictment forced the whole issue of church government squarely into the open. Declaring episcopal rule to be a cause of many evils in both church and state, the petition asked for its abolition 'with all its dependencies, roots and branches. . . .' A long litany of complaints set forth the bishops' misdeeds. They hindered preaching, persecuted good ministers, and suppressed the truth of God; they encouraged their dependents to contemn the nobility and gentry; they propagated Arminian and popish doctrines and fostered the increase of popery and Jesuits; of boundless ambition, they considered their office to be *jure divino* and possessed themselves of temporal dignities; they invaded liberty and property; they drove multitudes of Englishmen to exile; they incited the Scottish war.

Literal truth is not to be found in manifestos. If the Root-and-Branch petition charged the bishops with more than justice allowed, it contained just truth enough to make its accusations plausible. What was significant was that the petitioners accepted these statements. So low had the bishops' reputation fallen that no scandal against them was too extreme to be believed.

The petition displayed one striking omission. Entirely critical in substance, it proposed no alternative to prelacy except the ambiguous formula that 'the government according to God's Word may be . . . placed amongst us.' The means to redress the evils complained of, said the petitioners, they referred 'to the consideration of this Honourable Assembly. . . .'[2]

The Root-and-Branch petition was a blazing star that brought a swarm of satellites in its train: for in the following months petitions on church government came in from all parts of the kingdom—some favouring episcopacy, but many more against. Up and down the counties men promoted subscriptions demanding the hierarchy's overthrow. Members of parliament presented petitions from their constituencies signed by hundreds and thousands.[3] People of every

[1] Notestein, *D'Ewes*, 138.

[2] The Root-and-Branch petition is printed in S. R. Gardiner, *Constitutional documents of the Puritan revolution*, 137–44.

[3] Cf., e.g., the petitions submitted on 25 January 1641 by the county members for Hertford, Bedford, Sussex, Surrey, Cheshire, Warwick,

rank were solicited, from noblemen to poor tenants: a Cheshire petition against the bishops, for instance, professed to be signed by more than twelve thousand freeholders and such like, as well as several lords and many knights, esquires, and gentlemen.[1] In their zeal, the bishops' enemies took the hands of ignorant persons who had no idea of what they were endorsing. Very likely fraudulent signatures were not infrequently included.[2]

Yet even allowing for these practices, such a mass outpouring against the church was beyond example. From every quarter the popular anger snapped and bit. In the press, intemperate pamphleteers assailed the hierarchy without restraint. Bishop Hall indignantly appealed to parliament against their violence. '. . . how many furious persons,' he wrote in January 1641, '. . . have burst forth into slanderous libels, bitter pasquins, railing pamphlets . . . wherein they have endeavoured . . . to wound that sacred government, which . . . derives itself from the times of the blessed Apostles. . . .' Three months later he estimated the number of 'late seditious pamphlets' to equal at least one hundred and forty since the beginning of parliament.[3]

At the same time, encouraged by the Commons' grand committee on religion, which created a sub-committee for scandalous ministers, many parishes were complaining against their own clergymen. On 19 December 1640 the sub-committee was made into a separate committee, and during the first months of its existence it received more than eight hundred petitions.[4] Their drift appears in some from Kentish parishes. Petitioners denounced their ministers for being too ceremonial; for preaching against the Scots and Puritans; for burdening men's consciences with superstitious observances; for ridiculing 'sincerity and forwardness in profession, under the names of faction, schisme, and singularity.'[5] In view of this fusillade of criticism, it was no wonder that the county's M.P., Sir Edward Dering, was told by a

[1] *C.S.P.D. 1640–41*, 529.

[2] This was acknowledged by Lady Brilliana Harley, who thought only 'such hands should be taken as understand it, and will stand to what they have done' (*Letters of Lady Brilliana Harley*, 113–14). On 18 November 1641, the House of Commons referred to a committee the consideration of irregularities in petitions collected for and against episcopacy, *C.J.*, II, 319.

[3] Joseph Hall, *A humble remonstrance to the high court of parliament*, 1641, *Works*, new ed., 12v., Oxford, 1837, X, 275; *A defence of the humble remonstrance*, 1641, *ibid.*, X, 290.

[4] *C.J.*, II, 54; W. Shaw, *A history of the English Church . . . 1640–1660*, 2v., L., 1900, II, 177.

[5] *Proceedings in Kent*, 148–9, 158–60, 182–3, 192–3, 202–4.

Suffolk, Cambridge, Gloucester, Buckingham, and Norfolk, Notestein, *D'Ewes*, 282–3.

friend, '. . . the Monstrous Easye receipt of Petitions att the Standing Committees makes Authoritye declyne. . . .'[1]

So sudden a fall of Laud and his clergy made the Puritan mind almost giddy. Surely God's punishment was manifest in this reversal of fortune! And surely the divine favour that accomplished such a mercy to the faithful had fresh dispensations in store! Events nourished an expectation that grew in the church's antagonists with irresistible force. A mood as much as a hope, often inchoate in its yearning, it nevertheless infused religion with a dynamism that buoyed up the entire revolution and swept it on. Its substance was the presentiment of a mighty spiritual rebirth transfiguring the nation into a new Israel. Those whom it inspired felt themselves to be crusaders in a holy cause, their aim not merely the removal of particular evils but the institution of a perpetual sabbath in the land. This glowing hope, the myth of a pious generation, was already voiced at the beginning of parliament when the Rev. Stephen Marshall preached to the House of Commons on 17 November 1640, the first parliamentary fast day, an occasion the more memorable as being also the anniversary of Queen Elizabeth's accession. His sermon exhorted the members that a religious reformation was their supreme task. They were to 'pluck up every plant that God hath not planted. . . . That it may be said of this Parliament . . . as . . . of Josiah, there was never any like him before . . . nor any after him. . . .'[2] Many Puritans came to share Marshall's expectations as the attack upon episcopacy broadened. In the summer of 1641, Milton, deep in controversy against the bishops, exultantly called his time 'an age of ages wherein God is manifestly come downe among us. . . .' 'O perfect, and accomplish thy glorious acts,' he implored the deity, and

When thou hast settled peace in the Church, and righteous judgment in the Kingdome, then shall all thy Saints addresse their voyces of joy . . . standing on the shoare of that red Sea into which our enemies had almost driven us.[3]

Soon after, Lord Brooke gave utterance in a similar vein:

. . . now . . . the Clouds begin to breake away. . . . Now the Sun againe mounteth up in our Horizon. . . . God hath raised up a more glorious Light among these Northerne Iles. . . . Light dilating, and enlarging it

[1] B.M. Stowe MSS. 184, f. 31.
[2] Stephen Marshall, *A sermon preached before the . . . Commons . . . November 17. 1640*, ed. 1645, 3, 40.
[3] John Milton, *Animadversions upon the remonstrants defence*, 1641, *Prose works*, 5v., Bohn ed., L., n.d., III, 72.

selfe, seemeth to become more pure, more Light, more Glorious; and yet it seemes not to be Noone. The Light, still, will, must, cannot but encrease. . . .[1]

The same enlarging vision was reaffirmed by Stephen Marshall when he preached again to the Commons on the eve of the September 1641 recess. Surveying recent developments, he was filled with gratitude:

This one yeer, this wonderful yeer, wherein God hath done more for us . . . then in fourscore years before, breaking so many yokes, giving such hopes and beginnings of a very Jubilee and Resurrection. . . .[2]

Of course, these utopian perspectives were destined to extinction with the years. Many were the would-be builders of the new Jerusalem; but so various were their designs that they could never reconcile their differences. Time would presently show that the opponents of episcopacy agreed only in what they rejected, not in what they would set in the bishops' place. Lord Brooke, killed early in the civil war, did not live to see the total disappointment of his hopes; but Marshall and Milton were to witness the steady fragmentation of religious life and to hear the babel of discord, as the kingdom fell prey to the bitter quarrels of denominational rivals who smote each other mercilessly in press and pulpit.

Yet this result was only to be expected. For how could the newly liberated thrust for reformation be cribb'd and cabin'd inside the canonical definitions of any orthodoxy? The revolution inaugurated the final age of faith among the English people. For the last time the still living spirit of the Protestant Reformation flared up in a fierce resolve to complete the work begun a century ago. Under its invincible pressure, the whole frame of ecclesiastical order gave way. Puritanism, looking forward to a purified national church backed by the state, discovered, however, that it was no longer in sole possession of the field. Within a few months of the opening of parliament, it was joined by a luxuriant growth of separatist bodies whose presence was henceforth fatal to any claim to supremacy by an exclusive state church.

This proliferation was ultimately due to the inspiration of Puritanism itself. For the separatist was a Puritan offspring, sharing the same imperative need for holiness, the same disillusion with the infirmities of the established church. But while the Puritan adhered steadfastly to the ideal of a national church, the separatist broke away, embodying his vision of a purified church order in the sect and congregation

[1] Lord Brooke, *A discourse opening the nature of . . . episcopacie*, 1641, ed. 1642, 94–5, 116.   [2] Stephen Marshall, *A peace-offering to God*, 1641, 40.

determined to live their independent life free of external constraint.[1] From Elizabeth's time on, there were sporadic secessions of this kind —small, persecuted bodies like those formed in the 1580s by Robert Browne, Henry Barrow, and John Greenwood, ardent men bent on reformation 'without tarrying for any.' What separatism represented in essence was the voluntaristic principle of religious association. It was totally opposed to a territorial church embracing the entire nation by compulsion. It would have no part in parish assemblies which mingled the regenerate and the profane in an ungodly hodge-podge. The only earthly church it recognized was the particular group of believers, called and chosen, who joined freely together for worship and discipline. Its polity was therefore irreconcilable not only with bishops and the crown's religious supremacy, but with any Puritan state-enforced ecclesiastical system as well.

Until 1641 separatism was numerically insignificant and without much influence upon religious life. It existed in such obscure bodies as the fissiparous Barrowist churches in England and Holland; in a few anabaptist sects; in the independent congregation which Henry Jacob founded at London in 1616; and in a few other scattered, some-times ephemeral groups of worshippers, like the conventicles detected at Newington, Surrey in 1632 or at Dover in 1639.[2] Its main centre was London. In 1611 a sectary before the High Commission declared that 'there were yet left six or seven churches in London which had not submitted themselves to the Antichristian rule ... of Lord byshops. ...' Nearly twenty years later, the bishop of Exeter told Laud that he knew of eleven congregations of separatists in the capital who met every Sunday in brew houses.[3]

Unlike the Puritan laity, which included a cross-section of the dominant class, separatism was constituted almost wholly of poor

---

[1] For the development and varieties of separatism prior to 1641, cf. C. Burrage, *op. cit.*, I, and W. K. Jordan, *The development of religious toleration in England*, II, 216–314. The separatists and pre-revolutionary congrega-tionalists have been distinguished on the ground that the latter would have retained some degree of communion between their own and other congrega-tions; cf. C. Burrage, *op. cit.*, I, ch. XII. While this was so, congregationalism belonged fundamentally to the separatist phenomenon, both because it abandoned the national church and because it defined the church as a particular body of believers not subject to any superior jurisdiction. The congregationalism of Massachusetts Bay was non-separatist, since there it established a state church; cf. P. Miller, *op. cit.* This was quite exceptional, however, and was never the case in the mother country. Both W. K. Jordan, *The development of religious toleration in England*, II, 219–20, and G. F. Nuttall, the most perceptive modern historian of congregationalism (cf. *Visible saints*, Oxford, 1957, ch. I) treat it as a manifestation of separatist principles. [2] C. Burrage, *op. cit.*, II, 320–2; *C.S.P.D. 1639–40*, 80–3. [3] R. G. Usher, *The rise and fall of the High Commission*, 208; *C.S.P.D. 1631–33*, 74.

and humble folk. A list of sixty-one separatists of Great Yarmouth in 1628 contained such representative occupations as shoemaker, brewer, tailor, carter, gardener, turner, grocer, and servants. Another list from the same town two years later described the richest separatist as a grocer worth £100 at most and heavily in debt; the rest were all poor and those in prison constrained to live 'on the baskett.'[1] To the same inferior strata belonged a group of Londoners arrested at a conventicle in 1638, who gave their trades as clothworker, lastmaker, weaver, and cordwainer.[2] The leader of the Dover conventicle discovered in 1639 was a London mason temporarily employed on some fortifications near the town. Though illiterate, he was a fluent preacher and expounder of Scripture.[3] In Bristol, the separatist group in the 1630s from which the Broadmead Baptist church later evolved, usually met at the house of a glover or a carpenter. The other members included a grocer, a 'writing-schoolmaster,' a farrier, and a victualler. The grocer's widow, Mrs. Kelley, 'was the first woman in this city of Bristol that practised the truth of the Lord, which was then hated and odious, namely separation.'[4]

During the Laudian repression, which fell with equal severity on every species of dissent, the differences between Puritans and separatists were obscured by their common sufferings and common hatred of the ecclesiastical regime. The archbishop's fall, however, altered the situation. As separatism began boldly to assert itself, its divergences from Puritanism became increasingly evident. Its opponents watched its growth in alarm, but could do nothing to check it. From numerous quarters came accounts of the multiplication of sects. A pamphleteer declared that 'the sectaries ... swell now beyond the reach of names and numbers. ...'[5] Nightly conventicles were reported in Norwich, 'as publickely knowne as the sermons in the day time, & ... much more frequented.'[6] A Kentish clergyman complained to Sir Edward Dering about the increase of separatists in the county and their extreme views:

They would have every particular congregation to be independent. ...

[1] P.R.O. S.P. 16/124/81; C. Burrage, *op. cit.*, II, 309–10.
[2] *Ibid.*, II, 323–4.
[3] *C.S.P.D. 1639–40*, 80–3. That the mason was illiterate appears from the fact that he had to make his mark to the report of his examination by the mayor and jurats.
[4] *The records of a church of Christ meeting in Broadmead, Bristol*, ed. E. B. Underhill, *Hanserd Knollys society*, L., 1847.
[5] *A survey of that foolish, seditious ... libell, the Protestation protested*, 1641, cited in B. Hanbury, *op. cit.*, II, 83.
[6] *The Knyvett letters*, ed. B. Schofield, *Norfolk record society*, XX, 1949, 98–9.

*They would have the votes about every matter of jurisdiction . . . to be
drawne up from the whole body of the church . . . both men and women.
They would have none enter communion but by solemne covenant: Not
y^t made in Baptisme, or renewed in the supper of the Lord, but another
for reformation after their owne way.*[1]

To Sir Robert Harley came a similar address from a Herefordshire
clergyman: 'I can assure yow the best ministers complayne in severall
countryes how much they suffer . . . with that schysme.'[2] D'Ewes
noted in his journal in June 1641 that the freedom of preaching by
'mechanicall men' in London redounded to parliament's dishonour,
as if while suppressing popery 'wee intended to bring in atheisme &
confusion.'[3]

There was a significant meaning to the appearance of this vigorous
outgrowth of sects and separatists. Demanding freedom to pursue
their spiritual purposes unimpeded, it was they who injected the
burning issue of religious toleration into the revolution. Hitherto
Puritanism had stood for liberty and reformation against the bishops.
The separatists now invoked the identical claim against the Puritans.
Already in May 1641, Prynne's fellow martyr, Henry Burton, now
become a separatist advocate, was writing:

*If a state will set up a National Church . . . let not this exclude and bar
out the free use of such Congregations . . . whereof the spiritual
commonwealth of Israel consisteth; over which, Christ, as King,
immediately reigneth. . . . Let not the conscience of God's people be
bound, where Christ hath purchased liberty. . . .*[4]

Here was a position the Puritan mind found deeply disturbing. 'Is it
fitting,' asked the Rev. Thomas Edwards, a *quondam* non-conformist,

*that well meaning Christians should be suffered to . . . make churches,
and . . . choose whom they will for Ministers; as some tailor, felt-
maker, button-maker. . . .*

Such a freedom would subvert both state and clergy. Were toleration
granted,

the most eminent ministers in this kingdom for parts, grace, and

[1] B.M. Stowe MSS. 184, ff. 27–9.
[2] *H.M.C. Portland*, III, 80.
[3] B.M. Harl. 163, f. 276a.
[4] Henry Burton, *The Protestation protested*, 1641, cited in B. Hanbury, *op.
cit.*, II, 75. For producing this pamphlet, its printer was committed by the
House of Commons, *C.J.*, II, 269–70.

labours will have but little assurance of the continuance of their flocks to them. We see within this nine months though there be no Toleration . . . how are [the separatists] increased and multiplied.[1]

Thus as early as 1641, toleration, the parent of all heresy and schism according to its opposers, was becoming a divisive issue amongst the proponents of reformation. Meanwhile, however, of far greater immediate importance was the question of episcopal church government. For two months following the presentation of the Root-and-Branch petition, the Commons postponed consideration of the matter; this was undoubtedly because the party managers wanted to delay a debate that might provoke strong differences.[2] Towards the end of January 1641 the House received an alternative outline of reform from some hundreds of clergy including leading Puritan divines. Known as the Ministers' Petition, this was equally critical of the bishops, but would have retained them in some form while stripping them of all their secular employments and most of their spiritual jurisdiction.[3] The House had then to decide which of the two petitions to refer to a committee. Over this apparently procedural point, which nevertheless reached to the heart of the church question, the first great ecclesiastical debate occurred on 8 and 9 February.[4]

The ensuing speeches on episcopacy presented the earliest signs of potential division within the broad ranks of the Country and on this account deserve close study.[5] The essential point of difference was not one of conscientious attachment to episcopal church government

[1] Thomas Edwards, *Reasons against independent government of particular congregations, as also against . . . toleration*, 1641, cited in B. Hanbury, *op. cit.*, II, 104, 105.

[2] When the Root-and-Branch petition was presented on 11 December, the response to it in the House revealed germs of discord on the subject. Consideration of it was set for the 17th, but nothing was said of it that day; *C.J.*, II, 49; Notestein, *D'Ewes*, 140. On 13 January 1641, Sir Edward Dering told the House that the petition slept and asked leave to awaken it. Debate was accordingly set for 25 January, but it was then put off again; *Proceedings in Kent*, 27; *C.J.*, II, 67, 73.

[3] *C.J.*, II, 72; Notestein, *D'Ewes*, 277. The Ministers' Petition was presented on 23 January. Among its sponsors were the Revs. Cornelius Burges, Stephen Marshall, and Calybute Downing, *ibid.*, 313. The text has not survived, but its substance has been carefully reconstructed by W. Shaw, *op. cit.*, I, 23–6.

[4] D'Ewes noted in his pedantic way that 'divers mistaking the Question fell unto other long and large disputes,' Notestein, *D'Ewes*, 335. The issue of episcopacy, however, could hardly be separated from that of whether to. commit the Root-and-Branch petition, since a favourable vote for the latter also meant that the Commons must at least consider the abolition of bishops. This was just what the petition's opponents wanted to prevent.

[5] The principal speeches are printed in J. Rushworth, IV, 170ff., out of order and sometimes with inaccurate date.

by those favouring its retention. Indeed, the latter vied with the advocates of abolition in the severity of their censure on the prelates and readily admitted the necessity of sharp reform. The crux of disagreement lay elsewhere. In the mass outcry against episcopacy its defenders scented something dangerous in the air: a rising breeze of popular initiative in religion; an attraction to the spirit of innovation; an impulsion towards a church order likely to be less effective than the bishops in buttressing the existing regime of privilege.

Lord Digby, referring to the crowd that brought the London Root-and-Branch petition, declared that it was unfit for a parliament under monarchy to countenance tumultuous assemblies of petitioners: all men of judgment, he added, knew the danger 'when either true, or pretended Stimulation of Conscience hath once given a multitude Agitation.' Sir Benjamin Rudyard asked whether 'a Popular Democratical Government of the Church ... will be ... suitable or acceptable to a Regal Monarchical Government of the State.' Sir John Strangeways stressed the prescriptive right of the bishops as members of the upper House and an estate of the realm. '... if we made a paritie in the church,' he asserted, 'wee must at last come to a paritie in the Commonwealth.' One and all, Lord Falkland and other opponents of the Root-and-Branch petition cautioned against the peril of 'great Mutations in Government,' of the folly of removing, like a scene in a masque, an institution of sixteen hundred years' duration.[1]

It was in their indifference to these considerations that the Root-and-Branch men showed their own political tendency. They disliked episcopacy too much to reckon with the dangers their opponents apprehended. They declined to rebuke the petitioning Londoners who pressed their views on parliament, since citizen action was an instrumentality they could put to use. Oliver Cromwell denied that parity in the church would lead to parity in the commonwealth. Nathaniel Fiennes, the main speaker on the anti-episcopal side, held that monarchy could well stand without bishops. Moreover, in civil government, he pointed out, all jurisdiction under the King was 'Aristocraticall, and placed in many,' as in parliament and county administration. Only in ecclesiastical government did one man in a diocese have full jurisdiction, to the exclusion of others entitled to share the rule of the church. Unless ecclesiastical and civil government were assimilated, he concluded, the former would always try to render the latter as arbitrary and absolute as itself.[2]

Fiennes's speech offered a striking glimpse of a form of ecclesiastical polity very different from episcopacy. At the moment, however,

[1] J. Rushworth, IV, 171, 172, 183, 186; Notestein, *D'Ewes*, 339–40.
[2] J. Rushworth, IV, 174–5, 176, 179; Notestein, *D'Ewes*, 339–40.

the party leaders themselves were not altogether clear how thorough-going a remedy the church required. While not only Fiennes, but Holles as well,[1] advocated abolition, Pym preferred a milder course if possible. Neither his nor Hampden's words in the debate have survived, a pretty sure sign that both said little and avoided inflammatory language. A summary of his remarks reported him to declare that 'he thought it was not the intention of the House to abolish either Episcopacy or the Book of Common Prayer, but to reform both wherein offence was given. . . . And if that could be effected . . . with the concurrence of the King and Lords, they should do a very acceptable work to the people; and such as had not been since the Reformation. . . .'[2] This was wholly in keeping with Pym's methods. He evidently hoped to solve the problem with a minimum of disagreement by measures that would make abolition unnecessary. Nevertheless, if he was more moderate than some of his friends, this was no cause for disagreement. All favoured the commitment of the Root-and-Branch petition both as a threat to hold over the bishops and as an encouragement to their supporters outside parliament. In a test of strength the opposition leaders had the power to work their will. Thus the end of the two-day debate was a vote to commit the Root-and-Branch and all other petitions on church government, with the proviso that the point of episcopacy itself should be reserved for the House's own consideration.[3]

The committee to which the petitions were referred was the 'committee of twenty-four,' a body including Pym and other oppositionist notables. Created on 10 November 1640, various important business had already been delegated to it.[4] It now set about its task with exemplary speed. Adopting the line which Pym had expressed during the church debate as the sense of the House, it reported a series of proposals in March that went unerringly to the core of the laity's grievances against the bishops. These provided that bishops and clergy should be deprived of all secular offices and employments —membership in the House of Lords, the Privy Council, the commission of the peace, the Star Chamber, and other courts. On 1 May a bill to this effect passed the House of Commons without a single negative vote.[5]

[1] D'Ewes noted that Holles spoke against bishops, Notestein, *D'Ewes*, 336.
[2] This was the summary of Edward Bagshawe, M.P. for Southwark; cf. B. Hanbury, *op. cit.*, II, 141–2.
[3] *C.J.*, II, 81. Cf. the notes of opinions in the debate in Notestein, *D'Ewes*, 335–42. Of the associates of the party leaders, Selden alone opposed committing the petition, *ibid.*, 337.
[4] *C.J.*, II, 25. Six members were added to the committee to consider the petitions on church reform, *ibid.*, II, 81.
[5] *Ibid.*, II, 100, 101, 102, 110, 131; D'Ewes, Journal, B.M. Harl. 163, f. 121a.

The Lords' reaction to the bill might have been predicted from the strained relations arising between the Houses as a result of Strafford's trial. Having been coerced into voting the attainder, the upper House was in no mood to alter its constitution at the will of the Commons. The bishops were an estate of the realm: to expel them from parliament, where they had sat for centuries, might be of dangerous consequence in unsettled times.[1] Accordingly, the Lords resolved on 24 May that the bishops should remain in parliament, though offering at the same time to exclude them from other temporal functions. The Commons refused this compromise. On 8 June, after the Houses had failed to reach agreement in a conference, the Lords rejected the bill against the secular employments of the clergy.[2]

Its defeat was a strong check to the policy Pym had prevailed on his more extreme colleagues and followers to adopt. The party managers naturally viewed the episcopate as a solid bloc of votes that would always support the King and oppose measures of church reform coming from the House of Commons. Hence, if bishops were to survive in any form, they must have no power to obstruct, and this required their expulsion from the House of Lords.[3] Hampden himself told Lord Falkland that such was the condition of their continuance.[4]

In the Commons the response to the Lords' resolution of 24 May was to bring into play the threat contained in the Root-and-Branch petition. It took the form of a bill for the abolition of episcopacy drafted by St. John and introduced on the 27th by Sir Edward Dering. Those Puritan intransigents, Cromwell, Haselrig, and the younger Vane, also had a hand in it.[5] As Dering later explained, the measure's purpose 'was to expedite the progresse of another Bill against the secular jurisdiction of the Bishops (at that very time) labouring in the House of Lords. . . .'[6] Having got a first and second reading the same day—the latter by a vote of 139 to 108, it was then referred after acrimonious debate to a committee of the whole House.[7]

[1] Cf. the arguments of Viscount Newark, *Two speeches . . . May 21 . . . 24th, 1641.* [2] *L.J.*, IV, 256, 265, 269.

[3] The Commons' reasons against the bishops' votes stressed their lack of independence and power of obstruction as grounds to expel them from parliament, *C.J.*, II, 167. The same argument was made by Lord Saye in a speech to the House of Lords, W. Cobbett, *Parliamentary history*, 36v., L., 1806–20, II, 810.

[4] Clarendon, *Rebellion*, III, 152.

[5] Clarendon said that St. John drew up the bill, *Rebellion*, III, 156. For the connection with it of Cromwell, Haselrig, and Vane, cf. E. Dering, *A collection of speeches*, 1642, 2.

[6] *Ibid.*, 3.

[7] *C.J.*, II, 159. This reverses the tellers in the vote and must be corrected by D'Ewes, Journal, B.M. Harl. 163, f. 237b.

The Country and the Constitutional Revolution

It did not reappear again until the peers disregarded its warning by their rejection on 8 June of the earlier bill against the secular employments of the clergy.[1] This action was decisive. On the night of the 10th, Pym, Hampden, Sir Robert Harley, and others, meeting privately, concluded that the Root-and-Branch bill against bishops should be moved in the Commons next day. Harley accordingly did so, thereby initiating the debate over episcopacy anew.[2]

The Root-and-Branch bill was considered by the Commons in a committee of the whole from 11 June to early August amidst a welter of other business.[3] The debate brought forth no fresh viewpoints beyond those already voiced the previous February. This time, however, the defenders of episcopacy were seriously embarrassed, since the upper House's action had clouded the prospect of a reform envisaging the bishops' retention. The bill's supporters formed the majority—so much so that in all the votes the House passed relating to it, not a single division occurred. Once more the prudent Rudyard spoke his apprehension at the removal of ancient institutions.[4] The poet, Edmund Waller, who sat for St. Ives, stressed again, as had Lord Digby in February, the danger of abolition to the regime of subordination and privilege.[5] Against such strictures, the younger Vane defended the bill in the accents of the Puritan visionary:

. . . hath not this parliament been called, continued, and preserved . . . by the immediate Finger of God . . . for this work?. . . . Hath not God left [the bishops] to themselves . . . in the evil adminstration of their government, that he might lay them open to us; and lead us . . . by the hand . . . to discern that their rooting up must be our only cure? Let us not then halt any longer between two opinions, but . . . give glory to God, in complying with his Providence. . . .[6]

Now fully committed to the policy of root-and-branch, the Commons' managers secured the enactment of various clauses of the bill against episcopacy in a six-week's procession of votes. These provided that archbishops, bishops, deans and chapters should cease to exist in the church; episcopal lands were to be conveyed to the crown, dean

---

[1] There were several postponements of debate on the Root-and-Branch bill while the Lords' decision was awaited, *C.J.*, II, 159, 165–6.

[2] Cf. *supra*, 202, and *C.J.*, II, 173.

[3] The debates and chronological progress of the bill are described by W. Shaw, *op. cit.*, I, 80–99, who leaves the mistaken impression, however, that its last consideration was on 27 July.

[4] Printed in W. Cobbett, *op. cit.*, II, 833.

[5] E. Waller, *A speech . . . concerning episcopacie*, 1641.

[6] W. Cobbett, *op. cit.*, II, 826.

and chapter lands to feoffees to be devoted to religious uses such as the maintenance of a preaching ministry; all impropriations and advowsons belonging to bishops, deans and chapters, were also to be vested in feoffees. There was thus to be no suspicion that a greedy laity was destroying the bishops in order to gorge itself on ecclesiastical property. Finally, a new scheme of church polity was outlined in a provision that 'such Ecclesiastical Power, as shall be exercised for the Government of the Church, shall be transferred ... into the Hands of Commissioners, to be named in this Act.'[1]

Although various details still lacked to its completion, the Root-and-Branch bill signified the victory of a revolutionary policy in the House of Commons towards the church. Its two notes were the removal of the religious organization from royal control and the subjection of the clergy and ecclesiastical property to parliamentary appointees. Yet even while the members were forging its provisions, the bill was a dead letter. For if the House of Lords had already refused to remove the bishops from parliament, why should it consent to their abolition? Indeed, the peers did not hesitate now to ignore the wishes of the lower House. On 29 July, for instance, they rejected a bill to make the Protestation of the previous May obligatory on all male subjects; they did this to prevent the expulsion from their body of the Catholic noblemen, who could not in conscience have taken the Protestation.[2] Their veto so incensed the lower House that it voted the Protestation, which many in the kingdom had already been subscribing voluntarily, fit to be taken by everyone and then, in a gesture of disrespect for the Lords, ordered its resolution printed.[3] Here was a clear expression of a tendency by the House of Commons towards unilateral action in defiance of the upper House.

In spite of such abrasive incidents, however, the party leaders in the Commons knew that they could not risk a serious quarrel with the Lords just then, for the political situation after Strafford's execution would have made a breach disastrous. The King's behaviour and obscure intentions continued to provoke deep mistrust. Parliament faced the task of disbanding the English and Scottish armies, whose long occupation in the north was becoming an unendurable burden. Moreover, vital measures of constitutional reform were in process which required the cooperation of the two Houses. These circumstances accounted for the otherwise inexplicable fate of the Root-and-Branch bill. Taken up in the Commons for the last time on 3

---

[1] *C.J.*, II, 173, 174, 176, 204, 205.

[2] *L.J.*, IV, 333. The bill, called an act for the security of true religion, passed the Commons on 19 July, *C.J.*, II, 216. The text is in *H.M.C. House of Lords*, XI, *Addenda 1514–1714*, 277–80.

[3] *C.J.*, II, 230.

August, it was then silently laid aside without further consideration.[1] The only possible conclusion is that Pym and his friends had decided the abolition of episcopacy was hopeless and the issue too provocative of disharmony to be pressed further.

Nevertheless, the fundamental antagonism between the Houses persisted. Even after the Root-and-Branch bill was dropped, another outburst of bad feeling occurred at the beginning of September when the two published contradictory orders concerning the performance of divine service. The quarrel was patched up on the eve of the parliamentary recess, as again the need for unity prevailed.[2] It was clear, however, that the pressure coming from the Commons threatened to derange the parity supposed to exist between the Houses. In any disagreement, the peers would insist on their independence and freedom of action; the Commons under its oppositionist leaders would demand the peers' concurrence. If cooperation finally broke down, what solution to the lack of concord could be found? Constitutionally there was none. All that remained was the subjection of the upper to the lower House, in fact if not in law. Should the conflict against the King dissolve the polity to atoms, the Commons' supremacy must fill the void. To such a possible outcome did the differences between the Houses point.

6

During these hectic months of attacks on the Court, alarums and excursions due to fear of plots and violence, controversy over church government, parliament was also busy passing a far-reaching series of reforms through which it hoped to provide future security against misrule. It achieved this in the face of an almost overwhelming mass of business pressing on it from all sides. By force of circumstances the two Houses had become the *de facto* focus of the state. To the Commons in particular all men now looked for redress, for favour, for action of every sort. The members were engulfed in petitions and the host of committees and sub-committees which they had created competed for their time. They had started so many lines of investigation, were occupied with such a variety of matters great and small, that they found their proceedings clogged and disordered by the mountainous weight of their affairs. As early as 8 January 1641 the House took cognizance of the problem, appointing a committee to propose what subjects should be given precedence and what committees

---

[1] *C.J.*, II, 234. On 13 August the House ordered that the bill should be discussed the next Monday, but on that day no mention was made of it, *ibid.*, II, 255.
[2] Cf. the account of this episode in S. R. Gardiner, *History*, X, 14–17.

continued.[1] This committee to lessen committees, as it became known, apparently helped somewhat by its periodic recommendations to accelerate the House's progress. The obstacles it encountered may be gathered from a report made on 28 May by its chairman, Sir John Hotham, who complained that committees for private bills 'tooke away all the companie from committees appointed for publike business soe as the verie committee to lessen committees could not sitt.'[2]

The confused and winding course of parliamentary transactions was unavoidable in view of the breakdown of royal and conciliar authority. Yet notwithstanding, behind the scenes the constructive direction of Pym and his associates was steadily at work. In their role of unofficial leaders they steered parliament as well as they could, preventing the Commons from losing itself in the welter of business and securing the enactment of a broad programme of statutory limitations on royal power. To these Charles was constrained to give his reluctant consent. Politically isolated, lacking influence over the members, responsible for the payment of two armies for which only the Houses could find the money, he had very little choice.

The first constitutional statute was the Triennial Act, passed in February to assure the regularity of parliamentary assemblies. It was introduced by the oppositionist, William Strode, in the form of a bill for annual parliaments. It was then modified in the Commons so as to provide that no longer than three years should elapse between successive parliaments. To secure this end, it established an elaborate procedure for summoning a parliament if the King failed to do so; and it further ordained that the act should be read publicly every year at the assizes and general sessions of the peace.[3]

In May, the act granting the King tonnage and poundage definitely placed this great branch of the revenue under parliament's control. Declaring the King's former exaction of the tax illegal, the preamble stated that impositions on merchandise could only be levied with consent of parliament. The grant was made from 20 May to 15 July, after which it was periodically reenacted for stated intervals. Since Charles I's predecessors had enjoyed tonnage and poundage for life, this was an emphatic assertion of its conditional and parliamentary character.[4]

---

[1] Notestein, *D'Ewes*, 233; *C.J.*, II, 65. The committee made its first report on the 12th, *ibid.*, II, 66–7.

[2] D'Ewes, Journal, B.M. Harl. 163, f. 241a. On 1 June and 15 July Hotham's committee reported long lists of committees to sit and of work to be done, *C.J.*, II, 162, 212.

[3] 16 Car. I, c. 1, *Statutes of the realm*, V, 54ff.; Notestein, *D'Ewes*, 188n., 196.

[4] 16 Car. I, c. 8, *Statutes of the realm*, V, 104–5; for other limited grants of tonnage and poundage, cf. *ibid.*, V, 114–15, 132–3, 135–7.

The Country and the Constitutional Revolution

Two further statutes deeply circumscribing the crown's authority became law on 5 July. The first stripped the King's Council of the greater part of its judicial jurisdiction so largely expanded in the preceding century. It abolished as contrary to law the Court of Star Chamber and most of the other prerogative tribunals of the King— the Council of the North, the Council in the Marches of Wales, the Court of the Duchy of Lancaster, and the Exchequer Court of the County Palatine of Chester. It also prohibited the King and Council from dealing with any matters touching the property of subjects, which were henceforth to be left to the ordinary courts. As a protection for liberty, it provided as well that persons committed by the King or Council should be entitled to *habeas corpus*; the royal prerogative to commit to prison without showing legal cause, which the judges had upheld in 1627 in the case arising from the forced loan, was thus annulled.[1]

The destruction of the Star Chamber took away one of the most formidable engines of the King's power. The second statute did the same by abolishing the Court of High Commission, the chief agency through which the crown enforced its religious supremacy. It further prohibited any persons exercising ecclesiastical jurisdiction from inflicting fines, prison, or corporal punishment on the King's subjects.[2] Although this legislation left the other church courts still intact, it so denuded them of coercive sanctions that they could neither suppress religious dissent nor even police the moral offences belonging to their charge.

In early August a last group of statutes were passed of only slightly less importance in controlling the royal prerogative. The first annulled the judgment in the ship-money case and pronounced the tax illegal.[3] Another regulated the abuses of the Stannary Courts in their jurisdiction over the tin miners and landlords in Devon and Cornwall.[4] A third, directed to recent exactions under the forest laws, voided all proceedings of the forest courts since 1624 and decreed that no ground should be accounted royal forest unless a court had been held there sixty years before Charles I's accession.[5] A fourth set rigorous limits to the crown's right of purveyance for the royal

---

[1] 16 Car. I, c. 10, *Statutes of the realm*, V, 110–12. St. John proposed that the Star Chamber officials who lost their place should be compensated, and both Houses appointed committees to consider the matter; D'Ewes, Journal, B.M. Harl. 163, f. 382b; *L.J.*, IV, 302, 312; *C.J.*, II, 231.
[2] 16 Car. I, c. 11, *Statutes of the realm*, V, 112–13. The act repealed section VIII of the Elizabethan statute of supremacy, 1 Eliz. c. 1, from which the Court of High Commission derived its legal being.
[3] 16 Car. I, c. 14, *Statutes of the realm*, V, 116–17.
[4] 16 Car. I, c. 15, *ibid.*, V, 117–18.
[5] 16 Car. I, c. 16, *ibid.*, V, 119–20.

household in order to stop extortions which had long been a matter of complaint.[1] The last, dealing with knighthood fines, extinguished still another royal right by ordaining that no person could be compelled to take knighthood or be fined for not doing so.[2]

There are political-constitutional revolutions as well as social ones: for no other description can be given to great alterations of governmental power, even if they should leave the existing order of society untouched. Such was the significance of the statutes of 1641. The effect of a crisis that paralysed the regime, a reflection of invincible public and parliamentary demand, attained under the leadership of an organized opposition, the work of parliament's first ten months meant a historic reversal of the relation between monarchy and subject. It took from the crown almost all the powers which enabled the Tudor rulers to exercise their unrivalled mastery. Although the King would continue to govern, his administration would be subject to new and unprecedented restrictions. No longer could he manifest his authority through administrative-judicial tribunals outside the reach of ordinary law. The being of parliament was placed beyond his will, and henceforth he must consult it regularly. He could acquire no important revenue independent of parliament's consent. The statutes amputated the strongest limbs of the prerogative. They instituted safeguards to protect liberty and property against further invasions by arbitrary power.

Yet great as were these reforms, they no longer sufficed to restore the breakdown in the state. Measures that would have been received with jubilation six months previously were ineffectual by the summer of 1641 to provide a ground of settlement. Even as they were in passage, the Country leaders were pressing fresh demands on the King, searching for guarantees to allay their fears, and gradually gathering the threads of governmental authority into parliament's hands.

It was the King who bore the main responsibility for this. Devoid of any consistent policy, Charles confronted the overturnings of the strife-ridden time in irresolution and uncertainty. Though strong in the consciousness of his regality, he was weak in political judgment and will. He was incapable either of firmly withstanding his opponents or of gaining them to him by genuine compliance. He understood no better than the Queen the true nature of the movement that beat against his throne and lacked all sympathetic sensitivity to the general sense of grievance that called it forth. Unable to identify himself with the feeling of his subjects, he regarded his assent to parliament's bills as something done of his grace for the benefit of

[1] 16 Car. I, c. 19, *ibid.*, V, 129–30.
[2] 16 Car. I, c. 20, *ibid.*, V, 131.

others rather than for himself and his kingdom's welfare.[1] The tribulations through which he was passing aggravated his indecision, suggesting to him the most contradictory lines of action. He oscillated between political concessions and the resort to intrigues which might gain him the upper hand over the parliamentary managers. His indulgence in the latter, however, lost him all the credit of the former.

In view of the bitter recollections of the past and the inflamed emotions of the present, it was essential for Charles to show irrefutably that he accepted the constitutional revolution. Yet with the blundering that marked the whole course of his political life, he signally failed to do so. From Strafford's trial on, a continuing crisis of confidence in his intentions undermined all feeling of security as to the permanence of his concessions. This lack of confidence arose from fear that he would try to use violence to restore his position. Pym's revelation of the army plot on 5 May and the ensuing parliamentary investigation of the conspiracy provided convincing reason for distrust.[2] It was doubtless true that Charles's sponsorship of the plot was only half-hearted and that the project of using the army against parliament had little chance of success. But Pym and his friends could not be expected to take that view. If they magnified the dangers of the conspiracy and exploited it to the full against the King, it was because in their circumstances they were bound to place the worst construction on his conduct. They were not impartial judges, but oppositionist politicians who had staked life and fortune against the regime.[3]

[1] Charles's speech of assent to the Triennial Bill on 16 February was a characteristic display of his want of political judgment and inability to identify himself with public and parliamentary sentiment. '. . . never Bill passed here . . . of more Favour to the Subjects, than this is. . . . I mention this, to shew unto you . . . the Obligation . . . that you have to me for it. . . . Hitherto you have gone on in that which concerns your selves to amend, and not in those things that nearly concerns the Strength of this Kingdom, neither for the State, nor my own particular. . . . You have taken the Government all in Pieces, and I may say it is almost off the Hinges. . . . this is the greatest Expression of Trust, that before you do anything for me, I do put such a confidence in you.' (J. Rushworth, IV, 188, misdated the 15th).

[2] Cf. *supra*, 219. Committees of both Houses authorized to proceed in secrecy were established to investigate the army plot. The committee of the Commons contained the leading oppositionists; cf. S. R. Gardiner, *History*, IX, 358. For the committee's reports, cf. *Verney notes*, 86–91, 93, 94–9, 110–11.

[3] Clarendon's account of the army plot, like that of Charles's modern apologist, E. Wingfield-Stratford, is vitiated by the assumption that Pym cynically exploited the plot without believing in it. This represents a complete failure to understand how the men in Pym's position regarded the King's activities. There can be no question that they believed in the conspiracy and that Charles's behaviour, and the Queen's even more, justified

Moreover, in the early summer of 1641 Charles aroused new suspicions when he announced that he intended to go to Scotland to attend personally at the approaching meeting of the Scottish parliament. This news caused much disquiet. It was generally thought the King had some hidden purpose in his visit. The peace treaty in negotiation at London between England and Scotland was not yet completed and the armies in the north remained undisbanded. The opposition leaders felt real alarm when they thought of the King passing amid the troops. They further suspected that he hoped to find support in Scotland. This, indeed, appeared to be Charles's idea. He evidently believed that if he granted the demands of the Scottish parliament and distributed liberal favours to the principal Covenanter politicians, he would secure their aid against his English opponents.[1]

The King, in fact, was doing nothing less than play at counter-revolution. No political basis for counter-revolution, however, existed as yet in England. The courtiers who devised the army plot were frivolous *coup d'étatists* representing no one. As for Scotland, it was pure delusion for Charles to imagine that any blandishments of his would induce the leaders of the rebellion to desert their English allies. Both kingdoms still preserved too fresh a memory of their recent grievances. The main effect of Charles's obscure behaviour, therefore, was to aggravate distrust. It repelled moderates and solidified the alliance around the opposition party leaders, while at the same time exciting fears that did not let the revolution come to rest.

To counter the threat of violence and conspiracy, the Houses entered on a quest for guarantees that entailed the assumption of extraordinary powers far exceeding the provisions of the reforming legislation they had in hand. It was the prevalence of this state of mind which resulted in the most innovative statute of the period at the time of the army plot's disclosure. The act against dissolving parliament without its own consent was not the redress of a grievance, but an aggressive encroachment on the sphere of the executive belonging to the crown. Nor was this the only such action on which the Houses ventured because of the public emergency. They also invaded the King's military authority, presuming to issue orders on

---

[1] The despatches of the Venetian ambassador contain numerous allusions to the King's hopes and secret purposes in going to Scotland and the adverse reaction in parliament to his prospective journey, *C.S.P.V. 1640–42*, 153, 171, 177, 193, 205–6.

---

their mistrust; cf. Clarendon, *Rebellion*, III, 218–26; E. Wingfield-Stratford, *King Charles and King Pym*, L., 1949, 114–16.

their own initiative for the movement of ships and trained bands and for the care of castles, arms, and munitions.[1]

These steps were the first in a sequence of usurpations by which parliament in self-defence gradually possessed itself of the powers of governing. On 24 June the Commons adopted ten propositions brought in by Pym, which were presented to the King after obtaining the peers' concurrence.[2] Several of them dealt with immediate issues of security: Charles was asked to bar Catholics from his attendance, to disband the English army, and to delay his Scottish journey until all military forces were demobilized. The other propositions were of wider import, since they cut at the very sinews of the crown's autonomy. The King was 'to take into his Council, and for Managing of the great affairs of the Kingdom, such Officers, and Counsellors, as his People and Parliament may have just Cause to confide in.' A parliamentary superintendence was required as well over the persons attending the Queen and royal children and over the lords lieutenants and their deputies in the counties.[3]

These audacious proposals went far beyond any earlier demands: in effect, they were a claim that the appointment and conduct of ministers should be subject to parliamentary approval. Novel as this was, it suggested itself as an obvious solution to the problem of confidence. Since Charles did not resort voluntarily to a policy of 'bridge appointments,' parliament endeavoured to impose it on him. The King, however, would not submit to be thus bound. Although he consented to disband the army and to defer his journey until 10 August,[4] he made clear that he would not surrender the power to choose his councillors at his discretion.[5] Thus the political impasse remained unresolved.

With Charles's departure impending, parliament hastened to conclude the peace with Scotland. The treaty was formally enacted on 10 August, the day he set out for the north.[6] It conceded the substance of the demands for which the Scots had risen in rebellion, and also provided that parliament should give them a 'friendly assistance' of £300,000 in compensation for their losses.[7] To raise this great sum,

---

[1] *C.J.*, II, 135, 138.
[2] *Ibid.*, II, 184–5; *L.J.*, IV, 285–7, 290. Pym reported these demands as spokesman for the committee of seven appointed to investigate the army plot.
[3] *C.J.*, II, 185.
[4] *C.J.*, II, 188, 192.
[5] Charles's message to the Houses on 12 July concerning the removal of evil councillors was in effect a denial of their demand to control the appointment of ministers; *L.J.*, IV, 310–11.
[6] *C.J.*, II, 249; *L.J.*, IV, 356.
[7] The treaty is printed in T. Rymer, *Foedera*, XX, 448ff.

of which £80,000 was payable at once, an act had already been passed imposing a poll tax in England.[1] Because the provisions for disbanding the armies could not be fully implemented till the end of the month, the Houses petitioned the King on the 7th to stay two weeks longer.[2] This he refused, for his hopes were now strongly fixed on Scotland. On 14 August he arrived in Edinburgh, having passed through the troops of both nations without incident.

Charles's Scottish journey, in adding to the prevailing insecurity, only invited fresh encroachments on his authority. Besides the anxieties which his activities in Scotland caused at Westminster, his departure left England without any effective government. Into this governmental vacuum parliament stepped. Persuaded of the necessity to provide for the kingdom's safety amidst the dangers arising from the King's absence, the Houses invested themselves with a virtual regency. On 14 August the Commons established a committee of defence to confer with the Lords about military preparedness. To this committee were given powers amounting to a supervision over the entire military and naval establishment of the realm.[3] The Houses further adopted a recommendation from Pym to send commissioners of their own to Scotland to preserve good relations between the two kingdoms.[4] These representatives were little less than parliamentary ambassadors. Six members, all trusted oppositionists, were selected, four from the Commons, two from the Lords. Two of the commissioners were Hampden and Fiennes.[5] Their assignment was proof of the extreme importance the party managers attached to the mission. While their instructions preserved the language of deference to the King, the commissioners' real task was to watch over Charles's doings and counter every move he made. Besides supervising the execution of the peace treaty, which had still to receive the Scottish parliament's ratification, they were to clear the proceedings of the English parliament from any false reports that might raise misunderstandings. They were also to inform the two Houses of all occurrences concerning the welfare of the kingdom.[6]

In deciding how to legalize the appointment and duties of the commissioners, parliament took a long stride towards the acquisition

---

[1] The poll tax was passed on 3 July; *L.J.*, IV, 298.

[2] *C.J.*, II, 241; *L.J.*, IV, 347.

[3] *C.J.*, II, 257, 258.

[4] *Ibid.*, II, 249.

[5] The others were Sir William Armyne, Sir Philip Stapleton, Lord Howard of Escrick, and the earl of Bedford.

[6] The commissioners' names and instructions are in *C.J.*, II, 265–6. Two earlier versions of these instructions show the commissioners' task even more clearly, *ibid.*, II, 259, 262–3. Pym probably helped draft them, since he reported them to the House.

of a legislative power independent of the crown. The earliest hint of
this momentous development occurred on 28 July during a debate in
the Commons concerning the effects of the King's approaching
departure. D'Ewes, whose deep but uncritical antiquarian erudition
was much respected, told the members that 'the two howses may in
the absence of the King make ordinances which are of the greatest
authoritie next Acts of Parliament. . . .'[1] He reverted to the idea
again on 16 August in connection with the procedure for authorizing
the commissioners. Some members had urged that the Houses could
order the Lord Keeper to grant them a commission under the great
seal, but this he denied. He proposed an ordinance instead: 'such
ordinances of Parliament,' he declared, 'have been of great authoritie
in former times. . . .'[2] His suggestion was accepted. Four days later
the Lords and Commons passed their first ordinance appointing their
commissioners to Scotland.[3]

Four more ordinances followed before the recess, including one to
confiscate arms belonging to recusants and another prohibiting the
King's subjects from taking military service with any foreign prince
or state.[4] Doubtless the Houses did not think that in enacting ordinances they were legislating. Yet at the least they were issuing
commands in solemn form about matters hitherto reserved exclusively
to the crown. These were already incipient acts of sovereignty very
near to actual legislation. When the lower House was considering the
ordinance to disarm recusants, Selden strongly criticized it, contending that 'it made new lawes, which it could not. . . .' To this, Henry
Marten, M.P. for Berkshire, one of the very few oppositionists
unconcerned about constitutional proprieties, rejoined that 'hee
wished wee might account such an Ordinance to be of equall force
and power with an Act of Parliament. . . .' D'Ewes, however, rebuked
this opinion as contrary to law and Magna Charta. An ordinance, he
said, 'was merely to binde the members of either howse, but never . . .
of any force to take from the free subiects of England their goods
against their will. . . .'; accordingly, if the proposed ordinance
contained anything contrary to common or statute law, let it be
removed. The House, nevertheless, passed the ordinance as it stood,
and so did the Lords after a committee of the Commons stated that
it was 'especiallie drawne in pursuit of those Lawes alreadie established. . . .'[5]

With the parliamentary recess upon them, the party leaders took

[1] D'Ewes, Journal, B.M. Harl. 163, f. 416b.
[2] *Ibid.*, B.M. Harl. 164, ff. 32b–33a.
[3] *C.J.*, II, 265–6.
[4] *Ibid.*, II, 277, 285.
[5] D'Ewes, Journal, B.M. Harl. 164, ff. 70a, 79a.

steps to continue their direction of affairs while the Houses were dispersed. They did not mean to leave the helm even for a few short weeks at so critical a time. Accordingly, parliament on 9 September created a committee beyond all precedent: a body of forty-seven commoners and seventeen peers to manage business during the recess. This committee was the germ of an executive government and the prototype of the machinery by which the Houses afterwards ruled during the civil war. Its instructions gave it broad authority. It was to supervise the demobilization of the English army then in progress, and to issue directions in the Houses' name to parliament's commissioners in Scotland. This latter power was opposed by several members as too great, but St. John defended it and the Commons passed it without alteration.[1] On information of riots or tumults, the committee was authorized to communicate with sheriffs, J.P.s, and other officials. It could also summon any persons, writings, or records. Its membership included the principal opposition men. Foremost was Pym, who reported on the committee's work to parliament when it reconvened in October. Amongst the rest were St. John, Clotworthy, Strode, the younger Vane, and a goodly number of other party adherents. The representatives of the House of Lords had not the same strong political colouring, though among them were Essex, Warwick, and Mandeville. This was no matter, however, since the committee's work was carried on mainly by Pym and some others of the lower House.[2]

When parliament recessed, the leaders of the Country still retained their ascendancy from the previous November. The political situation, in contrast, had altered considerably. Although a great programme of reforms had been enacted, distrust had nullified its benefits. The King and his opponents stood further from collaboration than ever. Charles refused to confer ministerial power on Pym and his friends, while they in their quest for security were insisting on arrangements he was scarcely likely to grant. Without acknowledging it to themselves or the world, the Houses were groping towards sovereignty. This was the purport of their recent demands and actions, little as they were disposed to recognize the fact. Ten months of unresolved conflict had brought the monarchical constitution to the verge of disintegration, and the opposition party was already forging the elements of a parliamentary governing power to replace the decaying supremacy of the crown.

[1] *Ibid.*, B.M. Harl. 164, ff. 107b–108a.
[2] *C.J.*, II, 288–9, prints the committee's instructions and the names of the members from the Commons; the list of Lords' representatives is in *L.J.*, IV, 395.

The End of the Country

Parliament's six-week recess gave only a momentary respite from the strife of the spring and summer. Nothing but a wisdom far beyond the King's capacity could have found the remedy to moderate the distempers of his sickly, tottering state. Boundless suspicion of Charles on the one side, his keen resentment of his opponents' incessant pressures on the other, were driving the polity towards dissolution.

The Country leaders employed the adjournment to prepare their strategy against the approaching reassembly of the Houses. Pym, who presided at the twice-weekly meetings of the committee appointed for the recess, was then lodging in Chelsea at Lord Mandeville's house.[1] There, as well as at the London residence of the earl of Northumberland and in Kensington at the earl of Holland's house, he and his party associates conferred.[2] Hampden, on mission in Scotland, was kept informed of their counsels through the letters that passed between the committee for the recess in London and parliament's commissioners in Edinburgh.[3]

The King himself was still in Scotland when parliament resumed on 20 October. For English political news, he depended heavily on the letters sent him by Edward Nicholas, Clerk of the Privy Council. Nicholas, a prudent and faithful servant, was not even a member of the Commons, but he did his best to learn all he could of the party managers' plans.[4] He soon warned Charles that they had fresh

---

[1] The committee for the recess met on Tuesdays and Saturdays in the Exchequer chamber at Westminster. D'Ewes, attending on 12 October, noted Pym in the chair. When Pym afterwards reported to the Commons on the committee's work, he referred to 'my Lodgings at Chelsea. . . .', *C.J.*, II, 288, 290; Coates, *D'Ewes*, 1–2.

[2] Edward Nicholas to the King, J. Evelyn, *Diary*, ed. W. Bray, 4v., L., 1908, IV, 76; *L.J.*, IV, 490; *C.S.P.V. 1640–42*, 215; Clarendon, *Rebellion*, IV, 14.

[3] Nicholas to the King, J. Evelyn, *op. cit.*, IV, 83, and cf. the references to the correspondence between the committee in London and the commissioners in Scotland in Pym's report on 20 October, *C.J.*, II, 289, 290.

[4] On Nicholas, cf. *D.N.B.*, *s.v.* In December 1641 he was knighted and created Secretary of State. J. Forster was mistaken in calling him a member of parliament, *The debates on the Grand Remonstrance*, L., 1860, 285.

demands in store and repeatedly urged the necessity of the King's presence in the capital. '... when ye awe of the Parliament is upon all in generall,' he wrote, '... it is almost impossible for ... your servauntes, to know what to doe or advise. ...'[1] Charles, intent on his Scottish schemes, paid no heed to this advice. He made scarcely any preparations for the reconvening of the Houses, nor did he return to London till the end of November. About the only step he took in anticipation of the end of the recess was that the Queen, who remained in England at Oatlands, told Nicholas to write the bishops and some friendly peers asking their presence when parliament reopened.[2]

The King went to Scotland in the fatuous belief that if he complied with the Covenanters he would gain their aid against his English opponents. His communications to Nicholas hinted obscurely at some design against the parliamentary leaders at Westminster. 'I believe before all be done that they will not have such great cause of joy,' he wrote, and '... some day they may repent of their severitie. ...'[3] From his expressions, it appears pretty plain that he was already revolving in his mind a way to settle scores with the opposition chiefs, which was to issue three months later in his attempt at a counter-revolutionary *coup.*

To the Scots Charles yielded much. He not only ratified the establishment of a Presbyterian state church, but made the even greater surrender of consenting to an act that subjected the royal choice of councillors in Scotland to the advice and approval of the Scottish parliament.[4] This legislation was naturally taken note of in England, and Nicholas shortly informed him that Pym would demand the same power for the English parliament. Charles replied, however, that he would never grant it.[5]

In spite of his concessions, the King failed completely of his purpose in Scotland. The dominant Covenanter party, with the earl of Argyle as its foremost figure, had no motive to separate itself from its English allies, nor did its leaders trust the King to any degree. Doubtless their discussions with the commissioners sent by the English parliament only confirmed their scepticism. Thus they extracted all they could from Charles, while giving nothing in return. The true position was sombrely described by a courtier who accompanied him to Edinburgh: '... his majesties businesses runn in the

---

[1] J. Evelyn, *op. cit.,* IV, 74, 77, 85, 89, 117.

[2] *Ibid.,* IV, 84–5.

[3] *Ibid.,* IV, 78, 79, 81.

[4] This act was passed on 17 September 1641. The first appointment under its provisions was ratified in another act of 15 November, *Acts of the parliament of Scotland,* V, 354–5, 388–9.

[5] J. Evelyn, *op. cit.,* IV, 74, 76, 80.

wonted channell, suttle designes of gaineing the popular opinion and weake executions for the uphowlding of monarkie.'[1] In mid-October, the disclosure of a plot against Argyle inflicted a severe blow on the King's anyway tenuous credit. Probably he possessed only a limited knowledge of the Incident, as the plot was named; but he was aware that some enterprise was afoot and was indiscreet enough to receive Scotsmen into his presence who hated Argyle's ascendancy. Moreover, one of his intimate personal servants was involved. This was sufficient to incite the worst suspicions which the King's enemies both at Edinburgh and London used to his utmost disadvantage.[2] He spent the rest of his sojourn as the helpless witness of his own weakness. The result of all his plans was that Scotland attained a virtual independence of the crown's authority, while the Covenanters consolidated their hold on the kingdom.

Meanwhile, the Country leaders at Westminster had revealed their aims on the reopening of parliament. They had two capital objectives: first, the passage of the previously defeated measure to expel the bishops from the House of Lords; second, the securing of a parliamentary supervision over the selection of the King's ministers. On 21 October, the second day of the sitting, the oppositionist Sir Gilbert Gerrard introduced a new bill against the secular employments of the clergy. It passed on the 23rd against little resistance and was transmitted to the Lords.[3] There it stuck, obstructed, like the former bill, by the dislike of the upper House for any proposal altering its constitution.[4] Thus once more the two Houses were stalemated over a critical issue.

The demand for a parliamentary approval of ministers was presented on the 28th, a revival of Pym's proposition of the previous June.[5] The oppositionist, Robert Goodwin, moved that parliament must have power to remove evil councillors, else 'all wee had done this Parliament would come to nothing, and wee should never be free from danger.' Strode seconded him—in a mostly premeditated speech, noted D'Ewes—contending that 'all wee had done this

---

[1] Endymion Porter to Nicholas, *The Nicholas papers*, ed. G. F. Warner, *Camden society*, XL, 1886, 40.

[2] On the Incident, cf. S. R. Gardiner, *History*, X, 23–7, and further details in C. V. Wedgwood, *The King's peace*, 459–66. The news of the Incident was immediately reported in England, where it did the King much harm, as Nicholas pointed out, J. Evelyn, *op. cit.*, IV, 92–3, 95, 97. A letter from parliament's commissioners to Pym about the Incident was read to the House of Commons on the day it reassembled and was also published as a pamphlet, Coates, *D'Ewes*, 8–9; *C.J.*, II, 290; *L.J.*, IV, 396.

[3] Coates, *D'Ewes*, 21, 30–2; *C.J.*, II, 293; Clarendon, *Rebellion*, IV, 94n.

[4] *L.J.*, IV, 402, 408. On 28 October the Lords deferred consideration of the bill to 10 November, on which day it failed to appear.

[5] Cf. *supra*, 247.

Parliament was nothing unless wee had a negative voice in the placing of the great officers of the King. . . .'[1] This time the proposal met with less agreement than in June. After the passions of the last months, there was evidently a sense of surfeit in the House and a reluctance to be driven at the pace prevailing before the recess. Some members held the legislation already passed to be safeguard enough. Others cautioned strongly against trenching on the King's hereditary rights. Edward Hyde, now in the process of withdrawing his support from the Country, declared that parliament 'had done verie much for the good of the subject' and that 'all particulars weere in a good condition if wee could but preserve them as they weere.' These reactions were danger signals inside the Country alliance. Nevertheless, the opposition leaders continued to sway the House, and the debate resulted in the appointment of a committee to draft a petition to the King about evil counsellors.[2]

It was at this juncture, with parliament not yet sitting two weeks, that the calculations of both the party managers and the King became entwined with an event as incalculable as an eruption or an earthquake, one whose occurrence none foresaw or even imagined, and which helped fan the English political conflict to a consuming heat. On Monday, 1 November, came the report from across the Irish sea of the outbreak of a rebellion in Ireland. The Houses learned the news in an agitated letter from the Irish Privy Council at Dublin. It related that the Catholics of Ulster had risen in a carefully-laid conspiracy, seizing stores of arms and numerous strong places. A rebel attempt to capture Dublin Castle had narrowly failed. The Irish Council feared the spread of the revolt throughout the kingdom. If so, Ireland would be

in the greatest Danger that ever it underwent, considering our Want of Men, Money, and Arms, to enable us to encounter so great Multitudes as they can make . . . against us; the rather because we have pregnant Cause to [think] that the Combination hath taken Force by the incitement of Jesuits, Priests, and Friars.[3]

Thus, the contagion of resistance had now seized the third of the King's realms. That it burst forth with such stupefying surprise was merely proof of English blindness to the true condition of Ireland.[4]

[1] Coates, *D'Ewes*, 44, 45.   [2] *Ibid.*, 45–7; *C.J.*, II, 297.

[3] The letter was written to the earl of Leicester, Strafford's successor as Lord Lieutenant, who transmitted it to parliament, *L.J.*, IV, 413–14, *C.J.*, II, 300. The King received the news in Edinburgh on 27 October, *The Nicholas papers*, I, 58–9.

[4] All contemporary accounts stressed the unexpectedness of the rebellion; cf. R. Dunlop, *Ireland under the Commonwealth*, 2v., Manchester, 1913, I,

A subject country, its indigenous population of native Irish and old English ruled by men of alien religion and nationality, Ireland suffered injustices beside which the grievances of England and Scotland paled. During the Anglo-Spanish war of Elizabeth's reign, the Ulster Irish revolted and were only suppressed after a long and terrible struggle. In the sequel, the royal government pursued the policy of promoting large-scale immigration in order to strengthen the English Protestant ascendancy. Since the time of James I it had expropriated vast tracts of Irish land as plantations for alien settlement. The natives were driven off to make way for English and Scotch colonists. Few Irishmen had secure possession of their soil. They lay exposed to the threat of confiscation from the crown on the pretext of defective title, and to the rapacity of English officials who exploited their position unscrupulously for their own enrichment. Catholicism, the religion of the majority of inhabitants, was illegal; and while the King and Strafford had permitted the Irish Catholics some practical toleration for their worship, the prohibition against their faith could be enforced at any time. Under Strafford, Ireland attained a measure of economic prosperity. Moreover, to promote the superior interests of the crown, the Lord Lieutenant also set a curb on the English adventurers and land-jobbers in the Irish administration. But his rigorous rule weighed heavier than that of all his predecessors. His autocratic methods and twisting of the law, his invasion of any right hindering his purpose, his confiscatory measures on the royal behalf, and his arrogant intolerance of the slightest opposition, incurred the mortal hatred of all Ireland, Irish and English alike.

Yet it was not the long-standing oppression in land and religion that precipitated the rebellion, but, rather, two more immediate causes. The first was the diffusion in 1641 of the insubordinate spirit of England and Scotland, which unsettled Ireland as well. The second was Irish Catholic fear of the Long Parliament.

Strafford's impeachment formed an epoch in Irish history. When the members gathered at Westminster in November 1640, the parliament of Ireland was also in session at Dublin. Immediately it joined the attack on the Lord Lieutenant in a remonstrance against his misgovernment which the Irish House of Commons passed on 7 November.[1] From that point on, the force of English authority declined. The

[1] *C.J. Ireland*, I, 279–82. The opposition in the Irish parliament is described by A. Clarke, *The old English in Ireland 1625–42*, Ithaca, 1966, ch. VIII.

cxii. The letter of the Irish Privy Council expressed the English wonderment (*L.J.*, IV, 413), as did the history written by Sir John Temple, *The Irish rebellion*, 1646, 16–17. Temple, Leicester's confidant, was in Ireland when the revolt began.

example of English agitation over grievances was not lost upon the Irish. Once free of Strafford's domination, the parliament of Ireland could not be stopped from giving voice to Irish sentiments and claims. These claims, which formed the constitutional background to the rebellion, were incompatible with English supremacy. In effect, they would have placed Ireland in a position similar to Scotland's by ending all subjection to England and retaining only the tie of a common crown. The Irish parliament petitioned the King for 'the taking away of ... national distinctions heretofore in policy observed. ...' It asserted that Ireland should not be bound by legislation enacted in England. It further condemned as a grievance Poynings' Law, the famous Irish statute of 1494, which secured English control over the parliament of Ireland by ordaining that all projected legislation in the latter must first receive the approval of the King's Council in England.[1] Pursuant to these views, the Irish House of Commons solemnly resolved on 26 July 1641 that

The subjects of this his Majesty's Kingdom are a free People, and to be governed only according to the common law of England, and statutes made and established in this Kingdom of Ireland, and according to the lawful customs used in the same.[2]

The irony of the Irish parliament's case was that it appealed to constitutional principles much like those the English opposition proclaimed against Charles I. But the Country leaders at Westminster were completely incapable of sympathy with Irish grievances. Reformers and revolutionaries in the context of English politics, towards Catholic Ireland they were the reverse. They could only see Ireland through the eyes of the Protestant minority of officials and landowners who formed the most durable element of the English ascendancy. They took for granted its dependent status under both the crown and the parliament of England.[3] They could not feel the

[1] *C.S.P. Ireland 1633–47*, 286, 321.

[2] *C.J. Ireland*, I, 501. This resolution was preceded by queries which the Irish Commons adopted in February to assert Irish legislative independence and the liberty of the subject. The queries were defended in June by Patrick Darcy, an M.P., in a speech to the Irish House of Lords; cf. P. Darcy, *An argument*, Dublin, ed. 1746. The resemblance of Darcy's *Argument* and Irish constitutional claims to those of the American colonists before the American revolution has been stressed by C. H. McIlwain, *The American revolution: a constitutional interpretation*, N.Y., 1923, ch. II; cf. also T. Coonan, *The Irish Catholic confederacy and the Puritan revolution*, N.Y., 1954, ch. I and 74–5, 78–9.

[3] In his speech on Strafford's attainder, St. John said, 'The Parliaments of England do bind in Ireland, if Ireland be particularly mentioned. ...'; J. Rushworth, III, 698.

slightest doubt that English security required the subjection of the Irish Catholics, otherwise Ireland, Spain's ally in Elizabeth's time, would become 'a backe doore to open a conquest to England. . . .'[1]

To Irish Catholicism, accordingly, the dominance of the Country-Puritan opposition in the Long Parliament appeared a serious danger. As early as February 1641 the Catholic gentlemen who organized the rebellion began their first hidden preparations, already convinced that the English parliament intended the total extirpation of their religion. Why then, they considered, should not the Irish imitate the Scots, who had secured themselves by a resort to arms?[2]

Indirectly, the King himself abetted their design. He was well aware of Irish fears and in the summer of 1641 he secretly negotiated with some of the chief Irish Catholics to whom he held out the hope of toleration in return for their assistance; possibly he even suggested that they should seize Dublin Castle on his behalf with the help of elements of the Irish army raised by Strafford which was at last being disbanded. If Charles ever made this extremely risky proposal, nothing came of it. Yet by treating with the Irish he unconsciously encouraged the coming revolt and assured that its supporters would not think their purpose displeasing to him.[3] Meanwhile, as the English House of Commons resounded daily with calls for the suppression of papists and the execution of priests, apprehension in Ireland increased. The Irish Catholics became convinced that if ever in control, Pym's party would bind them with iron fetters. Neither their lives, lands, nor religion would be safe, and they would be forced to conform to the Protestant state church on pain of death or banishment. Rumours ran among them too that the Scottish Covenanters would send an army to cut out Catholicism with the sword.

[1] A consideration which members of the English Commons stressed when discussing the danger of Strafford's undisbanded Irish army, Notestein, *D'Ewes*, 229–30.

[2] Cf. Roger More's arguments to persuade Lord Maguire to join the rebellion, *The relation of Lord Maguire. A contemporary history of affairs in Ireland from 1641 to 1652*, ed. J. T. Gilbert, 3v., Dublin, 1879–80, I, pt. 2, 501–2.

[3] Cf. Gardiner's observations and review of the evidence on the King's negotiations with the Irish Catholics, *History*, X, 7n. It is impossible to determine exactly what Charles proposed. The story told in 1650 by the earl of Antrim (printed in R. Cox, *Hibernia Anglicana*, 1689, pt. 2, 206–8) that he suggested the seizure of Dublin Castle must be taken with caution because of its improbabilities, which are mentioned by Cox. Probably the King did not instigate the rebellion, but he did play with the possibility of getting Irish help. This was another of the dangerously imprudent expedients to which he resorted in the hope of restoring his position, and it led to consequences far beyond his anticipations; cf. also R. Dunlop, *op. cit.*, I, cxvi–cxvii.

Herein lay the imperative motive for resistance.[1] Conceiving themselves and their faith to be in direst peril, the despairing Irish rose. The outbreak began in Ulster, where the greatest land confiscations had occurred, and rapidly spread. Before the year's end it was joined by the old English, the lords and gentry of the Pale, the one component of Irish society which, though Catholic, had been strongly disposed to the support of English rule in the earlier century. English power found itself facing the avenging fury of a subject population bent on driving it from Ireland.

The Irish rebellion produced a profound shock in England. Nothing had prepared Englishmen to understand such a defection. Under the stress of the worsening news from beyond the Irish sea in the fall and winter of 1641, the Protestant-Puritan mind became as if possessed with wrath and fear. Its ever-lurking dread of Catholicism, often stirred during the past year, leaped into panic-stricken life. Retaining vivid imaginations of the lurid history of Jesuit treason and the Gunpowder conspiracy, it discovered its most nightmarish fantasies come true in Ireland. It had no conception of the real causes of the revolt, which it attributed exclusively to the malignity of priests. Prone to accept the wildest exaggerations, it was certain that the brutalities and slaughter committed by the Irish meant no less than a deliberate plot to massacre every Protestant man, woman, and child in Ireland.[2]

Before the spectre of treachery and terror in Ireland, the crisis of confidence in England assumed a graver urgency. The opposition leaders knew nothing of the King's communications to the Irish, yet harboured the darkest suspicions. They were persuaded that without secret support from Charles or the Queen the rebellion could not have occurred.[3] This seemed the likelier because only the King could

---

[1] The manifestos of the Irish rebels were unanimous in mentioning fear of the English parliament as a principal cause of the revolt; cf. *The generall remonstrance . . . of the Catholikes of Ireland*, 1641, *The humble remonstrance of the northern Catholicks of Ireland, now in arms*, 1642, and *The true demands of the rebells in Ireland*, 1642. The belief in the coming of a Covenanter army is referred to in *The relation of Lord Maguire, loc. cit.* and by Richard Bellings, the contemporary Irish historian of the Catholic confederation, *History of the Irish confederation*, ed. J. T. Gilbert, 7v., Dublin, 1882–91, I, 15–17.

[2] Lecky's remarks concerning Irish actions may still be accepted; W. E. H. Lecky, *A history of England in the eighteenth century*, 8v., N.Y., ed. 1879, II, 140–85. Although the Irish were guilty of many atrocities, there was no massacre, and contemporary English opinion exaggerated to fantastic proportions the number of victims; cf. also R. Dunlop, *op. cit.*, I, cxvii–cxviii.

[3] Cf. the Venetian ambassador's remarks concerning the party leaders' suspicions, *C.S.P.V. 1640–42*, 241.

take any advantage by it. From the outset the Irish rebels proclaimed themselves his faithful subjects and linked their grievances with his in severe condemnation of the English parliament. Their first manifesto, issued immediately after the start of the revolt, declared that the 'Puritan faction' and the English Commons had invaded the King's prerogative, usurped his authority, and left him naught 'but the bare name of a King.'[1] Believing Charles disposed to tolerate their religion, and having identified their cause with his, the Irish Catholics might easily decide to lend him armed assistance; or, on the other hand, since an army would have to be raised to suppress the rebellion, such a force, if the King controlled it, might well provide him with a sword to destroy his opponents in England.

In these ominous alternatives lay Ireland's tragedy: the Irish struggle could never fuse with the revolution in England nor obtain its help, but, on the contrary, must imperil its very survival. Once more Pym and his friends foresaw the prospect of violence and counter-revolution. To provide against it was now their overriding concern. More than ever they were resolved to render the King harmless by removing all influences but their own from his government; that the sole way to safety lay in investing parliament with the approval and oversight of councillors and thus of every aspect of executive policy.

Within a few days of the news of the rebellion the House of Commons saw the party managers' determination. On 5 November, Pym, reporting for a newly established committee on Irish affairs,[2] submitted a number of propositions which the parliamentary commissioners in Scotland were instructed to present to the King. After these had been accepted, he stood up to offer the members a further motion on his own account. All their efforts to preserve Ireland would be in vain, he said, so long as the King listened to evil counsels. Let them accordingly make a declaration that

howsoever wee had ingaged our selves for the assistance of Ireland yet unles the King would remove his evill counsellors and take such councellors as might be approved by Parliament wee should account our selves absolved from this ingagement.[3]

This proposal to coerce the King with conditions was too audacious to prevail at once, and a debate arose which continued till

[1] *The generall remonstrance of the Catholikes of Ireland*, 1641. This must have appeared in London early in November, judging from what looks like a reference to it in the Venetian ambassador's despatch of the 15th, *C.S.P.V. 1640–42*, 240.
[2] A standing committee for Irish affairs was appointed by the House on 2 November, *C.J.*, II, 302.   [3] Coates, *D'Ewes*, 94.

evening without result. Next day Pym submitted his motion again, now as a recommendation of the committee for Irish affairs.[1] Another debate ensued in which once more the House reached no conclusion.[2] Members felt themselves caught in the crux they were to experience repeatedly as the conflict with the crown completed its parliamentary phase and moved ineluctably towards civil war. They had to choose between the rights which the law and precedent gave the King and the severe and novel course dictated by the dangerous situation. On Monday, the 8th, Pym's motion reappeared slightly altered in language but its substance unimpaired. It now professed fidelity and obedience to Charles, yet told him plainly that the Irish rebellion and all the kingdom's evils for many years proceeded from the practices of persons near him in authority and counsel. Unless he would employ such ministers as parliament approved, the declaration continued,

we shall be forced, by Discharge of the Trust which we owe to the State, and to those whom we represent, to resolve upon some such Way of defending Ireland . . . as may concur to the securing of ourselves from . . . mischievous Counsels and Designs . . . and to commend those Aids and Contributions which this great Necessity shall require, to the Custody and Disposing of such Persons of Honour and Fidelity as we have Cause to confide in.[3]

Under the form of a petitionary request this proposal was nearly an ultimatum. It dissociated the King from the state, asserted the paramountcy of parliament's trust to those it represented, and threatened in the name of that trust to assume for parliament a power of command and appointment that did not belong to it. Again a long debate occurred during which the House finally became ready to decide. In the division that followed, Pym's revolutionary article passed by 151 to 110.[4]

This vote disclosed a sizeable movement away from the leadership of the Commons managers. In their search for guarantees, they were demanding endorsement of a step which many members thought both inflammatory and legally impermissible. Even D'Ewes, a pretty

---

[1] Whereas on 5 November Pym introduced his motion from the floor following the report of the committee for Irish affairs, on the 6th he reported it to the House as one of the committee's recommendations. The committee had met the previous evening, and it looks as if Pym had prevailed on it to adopt his proposal; Coates, *D'Ewes*, 94, 95, 99.

[2] *C.J.*, II, 307; Coates, *D'Ewes*, 102.

[3] The text of the declaration appears as nos. 7 and 8 in the instructions to be sent to the parliamentary commissioners in Scotland for presentation to the King, *L.J.*, IV, 431.　　　　[4] *C.J.*, II, 307; Coates, *D'Ewes*, 104, 105.

consistent Country adherent, voted negatively, noting in his journal in the cipher reserved for his most private thoughts that the motion was 'of verie dangerous consequence.'[1] The House of Lords also refused to adopt the declaration, despite Pym's vigorous speech at a joint committee urging its necessity. As a consequence the lower House notified the peers that it would send the King the declaration in its own name if they would not concur.[2]

It was evident that parliament's former unanimity in accomplishing the constitutional reforms of previous months could not stand the strain of the opposition leaders' pressure. Beset by reservations, doubts, and downright disaffection, the great Country alliance was cracking. The King, taking note of this, felt his position stronger and was thus less likely to grant additional concessions. He now counted on the obstructiveness of the House of Lords, which he did his best to encourage in his messages from Scotland.[3] Heartened that voices in the Commons championed his right to choose his own councillors, he conveyed his appreciation through Nicholas to Edward Hyde, Lord Falkland, and other upholders of his prerogative.[4] He let it be known that he would never consent to any alteration in the doctrine and government of the church; and several days after the House of Commons passed its second bill against the secular employments of the clergy he created five new bishops. He could not have expressed more bluntly his determination to preserve the episcopal votes in the House of Lords.[5]

There can be little doubt that Pym and his friends fully realized in the first days of November that their hard line was generating resistance in the Commons. They could hardly have failed to consider that they might face a reaction against their sway if they persisted in their demands. Even in the obscurity shrouding their deliberations, it may be surmised that they reviewed the situation and concluded not to recede from their position. Having come so far in their fight, they refused to leave what they had won at the hazard of an unfettered royal executive whose every action they distrusted. Nor could they for a moment overlook Ireland, now the heart of all their anxieties, where any projected counter-revolution possessed a potential military base. The opposition leaders must have agreed to intensify their pressure on the King, resolved to gain their object despite the risk that some of their parliamentary support might split away.

---

[1] *Ibid.*, 105.   [2] *L.J.*, IV, 431–2, 438; *C.J.*, II, 315.

[3] J. Evelyn, *op. cit.*, IV, 95.

[4] *Ibid.*, IV, 101. The other M.P.s mentioned by the King were Sir John Strangeways, Edmund Waller, and Sir Robert Holborne.

[5] *Ibid.*, IV, 88, 102. The King told Nicholas that the new bishops should take their seats in parliament as soon as possible.

The means for their purpose lay at hand in a proposal first advanced twelve months before in their consultations at the beginning of the Long Parliament. At that time they intended, according to Mandeville's memoirs, that the House of Commons, 'as the Grand Inquest of the Kingdome' should draw up a remonstrance to the King 'as . . . a faithfull and lively representation . . . of the deplorable Estate of his Kingdome. . . .'; and on 10 November 1640, after motions by St. John and Lord Digby, the House actually named a committee to this end.[1] Although the committee met a few times, the party managers apparently decided to hold the remonstrance in reserve: hence it made no appearance prior to the September recess.[2] But soon after parliament's reassembling they judged the moment had come to bring it forward.[3] On 8 November 1641, accordingly, at the close of the same afternoon that saw the passage of Pym's revolutionary motion on Ireland, the remonstrance was read the first time in the House,[4] to become at once an issue over which the members quarrelled with rising passion until the final vote of 22 November, when the Country alliance broke to pieces.

The *Remonstrance of the state of the kingdom*—later known as the Grand Remonstrance—was the manifesto and apologia alike of the House of Commons and of its steersmen, the leaders of the Country opposition.[5] It was at once an unsparing indictment of the King's reign, a vindication of all parliament had done or yet hoped to do against 'the multiplied evils and corruptions of fifteen years,' and an appeal addressed to the entire political nation. Of its authorship nothing definite can be ascertained. Though containing some expressions that seemingly came straight from Pym,[6] the whole was most

[1] B.M. Add. 15, 567, f. 30v.; Notestein, *D'Ewes*, 27 and n., 532; *C.J.*, II, 25.
[2] The House several times ordered the committee on the remonstrance to meet and bring in its work, e.g., on 28 April, 23 July, and 3 August, *C.J.*, II, 130, 221, 234.
[3] On 25 October the House ordered the remonstrance to be brought in on the 29th, and on the latter day the matter was moved again by the Buckinghamshire oppositionist, Arthur Goodwin. Discussion on it would have begun on 1 November, in accord with Goodwin's motion, had not the news of the Irish rebellion resulted in a week's postponement; *C.J.*, II, 294, 298; Coates, *D'Ewes*, 51.
[4] Coates, *D'Ewes*, 106; cf. also W. Coates, 'Some observations on the "Grand Remonstrance",' *Journal of modern history*, IV, 1 (1932).
[5] I cite the *Remonstrance* from S. R. Gardiner, *Constitutional documents of the Puritan revolution*, 205ff., which reprints the text contained in J. Rushworth, IV, 438ff. Rushworth's and Gardiner's version unaccountably omits almost the entire last page, amounting to nineteen and one-half lines, of the *Remonstrance* as printed in 1641 by authority of the House of Commons. Their numbering of the paragraphs is not always in accord and has no authority in the published text of 1641, but I retain it to facilitate reference.
[6] Cf. the close resemblances between the passage beginning, 'As in all

probably the common product of the small committee of opposition-ist notables to which the House had last given the *Remonstrance* in charge.[1] In spite of its inevitable propagandist tone and aim, it mirrored with perfect fidelity the political mind of the men who long had stood in the front of resistance to Charles's rule and who now felt impelled to circumscribe the King still further in order to preserve the kingdom from impending ruin.

Traced out at length in the *Remonstrance*'s pages was a grim picture of England's decline: the subversion of its liberty and law, the destruction of its traditional principles of government, and the corruption of the power and purity of its Protestant religion. All this it ascribed to a pernicious design of papists abetted by the Arminian clergy and royal councillors who had made the King the unwitting accessory of their nefarious ends. The *Remonstrance* claimed credit for the great benefits conferred by parliament's recent legislation, but pointed out that the forces of treason continued active and powerful. Still infusing their influence upon the King, incessantly plotting against parliament, it was they who kindled the Irish rebellion. Possessed of a party of bishops and Catholic peers in the House of Lords, they misrepresented the House of Commons' purposes as to religion and obstructed its efforts to secure further reforms. Having thus utterly discredited the King's reliability, the *Remonstrance* concluded on the one point its framers deemed needful beyond all others. It called on Charles to entrust the business of government only to persons who had parliament's confidence; in the event of refusal, it threatened to deny him further financial support and to deal with Ireland without his concurrence. It need scarcely be said that the attribution of the woes of Charles's reign to the plots of Romanists and crypto-Romanists was grotesquely mistaken. Yet such indeed was the genuine belief of the *Remonstrance*'s authors. These narrow-minded patriots, prejudiced Puritans, rigid defenders of parliament's

---

[1] The House on 3 August named a much smaller committee to bring in the remonstrance than had been appointed the past November. Except for Sir John Culpepper, all its members were opposition party intimates: Pym, Vane jr., St. John, Strode, Erle, Hampden, and Nathaniel Fiennes. From the task set this committee, it appears that two remonstrances were then contemplated, one on the state of the kingdom, the other on the church; *C.J.*, II, 234, 253. In the draft submitted after the recess, the two were consolidated in a single declaration. Neither Hampden nor Fiennes could have worked on the text presented on 8 November, since they were both still in Scotland, I assume. Hampden, however, was back in the House of Commons by 11 November, Coates, *D'Ewes*, 118. On 16 November, Lord Falkland was added to the committee, *C.J.*, II, 317.

compounded bodies,' (S. R. Gardiner, *Constitutional documents*, 207) and Pym's speech on evil counsellors to the Lords' committee on 13 November 1641, *L.J.*, IV, 431–2.

liberty—in short, these arch-conservative revolutionists—could make no other sense of events, so great was the incomprehension between them and the King. He had done nothing to win their personal sympathy or affection. He neither understood their point of view nor appeared concerned to set their fears at rest. The doubleness of his conduct baffled and dismayed them: the army plot, his Scottish intrigues, the Irish rebellion, all seemed to them aspects of the same ramifying pattern. In the *Remonstrance*, respect for convention restrained them from attacking the King personally or mentioning the Queen. If not for this, they would have laid every grievance at Charles's own door and openly branded Henrietta Maria as the agent-in-chief of the Catholic conspiracy. Instead, they left the matter in the Aesopian obscurity of allusions to the favour and influence enjoyed by Catholics, the non-enforcement of the penal laws, and the reception of a pope's nuncio in England.[1] But precisely because the King himself was untouchable, it seemed all the more essential to the *Remonstrance*'s partisans that parliament for its own security should control the choice of ministers.

On seven separate days between 9 and 22 November the House of Commons discussed the declaration, deleting and amending clauses here and there, but leaving its harsh, strong-spoken substance intact.[2] Finally, on the 22nd the draft was brought in for its fate to be determined, and its proponents and adversaries strove fiercely against each other from noon till after midnight, bent on winning a majority for their side. The members sustained the lengthy debate without intermission, altogether intent on the great argument waged in their midst. The light of the short afternoon faded and candles were brought, as one speaker followed another in the gloom. At last the question was put whether the declaration should pass. The ayes left the chamber, and the party managers learned that they had carried their *Remonstrance* by the slender majority of eleven in a vote of 159 to 148.[3] The division over, one of their side called for the *Remonstrance* to be printed.[4] Immediately a new quarrel flared up despite the late hour. Members who had attacked the declaration all day hotly demanded the right to enter a protest against any vote to print, and were as hotly denied. In the anger of the moment some drew swords: an intimation of the time not many months off when all

---

[1] Para. 88–94.

[2] The *Remonstrance* was before the Commons on the 9th, 10th, 15th, 16th, 19th, 20th, and 22nd; cf. *C.J.*, II, 309, 311, 316, 317, 320, 321.

[3] Coates, *D'Ewes*, 183–7; *C.J.*, II, 322. D'Ewes left the House about 4 p.m. but later entered into his journal an account of what occurred in his absence. Prof. Coates's editorial notes from other sources piece out D'Ewes's record.

[4] Moved by George Peard, M.P. for Barnstaple, Coates, *D'Ewes*, 186.

England must perforce take up the sword in a controversy become irremediable. A fortunate intervention from Hampden, however, helped to quiet the House's temper. It was then agreed to put aside the question of printing for that night, and as the clock struck two the weary members departed.[1]

A comparison of the vote on the *Remonstrance* with the one taken in April on Strafford's attainder makes instantly clear how far the balance in the House of Commons had shifted. Each of these votes represented a supreme commitment by the opposition leaders from which there was no backing away; on both they staked their parliamentary ascendancy. They had won Strafford's condemnation by 204 to 59; seven months later, in a better-attended House and in one of the biggest dvisions recorded during the Long Parliament, they obtained their victory by a mere majority of eleven.[2] Thus, while they still controlled the Commons, still possessed its sanction for their policy, the alliance they commanded was broken. A whole detachment of their support had abandoned them in a decisive trial of political opinion and parliamentary strength. This large minority now formed the basis of a new party favourable to the King. Rejecting Pym's appeal and warnings, it had made a sharp turn to the right, thereby promising the end of the King's long isolation. Most of its members undoubtedly regretted the breach in the House. They had acted with reluctance, and would still momentarily hesitate and halt on their way. Nevertheless, from the moment of the vote on the *Remonstrance*, their course was set towards the Royalism newly born of the Country alliance's disruption.[3]

---

[1] *Ibid.*, 186–7; *C.J.*, II, 322. Hampden had returned from Scotland by the 11th; cf. *supra*, 263.

[2] In proportion to the number of divisions in the House of Commons, the occasions on which 300 or more members voted was very small. There were only three between the beginning of parliament and the September 1641 recess. These were divisions totalling 325, 320, and 361 on 9 February, 5 March, and 9 June 1641, *C.J.*, II, 81, 97, 171. Two divisions on 22 November preceding the actual vote on the *Remonstrance* numbered 310 and 308, *ibid.*, II, 322. Thus, the vote of 307 on the *Remonstrance* was exceptionally large and shows that members were not deterred by the length of the debate from staying to the end. The last division of the night, however, on a point of detail gave a total of 225, indicating that over 80 members had now left. Some remarks on attendance will be found in V. Snow, 'Attendance trends and absenteeism in the Long Parliament,' *Huntington Library quarterly*, XVIII, 3 (1955).

[3] In the absence of division lists at this period, only a few of the members voting against the *Remonstrance* can be identified by name. It is highly probable, nevertheless, that the minority opposed to the *Remonstrance* comprised pretty nearly the same members who are known to have joined the King subsequently. There were, however, a few exceptions. Sir John Coke, M.P. for Derbyshire, wrote about the vote, 'If you sett Pimme Hollis

What caused this development? The King was still what he had been, and in view of the Irish rebellion the crisis of confidence in his intentions more acute, not less. What, then, prompted the defection that split the Country and led to the gradual emergence from its divided parts of a new political alignment in parliament and the kingdom?

It was the judgment of Gardiner, followed therein by nearly all subsequent historians of the subject since,[1] that the reason lay in the religious differences within the Country. According to him, '... if no other question had been at issue than the political one, there would have been no permanent division of parties, and no Civil War. ...'[2] Gardiner held that those who turned towards Charles were the favourers of episcopacy reacting not against the political line of the Commons managers but against their determination to remodel the church. Hence Pym's motion of 8 November and the sequel of the *Remonstrance* resulted in the

final conversion of the Episcopalian party into a Royalist party. ... To baffle the Puritans had now become its chief object. For the sake of that it was ready to trust the King, and to take its chance of what the Irish campaign might bring forth.[3]

Noting Charles's resistance to any alteration in the church and the opposition leaders' contrary aim of reformation, Gardiner characterized the situation consequent on the *Remonstrance*'s passage thus:

... the struggle which was at hand was not to be waged on mere political grounds. ... No king, said one party, shall rob us of our religion. No Parliamentary majority, said the other party, shall rob us of our religion. It was this, and this only, which gave to the great struggle its supreme importance.[4]

This view, however, in fact misstates the effect of religious differences in the breach over the *Remonstrance*, and on that account must be emphatically rejected. Doubtless Gardiner conceived it more fittingly ideal that Englishmen should quarrel over religion than on 'mere political grounds.' The reality, nevertheless, was rather differ-

---

[1] A notable exception is B. H. G. Wormald's study of Clarendon, *op. cit.*
[2] *History*, X, 32.   [3] *Ibid.*, X, 59.   [4] *Ibid.*, X, 78–9.

---

and Hambdin aside, the best of the House voted against it, as Sᵣ John Culpeper, Lᵈ. Faulkland, Mᵣ Crewe, Sir Robert Pye, Sᵣ John Strangewaies, all the best lawyers, Alderman Somes, Sir Edward Deering, Mᵣ Waller, Sᵣ Ralfe Hopton &c.' (*H.M.C. Cowper*, II, 295). Of this group, Crewe, Pye, and Soame became Parliamentarians.

ent. Severely as the *Remonstrance* criticized the church and bishops, its religious clauses contained nothing revolutionary. In particular, no attempt was made in it to revive the campaign against episcopacy, which the Commons managers abandoned when they dropped the Root-and-Branch bill in the summer.[1] Premissed indeed on the continuance of bishops, it promised further measures to reduce their power and, especially, to abolish their secular employments 'that so the better they might with meekness apply themselves to the discharge of their functions. . . .'[2] In addition, during the preliminary debates on the *Remonstrance* its promoters yielded to the sentiment in the House for deleting all statements derogatory to the prayer book. The document also expressed a vigorous condemnation of sectarianism and a pledge to enforce conformity to the church order established by law.[3] Accordingly, on its religious side the final version of the *Remonstrance* was to a certain extent a compromise. Besides the expulsion of the bishops from parliament, it committed the Commons to three principal reforms: the suppression of superstitious ceremonies, the removal of incompetent clergy, and the provision of a preaching ministry throughout the kingdom.[4] These were about the minimum steps towards the reformation impatiently expected by parliament's Puritan supporters, and came well short of the desires of those who wanted the destruction of episcopacy. Under other circumstances their substance might have been acceptable to many moderate churchmen—persons whom in distinction to the Arminians the *Remonstrance* called 'common Protestants.'[5] But religious questions could no longer be looked at except in their entanglement with the overshadowing political issues posed by the opposition leaders' course.

During the arguments over the *Remonstrance*'s ecclesiastical provisions, the Puritan D'Ewes noted the existence of an 'episcopall partie' in the Commons.[6] His own conduct accordingly demonstrated the weight of political over religious sentiments. Intensely as he disliked bishops and wished for church reform, his reservations towards the *Remonstrance* were stronger still. And so on 22 November, unwilling to take part in the final vote, he quit the House at four in

---

[1] Cf. *supra*, 240–1.

[2] Para. 183. The clause quoted was opposed but carried in a division of 161–147, *C.J.*, II, 322. Para. 137 is similar to it and also indicated the reform of bishops, not their uprooting.

[3] *C.J.*, II, 317; Coates, *D'Ewes*, 151; para. 184. An attempt to secure the deletion of a statement in para. 189 that the bishops had introduced idolatry was defeated by 124 to 99, *C.J.*, II, 317.

[4] Para. 137, 184, 186.

[5] S. R. Gardiner, *Constitutional documents*, 207.

[6] Coates, *D'Ewes*, 149, 150, 151, 152.

the afternoon because, he wrote, 'there were some particulars in the said declaration which I . . . could not in my conscience assent unto although otherwise my heart and vote went with it in the mayne.'[1]

But what, after all, was this 'episcopall partie' and what did its ecclesiastical conceptions signify? Falkland, Hyde, Sir John Culpepper, and Dering, four prominent voices among those to whom D'Ewes referred, feared less for the church in itself than for the monarchical order which it supported and which was now challenged by the incitements and demands in the *Remonstrance*. In every previous debate on church government before the recess, the defenders of the Anglican establishment had shown the keenest solicitude for the mutual dependence between the ecclesiastical system and the prevailing regime of privilege and subordination. That concern was now of sovereign import to them. In the context of the constitutional innovations and aggressive methods pursued by the Commons managers, religious changes also became dangerous and undesirable. This, rather than intransigent dislike of church reform, defined the nature of the religious question after the Houses reassembled. In May Lord Falkland voted in favour of the first bill against the secular employments of the clergy; in October he voted against the second, having ceased to be in sympathy any longer with the general policy of the opposition leaders.[2] Edward Hyde had always disliked the bill as overturning 'the whole frame and constitution of the kingdom,' but otherwise had actively concurred in the statutes enacted against the prerogative. He was now unqualifiedly hostile to Pym, whose aggression on the crown's legal rights he considered a grave provocation.[3] Sir John Culpepper felt no conscientious attachment to the church, but 'inclined to what was established to avoid the accidents which commonly attend a change.'[4] As for Sir Edward Dering, it was he who introduced the Root-and-Branch bill in May, yet now he was one of the bishops' defenders.[5] Commenting on the disturbed situation and the growth of sectarianism, he warned of the 'wicked sweetnesse of a popular parity,' foresaw the decline of kingship and nobility, and then, he concluded,

All's done. No rather, all's undone, by breaking asunder that well ordered chain of government, which from the chair of Jupiter reacheth

[1] *Ibid.*, 185.
[2] Clarendon, *Rebellion*, III, 151–2, IV, 94n.
[3] *Ibid.*, III, 149–50. Cf. B. H. G. Wormald, *op. cit.*, 3–11, 282–8, for an account of Hyde's 'episcopalianism.' He denies that Hyde separated from the opposition leaders over ecclesiastical issues.
[4] Clarendon, *Life*, 940.
[5] Coates, *D'Ewes*, 151; Sir E. Dering, *A collection of speeches*, 110–11.

down by severall golden links even to the protection of the poorest creature that now lives amongst us.[1]

These were the considerations dominating the alignment on the *Remonstrance*. Its adversaries recognized in it an inflammatory spirit which they believed would set the polity alight. That spirit was apparent in its harsh language and its embittered review of the past; in its revolutionary insistence that parliament should approve ministerial appointments; and finally, in the purpose it was meant to serve. The *Remonstrance* was not a petition to obtain the King's grace, but a device of threat and intimidation. Composed for the general eye, it was intended to mobilize popular passion for the party managers' demands. Hence in the last, decisive debate, Hyde roundly condemned it as destructive to peace, while Culpepper and Dering denounced 'the forme of itt.'[2] 'When I first heard of a Remonstrance,' said Dering, '. . . I did not dream that we should remonstrate downward, tell stories to the people, and talke of the King as of a third person.'[3] 'This [is] a Remonstrance to the people,' Culpepper told the House. 'Remonstrances ought to bee to the king for redresse; this may exasperate. . . . The humours [are] much stirred; and . . . this kingdome much distracted. . . . Wee [are] nott sent to please the people.'[4] Pym met these objections head on. '. . . The honour of the king lies in the saifty of the people,' he replied; '. . . all the plotts and designes [have been] thrust home . . . to the Court, and its time to speake playne English, least posterity shall say that England was lost and noe man durst speak truth. . . . This declaration will binde the peoples hearts to us, when they see how we have been used.'[5]

No compromise was possible over a difference of such magnitude, and the Country split apart.

2

In these altered circumstances the King returned to London on 25 November after his lengthy stay amongst the Scots. Conscious of his access of strength from the recalcitrance of the Lords and the breach in the Commons, he was ready to make an unyielding stand against the further demands of his opponents. His cordial reception by the

[1] *Ibid.*, 165–6. These remarks, written in 1642 as the concluding note to his speeches, were Dering's comment on the state of affairs in the fall and winter of 1641.
[2] Coates, *D'Ewes*, 183n., 184n.
[3] Sir E. Dering, *op. cit.*, 109.
[4] Coates, *D'Ewes*, 184n.
[5] Conflated from the notes of Pym's speech in *ibid.*, 184n. and *Verney notes*, 122–3.

lord mayor and aldermen fortified his firmness. The city's governing body was profuse in its expressions of loyalty and support, and made plain that it looked to him to sustain its authority against any challenge in these insurgent times.[1] The next weeks were to be climacteric. The revolution swayed dangerously, locked between the thrust of the Commons leaders to drive it on and the counter-thrust of the King to halt its advance. Amidst such fiercely contending stresses, it could not remain where it was. Either it must recede to be overwhelmed by a reaction in the royal favour, or it must go forward to invest itself with that supervisory power over the executive which was the core proposition of the *Remonstrance*.

On Pym's side there was no hesitation. Often in the past year he had shown his moderation and desire to achieve a consensus. Now consensus was absent and he stood forth as the advocate of uncompromising, radical measures. But the great parliamentary leader, grey-bearded and in his fifty-eighth year, did not pursue his way as an enthusiast or visionary. Sober and watchful as ever, he held to his course because he recognized no other alternative and was too clear sighted to shrink from accepting the consequences of his own commitments and previous actions.

Three days after the vote on the *Remonstrance*, the party managers demonstrated their continued hold on the Commons. The members who had claimed the right of protestation were sharply rebuked and Geoffrey Palmer, their spokesman, was voted to the Tower.[2] On 1 December the House presented the *Remonstrance* to the King, together with a petition reiterating the necessity of his consent to the bishops' removal from the House of Lords and to the employment in public affairs of persons who possessed parliament's confidence.[3] Although not yet in print, the declaration was known to the Londoners on account of the publicity continually surrounding parliament's doings. A report of it also appeared in the first number of *The heads of severall proceedings in this present parliament*, which came on sale at the end of November, the earliest forerunner of a host of revolutionary newspapers.[4] On 15 December the Commons managers

[1] Cf. *infra*, 285.

[2] *C.J.*, II, 324; Coates, *D'Ewes*, 192–5, 197–9. The divisions taken on 24 and 25 November revealed the alignment in the House. Palmer was committed to the Tower by a vote of 169–128. A motion of the oppositionist, Sir John Hotham, to expel him from membership was defeated, however, by 163–131. The question of protestation in general was definitively settled on 20 December in the House's resolution that no member had the right to protest the action of the majority, whose decision was binding upon all; *C.J.*, II, 350; Coates, *D'Ewes*, 320–3.

[3] *C.J.*, II, 328, 330; S. R. Gardiner, *Constitutional documents*, 202–5. Pym was the petition's main draftsman, Coates, *D'Ewes*, 206n.

[4] Cf. *supra*, 206.

decided to renew their proposal to publish the *Remonstrance*. The motion was put by a couple of oppositionists with the privity of many members, according to D'Ewes. He himself again left the chamber to avoid voting. Although vehemently attacked, the motion was carried by 134 to 83.[1] A few days after the incendiary declaration was blazoned to the world.

It fell upon a disturbed, distempered London amidst an atmosphere close with tension. The capital was on the brink of a revolution in its own internal government,[2] which was foreshadowed by the unruly crowds favourable to the opposition leaders that had been assembling at Westminster. One who witnessed the mob gloomily commented, 'Sects in the body and factions in the head ... do desperately threaten the dissolution of a well-governed estate.'[3] In the House of Lords the bill against the secular employments of the clergy lay stalled and disregarded. The Commons could do nothing but vainly threaten the peers with unilateral action on the measure, 'this House being the Representative Body of the whole kingdom, and their Lordships being but as particular Persons and coming to Parliament in a particular Capacity. . . .'[4]

This dangerous and innovative doctrine merely helped to strengthen the upper House's obstinacy. The majority of its members in their antagonism to the policy of the Commons were only following the King's lead. From the moment of his return, Charles had decided to make no further concessions. In his first public speech in London, he pledged to maintain the church as it was under Elizabeth and his father.[5] A few days later he pointedly snubbed a recommendation from the Commons that he give offices to the earls of Pembroke and Salisbury as persons who possessed the House's confidence.[6] Finally, in his answer on 23 December to the petition submitted with the *Remonstrance* he gave his verdict conclusively against its demands. The bishops' membership in parliament, he stated, is 'grounded upon the Fundamental Law of the Kingdom, and Constitution of Parliament;' as to the 'Choice of Our Counsellors and Ministers of State. . . . it is the undoubted Right of the Crown of England, to call such Persons to our secret Councils, to publick Employment, and Our particular Service, as We shall think fit. . . .'[7]

---

[1] *C.J.*, II, 344; Coates, *D'Ewes*, 294–5.
[2] Cf. *infra*, 287ff.   [3] *H.M.C. Buccleuch*, I, 287.
[4] *C.J.*, II, 330.   [5] J. Rushworth, IV, 430.
[6] The House recommended Pembroke's appointment as Lord Steward and Salisbury's as Treasurer. On 5 December Charles gave the office of Steward to the duke of Richmond instead; that of Treasurer remained unfilled; *C.J.*, II, 336; G. E. Cokayne, *op. cit.*, X, 832. Cf. the Venetian ambassador's remarks on the episode, *C.S.P.V. 1640–42*, 261.
[7] J. Rushworth, IV, 452–3; *C.J.*, II, 354.

Together with the evident hardening of the King's will appeared signs that he was preparing for a showdown with his opponents. Reports came to the House of Commons that certain of its members would shortly be accused of treason. Charles's partisans were predicting the early end of the opposition's sway and the victory of the 'King's party.'[1] 'The Parliament fly high yet,' wrote one on 9 December, 'but it is conceived it will every day grow more temperate.'[2] Charles now felt strong enough to dismiss the elder Vane, whom he had distrusted ever since Strafford's trial, replacing him as Secretary of State by Edward Nicholas.[3] Repeated rumours spoke of the dismissal of other unfaithful servants and of the forthcoming conferment of ministerial offices on members of parliament hostile to Pym's party.[4] These forecasts were confirmed on 1 January 1642 when the King appointed Lord Falkland as co-Secretary of State and Sir John Culpepper as Chancellor of the Exchequer.[5]

A prey to fears of every sort, the House of Commons was defenceless in the event of violence. Although a guard under the earl of Essex had been posted by parliament at Westminster during the King's absence in Scotland, Charles dismissed it immediately on his return.[6] He meant to keep all military force in the capital at his own disposition and was adamant against the Commons' pleas for its restoration.[7] The party managers naturally placed a sinister interpre-

---

[1] Coates, *D'Ewes*, 212, 213, 215; *C.S.P.D. 1641–43*, 188.   [2] *Ibid.*, 192–3.
[3] *Ibid.*, 193–4. Nicholas had sent the King in Scotland numerous hints of Secretary Vane's disloyalty and communications with the opposition party in England, J. Evelyn, *op. cit.*, IV, 68, 77, 92.
[4] *C.S.P.D. 1641–43*, 192, 201, 211. On the strength of a remark made in a letter by Sir Edward Dering, Gardiner declared that the King first offered the chancellorship of the Exchequer to Pym before appointing Culpepper to the place; *History*, X, 127. J. Forster, *The arrest of the five members*, L., 1860, 48–9, and C. V. Wedgwood, *The King's war*, L., 1958, 55, also accept this story. I know of no other evidence in its favour, however, and reject it as most improbable. At the moment of his alleged offer, Charles was about to launch his long meditated *coup* against Pym's group.
[5] According to Clarendon, Falkland accepted office with the greatest reluctance. One reason was his fear that the world might think he had opposed the dominant party in parliament in order to gain promotion from the King. Both his and Culpepper's preferment aroused the strong disapproval of 'the angry part of the House'; *Rebellion*, IV, 123–5. This would seem sufficient to expose the fallacy of Wormald's suggestion (*Clarendon*, 41) that in the appointment of these former allies of the oppositionists the King now had advisers 'to whom it was difficult to deny confidence. . . .' In fact, because of the tense situation prevailing on the eve of the King's *coup*, the promotion of M.P.s conspicuously separated from Pym could have had no such effect.   [6] Coates, *D'Ewes*, 18n., 70; *L.J.*, IV, 398–9; *C.J.*, II, 325.
[7] *C.J.*, II, 327–8. On 29–30 November, because of the crowds at Westminster, Charles despatched a guard under the earl of Dorset's command with whom the citizens almost came to blows. He then withdrew it, *L.J.*, IV, 455.

tation on his refusal. It served to emphasize the extent of the danger as long as control of armed force rested with the King. The relief of Ireland, the security of parliament, the entire crisis of confidence lay centred in this issue. In consequence the House initiated a fresh aggression on the crown's authority. It was foreshadowed in a motion made by the oppositionist Strode at the end of November that a course be taken to remove the military power from the King. This proposal was the germ of the bill which Sir Arthur Haselrig introduced on 7 December to place command of the kingdom's militia in a general to be named by parliament.[1] In essence, the bill was an application of the principle that ministerial appointments should be subject to parliament's approval. Thus far, however, the House had only advanced this demand by way of petition, and had claimed a right of veto, not of direct nomination. Haselrig's bill went further in proposing by means of statute to invest parliament with complete supervision of the military. Radical as this was, it did not deter the members, and against the clamour of those who urged the militia bill's rejection as an unlawful invasion of the prerogative, a majority voted to receive it.[2] With this decision the House of Commons committed itself to wrest from the King the *ultima ratio* of his monarchical sovereignty.

Charles did not intend to hold to a merely defensive posture against these latest assaults on his crown. Ever since his Scottish journey he had been considering how to master his opponents by a decisive stroke. After his return to London he judged the situation favourable for such an attempt. Whether the plan for the *coup* he had in mind was conceived then, or earlier in Scotland, cannot be determined. Perhaps he had long entertained it in a general way, since it closely resembled Strafford's scheme at the opening of the Long Parliament to get rid of the opposition leaders by accusing them of treason.[3] Possibly he made the decision for its execution because of the urgings of Lord Digby in London: for that brilliant but imprudent gentleman, having deserted the Country during Strafford's attainder, had become Charles's and the Queen's trusted confidant.[4]

---

[1] Coates, *D'Ewes*, 202, 244. The bill also provided that parliament should appoint an admiral.

[2] *C.J.*, II, 334; Coates, *D'Ewes*, 244–8. The vote in favour of receiving the militia bill was 158–125.

[3] Cf. *supra*, 209.

[4] Clarendon attributed the responsibility to Lord Digby, *Rebellion*, IV, 127, 154. His statement, however, that Digby persuaded the King 'to depart from his purpose of doing nothing' (*ibid.*, IV, 146) is unbelievable. Charles's refusal to allow parliament a guard and the rumours that members would be accused of treason were but two of the indications that he was preparing a stroke against his enemies.

The counter-revolution—for this was the King's aim—was to proceed in duly legal form. Pym and several of his near associates were to be charged with treason and placed in confinement; once removed from parliament to face trial, their party supporters would be thoroughly intimidated and their ascendancy at an end. Undoubtedly Charles held himself justified both morally and legally in taking this action. His sense of the rights confided him by God and his royal predecessors was the deepest conviction he possessed. He really did believe the parliamentary managers guilty of treason. If Strafford, his faithful servant, had been condemned to suffer for subverting the law, then so much the more did Pym merit condemnation who in violation of the law was traitorously endeavouring to deprive the King of his regal power.

To effect his aim the King knew that he must cow the London crowd and even suppress it by force if necessary. He therefore acted to secure the Tower, the key to military control of the capital. On 22 December he dismissed the Lieutenant of the Tower, Sir William Balfour, and replaced him with a professional soldier, Col. Lunsford, on whom he felt he could rely.[1] Perhaps Charles imagined that this step, the opening move in his *coup*, would pass unnoticed. Incredible if he thought so! Lunsford, who had served in France and with the royal army in the north, was a swaggerer of notorious reputation.[2] His installation in the Tower at such a time of wrought-up nerves and political fears could not fail to provoke an explosion of suspicion.

The next day, the House of Commons, alarmed by the reports of Lunsford's appointment, asked the Lords to join in remonstrating against it to the King. The upper House refused; it would do nothing to challenge Charles's exercise of his lawful prerogative.[3] The members reacted sharply to this rebuff. On the 24th they gave the militia bill a second reading and resolved that 'This House holds Colonel Lunsford unfit to be . . . Lieutenant of the Tower of London; as a Person in whom the Commons of England cannot confide.'[4] They also addressed a stinging declaration to the Lords, in which they condemned the 'Delays and Interruption . . . we have received in the House of Peers . . . by the great Number of Bishops and Papists, notoriously disaffected to the common Good. . . .' They had done their uttermost, they said, to save the commonwealth from ruin; but if Lunsford continued in his charge, we 'hold ourselves bound in

---

[1] *C.S.P.D. 1641–43*, 210; Balfour was to receive £3,000, payable by the Queen's treasurer, for resigning his office in Lunsford's favour.
[2] Cf. *D.N.B., s.v.*
[3] *C.J.*, II, 355; *L.J.*, IV, 487.
[4] *C.J.*, II, 356; the militia bill received a first reading three days earlier, on 21 December, *ibid.*, II, 351.

Conscience to declare and protest, that we are innocent of the Blood which is like to be spilt, and of the Confusion which may overwhelm this State. . . .'[1]

The noblemen received this statement with extreme resentment, which they showed by voting to put off consideration of it for three days to 27 December. A minority of twenty-two opposition lords and their friends, however, entered a vigorous protest against the vote, declaring that the Commons' declaration concerned 'the instant Good and Safety of the King and Kingdom.'[2] Deprived of the peers' cooperation, the lower House then sent a message to the earl of Newport, Constable of the Tower, who was above the Lieutenant in rank, asking him to take immediate custody of the fortress. Newport replied that he could not do so, as on that same day, the 24th, the King had discharged him from his office.[3]

Constitutionally, the House of Commons was at a standstill. Although the thought of acting alone had undoubtedly occurred to its leaders, they did not venture to propose this course; while even with the Lords' support, the House had no legal power to hinder the King's choice of officers. But at this point the London populace took a hand. A revolution against the lord mayor's authority had just begun in the city with the common council election of 21 December.[4] On the 23rd some of the activists in that movement petitioned the Commons against Lunsford's appointment. Another petition with a roll of thirty thousand signatures, which some apprentices delivered, complained of the presence of bishops and Catholic peers in the House of Lords. The apprentices stated their determination 'if need bee to over-match a Royal Coupe.'[5]

Nothing could have been more welcome to the opposition leaders than the spreading agitation in the city. Lacking any means of defence, the Londoners were their sole recourse. Probably the London M.P.s and their citizen friends helped to organize the public reaction. But however it may have been done, it was neither contrived nor artificial. Pym's group enjoyed widespread support in the capital, and popular disapproval of the King's conduct was both broad and deep.

While the Houses stood briefly adjourned over Christmas, London's unrest grew. On Sunday, the 26th, the mayor, Sir Richard Gurney, went to Whitehall to tell the King that if he did not remove Lunsford, the apprentices would attack the Tower. Charles had no

[1] *Ibid.*, II, 356–7; *L.J.*, IV, 489.
[2] *L.J.*, IV, 489–90.
[3] *C.J.*, II, 357; *L.J.*, IV, 490.
[4] Cf. *infra*, 288–9.
[5] *C.J.*, II, 354; Coates, *D'Ewes*, 337 and n.; J. Rushworth, IV, 459, 462.

choice but to retreat. That night he dismissed Lunsford and replaced him by Sir John Byron, a man of far better reputation.[1] Nevertheless, the concession came too late to calm the whirlwind his actions had stirred up. During the next three days London was overwhelmed in turmoil that portended a civil war. Rioting crowds crying out against bishops and 'rotten-hearted lords' surged through the neighbourhood of parliament. Fights broke out between citizens and the trained bands summoned by the mayor and the King. A throng of apprentices assaulted Lunsford and some friends in Westminster Hall and were beaten off with swords. A mob attacked Archbishop Williams of York, and, invading Westminster Abbey, tried to pull down the altar and organ. At Whitehall scores of courtiers and ex-officers gathered to defend the King's person.[2] On the 28th a royal proclamation commanded an end to the rioting, but further disorders continued the next day.[3]

The Lords, whose episcopal members were the special object of the mob's anger, had already asked the Commons to join in petitioning the King for a guard and in publishing a declaration against the crowds at Westminster. The lower House replied with a refusal on the 29th. It would have no guard except one approved by parliament and commanded by the earl of Essex—a condition which the peers in their turn refused as invading the King's military authority. The proposed declaration the Commons also rejected, unwilling, noted D'Ewes, 'at this time to discontent the Cittizens of London our surest friends when soe many designes and plotts were daily consulted of against our safetie. . . .'[4]

But even before this reply was received, Lord Digby, who had received a peerage after Strafford's trial, offered an incendiary motion in the House of Lords. Sure that the House of Commons would not rebuke the rioters, he moved that because of the mob's threats parliament was no longer free. He seized here on a possibility that had probably been floating before the King's partisans for some time. Only recently a pamphlet circulating in London had impugned the validity of acts passed during the Scottish occupation in the north.[5] Digby's motion pursued the same purpose and with the riskiest

---

[1] J. Rushworth, IV, 464; *C.S.P.D. 1641–43*, 216.
[2] Clarendon, *Rebellion*, IV, 111; *C.S.P.D. 1641–43*, 214–18.
[3] J. Rushworth, IV, 466; cf. the Commons' complaints of attacks by ex-officers of the King's army on the citizens at Whitehall, *L.J.*, IV, 496.
[4] *L.J.*, IV, 493, 494, 496; *C.J.*, II, 358–9; Coates, *D'Ewes*, 356.
[5] 'Whether any laws, divine or human, allow subjects to keep an army of Strangers to master their King? Whether statutes enforced upon the King with the awe of an army will be of any force hereafter?', *C.S.P.D. 1641–43*, 113, misdated August. On 18 November the Commons appointed a committee to investigate the origin of this pamphlet, Coates, *D'Ewes*, 165.

implications. If parliament were unfree in December, as he contended, then it had been equally unfree in May when mob intimidation forced the Lords and King to agree to Strafford's attainder and to the act against dissolving parliament without its own consent. The road would be open to infinite questionings and the unsettlement of the very foundations of the constitutional revolution.[1] Although the peers detested the mob, they nevertheless shrank from the vertiginous consequences of Digby's motion, and they resolved by a majority of four 'That this Parliament is at this present a Free Parliament.'[2]

Digby's tactic, however, was immediately renewed by the clerical politician, Archbishop Williams. Formerly bishop of Lincoln, the bustling Williams had returned to public activity in the Long Parliament after many years of royal disfavour and had just been promoted to York. On the 29th he brought the King a protest from twelve bishops declaring that fear of the mob prevented them from attending parliament and pronouncing null all 'Laws, Orders, Votes, Resolutions, and Determinations' passed during their 'forced and violent Absence. . . .' Williams begged the King to send the protest to the upper House, and Charles did so the next morning.[3]

The peers' response, contrary to Charles's expectation, was one of anger and alarm. Placed between the King and the Commons, most wished to support the King, yet condemned this new attempt to invalidate parliament's authority. They promptly transmitted the bishops' statement to the Commons as a matter of 'high and dangerous Consequence . . . entrenching upon the fundamental Privileges and Being of Parliament. . . .' That afternoon the lower House impeached all twelve episcopal signatories for high treason and the Lords ordered them jailed. But at the same time, to express their continued care for the crown's rights, the noblemen denied a further request from the Commons that both Houses petition the King for a guard under the earl of Essex.[4]

As December came to a close, a showdown clearly impended. Fear was general and most of the city's shops were shut. '. . . it is a wonder there is no more blood yet spilt,' a news letter said on the 30th, 'seeing how earnest both sides are. There is no doubt but if the King do not comply with the Commons in all things they desire, a sudden

---

[1] Cf. the observations of a news writer that Digby's motion was a plot 'to make this Parliament no Parliament, and so to overthrow all Acts passed and to cause a dissolution of it for the present. . . .', *C.S.P.D. 1641–43*, 216–17.

[2] *L.J.*, IV, 494, 495; S. R. Gardiner, *History*, X, 120n. The vote was 29–25.

[3] Clarendon, *Rebellion*, IV, 130, 139; *L.J.*, IV, 496–7. The bishop of Peterborough's name is omitted from the list of signers.

[4] *Ibid.*, IV, 497, 498–9; *C.J.*, II, 363–4.

civil war must ensue. . . .'[1] The King felt himself menaced by disorderly mobs whom the Commons encouraged. On their side, the opposition leaders dreaded Charles's intentions. Observing the numbers of demobilized army officers around him at Whitehall, they expected an outbreak of violence at any time.[2] On Friday the 31st, the House of Commons met amidst the keenest apprehensions. The members decided to adjourn until 3 January and meanwhile to sit as a committee of the whole at the London Guildhall, where the strength of the city would surround them. Their last action before adjourning was to send a fresh message to the King reiterating their appeal for a guard under the earl of Essex: 'their [own] Safety,' they declared, 'and the Safety of the whole Kingdom depends upon it, and will not admit of any Delay.'[3]

To this request Charles returned a flat denial, coupled with a solemn assurance that he knew of no violent design against the Commons and would be as careful of the members' security as of his own.[4] His asseverations were worthless: for on Monday, 3 January, when the Houses resumed sitting at Westminster after the weekend adjournment, he launched his blow.[5] That afternoon he ordered the Attorney General, Sir Edward Herbert, to impeach the opposition leaders of high treason and Herbert laid the accusation before the House of Lords. It charged Pym, Hampden, Holles, Strode, Haselrig, and Viscount Mandeville[6] with a formidable list of crimes: they had endeavoured to subvert the fundamental laws and government of the kingdom and to deprive the King of his regal power; they had foully

[1] *C.S.P.D. 1641–43*, 218.

[2] Cf. Pym's statement to the House on 30 December, Coates, *D'Ewes*, 366, and the comments of the Venetian envoy on the situation, *C.S.P.V. 1640–42*, 271.

[3] *C.J.*, II, 365–6; Coates, *D'Ewes*, 373.

[4] J. Rushworth, IV, 471–2. The King's reply was sent to the committee of the whole at the Guildhall on Monday, the 3rd, and was reported to the House in the afternoon when it returned to Westminster, *C.J.*, II, 366; Coates, *D'Ewes*, 375.

[5] Gardiner thought Charles was led to act on hearing that the committee at the Guildhall had resolved to impeach the Queen. The main evidence for this is the story in the Venetian ambassador's despatch of 7 January (S. R. Gardiner, *History*, X, 128; *C.S.P.V. 1640–42*, 275–6). D'Ewes, however, mentions no such plan of the opposition leaders. It is true that he did not attend the committee at the Guildhall; but if the Queen's impeachment had been proposed, he would surely have known of it and referred to it subsequently in connection with the accusation of treason against Pym's group. The story of the proposed attack on the Queen may have been put about by the King's supporters as an excuse after the failure of his *coup*. On 14 January D'Ewes and Sir Hugh Cholmley spoke in the House of false rumours and fears instilled in the King that parliament meant to impeach the Queen, D'Ewes, Journal, B.M. Harl. 162, ff. 325b, 326b.

[6] Referred to in the impeachment by his title of Lord Kimbolton.

aspersed the King in order to alienate his subjects' affections; they had incited the royal army to disobedience and invited a foreign power—the Scots were meant—to invade England; they had attempted to subvert the rights and being of parliament and had raised tumults to force its compliance with their traitorous aims; finally, they had actually levied war against the King.[1]

At last the confrontation between the King and his opponents was at hand! But Charles had seriously miscalculated the effect of his accusation. Beneath the show of constitutional form, the House of Lords, largely Royalist though it now was, smelled something unwholesome and menacing to parliament's life. Hence, instead of commanding the members' arrest, the peers voted to consider whether the charge accorded with law.[2] The Commons in its turn received the news of the impeachment with indignation as a high breach of privilege. Late in the day Charles sent the Sergeant-at-Arms with an order to the Speaker demanding the accused men. The House refused to give them up. The matter, it told the King, required further deliberation as affecting the privilege of parliament and all the commons of England; in the meantime, the five M.P.s would attend daily in readiness to answer a legal charge.[3]

With each passing hour the impeached members remained at liberty the King's *coup* lost some of its impact. Delay was fatal to his enterprise. He therefore decided to go to parliament in person to seize the traitors. The next afternoon, 4 January, Pym and the others were in their places when news came that the King with several hundred armed men was on his way from Whitehall. They were immediately permitted to depart. Leaving the chamber just in time, they were joined by Mandeville and the six fled into the precincts of the city for safety.[4]

A few minutes later Charles arrived at the Commons. Commanding his followers to remain outside, he walked through the standing and uncovered House to the Speaker's chair and there called for the accused men. When it became evident they were gone, he addressed the House in a self-justifying speech. No one, he said, cared more for parliament's privileges than himself. He was determined, however, to have the members, who stood charged with crimes in which a plea of privilege was inadmissible. But he never intended force, and promised 'on the word of a King' to proceed only in a 'legal and fair way.' Having concluded these remarks, he left the chamber amidst cries of 'Privilege, Privilege,' from his auditors. Shortly afterward, too shaken

---

[1] *L.J.*, IV, 501.
[2] *Ibid.*
[3] Coates, *D'Ewes*, 377; *C.J.*, II, 366–7.
[4] Coates, *D'Ewes*, 381; *Verney notes*, 138.

for further business and feeling that it had missed calamity by a hair, the House adjourned for the day.[1]

This was failure. Charles had lost his quarry, while the armed presence accompanying him belied all his professions of legality. There was no question in anyone's mind that he would have taken the members by force had the House refused to give them up.[2] The next day deepened his reversal. Going into the city in the hope of seizing the accused, he had to pass large crowds which stood by shouting, 'Privilege.' A speech in defence of his proceedings which he delivered to the aldermen and common council was received with strong hostility.[3] On 8 January he issued a proclamation for the apprehension of the accused members. It was to no effect, since no one would execute his order.[4]

Meanwhile, the House of Commons was busy passing judgment on his conduct. Albeit a few voices sought to excuse it, the prevailing sense was one of unqualified condemnation.[5] On the 4th, the House voted the King's warlike coming the day before to be a 'High Breach of the Rights and Privilege of Parliament, and inconsistent with the Liberties and Freedom thereof. . . .' Declaring that it could not remain safely at Westminster, it adjourned until 11 January. In the interval it ordered that a committee of the whole should meet in the city. The Lords followed suit by also adjourning to the same day.[6]

The Commons' committee began sitting at the Guildhall on the 6th.[7] Its main business, naturally, was the legality of the King's proceedings. The impeachment and the order for the members' arrest without the House's consent it pronounced unlawful and a breach of privilege on grounds cogently formulated by D'Ewes. In a charge of treason, he said,

the howse must bee first satisfied with the matter of fact before they part with their members for else all priviledge of Parliament must of necessitie bee destroied for by the same reason that they accuse one of the said members they may accuse 40 or 50 upon imaginarie and false Treasons and soe committ them to custodie. . . .[8]

[1] J. Rushworth, IV, 477–8; Coates, *D'Ewes*, 381–4; *Verney notes*, 138–9.
[2] Cf. D'Ewes's comments, Coates, *D'Ewes*, 382–3.
[3] *Ibid.*, 387; J. Rushworth, IV, 479–80; *C.S.P.D. 1641–43*, 242–3.
[4] R. Steele, *op. cit.*, I, 1919. Oddly, the proclamation named only the Commons' members and omitted Mandeville.
[5] Coates, *D'Ewes*, 386.
[6] *C.J.*, II, 368–9; *L.J.*, IV, 504.
[7] The next day the committee sat at the hall of the Grocers Company, where it remained until the House returned to Westminster on the 11th, Coates, *D'Ewes*, 389, 392.
[8] Coates, *D'Ewes*, 389, 391.

The committee then turned to the King's descent upon the Commons. On the 7th it resolved that his coming with soldiers was 'a traiterous designe against the King and Parliament.'[1] The distinction entailed in this resolution between Charles's personal and regal capacity was noteworthy. It meant that he separated himself from his office in acting illegally. As an implied corollary, resistance to him in such a case would be resistance to Charles Stuart, not the King. With this comforting doctrine the men moving down the road to civil war could at necessity resort to arms in good conscience. No rebels, they could proclaim that they defended the King and parliament even as they fired their cannons against Charles's forces.

These votes by the committee amounted to a vindication of the impeached members, who were thereupon invited to return to their parliamentary duties, 'notwithstanding any warrant ... or other matter or accusation against them.'[2] The committee's last important action was to settle the disputed point of a guard for parliament. In the wake of the terror engendered by the King's attempt, it ordered the sheriffs of London to raise a force in the city for parliament's defence. This plain usurpation on the crown's military prerogative was justified by a plea of necessity and was endorsed by both Houses as soon as they reconvened after the adjournment.[3]

The collapse of his scheme to remove the opposition leaders left the King in a situation of humiliating weakness. However he pleaded his good faith, few believed him. His partisans would doubtless have justified the *coup*, had it succeeded; in failure, he incurred only opprobrium. Those moderates who had broken away from the Country in the fall stood momentarily perplexed and vacillating. Now the King, rather than his parliamentary opponents, appeared the aggressor. The House of Lords, too, had been subjected to great provocation by his attempt and accordingly inclined to be somewhat more compliant with the Commons than in recent months.

On 10 January, Pym, Hampden, Holles, Haselrig, and Strode emerged from hiding to attend the committee in the city.[4] Next day, when the Houses met again at Westminster, they returned to parliament in triumph. Huge crowds applauded them on the way, and on the river the mariners and vessels shot salvoes in their honour. The citizen guard raised by the civic authorities was already disposed about the streets and parliament buildings. 'And I saw,' wrote D'Ewes,

upon the topp of the pikes of divers of the Londoners the Protestation[5]

---

[1] Coates, *D'Ewes*, 394.   [2] *Verney notes*, 140.

[3] *C.S.P.D. 1641–43*, 247–8; *C.J.*, II, 370; *L.J.*, IV, 504.

[4] Coates, *D'Ewes*, 399.

[5] The pledge to preserve religion, liberty, the rights of parliament and the

281

formerlie framed and taken by members of the howse . . . and afterwards by most of the citizens, hanging like a little square banner. Some had them also affixed . . . to ther muskets, one had it fastened upon his breast. . . .[1]

To be the witness of his own abasement was more than the King could stomach. He did not wish to remain in London amidst the immense demonstration for the oppositionist members which, commented the Venetian ambassador, 'strikes to the quick the dignity of his name and the greatness of his royal fortunes.'[2] Taking a sudden resolution, he left Whitehall for Hampton Court on 10 January accompanied by the Queen and royal children.[3] It was the first stage of a journey that would not see his return to his capital until he came to face trial and execution there seven years later. He felt no doubt that the kingdom was on the threshold of rebellion: the defiance of his treason accusation and the affronts to his authority meant nothing else.[4] Thus it was with the idea of meeting a rebellion that he now set out to secure a military base and means of war.

3

To London—'The proud, unthankefull, Schismaticall, Rebellious . . . City of London'[5]—the parliamentary managers owed the defeat of the King's *coup*. But the intervention that preserved the revolution was the work of the politically conscious populace, not of the civic government. Not only did the latter give no sign; it was, in fact, more decidedly partial to the King in the fall of 1641 than it had been a year earlier.

A divergence of political sentiment between the magistrates and the citizenry had existed from the time parliament began. Individually, a handful of aldermen supported the Country, and had they controlled the civic corporation they would doubtless have secured its endorsement of Pym's programme. But they did not speak for the court of

[1] J. Rushworth, IV, 484; *C.S.P.V. 1640–42*, 281; *C.S.P.D. 1641–43*, 252; D'Ewes, Journal, B.M. Harl. 162, f. 318a.
[2] *C.S.P.V. 1640–42*, 281.
[3] *C.S.P.D. 1641–43*, 252.
[4] The Queen told Heenvliet, the agent of the Prince of Orange, on 11 January that 'tout se préparoit à une rebellion,' and that neither she nor the King 'ne poulvoyent plus endurer ces grandes affrontes . . .'; *Archives . . . de la maison d'Orange-Nassau*, ed. G. Groen van Prinsterer, 2nd ser., 5v., Utrecht, 1858–62, III, 501.
[5] *A letter from Mercurius Civicus to Mercurius Rusticus*, 32.

subject, which the House of Commons adopted in the crisis of Strafford's attainder; cf. *supra*, 223.

aldermen.[1] As a body, the mayor and his brethren, including most of those senior in service and prestige, were unwilling to associate the official municipality with any action hostile to the crown. Their refusal sprang from a rooted disposition in favour of everything established that was entirely intelligible in such men as these. Belonging to the select stratum of wealthy traders which had provided the city's ruling group for generations, they observed with intense dislike the insubordinate temper rampant among the citizenry. The notion of a tranquillity based on unconditional submission to the authority of the magistrates was all but axiomatic in their mentality; and with them it was not outweighed, as it was with other men of substance in the city, by zeal for religious or political reform. Hence, when the Londoners petitioned against the bishops by the thousands, or when they mobbed the streets in a riotous outcry for Strafford's death and Lunsford's removal from the Tower, they did not receive the slightest sanction from the civic government. Faithful to its tradition of dependence on the crown, the official municipality refrained from all support of the King's opponents in the public controversies of 1641.

Because of this, the main channel of communication between the parliamentary managers and their citizen supporters was London's M.P.s. All four chosen in October 1640 favoured the Country.[2] This outcome was not surprising, since common hall, the electing body, was the most popularly constituted assembly in the municipal government and thus likeliest to reflect general opinion. In May 1641, on the death of Mathew Cradock, John Venn succeeded him as member. The speed of Venn's return—he took his seat in the House of Commons within eight days of Cradock's decease—suggests that the oppositionists desired his presence and perhaps even planned his election.[3] A well-to-do cloth merchant and Puritan, he was to take a considerable part in organizing the citizens' demonstrations and the subsequent revolution against the mayor's authority.

An intimation of that revolution occurred soon after Venn's election in a quarrel between the mayor and commonalty over the choice of the city's sheriffs. The latter together with certain other officials were appointed annually at a common hall in June, and on the usual day, the liverymen, who formed the commonalty under the municipal constitution, assembled for this purpose. According to custom, the mayor was to name one sheriff and common hall the

[1] Cf. the survey of the political outlook of the aldermanic bench in 1640–1 in V. Pearl, op. cit., 113–14.

[2] Cf. supra, 146.

[3] Cradock died on 27 May, and the first appearance of Venn's name in the Journal was 4 June, M. Keeler, op. cit., 144; C.J., II, 168. I have found no order of the House authorizing an election in London for Cradock's successor.

other. Nevertheless, when Sir Edmund Wright attempted to exercise his prerogative of office, common hall refused to allow it and demanded the power to choose both sheriffs itself. No election could be held. Wright and his aldermanic colleagues then appealed to the King to uphold the mayor's privilege. Charles, perhaps from reluctance to antagonize either side, referred the dispute to the mediation of the House of Lords. The House first commanded the parties to try to settle their difference peaceably amongst themselves. When they proved unable to do so, it decreed that for the coming year the commonalty should choose both sheriffs. It added the hope that one of the two so designated would be the mayor's nominee.[1] Notwithstanding this suggestion, which common hall adopted,[2] the mayor and aldermen protested vehemently against the upper House's judgment. Expressing the fear that the commons of London would throw off the municipal government, they threatened to resign if their authority were not sustained. The peers, however, adhered to their award as best conducive to the city's peace.[3] Their order was entered in the Journal of the common council;[4] furthermore, at the shrievalty election of 1642, the mayor conceded to common hall the appointment of both sheriffs, though with a saving of his prerogative.[5]

Encouraged no doubt by this success, London oppositionists prepared for a fresh contest when common hall met in September 1641 for the annual election of the lord mayor. As in the year before, so again they tried to elect Alderman Soame, one of the city M.P.s. Established usage, however, required that the mayoralty should go to the nominee who was senior alderman. The latter in 1641 was Richard Gurney, a merchant 'well affected & stout' for the King.[6] The defenders of the constitutional *status quo* took care to see that Gurney as legitimate candidate should be victorious. As soon as his name was proposed, the mayor and aldermen pronounced him elected. The presiding sheriff, Clark, the mayor's nominee of the previous summer, then dissolved the meeting, despite indignant calls of 'no election' from Soame's supporters. So to the jubiliation of the King's friends, a royal partisan succeeded as mayor, and Nicholas was able to inform Charles of the defeat of the 'Schismaticks' and 'factious party' in the city.[7]

[1] *L.J.*, IV, 292, 293, 373.
[2] The two sheriffs appointed were George Garret and George Clark, the latter the mayor's nominee.
[3] *L.J.*, IV, 376–7; *H.M.C. Fourth report*, pt. 1, 99.
[4] 29 September 1641, Journal, 39, f. 230b. A note on the same page states, 'no other officers elected now because of ye difference.'
[5] *Ibid.*, 39, f. 328b.   [6] Nicholas to the King, J. Evelyn, *op. cit.*, IV, 82.
[7] *C.S.P.D. 1641–43* 132: J. Evelyn, *op. cit.*, IV, 82.

That fall, with political differences more inflamed than ever, the restlessness of London caused the new mayor and his colleagues much anxiety. Disaffection spread abroad against the King undermined their own authority as well. Early in November they complained pointedly to parliament about the condition of the city. Their warrants, they said, were not obeyed, and their government so slighted 'that there is an Equality between the Mayor and the Commons, the Power of the Mayor no more than that of the Commoners of the City.'[1]

Small wonder, then, that when the King returned from Scotland the civic government decided to make the occasion into a resounding manifestation of support. '. . . yor Matie,' Nicholas wrote him, 'was never more welcome to ye better sorte of Londoners than you will now be. . . .'[2] Re-entering the capital on 25 November, Charles received a sumptuous reception.[3] The display of loyalty, however, was more expressive of the official attitude than of the feeling prevalent in the citizen populace. Charles and the magistrates had every reason to turn towards each other at such a time. Addressing the monarch, the recorder begged him

to uphold and countenance that ancient form and frame of Government which hath been long established in the City; that Power and Authority of yours, which you have committed to your Lord Mayor, your true and faithful Subject and Servant, and the fit Reverence and Respect due to the Aldermen his brethren. . . . we shall be thereby the better enabled to serve your Majesty, and constantly to render to you the Fruits of a true Obedience. . . .[4]

Charles on his part took the city's demonstration as strengthening his hand for his approaching dénouement with Pym's group. '. . . now I see,' he said in reply,

that all . . . tumults and disorders have only risen from the meaner sort of people, and that the Affections of the better, and main part of the City, have ever been Loyal to my Person and Government.

He promised to do all in his power to promote London's prosperity and to grant its reasonable demands. As a sign of grace, he knighted the lord mayor and recorder and conferred the same honour a week later on the sheriffs and five aldermen as well.[5]

[1] *C.J.*, II, 304; *L.J.*, IV, 420.
[2] J. Evelyn, *op. cit.*, IV, 115.
[3] Cf. the description in *Ovatio Carolina*, 1641.
[4] J. Rushworth, IV, 429–30.   [5] *Ibid.*, IV, 430–1, 434.

To counteract the effect of the King's reception, the city oppositionists got up a petition attesting London's attachment to the House of Commons. It was delivered to the House on 11 December, a paper twenty-four yards long containing fifteen thousand names, including those of several aldermen and of some of the members of the common council.[1] The petitioners condemned malicious attempts 'to misconstrue the citizens' loyal entertainment of his Majesty' as 'a deserting of this honourable assembly. . . .' They acknowledged thankfully the benefits the Commons had done the church and kingdom, endorsed the bill for the bishops' expulsion from parliament, and asked the House also to take into consideration 'the abuses that are crept into the ancient government of the City. . . .' They were ready, they said, to hazard their lives against 'all wicked counsellors and malignant opposers' who try to divide the King from parliament.[2]

The manner of promoting this petition, which the mayor did his best to discourage,[3] points to a considerable background of organization. There must have been a network of sympathizers across the metropolis, since four men from each of London's twenty-six wards accompanied the petition to the House of Commons.[4] A sight of the apparatus the city oppositionists built was given by a pamphleteer who said that they had

Taverne clubs in each Ward, communicating intelligence to, and from their table Juncto's, or Sub-Committees sitting in divers private houses . . . [as] Brownes house a Grocer neare Cheap-side crosse; also a Drapers house in Watling street[5] . . . to prepare results of each dayes passages in the City to report to Mr. Pym. . . .[6]

One of the places where the petition was exhibited for signatures was the White Lion tavern in Canning Street. In several wards its sponsors summoned most of the residents of the parish to their house and exhorted them as Christians and patriots to sign.[7]

The same machinery was set going to call out the London crowds.

---

[1] Coates, *D'Ewes*, 271.
[2] Text in *C.S.P.D. 1641–43*, 195–6.
[3] Coates, *D'Ewes*, 319–20; *C.J.*, II, 350.
[4] Coates, *D'Ewes*, 271.
[5] This draper was probably Francis Peck, a common council member; cf. V. Pearl, *op. cit.*, 323, for an account of him.
[6] *Persecutio undecima*, 60. Internal evidence suggests (cf. 4, 34) that the author of this pamphlet was the Rev. Robert Chestlin, rector of St. Matthew Friday Street in London, a great hater of the Puritans whose tactics he had seen at first hand.
[7] *C.S.P.D. 1641–43*, 193, 197.

Venn, with his connections in the city, was probably the key figure in this. When he passed the word, Pym's supporters flocked in multitudes to Westminster. According to one account, he and the Rev. Cornelius Burges, a great man in the Puritan ministry, 'sent tickets by Porters and Emissaries' to mobilize their 'Mermidons.'[1] On a night at the end of November, Venn was able at short notice to bring down more than a thousand armed citizens to the House of Commons. Mrs. Venn also helped, 'and with great industry solicited many people to go down with their arms. . . .' Following this occurrence, Sir John Strangeways and Edward Kirton accused Venn publicly in the Commons of inciting the crowds to intimidate members, an offence, they said, little less than treason. The House, however, with its majority favourable to Pym, treated the charge as unproved.[2]

Revolution is a stern test not only of political will and strategy, but also of organizational resource. The party that knows how to coordinate its forces, to exploit its followers' zeal to most effect, to harness popular passion to its programme, will always be stronger than an opponent less efficient in these arts. As regards the latter, the London oppositionists were incontestably superior to the King's sympathizers. But between them and the subjection of the capital to their political purpose stood Gurney, the mayor, and his brother aldermen. If the official municipality were to take a different political direction, the authority of its governors, to whom the King looked for aid, had first to be overthrown. In that tense December, amidst increasing disorder and expectation of an approaching dénouement, Pym's citizen allies girded themselves for an attempt to capture the civic government.

The preparations they made are hidden in darkness. Two years later, however, an anonymous tract, *A letter from Mercurius Civicus to Mercurius Rusticus* (1643),[3] gave a circumstantial account of the whole affair which described the oppositionists' tactics:

But because it was impossible to disarme the King, as long as the Lord Major stood firme in his Loyalty, and invested in his power; their maine worke therefore was, first, to pack a Common-Councell of men of their own Faction, and then by advancing the power of their Common-Councell (by the assistance of the House of Commons) above the Lord Majors, to draw the voting of all Queryes, and the Resolution of all

[1] *Persecutio undecima*, 64.

[2] Coates, *D'Ewes*, 214–16; Clarendon, *Rebellion*, IV, 120.

[3] The tract is dated at the end 5 August 1643. It is reprinted in *Somers tracts*, 2nd ed., ed. W. Scott, 13v., L., 1810, IV, 580–98. Its authorship has occasionally been ascribed to the satirist, Samuel Butler, but there is no evidence for this.

Doubts, or matters under debate, unto the decision of a Major part; and if any Obstacle lay in their way to these ends, which was not in their power to remove, presently at a dead lift, Penington or Ven or Vassels bring an order from the House of Commons, which never failed to determine all things, for their own Creatures.[1]

Mercurius Civicus stated nothing more than the truth. The city oppositionists set out to deprive the mayor of power and win control of the official municipality; and as the sequel showed, by skilful organization and adroit manoeuvre, they succeeded.

The revolution in London's government occurred in several stages. It began on 21 December with the annual election by the wards of their representatives to the common council. On this occasion the opposition party made a strenuous effort to secure the return of its own activists and the defeat of men of adverse view. Evidently some hard electioneering went on: in Langborne Ward, for instance, the Puritans were pictured as '... infinitely busie at an election of a Common-Councell man ... (and from such meetings none of the Faction would be absent). ...'[2] Common council members favourable to the King were attacked as corrupt and accused of levying unequal parish rates which discriminated against the poorer inhabitants.[3] Undoubtedly, the atmosphere in the capital affected the election. Fear of violence, the Irish scare, alarms from the House of Commons, had jolted the Londoners out of their workaday routine and roused them to intense excitement. With a partisanship rare in municipal politics, it was not difficult, said Mercurius Civicus, for the 'active faction, to instill into their fellow Citizens how much it Concerned them to make choyce of Godly men (so they miscall themselves). ...'[4]

The election resulted in an emphatic reversal for the royal supporters in the city government. Mercurius Civicus declared that 'in most Wards, the old Common-Councell men were turned out, and new chosen in, wholy devoted to the Puritan faction. ...'[5] This was an exaggeration, but the vote unquestionably made a noticeable alteration in the common council's composition. Out of a total body of approximately two hundred and fifty, there is evidence for fifty-seven returns, of which twenty-five were new members.[6] Thus, the

---

[1] *A letter from Mercurius Civicus*, 14.

[2] *Persecutio undecima*, 59. The author adds that in Langborne Ward with its three hundred householders, the Puritans could not muster sixty.

[3] Cf. John Bond, *The downfal of old common-counsel-men*, 1641.

[4] *A letter from Mercurius Civicus*, 15.   [5] *Ibid.*, 15.

[6] Cf. the discussion of the election in M. Wren, 'The disputed elections in London in 1641,' *E.H.R.*, LXIV, 250 (1949) and, more precisely, with a correction of several of the former's conclusions, in V. Pearl, *op. cit.*, 132–9.

turnover of membership in the common council amounted to at least ten per cent, probably an unprecedented figure for a single election. Amongst the men elected were Owen Rowe, Nathaniel Wright, and William Perkins, militants connected of old with the opposition movement through their membership in the Massachusetts Bay Company. These new councilmen were merchants and tradesmen, masters of shops, great enemies of the bishops, ready to assist the parliamentary leaders by every means. Some occupied a very middling status in the city, as Mercurius Civicus contemptuously recorded: 'Perkins the Taylor, Norminton the Cutler, young beardlesse Coulson the Dyer, Gill the Wine-Cooper, and Jupe the Laten-man in Crooked-Lane. . . .' The richest and most prominent was John Fowke—'Fowke the Traytor'—a successful merchant whose resistance to Charles I's government had begun in 1627 and continued ever since.[1]

The oppositionists in the common council showed their militancy at once. It was due to them that a petition protesting the King's appointment of Lunsford as Lieutenant of the Tower was submitted on 23 December to the House of Commons in the name of 'divers Common-Council men, and others, of the City of London.'[2] According to custom, however, the new members ought not to have assumed their seats until the Monday after Twelfth Day, 10 January 1642. Nevertheless, they took advantage of the prevailing disorder to attend the common council before time, even those of them whose election was in dispute. The complaints voiced against their intrusion by the defenders of 'the ancient order . . . of the city' were overborne.[3] Thus installed in strength, the oppositionist faction was in a position to affect the official municipality's conduct at the moment of deepest crisis when the King impeached the parliamentary managers.

The next and decisive step in the revolution of the city government occurred on 4 January, the day after the impeachment, and directly in consequence of the King's preparations to seize the accused members at Westminster by force. That morning at the instance of Pym himself, the House of Commons sent three of London's M.P.s with an urgent message to the mayor and common council warning that parliament and the city were in danger.[4] The sequel is revealed in the municipal records. On receipt of the House's message, the common council proceeded to establish a committee of safety to institute measures for the city's defence and security 'in these tymes of feares and daungers. . . .'[5] Six aldermen and twelve councilmen

---

[1] *A letter from Mercurius Civicus*, 15; for an account of Fowke and some of the new oppositionist councilmen, cf. V. Pearl, *op. cit.*, App. II.
[2] *C.J.*, II, 354; J. Rushworth, IV, 459; for this petition, cf. *supra*, 275.
[3] *A letter from Mercurius Civicus*, 16.
[4] *C.J.*, II, 367–8; Coates, *D'Ewes*, 379.   [5] Journal, 40, f. 11.

were appointed to it:[1] three of the former and all of the latter belonged to the opposition faction; the contingent of councilmen, in particular, contained some of the keenest activists in London.[2]

Was the committee of safety a stratagem conceived and prepared for in advance? There is no way of knowing. Real as was the emergency that led to its creation, such a body, standing completely outside the regular machinery of administration, had no precedent in the city. In any case, whether it was an invention of the moment or the product of a well-laid plan, the committee became the instrument by which, with the help of the House of Commons, the London oppositionists made themselves the masters of the municipal government.

The encroachments by the committee of safety started at once. Immediately on its establishment a precept from the lord mayor concerning the security of the wards came forth 'By advise of the Committee assigned by Common Councell assembled this day at the Guildhall.' Other precepts issued subsequently bore such formulae as 'According to direction of the Committee of late appointed by Act of Common Councell.'[3] The ensuing day, 5 January, was the one on which the King, coming into the city, addressed the mayor, aldermen, and common council in defence of his proceedings against the accused members. The antagonism shown him on this occasion was a suitable prelude to what followed. After his withdrawal the committee of safety brought in a petition strongly condemning his actions. This was adopted and submitted to the King in the name of the mayor, aldermen, and common council.[4] It was noteworthy as the first official declaration of the city government which placed it squarely on the side of Charles's opponents. Another petition followed later in the month supporting the bills to exclude the bishops from parliament and to give the Houses control of the kingdom's militia.[5] Since the mayor, Sir Richard Gurney, and his fellow aldermen could hardly have endorsed these statements, their right to veto the common council's proceedings and to serve as sole spokesmen of the municipality was evidently no longer operative.

From this moment on, the oppositionists steadily expanded their grip. It was by agreement with the committee of safety that on 8 January the Commons' committee sitting in the city directed Lon-

---

[1] *Ibid.* The aldermen: Rainton, Gayer, Garrard, Atkin, Wollaston, Towse. The councilmen: Manwaring, Gibbs, Fowke, Bunce, Peck, S. Warner, Russell, N. Wright, Barkley, Normington, Estwick, Rowe.
[2] The opposition aldermen were Atkins, Wollaston, and Towse; perhaps Gayer should be added. There are biographical sketches of the members of the committee of safety in V. Pearl, *op. cit.*, App. I & II.
[3] Journal, 39, ff. 264, 279b.
[4] Journal, 40, f. 12; cf. the text in J. Rushworth, IV, 480–1.
[5] Journal, 40, f. 18; *L.J.*, IV, 534–5.

don's sheriffs to raise a guard for parliament's defence.[1] The common council did not permit the guard to come under the mayor's authority, but entrusted its command to Philip Skippon, an officer of the Artillery Company who was 'a confiding brother to the Cause.'[2] Two weeks later, pursuant to an order brought down by Venn from the House of Commons, the common council gave its committee of safety full supervision of the London militia.[3] This action delivered up the military resources of the city to Pym's party. A blatant violation of the mayor's prerogative, it exactly paralleled the effort the parliamentary leaders were then making, in fear of a civil war, to strip the King of his authority over the kingdom's armed forces.[4]

Charles's citizen supporters did not let the committee of safety's usurpation of the militia pass without a fight. First, the mayor and aldermen petitioned the House of Lords on 16 February for the restoration of their military jurisdiction which had belonged to them, they said, 'time out of mind. . . .'[5] The House, in which the Royalist peers were by now the weaker party,[6] rejected the petition. Sir Richard Gurney's loyalty, commented Mercurius Civicus, 'was too well knowne, to be admitted, to have any share in that power which was intended to be imployed against the King.'[7]

At the same time, some citizens headed by Sir George Benyon, a rich silk merchant and royal financial official, were busy circulating another petition in favour of the mayor's right over the city militia. Benyon disliked the opposition faction with good reason, as he was one of the 'grave, discreet' councilmen defeated at the recent election.[8] He had said of the House of Commons that its members 'much complained of the King's arbitrary Power; and yet . . . go about an arbitrary Government themselves, which, being Four Hundred, will be more grievous than the other.'[9] On 17 February its sponsors brought the petition to the common council. There it was denied a reading by a vote of ninety to sixty-nine. Although the mayor and most of the aldermen favoured it, their votes were included with the whole instead of counted separately.[10] Mercurius Civicus noted the meaning of this development with indignation:

[1] Journal, 40, f. 14. [2] *Ibid.*, 40, f. 15; *Persecutio undecima*, 56.
[3] Journal, 40, f. 17b. [4] Cf. *infra*, ch. IX.
[5] *H.M.C. Fifth report*, pt. 1, 8; *L.J.*, IV, 590.
[6] Cf. *infra*, 299. [7] *A letter from Mercurius Civicus*, 24.
[8] *L.J.*, IV, 683; *A letter from Mercurius Civicus*, 15. In 1631, Benyon became receiver general for Rutland and Northants, *H.M.C. Fourth report*, pt. 1, 97.
[9] *L.J.*, IV, 684.
[10] Journal, 40, ff. 20b–21. The mayor and seven aldermen voted to read the petition, five aldermen voted against. In 1645 John Bellamie cited this vote to support his contention that the aldermanic veto, while never formally abolished, had ceased to hold, *A plea for the commonalty of London*, 11–12.

... whereas the Lord Mayor and Aldermen sit apart, from the Commons, and are Covered, when the others are bareheaded, and have a Negative Voice ... the faction here ... have cast all into a common huddle, blending the Court of Aldermen with the Commons. And though in outward appearance, they remain two distinct Members of one body, yet, in power, they have made both Levell, Involving the Votes of the Mayor and Aldermen in the major part of the Commons.[1]

Rebuffed by the common council, Benyon and his friends nevertheless persisted with their petition. After soliciting further signatures in shops and at the London Exchange, they presented it to parliament on 24 February. It bore the names of more than two hundred citizens, 'divers of them verie wealthie men,' the House of Commons was told. The petitioners declared that the ordering of the London militia belonged by ancient charter to the mayor and that it was against the freedom of the city to put this power into any other hands.[2]

For Benyon the consequences of his political resistance were ruinous. The Houses, then preparing for possible civil war, considered his conduct far too dangerous to go unpunished and decided to make an example of him. Accordingly, in March the Commons impeached him for his 'false and seditious' petition, as well as for other acts of disaffection against parliament. The Lords, adjudging him guilty, then sentenced him to disenfranchisement, £3,000 fine, and two years' imprisonment.[3] The civic government had already disavowed Benyon's petition with one of its own which, through the victory of the majority principle, was presented—supreme irony—in the name of the mayor, aldermen, and common council.[4] Thus, the oppositionist faction quashed the defiance of the royalist citizens, and Pym could feel sure that London's government was in safe hands if civil war proved unavoidable.

While the conquest of the militia was perhaps the main achievement of the London oppositionists, they annexed the prerogatives of the mayor and aldermen in other regions as well. Constitutionally, the right of summoning a common council pertained to the mayor alone: but on 13 January, an order of the Houses originating with the city's M.P., Alderman Penington, commanded the mayor to convene a common council whenever the committee of safety desired.[5] The

[1] *A letter from Mercurius Civicus*, 21.
[2] *C.J.*, II, 451–2; *L.J.*, IV, 609, 684, 701–2; D'Ewes, Journal, B.M. Harl. 162, f. 402b.
[3] *L.J.*, IV, 683–4. 705.
[4] Cf. the city's petition presented to the Houses on 18 March, *C.J.*, II, 485; *L.J.*, IV, 651.
[5] *C.J.*, II, 376; *L.J.*, IV, 508; D'Ewes, Journal, B.M. Harl. 162, f. 321a.

latter used this usurped power so insolently, declared Mercurius Civicus,

that when they have required Sir Richard Gurney to call a Common-councell, and he hath demanded a reason, they have vouchsafed him no other answer, then this saucy one, that when he came thither he should know.[1]

The common council also charged its committee of safety to investigate disputed returns of councilmen in the recent election, a function hitherto reserved to the mayor and aldermen.[2] On 2 March the committee of safety made its report, which received the common council's approval. Besides ordering a number of new elections, it condemned the practice in certain wards by which small groups of citizens at precinct meetings presumed to elect the members of the common council themselves against the rights of the generality of freemen. Although the precincts might meet to consider suitable persons, the report stated,

yet their power therein extends onely to present the names of such persons to the Wardmote, And that then the said inhabitants of the Ward may in part or in whole approve or reiect that nomination or name others to put in election with them as they finde cause.[3]

Eventually the city oppositionists succeeded in removing Sir Richard Gurney from office altogether. At the end of June, with civil war beginning, the lord mayor attempted to raise forces for the King in London. For this and other Royalist acts, the House of Commons impeached him. His trial followed, in which the militants on the common council and committee of safety testified abundantly against him. On 10 August the House of Lords pronounced him guilty. The unfortunate Gurney was expelled from his mayoralty, pronounced incapable of any future honour, and committed to the Tower.[4] At the peers' order a common hall promptly assembled to name his successor. The choice fell upon Alderman Penington, a man to delight all reformers in church and state.[5] Six weeks later when his interim term expired, Penington was re-elected mayor for the ensuing year.[6]

[1] *A letter from Mercurius Civicus*, 21.
[2] Journal, 40, f. 16, order of 19 January 1642.
[3] Journal, 40, f. 21b. The committee of safety's report was published, no doubt, to secure greater publicity; cf. *Articles comprised ... in a report confirmed by Common Councell the second day of March 1641* [1642].
[4] *L.J.*, V, 182, 230–1, 240–1, 246–8, 280.
[5] *Ibid.*, V, 297.
[6] R. Sharpe, *op. cit.*, II, 173.

This signal triumph made the oppositionists' domination of the municipality complete. In seizing power, however, their primary aim was not to liberalize the civic constitution, but to suppress the authority of the Royalist magistrates. If Sir Richard Gurney had shared their political convictions, he would likely have retained his mayoral prerogatives unimpaired. The reforms they introduced, all tending to establish the common council's supremacy, were indeed considerable. Yet they made no attempt to vindicate these innovations by invoking principles of popular government that might have justified their breach of the city's charters and customs. Neither did they try to make their reforms permanent by enacting them into municipal law. The oppositionists' measures all bore an *ad hoc* character; they were the offspring of expediency and emergency and incident to another purpose.

The importance of the revolution in the capital, however, can scarcely be overrated. The oppositionists won power at the moment of showdown between the King and his parliamentary antagonists. Charles counted heavily on the city government's moral and material support for his intended *coup*. He was deprived of both when he needed them most, a loss of incalculable disadvantage. Henceforth, as both sides prepared for the eventuality of war, the official municipality was devoted wholly to Pym's party.

Parliamentarians and Royalists
The Civil War

The King's withdrawal from London on 10 January initiated the final phase of England's ebbing peace. A resort to arms was still avoidable, perhaps, but its dark prospect loomed clearly before every mind. In the House of Commons, D'Ewes reflected the general sense when he spoke of evil auguries and voiced his concern lest the 'misunderstanding betweene us and his Majestie' grow into a flame.[1] Charles's departure was more than a physical remove from the scene of his ignominy and repulse. It signified an act of secession on his part, a bill of divorcement delivered to the Houses and the unfaithful city that had defied and contemned him. He intended not to return until he could do so from a position of strength. Meanwhile, he left his enemies in triumphant occupation at Westminster, loudly acclaimed by the popular voice. From this time he dealt with parliament from afar, their relation increasingly like that of independent states who in a last negotiation stand poised between the alternatives of treaty and the sword.

The situation now, however, did not admit of compromise. Parliament was separated from the King not only by specific differences, but by a mistrust so enveloping that only total acquiescence on his part could dispel it. His attempt against the opposition members was seen as a display of bad faith that justified the exaction of steel-clad guarantees for the sake of future security. His power had to be clipped and contracted to the narrowest limits. Of course, to press him thus meant risking the chance of civil war. Yet Pym and his party felt that their own and the kingdom's safety required nothing less, and very likely calculated that by driving on determinedly they would overbear all opposition as before, and force the King to submit.

Charles, too, suffered from fears. He had heard reports that the Queen would be impeached or separated from him[2]—a story that

[1] On 20 January: Journal, B.M. Harl. 162, ff. 336a–b.
[2] Cf. the Queen's statement mentioned by the Dutch agent in his despatch of 11 January, *Archives . . . de la maison d'Orange-Nassau*, 2nd ser., III, 502.

perhaps arose amongst his own followers to justify or palliate his attempt against the opposition leaders.[1] Perhaps the account also came to his ears of an intention to depose him in favour of his elder son.[2] On 14 January all these rumours were denounced as false in the Commons, and Pym, as an offer of reassurance, suggested a declaration expressing the House's care for the King's safety and honour.[3] But Charles and Henrietta Maria doubtless put little faith in these professions, since they considered their opponents would stop at nothing to attain their ends.

Charles's immediate thought on quitting London was to get possession of Hull in Yorkshire, where the largest magazine in the kingdom with arms for 16,000 men lay stored. From Hampton Court on 11 January he issued secret orders to the earl of Newcastle, Strafford's former friend, to hasten northward to assume the government of the town.[4] The Houses anticipated the King's purpose, however, and that same day commanded Sir John Hotham, M.P. for Beverly, to secure Hull and not to yield it 'without the King's Authority, signified ... by the Lords and Commons ... in Parliament.'[5] The tenor of this instruction indicated plainly that every move towards force on Charles's part was bound to incite the Houses in self-defence to further restrictions on his powers. Several days later they also presumed to direct a general command to the sheriffs and justices of England to suppress assemblies dangerous to the peace.[6] Meanwhile at Hull the position remained undecided, as the mayor would admit neither Newcastle nor Hotham's son, who had come as his father's representative. The Houses dealt with the situation by curtly summoning both the earl and the mayor to explain their conduct.[7] This sufficed to procure obedience, and before the end of January Hotham with three companies of Yorkshire militia was master of the town.[8]

In the face of these resolute measures, Charles made his first conciliatory gesture since the failure of his *coup*. On 20 January he sent the Houses a message lamenting the dangerous state of affairs

---

[1] Cf. *supra*, 278.

[2] Sir John Northcote told the House that this rumour was current, D'Ewes, Journal, B.M. Harl. 162, f. 324b.

[3] *Ibid.*, ff. 325b, 326b.

[4] The order to Newcastle is printed in *L.J.*, IV, 585. The text attests its secrecy as does the King's warrant to Secretary Nicholas not to make a record of it in the Signet Office, *C.S.P.D. 1641–43*, 251.

[5] *L.J.*, IV, 505. Hotham had actually received a patent from the King in 1639 appointing him governor of Hull; cf. *ibid.* and *D.N.B.*, *s.v.*

[6] *L.J.*, IV, 512.

[7] On 20 January: D'Ewes, Journal, B.M. Harl. 162, f. 337b; *L.J.*, IV, 526, 527.

[8] *C.J.*, II, 407; J. Rushworth, IV, 565.

and protesting his desire for an accommodation. Let them submit proposals, he asked, for the maintenance of his regal authority, the establishment of their privileges, the security of true religion, and the settlement of church ceremonies so as to remove all just cause of offence. For his part, he was ready to consider their views and to exceed 'the most indulgent Princes in their Acts of Grace and Favour to their People. . . .'[1]

Although Charles may have been sincere, his mind was not directed entirely towards conciliation. Knowing his weakness while he continued so near London, he sought time to improve his situation, and the Queen informed the Dutch envoy that he would go into Yorkshire to provide himself with means of defence if parliament refused him satisfaction.[2] In any case, however, his offer came too late. The opposition party, convinced that he would try to crush it at the first opportunity, did not look for grace and favour, but for infallible guarantees. The Commons therefore replied to the King's message with a request that he 'raise up . . . a sure Ground of Safety and Confidence' by giving command of the forts and militia to persons recommended by both Houses. The mover of this proposition was Hampden.[3] The peers in their turn refused to adopt it, and the answer accordingly went to the King on 25 January in the name of the Commons alone.[4]

The peers' non-cooperation was merely a further effort on the part of the majority to retain a shred of political independence and to preserve some ground of legality in relation to the King. But to the Commons their actions constituted an intolerable obstruction which must be overcome. Since October the upper House had neglected the bill against the secular employments of the clergy, despite the strong outcry for the bishops' expulsion from parliament;[5] it had obstinately refrained as well from endorsing the demand that the King surrender his authority over the militia. The Commons managers, buoyed up by their recent triumph over Charles, were determined to break the deadlock between the Houses and to force the peers to submit.

In the last week of January the House of Lords was subjected to every form of pressure the oppositionists' supporters could devise. Petitions came in from many counties exhorting the Lords to comply with the Commons lest the kingdom be lost. Petitions to the same effect were submitted by the city governments of Exeter and London. The latter, now fallen under the domination of Pym's allies, declared that the citizens would lend no money for the relief of Ireland till the

[1] *L.J.*, IV, 523–4.
[2] *Archives . . . de la maison d'Orange-Nassau*, 2nd ser., IV, 7.
[3] D'Ewes, Journal, B.M. Harl. 162, f. 340b.
[4] *L.J.*, IV, 533; *C.J.*, II, 395–6.   [5] Cf. *supra*, 253.

peers ceased their obstruction; its statement spoke also of the decay of trade and hinted pointedly at an outbreak by the poor if the peers did not promptly pass the bill against the secular employments of the clergy and agree to place the militia in safe hands.[1]

The party leaders shrewdly exploited these importunities to overbear the upper House. At a joint conference on the 25th Pym expressed a note of utmost urgency. In the petitions, he said, 'your Lordships might hear the Voice . . . of all England. . . . the Agony, Terror, and Perplexity, in which the Kingdom labours, is universal. . . .' He intimated plainly that the peers were failing in their duty and appealed for their cooperation lest the Commons 'should be inforced to save the Kingdom alone. . . .'[2]

The business slump arising from political unsettlement was used to frighten the Lords with the threat of social insurrection. On 31 January the Commons accepted without a sign of disapproval an inflammatory petition in the name of thousands of London poor warning of the extremities to which want and unemployment might drive them. At the House's bar, the city M.P. Venn introduced the spokesmen for the petitioners. They 'boldlie . . . desired to know,' noted D'Ewes, 'who weere the obstructours of our happines.'[3] That evening in a joint conference Holles drove home the point to the Lords. The petition was extraordinary, he acknowledged: 'but now consider the necessity of a multitude, a sleeping lyon, not good to awaken. . . .' Rents were unpaid and public distractions had weakened authority. If the worst came, he admonished, the fault would lie with the peers for withholding their cooperation.[4]

Any nobleman who showed his dislike of these pressures exposed himself to risk. The youthful duke of Richmond brought a storm upon himself when he offered a motion that the House of Lords adjourn for six months. His fellow peers compelled him to retract and apologize, but the Commons, thinking the penalty too light, branded Richmond 'one of the malignant Party' and launched an investigation into his use of electoral patronage as Warden of the Cinque Ports.[5] This was as good as to tell the upper House that no defiance of the Commons would be tolerated.

[1] *L.J.*, IV, 534–40, *passim*. Petitions of support also came in to the House of Commons. One from Suffolk on 31 January had over fourteen thousand signatures, D'Ewes, Journal, B.M. Harl. 162, f. 360b.

[2] *L.J.*, IV, 540–3.

[3] D'Ewes, Journal, B.M. Harl. 162, f. 360b; *C.J.*, II, 404. The petition circulated as a printed broadside 'for the use of the Petitioners who are to meet in More Fields and from thence go to the House of Parliament with it in their hands.'; cf. *Catalogue of the Thomason tracts*, I, 67.

[4] *L.J.*, IV, 559; *H.M.C. House of Lords*, n.s., XI, *Addenda, 1514–1714*, 306–7.

[5] *L.J.*, IV, 549–53, 555–6; *C.J.*, II, 400; D'Ewes, Journal, B.M. Harl. 162,

Parliamentarians and Royalists

The House of Lords had no means to counter this campaign. Feeling itself surrounded by hostility and lacking any organized support, it could do nothing but bow to superior strength. On 1 February it accepted the Commons' demand to the King for parliamentary control of the militia; on the 5th it passed the bill expelling the bishops from parliament.[1] The Venetian ambassador ascribed its submission to 'fresh movements among the common people, who openly support the designs of the most seditious. . . .' Another news writer spoke of its 'panic fear of the multitude, who from all the counties come daily in thousands with petitions. . . .'[2]

These votes meant surrender all along the line. They signified the total defeat of the upper House's attempts to take an independent or mediating position between the Commons and the King. The Royalist and more moderate noblemen, no longer hopeful of rendering any service after such a reverse, began to withdraw from parliamentary activity. The peers who favoured the opposition put no obstacles in their way. On 4 February the earl of Southampton, conspicuously loyal to the King, obtained leave to be absent, as did also the earl of Carnarvon.[3] Other noblemen followed their example over the next days and weeks, so that the upper House was left much reduced in numbers. During February the average attendance was forty, compared with about sixty in the previous month. At a call of the House on the 9th, sixty-seven members were recorded absent.[4] It was a body thinned by desertion and disaffection that now confronted the King in union with the House of Commons.

Meanwhile, Charles had given his reply on 29 January to the Commons' petition on the militia. He denied the House's demand, declaring that the military prerogative was an 'inseparable . . . Flower of his Crowne . . . derived unto Him . . . by the fundamentall Lawes of the Kingdome. . . .'[5] His answer was vehemently attacked by

---

[1] *L.J.*, IV, 558, 564. The *Journal* does not record the figures in the vote on the bill, but observers gave them as 36–23 in favour; *Archives . . . de la maison d'Orange Nassau*, 2nd ser., IV, 18; *H.M.C. Buccleuch*, I, 290.

[2] *C.S.P.V. 1640–42*, 290; *C.S.P.D. 1641–43*, 278.

[3] *L.J.*, IV, 562. Southampton returned to the House for a time in March in order to protest against parliament's seizure of the militia power, *L.J.*, IV, 628, 646.

[4] C. H. Firth, *The House of Lords during the Civil War*, 111 and n.; *L.J.*, IV, 571.   [5] *C.J.*, II, 402; *An exact collection*, 60–1.

---

f. 355a. This was not the first time the Commons intervened against the electoral influence of the nobility. In December 1641, because of a 'commendatorie letter' from the earl of Arundel in favour of a candidate in a by-election in his own borough of Arundel, the House passed an order to prohibit such letters by peers as an infringement on the freedom of election; Coates, *D'Ewes*, 236–7; *C.J.*, II, 337.

299

Holles, Strode, and other oppositionist speakers; and two days later the House responded by passing the militia ordinance, which provided that parliament 'in this Time of so imminent Danger' should exercise authority over the militia through lords lieutenants to be appointed by it in every county.[1] A lone voice, that of Sir Ralph Hopton, M.P. for Wells, pointed out that 'wee could not doe this but by an Act of Parliament. . . .', but to no effect.[2]

The militia ordinance was the most extreme measure that the Commons had thus far sponsored. Yet it represented nothing more than a logical progression from earlier positions. As far back as the previous August the Houses had passed their first ordinance: even then they were reaching towards a legislative power fixed solely in themselves. The party leaders, believing the care of the commonwealth to devolve principally on parliament, had repeatedly used the public emergency to launch encroachments on the executive. For months, moreover, the lower House had been straining to win a parliamentary supervision of the choice of ministers, while latterly the Irish rebellion had led it to challenge the King's military authority both by petition and by bill. If it now took the revolutionary step of preparing to seize control of the militia by the legislative fiat of the Houses alone, it had fully prepared the way for such a development.

To the King's misfortune, the two Houses had finally reached accord just as the thrust of the revolt against his regime was becoming concentrated on the decisive issue of military supremacy. The House of Lords having already consented on 1 February to the Commons' petition for the militia, there was every likelihood that it would also agree to the militia ordinance. On the 7th Charles indicated that he might allow parliament to appoint the militia's commanders for a certain time, on condition that he retained a veto on the persons recommended and was satisfied as to the extent of power they would exercise.[3] This gleam of possible concession did not dissuade the Commons from its course. It went on in the next few days'to complete the nomination of lords lieutenants over the militia of the counties and sent their names to the upper House. The persons selected were mainly noblemen believed favourable to the oppositionist side. None was to have more than two English counties under his command, and 'if . . . wee cannot . . . find Lords enough in whom wee may confide,' declared D'Ewes, '. . . wee may . . . take Commoners, men of prime qualitie and faire estates. . . .'[4] For London, the ordering of the militia was confirmed in the city's newly-established committee

[1] D'Ewes, Journal, B.M. Harl. 162, f. 356b (in cipher); *C.J.*, II, 406.
[2] D'Ewes, Journal, B.M. Harl. 162, f. 362b.
[3] *C.J.*, II, 416.
[4] D'Ewes, Journal, B.M. Harl. 162, f. 376b.

of safety. The peers accepted this list of appointments on 12 February; on the 15th they passed the militia ordinance itself.[1] The two Houses in cooperation thus completed the basis for investing themselves under the title of parliament with supremacy over the kingdom's military establishment.

Whether or not the parliamentary leaders would proceed further on their unilateral line now depended on the King. With or against his will they meant to deprive him of his military power. Nevertheless, they still hoped that the threat of the militia ordinance would cause him to submit voluntarily to their demand. Charles had, indeed, already yielded several substantial points while the ordinance was passing through the House of Lords. Not only did he agree to appoint parliament's nominee, Sir John Conyers, as Lieutenant of the Tower; more important still, on the 14th he consented to the bill against the secular employments of the clergy. He also accepted an impressment bill by which he relinquished his prerogative right to conscript men for military service outside their counties without parliament's authorization.[2] After these renunciations, it was less than likely that he would offer anything more to secure an accommodation. Even the bill against the secular employments of the clergy was agreed to by him with the greatest reluctance. He did so only after repeated persuasions from the Queen and Sir John Culpepper, who urged that the removal of the bishops from parliament was the sole way to preserve episcopacy itself, and that if he satisfied the Houses in this he could the more firmly deny them the militia.[3]

Probably the King and Queen decided on these last concessions, however, not so much to draw parliament to a compromise as to spin out the time till they obtained the means of effective resistance. Henrietta Maria was convinced that only the force of arms could reestablish royal authority and she told the Venetian envoy that 'to settle affairs it was necessary to unsettle them first. . . .'[4] With this end in view she and the King were making fresh plans. At the end of January they concluded that she should go to Holland with her daughter, Princess Mary, who had been married the previous year to the son of the Prince of Orange. While abroad, she was to try to procure foreign military assistance for the King. He on his side would betake himself to Yorkshire to rally the loyal gentry and make another attempt to seize Hull or some other stronghold

[1] *L.J.*, IV, 577–8, 586.

[2] *L.J.*, IV, 577, 580; 16 Car. I, c.27, c.28, *Statutes of the realm*, V, 138.

[3] Clarendon, *Life*, 942; *Rebellion*, IV, 299–301.

[4] On 10 February, *C.S.P.V. 1640–42*, 295. A little earlier, Charles's nephew, the Elector Palatine, reported that the Queen was against any reconciliation with parliament, since it could only be got on dishonourable conditions, *C.S.P.D. 1641–43*, 276.

from which he could maintain regular communication with the continent.[1]

On 7 February the King, then at Windsor, notified parliament of the Queen's approaching journey.[2] Till she was safely away, he put off his answer to the militia ordinance. Accompanied by him to Dover, Henrietta Maria embarked on the 23rd for Holland where, during the year of her absence, she did everything in her power to sustain her husband's cause. As soon as she was gone, the King set out to execute the measures of resistance he had in mind. On 28 February, just as he was about to start for the north, he delivered his opinion of the militia ordinance. His message, with its tart language and emphatic assertion of his own wishes, offered little hope of his compliance. He was willing to appoint their nominees as lords lieutenants, he informed the Houses, but only if all commissions came from himself and terminated at his discretion. This was the sole arrangement consistent with the authority given him by God and the law for the defence of his people. Further, he would not consent to deprive the mayor and aldermen of London of their rights over the citizen militia. As for any future provisions concerning the militia, they must be effected by statute, not ordinance. Finally, he demanded that anyone who meddled with the militia without authority should be proceeded against by law.[3]

The House of Commons immediately rejected the King's answer in every particular as a denial of parliament's desires. If he persisted in his stand, the members declared, he would hazard the peace and safety of the kingdom; they also warned of the danger to peace if he removed to distant parts and asked him to remain near parliament. D'Ewes, who did not dissent from this intransigence but had no stomach for its risks, entered bleakly in his journal: 'This was soe sadd a dayes work to mee as I withdrew out of the howse . . . the rest of the day. . . .' The Commons' resolutions were promptly carried to the House of Lords, which accepted them without demur.[4]

The opposition party was following a line from which it refused to budge by even a hair's breadth. On 1 March a joint committee brought the King the Houses' resolutions of the previous day along

[1] The Queen first told the Dutch agent on 29 January of her intention to go to Holland, *Archives . . . de la maison d'Orange-Nassau*, 2nd ser., IV, 12–13. The plans she and the King made prior to her departure are summarized in a letter she sent him from abroad on 29 September 1642, *Letters of Queen Henrietta Maria*, ed. M. A. E. Green, L., 1857, 112. The entire tenor of her correspondence while away was aimed at stiffening the King's will against any concession to parliament.
[2] *L.J.*, IV, 567.   [3] *C.J.*, II, 459–60.
[4] *Ibid.*, II, 460; D'Ewes, Journal, B.M. Harl. 163, ff. 10b–11a; *L.J.*, IV, 619–20.

with a virtual ultimatum: unless he speedily granted their demands, 'they shall be enforced . . . to dispose of the militia by the Authority of both Houses . . . and they resolve to do it accordingly.' Charles, then stopping in Hertfordshire on his way northward, returned an equally unyielding answer. He declined to modify his stand on the militia in any respect, he said, nor did he hold it consistent with his safety or honour to reside near parliament.[1]

This was very nearly the breaking point. With the King's last message before them, the Houses on 2 March voted to put the kingdom in a state of defence by means of the militia ordinance. Consonant to this, they again passed the ordinance on the 5th with the names of their lords lieutenants included. Another vote decreed the nullity of all commissions of lieutenancy issued by the King.[2] These actions breached the inmost citadel of the King's executive authority, yet still the Houses made one more effort to gain his concurrence. At Newmarket on the 9th a joint committee presented him with a declaration expressing the just causes of the Houses' fears and urging that he grant them the security they desired. The appeal was futile, its recriminatory tone more apt to inflame than assuage. '. . . wee might have declared the whole and naked Truth,' noted D'Ewes, 'as well in reverentiall and humble words, as in soe high and asperous termes.'[3] Charles's response was an indignant refusal. He too had grounds for fear, he said; moreover, he had passed all bills for his subjects' ease, granted all that the Houses could reasonably ask; they had done nothing for him in return. To a question from the earl of Pembroke, one of the committee, whether he might not accept the terms of the militia ordinance for a time, he retorted angrily, 'By God, not for an houre; you have askt that of me in this, was never askt of a King. . . .'[4]

The King was nearing York when the Houses on 15 March proclaimed that the militia ordinance 'doth oblige the People, and ought to be obeyed by the fundamental Laws of this Kingdom.' The proposition was reported to the Commons by Pym. Certain members objected to it that only a law with the royal assent could oblige the subject. Nevertheless, it passed without a division, its defenders contending that the militia ordinance was 'warranted by the law of God . . . the law of nature and of necessity. . . .'[5] The King countered with a declaration that any ordinance lacking his consent was

[1] *Ibid.*, IV, 620–2.

[2] *Ibid.*, IV, 622, 625–6, 628.

[3] *Ibid.*, IV, 629–31; D'Ewes, Journal, B.M. Harl. 163, f. 19a.

[4] *L.J.*, IV, 640–1; *An exact collection*, 105.

[5] *C.J.*, II, 479; D'Ewes, Journal, B.M. Harl. 163, f. 33a; *L.J.*, IV, 646. Six noblemen entered their protest against the declaration in the House of Lords.

unlawful and of no force to bind his subjects.[1] To this the Houses replied with the most far-reaching claim ever propounded by the imperious politicians who governed their deliberations. 'When the Lords and Commons in Parliament,' they asserted,

which is the supreme Court of Judicature in the Kingdom, shall declare what the Law of the Land is; to have This not only questioned and controverted, and a Command that it should not be obeyed, is a high Breach of the Privilege of Parliament.

The peers first tried to soften this statement by deleting 'Lords and Commons,' thus tacitly allowing that the crown, too, had a part in parliament. The Commons would have none of the amendment. Even D'Ewes spoke against it, arguing that the disputed proposition meant 'not *ius dare*, but *ius dicere*.' The conceited antiquarian preened himself on the parchment learning that frequently enabled him to furnish his fellow members with a legal excuse for their actions. '... the onlie question now is,' he said, 'whether both howses may not declare what the ancient law is, which I hold stronglie the Howse of Commons [may] doe alone.' The peers acquiesced and on 22 March the two Houses adopted the declaration as their official view.[2]

The split was absolute. The fig leaf of constitutional propriety with which D'Ewes tried to cover the nakedness of the Houses' assumption of legislative power could hardly have deceived anyone. Under the title of parliament the Houses were claiming sovereignty for themselves. All that now remained was for them and the King to prepare to impose their will on each other by whatever means they could.

The King arrived in York on the 19th, hopeful of gathering support about him in the northern counties to withstand a rebellion.[3] At Westminster the Houses were already giving effect to the militia ordinance.[4] In their latest declarations, the irreconcilable antagonists were no longer speaking to, but past, each other. These statements, like their ensuing manifestoes of the spring and summer, were communications to the kingdom and the governing class, appeals from both sides to enlist popular strength for the approaching 'continuation of politics by other means.'

[1] *L.J.*, IV, 647.
[2] *C.J.*, II, 481; *L.J.*, IV, 650, 663; D'Ewes, Journal, B.M. Harl. 163, ff. 37a–b.
[3] The King's itinerary from the Queen's departure to his arrival in York is given in J. Rushworth, IV, 484.
[4] Pym, for instance, moved on 21 March that Sir Edward Hungerford, M.P. for Chippenham, should have 'leave to go into the cuntrie ... where he would be able to doe us much service ... for the settling of the Militia.'; D'Ewes, Journal, B.M. Harl. 163, f. 39b.

As the tide of public differences swept steadily on towards civil war, a massive political realignment occurred in the kingdom. The breakup of the Country, signalized in the past November's vote on the Grand Remonstrance, continued without reversal during the winter and spring of 1641–2. Out of the Country's split, and from its sundered segments, arose the two parties that were shortly to engage each other in blood on the field of battle.

The appearance of the Royalist and Parliamentarian parties marked a fresh stage in the revolution's progress. In no sense did they correspond to the preceding Court-Country division whose conflict dominated Charles's earlier reign and the first period of the Long Parliament's history. The Court, isolated and powerless when parliament assembled, had disintegrated as a political factor. The Country, with public opinion and the governing class largely united in its support, had enacted a far-reaching programme of reforms. But owing to the crisis of confidence in the King, these reforms had failed to end the revolution. The Country leaders embarked on a quest for guarantees that led to ever bolder encroachments on the crown's executive authority. Under their direction parliament was moving steadily, in fact, to take over both the work of government and the legislative power. The unremitting demands of Pym and his associates, their grasping for control of ministerial appointments and the military establishment, their exploitation of the London populace, all strained their public and parliamentary backing to the breaking point. Every politically-conscious person who had acknowledged their ascendancy was compelled to consider whether to accompany the party managers further on a road that was taking England away from its old landmarks and very probably towards armed struggle against its lawful prince.

It was the strength of the oppositionist leaders that they had faced the issue squarely and made their deliberate choice. These men, profoundly conservative as they were at heart, stood ready if necessary to endure the stigma of rebellion and to chance the trials of war rather than leave the King the slightest power to destroy what parliament had won. Many others in the political nation, however, would not consent to follow them in this. Thus, the Country disintegrated, and in the re-groupment of its dismembered elements the Parliamentarian and Royalist parties gradually took shape.

'. . . that which was called the King's party in both Houses,' said one of its foremost adherents,

was made up of persons who were strangers to the Court, of the best fortunes and the best reputation in their several countries, where they were known as having always appeared very zealous in the maintenance of their just rights and opposed as much as in them lay all illegal and grievous impositions.[1]

The author of this description of the newly-emerged Royalism was Edward Hyde, the future historian of the revolution. A Royalist convert himself, his conduct was emblematic of the break of ranks in the governing class that disrupted the Country and gave the King a party. Hyde's personal acquaintance with the King only began in the summer of 1641, when Charles received him in a private interview to acknowledge his parliamentary services on the monarchy's behalf.[2] Already in the process of withdrawing from cooperation with the opposition leaders, his secession became complete during the debate on the Grand Remonstrance.[3] The same political transition was made by his friends, Lord Falkland and Sir John Culpepper, who, like himself, enjoyed some esteem and prominence in the House of Commons. Accordingly, when the King conferred office upon the latter two in January 1642, he offered Hyde promotion as well. Hyde declined it on the ground that he could assist the royal cause better for the time if he remained a private member of parliament. He promised, nevertheless, to send Charles advice and to consult regularly with Falkland and Culpepper about affairs.[4] Henceforward he was effectively in the King's employ notwithstanding his non-official capacity.

His most recent and discerning historian has argued that in thus joining the King Hyde did not change his political position: that what changed was the situation in which Pym pursued a policy incompatible with peace and compromise, while Hyde himself continued to desire a legal settlement based on the statutes passed before the September 1641 recess.[5] This view, however, is a misleading and partial one. In the context of the acute and unbroken crisis of confidence, it was Pym's judgment that there could be no guarantee of permanence for parliament's reforming work nor of the personal safety of the oppositionist leaders without additional securities from the King. The House of Commons' insistence on these securities was, indeed, the practical basis for the formation of the Parliamentarian

---

[1] Clarendon, *Rebellion*, IV, 94. This statement noting the formation of a Royalist party refers to late January 1642. In a subsequent reference to April and the militia controversy, Clarendon mentions the King's 'own party (for so those began now to be called who preserved their duty and allegiance entire). . . .', *ibid.*, V, 87.
[2] Clarendon, *Life*, 937.   [3] Cf. *supra*, 268.
[4] Clarendon, *Rebellion*, IV, 126; *Life*, 938–9.
[5] Cf. B. H. G. Wormald, *op. cit.*, 13, 17–18, 45–6, 83–4.

party. To diverge from Pym in this, to opt for the King in the contest of wills over the control of ministerial appointments and the militia, meant a change of sides to Royalism. That Hyde acted out of principle need not be denied. Yet the Royalist perspective from which he now saw events, and which afterwards also shaped his *History of the rebellion*, gave him a prejudiced and therefore very inadequate conception of the motives of the Parliamentarian leaders. In particular, it inclined him grossly to underrate the depth and extent of distrust of the King. He treated the crisis of confidence as one of Pym's deliberate contriving, rather than as the authentic consequence of the King's repeated actions. This failing led him into disingenuousness and misrepresentation when he wrote his *History*.[1] Hence, he even explained away the King's attempted *coup d'état* (for which he himself bore no responsibility) as a mere misjudgment, and attributed parliament's breach with the King almost entirely to the artful machinations and unprincipled ambition of Pym's group.[2]

As England's peace expired, it was Hyde who framed the emerging Royalist party's doctrine and therewith enabled the King to assume the unfamiliar role of defender of the legal constitution against the transgressions of the Parliamentarians. He performed this unique service as author of the declarations which the King put forth in answer to parliament's messages. Hyde undertook the task of composing the King's replies at the end of February 1642. As long as he stayed at Westminster, he transmitted the drafts to Charles secretly, who then communicated the result to the Houses as his own. The same ghost-writing arrangement continued when Hyde arrived in York in May to attend Charles in person. With one exception, he was responsible for every important statement of constitutional doctrine which the King published in the wordy war of manifestoes preceding the war of arms—a contribution of inestimable value to the refurbishing and renewal of the monarch's public image.[3]

The policy Hyde advocated for the King in the face of germinating

---

[1] The method and chronology of Clarendon's composition of his *History* have been analysed by C. H. Firth, 'Clarendon's *History of the rebellion*,' 3 pts., *E.H.R.*, XIX, 63–5 (1904). Firth's verdict on Clarendon's account of the coming of the civil war (*ibid.*, pt. 1, 37–8) is severe, but not unfairly so.
[2] The King consulted neither Hyde, Falkland, nor Culpepper before his impeachment of the opposition members. But Hyde, though disapproving the action as ill-advised and unseasonable, believed Pym guilty and considered that the King might have proceeded against the oppositionists more effectively. Charles, he declared, did 'rather what was just than what was expedient. . . .'; *Rebellion*, IV, 149n., 158, 192, 218.
[3] Clarendon, *Life*, 943–4. Before engaging himself to write the King's declarations, Hyde had shown his talent by drafting Charles's reply to the Grand Remonstrance. The only important royal declaration not composed

rebellion was one of non-violence and reliance on the law to preserve his authority. He was

to grant anything that by the law he was obliged to grant, and to deny what by the law was in his own power and which he found inconvenient to consent to, and to oppose and punish any extravagant attempt by the force and power of the law.[1]

How the King was to do this amidst the breakdown of the monarchical constitution and parliament's step-by-step erection of a competing sovereignty Hyde did not explain. In any event, Charles had decided with the Queen on resistance; even then he was in the north to make a further try to secure the arsenal at Hull. Hyde, however, had no knowledge of these counsels when they were first adopted, while later he was plausibly able to represent the King's actions as defensive measures against the seditious conduct of the Houses.[2]

It was therefore to the law that Charles appealed in the declarations Hyde penned on his behalf. These royal utterances contained no recondite theorizing. The sentiments to which they addressed themselves were the long-engrafted ones of honourable loyalty to the crown and deference for established principles. They were directed especially to those men antagonized by parliament's latest demands and the prospect of further unsettlement: persons, as Hyde told the King, 'who have been the severest assertors of the publick liberties, and so besides their duty and loyalty to your person . . . value their own interests upon the preservation of your rights.'[3] The themes which the declarations reiterated were the King's innocence of any evil intention towards parliament and the falsity of accusations that he had plotted to destroy its privileges; the many concessions he had made to demonstrate his desire for political reconciliation and the public good; the justifiable reasons he had to fear the popular tumults and seditious language that had driven him from London; above all the King invoked the law—'the Law,' he asserted, '. . .which We always intend shall bee the measure of Our owne power, and expect it shall be the rule of Our Subjects obedience.'[4] Once he quoted shrewdly from a great panegyric on the law which Pym had delivered

[1] Clarendon, *Rebellion*, V, 12.
[2] Hyde recorded that only Culpepper, neither he nor Falkland, knew of the King's design upon Hull, Clarendon, *Life*, 941.
[3] Hyde to the King at York, March 1642, *Clarendon state papers*, II, 138–9.
[4] *An exact collection*, 109.

by him before the civil war was the answer to parliament's Nineteen Propositions (for which cf. *infra*, 318–19), which Falkland and Culpepper wrote, *ibid.*, 937, 953.

a year previously against Strafford and told the Houses to take the words to heart: 'the Law of the Land,' he admonished, 'is the only Rule which preserves the Publick. ... Preserve the Dignity, and Reverence due to that.'[1] From this high ground he denounced the Houses' ordinance power as a subversion of the kingdom's constitution. '... We must declare to all the World,' said the King,

That we are not satisfied, or shall ever allow Our Subjects to be bound by your printed Votes ... or that under pretence of declaring what the Law of the Land is, you shall without us make a new Law, which is plainly the case of the Militia: And what is this but to introduce an Arbitrary way of Government?[2]

Against the legalist arguments of the King, the Houses did not avow any fundamental political or constitutional theory, at least not in explicit terms. Steeped in reverence for the law themselves, the party leaders had no mind to argue the Parliamentarian case on the ground of first principles. Besides, they believed that they were the true defenders of the legal order against arbitrary government, whatever Charles might say, and that practical exigencies existed which amply warranted their programme. Accordingly, the Houses' declarations expressed no awareness or acknowledgment that they were propounding opinions of any novelty. Yet despite this, they implicitly presented the elements of a revolutionary redefinition of the polity, wherein monarchy became no more than the obedient and answerable agency of the community's will expressed through parliament.[3]

The root of Parliamentarian doctrine was the conception of parliament as the organ supremely responsible for the care of the commonwealth—for the preservation of law, liberty, property, and a rightly limited prerogative. Such had been the Country's creed from the beginning. Parliament, of course, included the King: but with the progressive breakdown of the constitution in 1641-2, the Houses claimed the responsibility of parliament for themselves alone. Partly they sought the sanction of law to justify their position. Thus, to refute the King's accusations of illegality they cited both medieval precedents and the 'fundamental law' as grounds for the militia ordinance. '... the two Houses of Parliament,' they said,

... were enabled by their own authority to provide for the repulsing of ... imminent, and evident danger not by any new Law of their own

[1] *Ibid.*, 140.   [2] *Ibid.*, 126.
[3] Cf. the discussion of the Houses' views by J. W. Allen, *English political thought*, pt. VI, ch. IV and J. W. Gough, *Fundamental law in English history*, ch. VI.

making as hath been untruly suggested . . . but by the most ancient Law of this Kingdome, even that which is fundamentall and essential to the constitution and subsistance of it.[1]

As these remarks illustrate, the Houses did not admit that their militia ordinance entailed an exercise of legislative power. For the same reason they referred to themselves as a council and as a court—traditional designations of parliament—without ever straightforwardly asserting that they were sovereign. All the same, their reasoning implied no less. For underlying their arguments was the notion that they, as the kingdom's representative body, were entitled to declare the law and to determine public policy in the commonwealth's interest. It was therefore the idea of the Houses as representative—as being, quintessentially, the community itself—that constituted the tacit theoretical basis of the Parliamentarian case.

Repeatedly, the Houses described themselves as 'entrusted' by and for the kingdom. While they allowed that the King also possessed a trust, they pronounced theirs to be superior and controlling. '. . . the Wisedome of this State,' they affirmed, 'hath intrusted the Houses of Parliament with a power to supply what shall be wanting on the part of the Prince. . . .' In their discharge of this trust they proclaimed their judgment binding upon all, the King included: what is 'declared by the Lords and Commons in Parliament needs not the authority of any person . . . to affirme; nor is it in the power of any person . . . to revoke that judgment.'[2]

More than once, indeed, the opinion had been expressed in the Commons that the King possessed no negative voice in legislation. Henry Marten, M.P. for Berkshire, advanced the suggestion that Charles must pass all bills, since his vote 'was included in the Lords votes as the whole Commons of England weere included in ours; because hee elected the Peeres as the Commons did us,'[3] On another occasion, Nathaniel Fiennes said in defence of the militia ordinance that the King was obliged to assent to all measures on which the Houses agreed. It made no difference that D'Ewes replied that the King had always assented to acts—that records would show the kings of England to have rejected more bills than they had passed.[4] The Commons eventually adopted Fiennes's opinion when it voted on 19 May that the King was bound by his coronation oath to pass all bills presented by the Houses for the good of the kingdom.[5]

---

[1] *An exact collection*, 197, 205–6.
[2] Declaration of 19 May 1642, *An exact collection*, 204, 206, 207–8.
[3] D'Ewes, Journal, B.M. Harl. 162, f. 375b. This was on 7 February.
[4] On 1 April, *ibid.*, B.M. Harl. 163, f. 58b.
[5] *C.J.*, II. 580. This was voted in a division of 103–61.

The Houses thus left the King no shred of independence from themselves. Completely severing his monarchical from his personal capacity, they declared that his politic will, as distinct from his merely personal one, was merged in theirs. Parliament, they informed the King, is

not onely a Court of Judicature . . . to adjudge and determine the Rights and Liberties of the Kingdome . . . but it is likewise a Councell to provide for the necessity, to prevent the imminent dangers, and preserve the . . . safety of the Kingdom, and to declare the King's pleasure in those things as are requisite thereunto, and what they doe herein hath the stampe of Royall authority, although his Majesty . . . do in his own person oppose or interrupt the same; for the Kings Supream . . . and Royal pleasure is exercised and declared in this high Court of Law and Councell after a more eminent and obligatory manner, then it can be by any personall Act or Resolution of his own.[1]

This bifurcation between the office of kingship and its personal incumbent was reminiscent of the rebellious magnates' declaration against Edward II in 1308, wherein they stated that they owed their subjection to the crown rather than to the person of the King.[2] The latter doctrine, however, found no warrant in the law. In the early seventeenth century, indeed, Bacon, Coke, and Ellesmere, the greatest lawyers of the age, all commented on it only to reject it emphatically as inferring 'execrable and detestable consequences.'[3] With the formulation of the same fiction in 1642, the Houses established a justification to annex both the recognized attributes of monarchical supremacy and a legislative power as well which the King had never possessed.

Perhaps the framers of their manifestoes did not perceive that under colour of declaring law they introduced the greatest innovation ever made in England's government. If so, the King at any rate knew better. In a critical review of the Houses' claims, he taxed them with making themselves absolute so as to become the sole disposers

---

[1] *An exact collection*, 304.
[2] Cf. M. McKisack, *The fourteenth century 1307–1399*, Oxford, 1959, 7, 64, and E. Kantorowicz, *The King's two bodies*, Princeton, 1957, 364–6.
[3] F. D. Wormuth, *op. cit.*, 51–2; Bacon, *Works*, XV, 233–5. The views of Bacon, Coke, and Ellesmere were expressed in the great constitutional case of the *post-nati*, 1607. Although English legal thought, as Kantorowicz, *op. cit.*, has shown, was rich in corporational concepts of kingship and made use of the distinction between the King's natural and politic bodies, it did not formulate this doctrine to justify rebellion or to set the crown against the King's person. Bacon said that King and crown could be distinguished but not separated, *Works*, XV, 234.

of all law and public matters by majority vote. He was not wrong. Nor did he exaggerate much in describing the import of the Houses' doctrine as nothing else than a design for

The ruine . . . of Monarchy it Self (Which Wee may justly say, is more than ever was offered in any of Our Predecessours times; for though the Person of the King hath been sometimes unjustly deposed, yet the Regall Power was never before this time stricken at). . . .[1]

3

The clangour of argument in official declarations only mirrored the furious debate which was spreading over the kingdom and eating away its peace. 'I finde all heere full of feares,' said a report from Kent. 'Parents and children, brothers, kindred . . . and deere frends have the seed of difference and division abundantly sowed in them. . . . All is at stake, and the rent is conceived to be so great that it can hardly bee drawne up. . . .'[2] One man praised Pym's 'herroicke courage' and thought parliament's statements enough to 'satisfie any resonable person'; another testified to the persuasive force of the King's views.[3] What mainly undermined Charles's case, however, was that many people did not believe him. There was a numerous body of Englishmen in whose eyes he stood convicted, despite his professions to the contrary, of double-dealing, conspiracy against parliament, complicity in the Irish rebellion. Such persons endorsed parliament's actions and the militia ordinance as measures essential to the security of the commonwealth in an extreme situation. Our invaluable diarist, D'Ewes, held this opinion. The anxious witness of the polity's disintegration, repeatedly pleading with his fellow members for moderation and compromise, he merely stated a widespread belief when, with civil war impending, he told the House of Commons:

. . . I cannot but much wonder what end any man can imagine wee can have in what wee have done of late but the publike good. . . . They must be more uncharitable then Turk or Heathen . . . that shall imagine that soe many persons as the Parliament now consisteth of can bee united in one Act of disloyalty but that what wee have done was of meer necessity and for the preservation of the King and Kingdome.[4]

[1] *An exact collection*, 297–8.
[2] *The Oxinden letters 1607–1642*, 272, 306.
[3] *Ibid.*, 271, 307; *Sir Roger Twysden's journal*, ed. L. B. Larking, *Archaeologia Cantiana*, I, 1858, 200.
[4] D'Ewes, Journal, B.M. Harl. 163, f. 121b, 16 May 1642.

Parliamentarians and Royalists

One of the earliest expressions of a popular Royalism was Sir George Benyon's attempt in February 1642 to get up a petition in London against the Houses' claim to dispose of the militia. Benyon was severely punished for his temerity in challenging the Houses' actions.[1] A still more significant outbreak of Royalist sentiment occurred in Kent at the end of March. Although the county and its gentry had been generally favourable to the Country opposition when parliament began, since the autumn of 1641 they were experiencing the same fissiparous process that was dividing all England into hostile camps.[2] Of the two Kent M.P.s, Sir John Culpepper, changing from reformer to Royalist, had entered the King's employment, while Sir Edward Dering had broken his connections with the opposition leaders in the Commons. Early in 1642 Dering published a volume of his parliamentary speeches, thereby so incensing the House that it disabled him from sitting.[3] Parliamentarians considered him to be no better than a turncoat. A pamphlet addressed to him in February 1642 declared:

You have given such a president, that putting my Lord Digbie aside . . . you shall never twice be parallel'd . . . hypocrizing and deluding the expectation of all right honest men . . . as to betray . . . the cause of God, the Church, and the Country . . . forgetting wholly what you were. . . .[4]

Sir Roger Twysden, another Kentishman and friend of Dering, described the progress of his own disillusionment with Pym's party in his autobiography. He too had greeted the Long Parliament as the kingdom's salvation, only to become in time more and more critical of the *ultra vires* tendency of its actions. In this, Twysden, a learned antiquarian who admired England's ancient constitution as the best in the world, was typical of the moderate mentality that carried many gentlemen of his sort into Royalism.[5] '. . . I began to be much troubled,' he related, that 'if wee did change our Task Masters, our burthens would not be lesse. And what was it to me . . . whether the Earl of Strafford or Mr. Pym sate at the helme of government, if their commands carryed equall pressure?' He was completely against the

---

[1] Cf. *supra*, 291–2.
[2] The best account is now that by A. Everitt, *The community of Kent and the great rebellion, 1640–1660*, Leicester, 1966, which became available too late for me to use.
[3] *C.J.*, II, 411.
[4] [J.P.], *The copie of a letter written unto Sir Edward Dering*, 1642, 4.
[5] Cf. Twysden's *Certaine considerations upon the government of England*, ed. J. M. Kemble, *Camden society*, XLV, 1849, for the exposition of his constitutional views, and the account by J. W. Gough, *op. cit.*, 93–7.

militia ordinance: if the Houses acquired the military power despite the King's denial, 'they had in effect all yᵉ rights of Soveraignity, the people under an absolute arbitrary voting Tyrany. . . .'[1]

The ripening disaffection to parliament signallized in these sentiments manifested itself publicly on 25 March at the Kent assizes. Inspired by Dering, Twysden, and other local notables, a specially empanelled grand jury of justices and gentlemen drew up a Royalist petition to express the county's grievances. Dering himself was the jury's foreman. Addressed to the House of Commons, the petition touched a number of tender points, including the preservation of episcopal church government and the suppression of sects, lay preaching, and seditious sermons. But its sharpest sting was aimed at the militia ordinance which it attacked as arbitrary and illegal. '. . . no Order,' it said, 'in either or both Houses, not grounded on the Laws of the Land, may be enforced on the Subject. . . .'[2]

To attain the widest circulation, the petition's sponsors published it throughout the county and further arranged that a mass meeting should be held at the end of April at Blackheath to carry it to the House of Commons. But the House did not wait for the mutinous spirit in Kent to gather head. It promptly began an investigation into the petition's appearance and summoned Dering, Twysden, and several others as delinquents. For having a copy in his possession, the earl of Bristol was sent to the Tower by the Lords. On 26 April the Commons completed Dering's overthrow when it impeached him for 'high Crimes and Misdemeanors.'[3] Despite these discouragements, some of the petition's supporters delivered it on 30 April to the lower House. Their campaign had lost its impetus, however, and after making a subdued appearance they were patronizingly dismissed by the Speaker as 'young Gentlemen, misled by Some not affected to the Peace of the Kingdom. . . .' By this time, moreover, Parliamentarian sentiment was rapidly organizing itself in the county, so that on 5 May the Houses received a counter-petition of support from Kent containing six thousand signatures and the promise that 'many thousands more intend to subscribe. . . .'[4]

These Kentish episodes were subsidiary to the central conflict which the King and parliament were waging between York and Westminster. Although gestures of negotiation continued, they were overshadowed by invincible animosity which made each side look to

---

[1] *Sir Roger Twysden's journal*, I, 187, 188, 198. Twysden wrote this autobiographical account about 1657, cf. *ibid.*, *Archaeologia Cantiana*, IV, 1861, 195.

[2] *L.J.*, IV, 677–8. The circumstances of the Kentish petition's appearance are given in *ibid.*, V, 17–19 and in *Sir Roger Twysden's journal*, I, 200–13.

[3] *C.J.*, II, 507; *L.J.*, IV, 678, V, 17.

[4] *C.J.*, II, 550, 558; *L.J.*, V, 44.

its own strength. From abroad at the end of March and the beginning of April the Queen sent her husband urgent letters imploring him to occupy Hull without delay. His enemies still counted on his submitting to an accommodation, she wrote, but he was not to think of it: 'it is only trifling and losing time.' Let the Houses see him in action and 'they would speak after another fashion.'[1]

Charles's first view of Yorkshire opinion evidently made him pause. His presence evoked no instant outpouring of political support. Instead, a petition of 5 April drawn up at the county assizes expressed concern at the kingdom's division and begged him to devise expedients to reestablish union with parliament.[2] Meanwhile, as he considered how to secure Hull, he sent the Houses an unexpected proposition on 11 April which became the focus of new fears. In this he stated his intent to go to Ireland to suppress the rebellion and with this object to raise a body of some two thousand men whom he proposed to arm from the arsenal in Hull. In order to remove misunderstandings, he added, he would presently transmit a new bill for the settlement of the militia in a way that would give general satisfaction.[3]

When and how the King conceived this idea does not appear, unless he and the Queen canvassed it as a possibility prior to her departure.[4] Probably he believed that parliament would find it awkward to reject an offer aimed ostensibly at the relief of Ireland. If so it was a further sign of his inferior political judgment and lack of statesmanship, since the Houses would never consent to any scheme that entailed his having an army.

The King's messages naturally aroused speculation as to his real motives. A common opinion held that he wished to go to Ireland to make peace with the rebels on any terms so that he might return to England at the head of an army.[5] This, certainly, was the conjecture of the Parliamentarian leaders. They could imagine no other reason why the King proposed to leave his English realm at so critical a time. Accordingly, the Houses issued a declaration on the 15th rejecting his offer as dangerous and asserting that they would not allow him to levy any soldiers for Ireland.[6]

[1] *Letters of Queen Henrietta Maria*, 59–63.
[2] The petition was offered in the name of gentry, ministers, and freeholders, J. Rushworth, IV, 613.
[3] *L.J.*, IV, 709–10.
[4] Clarendon's explanation of the King's Irish project was that it was a 'stratagem' and a 'counsel . . . very suddenly taken, and communicated to very few, without consideration of the objections that would naturally arise against it. . . .', *Rebellion*, V, 78.
[5] Cf. the despatch of the Venetian envoy, *C.S.P.V. 1642–43*, 46.
[6] *L.J.*, IV, 719–20.

Pym's management of this incident gave proof of how persistently he tried to preserve agreement amongst the Parliamentarian members. It is D'Ewes who permits us a sight of his tactics. In his notes the troubled diarist had begun to refer for the first time to the 'fiery' and 'violent spirits' in the Commons. Thus, when Pym reported the draft of the reply to the King's message, D'Ewes suggested a few softening changes of language, only to be interrupted, he recorded, by 'some indiscreet and violent spirits.' This led him to tell the House to weigh its words well, lest 'wee ... leave the kingdome without all hope or possibilitie of an accomodation betweene his Matie and us. ...' Pym, however,

did with much discretion and modestie approve what I had spoken and comming himselfe to the Clarkes table did amend the said Declaration according to the advice I had given. ...[1]

The modified declaration remained sharp enough, but the episode was characteristic of Pym's methods. Essentially a man of the centre, with nothing in him of the *enragé*, the Parliamentarian chief moderated differences whenever possible. In his role as helmsman, he exerted his leadership to hold together left and right, the more and the less militant, on his own side. In addition, he wished it to be manifest that if peace gave way the fault would be the King's, not parliament's.

This appeared further in the sequel to the King's announcement in his recent message that he would propose a new militia bill. As the Houses were insisting on the legality of the militia ordinance, they might have refused to entertain the King's bill. Instead, the Lords received the bill on 19 April, amended it, and sent it to the Commons the next day. There, Henry Marten, one of D'Ewes's 'violent spirits,' urged its rejection. If the House accepted a bill, he said, 'wee shall condemne our own Act and vilify the ordinance wee had made ... and should seem to give way to the Kings evill counsellors who had ... advized this way of Bill. ...' Good logic, it would appear! Yet no support arose for Marten's view. Clearly, the House's managers were set on avoiding any impression of inflexibility. Then, with Marten alone dissenting, a motion by D'Ewes was carried to read the King's bill a second time and refer it to a committee of the whole.[2]

Despite this treatment, the King's bill had no effect on the course of events. By its provisions Charles offered to share the militia power

[1] D'Ewes, Journal, B.M. Harl. 163, f. 75b.
[2] *L.J.*, V, 5; *C.J.*, II, 535; D'Ewes, Journal, B.M. Harl. 163, f. 83b. D'Ewes contended that the militia ordinance was lawful, but that it would be safer to proceed by bill.

with the Houses for one year; during this time he would order the militia subject to their advice while he remained in England, and if he went to Ireland they were to dispose of it alone. In committee, the Commons extended the bill's term to two years and altered it in other particulars as well so as to deprive the King of any part in the militia. The amended bill passed both Houses on 22 April.[1] Six days later Charles denied it his assent, declaring that it excluded him from all power in that 'which God and the Law hath trusted Us solely. . . .'[2] The Houses accordingly proceeded to act on the basis of the militia ordinance. The entire transaction demonstrated that while the Parliamentarian leadership had no doctrinaire commitment to an ordinance, it was immovable in its determination to secure exclusive rule of the militia.

During the consideration of his Irish proposition and militia bill, the King held back from any attempt on Hull. Parliament's dismissal of his offer probably decided him to wait no longer as well as to lay aside further thought of going to Ireland. The Houses of course realized the danger of his proximity to the town. Because of this, they authorized Sir John Hotham to remove its magazine.[3] Before it could be done, the King came before Hull on 23 April with about three hundred men and demanded entrance. Hotham refused, replying that he could not admit the King against parliament's instructions. Again Charles commanded that the gates be thrown open, only to receive the same reply. Thereupon he caused Hotham and those adhering to him to be proclaimed traitors. Withdrawing for the night to Beverly a few miles off, he made a second fruitless attempt the next day to persuade Hull's defenders to open the town. His commands thus set at naught, there was nothing left for him for the time being but to return angrily to York.[4]

The events at Hull brought England's cracked and ailing peace *in articulo mortis*. Hotham's disobedience in parliament's name was proof that rival sovereignties were engaged at its walls. There was certainly no room for both in one realm. In subsequent declarations, the two sides argued acrimoniously over the rights and wrongs of the King's exclusion from Hull. The King as usual took refuge in legal considerations to justify a course of action which really tended

---

[1] *C.J.*, II, 537; *L.J.*, V, 10. The text of the King's militia bill has not survived, but its substance and the amendments made in it can be gathered from the subsequent arguments about it in the King's declaration of 28 April and the Houses' answer of 5 May, *An exact collection*, 158–9, 171–2. Cf. also the Venetian ambassador's description of the bill, *C.S.V.P. 1642–43*, 42.

[2] *An exact collection*, 159.

[3] *L.J.*, V, 4; *C.J.*, II, 533.

[4] Cf. the description of the events at Hull in Sir John Hotham's letter to parliament, *L.J.*, V, 28–9 and in J. Rushworth, IV, 567.

towards force. He affirmed Hull and its magazine to be his own property by the same lawful title that his subjects held their goods. Parliament retorted that the kingdom's towns and forts were not the King's, but a trust to be used by him for the public benefit.[1] Behind these contrary claims stood the stark reality, visible to all, that if the King got Hull he would be in a better position to wage war.

Charles, however, was resolved to take the town and punish the affront he had received there.[2] Over the following weeks he energetically solicited the assistance of the gentry and people of Yorkshire, whom he addressed at large open-air meetings in May and early June. He appealed to the gentry to provide him with a guard on the ground that he had to defend himself when parliament countenanced treason and detained his magazine. The mixed reception of approval and disapproval from the crowds revealed the fractured condition of the county, divided and at odds like all of England.[3] Still, his pleas had some success, so that by the end of May he had formed a troop of Yorkshire gentlemen to which he also added a regiment of about six hundred county militia that appeared in response to his summons.[4]

These were actually the first forces to be raised for civil war. In no other light did the Parliamentarians regard the King's activities at York. Accordingly on 20 May the Houses passed the momentous resolutions that the King, seduced by wicked counsel, intended to levy war on his parliament; that his doing so was 'a breach of the Trust reposed in him by his People' and tended 'to the Dissolution of this Government;' and that all assisting him were 'Traytors, by the fundamental Laws of this Kingdom. ...' The Commons adopted these votes after strong debate, 'the hotter and more violent spirits prevailing,' according to D'Ewes, 'although there were many negatives. ...'[5]

While pushing on its war preparations, parliament at the beginning of June drew up a final offer of conditions for an accommodation in the form of nineteen propositions. These, however, did not retrench its earlier demands in the slightest degree. They spelled out more fully, rather, the contemplated subjection of the King to the common-

---

[1] Cf. the King's declaration of 4 May and parliament's answer of the 26th, *An exact collection*, 163–4, 265–6.

[2] Cf. the Venetian ambassador's description of the King's state of mind, *C.S.V.P. 1642–43*, 53.

[3] The documents relating to these Yorkshire assemblies are printed in J. Rushworth, IV, 615–25.

[4] Clarendon, *Rebellion*, V, 140.

[5] *C.J.*, II, 581; D'Ewes, Journal, B.M. Harl. 163, f. 128b. The phrase, 'seduced by wicked counsel,' was included in the first of these resolutions on Pym's motion.

wealth's representative body. Parliament was to approve the appointment and removal of councillors, ministers, great officers of state, and the chief justices of the common-law courts; foreign alliances and marriage treaties were to be made with its advice; the King was to consent to such a reformation of church government and liturgy as it recommended; he was also to accept the militia ordinance, disband his forces, and grant the custody of forts and castles to persons whom parliament approved; and he was not to hinder the justice of parliament on all delinquents—a direct threat to Charles's closest and most loyal followers.[1]

The Nineteen Propositions defined a surrender, not terms framed to avoid a war. As such the King scornfully rejected them, avowing that they overthrew the law and robbed him of the substance of his regality. He added a sketch of England's traditional balanced constitution to enforce the lesson that neither House was entitled to any share in governing the kingdom.[2] On receipt of this answer, the House of Commons spent some time reviewing the propositions to see how they might be rendered more acceptable. After voting a few modifications, it let the matter drop, being too preoccupied with the imminent trial of arms. There was, in truth, no poultice left to apply against the civil infection epidemic in the kingdom. The Nineteen Propositions remained as the fullest outline of the revolutionary polity which parliament, under the justification of self-defence, was contending for against the King.[3]

Meanwhile, each party was making strong exertions to enlist the militia of the counties on its side. The Parliamentarian lords lieutenants and their deputies acted under the sanction of the Houses' militia ordinance; the Royalist lieutenants invoked the King's authority conveyed to them from June onward in the form of commissions of array, which bid them arm and muster the able-bodied in the counties and suppress all attempts at interference. Each party declared itself to be acting in self-defence; each proclaimed the nullity of the other's orders and the legitimacy of its own.[4]

In this way, people of every rank throughout the realm were put

[1] *C.J.*, II, 599–600.

[2] *An exact collection*, 311ff. The King's answer to the Nineteen Propositions was written by Culpepper and Falkland. Its importance in the evolution of the theory of mixed monarchy and its subsequent uses in controversy are stressed by C. C. Weston, *English constitutional theory and the House of Lords, 1556–1832*, N.Y., 1965, ch. I.

[3] The principal discussions of the propositions occurred on 24, 27, 28 June, and 2 July, *C.J.*, II, 638–9, 642, 643, 648. The Venetian ambassador's despatch of 24 June gave an exaggerated account of the changes the House was willing to make, *C.S.P.V. 1642–43*, 92.

[4] The documents pertaining to the execution of the militia ordinance and the royal commission of array are printed in J. Rushworth, IV, 655ff.

face to face with the contradictory decrees of rival sovereignties. To choose in such a crux was dangerous, yet inescapable. 'For mine own part,' declared the earl of Bristol, one of the last moderates in the House of Lords,

> ... I cannot find out, under the different Command of the King and Parliament, any such course of Caution and Wariness, by which I can promise to my self Security or Safety.[1]

It was the common dilemma of the governing class. A Kentish Parliamentarian expressed it similarly:

> ... my condition beetwixt the commission of Aray and ordinance of Parl: is like his that is between Silla and Carybdis, and nothing butt Omnipotence can bring mee clearely and reputably off. ...[2]

Brush fires of strife breaking out in many parts of England between the executants of the militia ordinance and the commission of array marked the actual beginning of the civil war. Contemporary writers reckoned that the first casualty fell at Manchester on 15 July when the townsmen were resisting the attempt of the Royalist son of the earl of Derby to implement the commission of array.[3] Prior to this, however, several of the King's supporters had already been slain at Hull.[4] Besides the contention over the militia that erupted in the counties, other martial actions ensued. In mid-June, the earl of Newcastle with troops raised from his own tenants and others, occupied Newcastle and the mouth of the Tyne for the King.[5] Ordnance and munitions also reached Charles from Holland, acquired by the Queen with money from the pawn of crown jewels. Early in June the King in a new move against Hull tried to blockade the town with about twenty-five hundred men, but was repulsed by the defenders and withdrew.[6]

On parliament's side the Houses took these occurrences as the definite initiation of a war. Accordingly on 4 July they appointed a joint committee of safety charged to prepare measures of defence.[7]

---

[1] Speech delivered 20 May 1642, J. Rushworth, IV, 717. The entire address is of great interest. In spite of Bristol's complaint about its publication, it is probably authentic (*L.J.*, V, 87). A few weeks later, Bristol withdrew from parliament and joined the King at York.

[2] *The Oxinden letters 1607–1642*, 312.

[3] J. Rushworth, IV, 680.

[4] Cf. a letter from Hull to the Speaker of the Commons on 13 July, *L.J.*, V 217.   [5] *Ibid.*, V, 170.

[6] *L.J.*, V, 126, 217; J. Rushworth, IV, 600–1, 610–11.

[7] *C.J.*, II, 651; *L.J.*, V, 178.

They followed this with a decision to raise an army of ten thousand volunteers out of London and the neighbouring counties. At the same time, the energetic activity of the earl of Warwick, whom the Houses had named by ordinance to command the fleet, secured the navy under parliament's control.[1] Finally, on 12 July they appointed the earl of Essex as general of parliament's army, and both the peers and the members of the lower House pledged themselves 'to live and die' with Essex in the common cause.[2]

Of these actions, the one of most political importance was the creation of the committee of safety. In this body parliament established a directive organ which gradually undertook many of the functions of a government. The Houses had already made several previous experiments in filling the governmental vacuum left by the disintegration of the King's power. Both the committee of defence and the committee for the recess, formed respectively in August and September the year before, resembled regencies, and the latter, in particular, possessed an extensive competence during its brief term.[3] The committee of safety, following on similar lines, lasted until the end of 1643 and developed into the first true parliamentary executive. With a much smaller membership than the committee for the recess— fifteen compared to sixty-four—it was easier managed and better fitted to cope with the emergencies of war. Ten of the Commons and five noblemen composed it at its inception. Pym, Hampden, Fiennes, Holles, the earl of Essex, and Lord Saye were of the number.[4] The committee began its work at once. It proposed the ordinance of 6 July to recruit two thousand men in and around London for immediate despatch to Hull. It was empowered to issue arms and ammunition as it saw need. To it fell the task of nominating the chief officers of parliament's army.[5] As the war continued, its business grew until it was handling not only army administration and innumerable military problems, but also a considerable part of war finance, the coordination of local defence under Parliamentarian county committees, and even the Houses' first ventures in diplomacy.[6]

4

So did domestic war possess England. Although the King and parliament had yet to form armies, both had accepted the gage of battle

[1] *C.J.*, II, 650, 654, 663; *L.J.*, V, 196; *Acts and ordinances of the interregnum*, I, 12.   [2] *C.J.*, II, 668; *L.J.*, V, 206.   [3] Cf. *supra*, 248, 250.
[4] *C.J.*, II, 651; *L.J.*, V, 178. Other members were subsequently added. A full list of the committee's membership until its demise is given by L. Glow, 'The committee of safety,' *E.H.R.*, LXXX, 315 (1965), 313.
[5] *C.J.*, II, 656, 657, 660.
[6] Cf. L. Glow, *op. cit.*, for an account of the committee's history.

and unsheathed their swords. On 9 August at York, Charles proclaimed the earl of Essex and all serving under him to be rebels and traitors. Another proclamation a few days after commanded the King's loyal subjects north of Trent to repair to him in arms at Nottingham.[1] There on 22 August before a company of lords and gentlemen and about two thousand troops, Charles ordered his royal standard erected to signify that he had taken the field. At its top flew a flag with the image of the King's arms and crown and the motto, 'Give Caesar his due.'[2] Parliament, in a manifesto of its reasons for taking arms, had already declared its own altogether different sense of the issue. To the people and the political nation—'those who have sent us hither and intrusted us with all they have, Estates, Liberty, and Life, and that which is the life of their lives, their religion,'—the Houses addressed a solemn monition:

. . . if the King may force this Parliament, they may bid farewell to all Parliaments, from ever receiving good by them; and if Parliaments be lost, they are lost; their Laws are lost, as well those lately made, as in former times, all which will be cut in sunder with the same sword now drawne for the destruction of this Parliament.[3]

Despite this utterance, which was the indubitable conviction of the majority at Westminster, every step towards war made for increased tension within the Parliamentarian party. Although Pym and his confidants doubtless would have preferred peace, they had known the risks of their policy and accepted its consequences without dismay. Men of D'Ewes's sort, on the other hand, having continually reckoned on the King's submission, became timorous and queasy when the opposite happened. But if the worthy diarist longed for peace, neither he nor any other of similar mind in the House of Commons knew how to attain it or had any serious proposals to offer. Reluctantly, yet with a growing sense of inevitability, parliament in the summer of 1642 was drawn to war. All D'Ewes could do as a peace advocate was to voice his scruples and plead for delay, while privately he memorialized his disapproval of the 'fiery spirits.'

Thus, when Edmund Waller moved the House at the end of May to consider means to preserve peace, and Strode attacked the motion as to no purpose, D'Ewes supported Waller.[4] In the midst of their war

[1] *An exact collection*, 503–7, 512–13.
[2] J. Rushworth, IV, 783–4.
[3] *An exact collection*, 496, 2 August 1642.
[4] D'Ewes, *Journal*, B.M. Harl. 163, f. 135. Waller's motion was carried and included in the instructions given a committee for the defence of the kingdom, *C.J.*, II, 589. The result was the Nineteen Propositions, hardly a platform of accommodation!

preparations, D'Ewes warned his fellow members that the civil conflict might lead to a social revolution:

... all right & propertie, all meum & tuum must cease in a civill warre & wee know not what advantage the meaner sort alsoe may take to divide the spoiles of the rich & noble amongst them, who begin alreadie to alledge, that all being of one mould ther is no reason that some should have soe much & others soe little.[1]

Because he disliked all measures looking towards arms, he also opposed a proposition on the same occasion that called for parliament's adherents to contribute money, plate, and horses. Nevertheless, it was carried, he noted, 'by those hott earnest men ... with those who commonlie followed them.' This proposition became parliament's first financial ordinance, passed on 9 June.[2]

The next day the House began polling its own members to state what they would give. Some answered with a direct refusal, like the Wiltshire Royalist William Pleydall, who said 'hee had given his No to the propositions & soe desired to be excused.' D'Ewes when named replied that he would declare himself in due time: in his journal, however, he commented that the calling of members in such a way was against the liberty of the House of Commons. As the roll continued, Denzil Holles suggested that members who wished to contribute and conceal their names might do so. The House revealed its state of mind by rejecting this as 'verie derogatorie to the worke. ...'[3]

The size of the Commons' minority representative of a peace tendency is difficult to estimate. It included both the Parliamentarians who felt scruples about an actual war with the King, and the rapidly dwindling number of Royalists who still continued to attend the House. Perhaps the best impression of its extent is obtained from several divisions. On 11 June, for instance, a motion to impeach nine peers who had deserted Westminster for York passed by 109 to 51.[4] Another motion on the 16th directed against the House's absentee members passed by 147 to 91. Most indicative of all was a division on 9 July on the motion to raise an army. It was carried by a vote of 125 to 45. The tellers in favour were Denzil Holles and Sir John Evelyn; the tellers against were the great scholar, John Selden, a peace Parliamentarian, and Sir John Strangeways, a Royalist.[5]

[1] D'Ewes, Journal, B.M. Harl. 163, f. 154b, 8 June 1642.
[2] *Ibid.*, f. 153b; *Acts and ordinances of the interregnum*, I, 6–9.
[3] D'Ewes, Journal, B.M. Harl. 163, ff. 157a (in cipher)–175b.
[4] *C.J.*, II, 620. Edmund Waller was a teller for the negative, Holles and Oliver Cromwell told for the affirmative.
[5] *C.J.*, II, 626, 663. Selden's views appear from glimpses in D'Ewes. On 2

Whatever his reservations, it was out of the question for one of D'Ewes's convictions ever to become a Royalist. But his feet-dragging arguments caused so much irritation that they finally led to a quarrel and the most distressing incident of his parliamentary life. The episode was fully recorded by him in his journal.

On 23 July he came into the House as the members were about to vote a 'long impertinent & dangerous declaration' against the King after but a single reading. Extremely provoked at the 'uniust and violent proceeding,' he attacked the declaration vehemently, only to get into an altercation with Strode, 'a notable prophaner of the Scriptures & a man doubtless void of all truth & pietie.' Shouts for his withdrawal arose which were joined in, he noted bitterly, by 'my formerlie seeming freind Mr Nathaniel Fynes,' and Holles, 'a proud ambitious man. . . .' Although Edmund Waller tried to speak on his behalf, while others caught at his cloak to restrain him, he had to leave the chamber. He was then recalled by Speaker Lenthall and ordered to acknowledge his fault. D'Ewes did so, yet without offering any real retraction, whereupon 'that firebrand Strode' denounced his apology as insufficient. He finally got off through the intervention of Fiennes, who 'did verie noblie expresse himself . . . that I had spoken enough to satisfie the Howse. . . .'

In his private communings D'Ewes poured out his grief and resentment at his treatment by the party leaders with whom 'I had alwaies concurred . . . & oftentimes helde up ther cause ever since the beginning of the Parliament except . . . ther last four months violent preparations for a civill warre.' He wished posterity to know

that when those furious spirits in the Howse of Commons weere iritated with my freedome of expression that had for about several months . . . resisted (& often alsoe alone without being seconded by anie who weere most of them overawed . . .) ther bitter and irreverentiall language towards his M^tie, & ther . . . hott preparations for a civill warre, they took this frivolous & uniust occasion to call in question what I said at this time. . . .

Concluding his account, the mortified diarist declared:

This horrible ingratitude for all my services . . . made me resolve to leave off further writing & speaking in the Howse & to come as

---

July, in a discussion of the Nineteen Propositions, he advised the House in vain against insisting on exclusive control of the militia and urged that means be found to accommodate differences with the King, D'Ewes, Journal, B.M. Harl. 163, f. 254b. It will be recalled that Selden also voted against Strafford's attainder.

seldom amongst them as I could seeing libertie of speech was taken away. . . .[1]

Fortunately, D'Ewes loved parliament too well to stick to his resolution. In the days immediately following, however, he attended less diligently, believing members were no longer free to speak their minds. An entry in his journal on 10 August, commenting on the thinness of the House, expressed his attitude at the time:

. . . the hott fierie spirits having begunn a civill warre carried all things now as they listed soe as men made no great hast to the Howse, neither did many at all assemble.[2]

If the imminence of war brought out doubts and scruples in members of the Commons, the same was no less true amongst the peers. The Parliamentarian Lord Paget, for instance, having been appointed lord lieutenant of Buckinghamshire by the Houses, was actively engaged during May in executing the militia ordinance. Then, wrote one of his deputies, he 'began to boggle, and was unfixed in his resolutions.' The publication in June of the royal commission of array made him change allegiances. A letter he sent the House of Lords *en route* to York announced his turnabout. While acknowledging his former zeal for reformation, Paget declared that he could not in conscience take arms against the King. 'I . . . am now on my Way to his Majesty, where I will throw myself down at His feet, and die a loyal Subject.'[3]

The most prominent of aristocratic vacillators was William Cecil, earl of Salisbury. The heir of a great political family which owed everything to the monarchy, Captain of the Gentlemen Pensioners at the Court, Salisbury had nonetheless joined the Court's opponents. Probably he was actuated in this by personal resentment. In 1635 the King denied him the great and profitable office of Master of the Wards, to which he held the reversion and which both his father and grandfather had occupied before him. The captaincy of the Gentlemen Pensioners was given him in compensation, but the loss must have rankled.[4] In August 1641 the House of Commons as a mark of

---

[1] D'Ewes, Journal, B.M. Harl. 163, ff. 291b–292b. The declaration to which D'Ewes excepted so strongly was parliament's statement of justification for taking arms, published 2 August, *An exact collection*, 491ff. One of his criticisms was that the declaration borrowed some of its arguments from a pamphlet, Henry Parker's *Observations upon some of his majesties late answers and expresses*, 1642.   [2] D'Ewes, Journal, B.M. Harl. 164, f. 260b.
[3] B. Whitelocke, *op. cit.*, I, 169–71; *L.J.*, V, 152.
[4] Cf. *H.M.C. Denbigh*, 8; *C.S.P.D. 1634–35*, 529–30; G. E. Aylmer, *The King's servants*, 114–17.

favour asked the King to create him Treasurer, a request which Charles, of course, refused. A little later, Salisbury was also one of the noblemen who supported the policy of the opposition leaders on the militia.[1] Thus, there was no little surprise in parliament when the earl suddenly turned up in York with the King at the end of May. A number of other lords summoned by Charles did the same, and after the Houses had vainly ordered their return to Westminster, the Commons impeached nine of them on 16 June as an example.[2] Salisbury, however, was spared this disgrace through the intercession of his Parliamentarian son-in-law, the earl of Northumberland. The latter believed the erring peer to be redeemable and began at once to try to woo him back to parliament.

As soon as Salisbury's departure became known, Northumberland wrote him in mingled reproach and persuasion:

Your Lo:ps going away in that manner was very unexpected to divers of your freinds, and I do not know how it will be possible in the way of justice to divide your Lop: from the other Lords that are faultie in the like kind; we have hitherto been very moderate in censuring this contempt, for we have only cited your Lop: and the rest to appeare against a certaine day. The opinion wch the world conceaves of this action is the greatest punishment we shall or can inflict upon your Lop: for this offence. The only way to redeeme what you have lost is . . . to returne hither again wth all convenient speede. . . .[3]

A week later, on 7 June, Northumberland wrote again. '. . . our house,' he informed Salisbury,

was more sensible of your leaving them then they were of the rest as lesse expecting it from your Lop: then from almost any of the other Lords; it were not answerable to the respect I have ever confessed unto your Lop: . . . what I conceave to be the true state of your condition, if you do not something to redeeme the good opinion of the Parl:. . . . If I can prevaile I will perswade wth some of my freinds that we may not proceede to hastely against those Lords that are gone from us, so as we may still have it in our powers to shew favor unto those that shall deserve well of the Parlament.[4]

[1] *L.J.*, IV, 355, 533.
[2] *L.J.*, V, 141. The impeached peers were the earls of Northampton, Devonshire, Dover, and Monmouth, and lords Howard of Charlton, Rich, Grey of Ruthyn, Coventry, and Capel. The constitutional foundation of the impeachment was that the duty imposed by the writ of summons to attend parliament took precedence over a personal letter from the King commanding attendance at York.
[3] Cecil MSS., v. 131, f. 176 (31 May).   [4] *Ibid.*, ff. 177–8.

Obviously the Parliamentarian leaders attached the highest importance to having a good presence of eminent noblemen on their side
when they were appealing to the nation for support in arms. To them
it was worth overlooking Salisbury's aberration if they could obtain
his further adherence. Hence, when he still remained at York,
Northumberland wrote him on 14 June that 'if your Lop: will speedily
returne I dare confidently say that you shall not suffer any kind of
censure from our house for what is past. . . .' To reinforce these
blandishments, he expatiated to Salisbury in a further letter on the
excellent success of parliament's financial ordinance:

*The monyes and plate are brought in faster upon our late propositions
for the peace and safetie of the kingdom than the treasurers that are
appointed can receave it.*[1]

These baits sufficed to lure the absent nobleman from York. On 20
June Northumberland was able to inform the House of Lords that
Salisbury was at his Hertfordshire residence in readiness to attend
parliament. The House immediately vacated a previous order citing
him as a delinquent and sent him a cordial invitation to 'come . . . and
sit in his Place as a Peer. . . .'[2] The earl's vagrant escapade was at an
end. It was his last. He remained a Parliamentarian, and so did his
two sons, both of whom had been returned to the House of Commons
in 1640 from family boroughs.[3]

One further ray, however, illumines the political calculations of
men of Salisbury's sort at this juncture. It comes from a friendly
letter—the last relating to the affair—sent him from York after his
departure by the Royalist earl of Dorset, who begged him to work
for moderation. '. . . this fatall fire once kindeled,' said Dorset,

*who knowes how to quench the flames, or where . . . the conflagration
may extend. I doe not apprehend yr Lshp. well tempered disposition,
can bee induced to ad fewell to the fire: men only . . . of desperat fames
or fortunes, cann promise themselves any ammelioration of condition,
by such broken and distracted ways. Those thatt inioy such a portion of
honor, and such a proportion of estate as (by Gods blessing) you doe,
cannot butt really mourn the desperate face of the times. . . . Good my
Lo . . . keepe the more violent spirits from passinge the Rubicon, Lett
them att London put nothing in execution that may give probable*

[1] *Ibid.*, ff. 179, 180.
[2] *L.J.*, V, 151.
[3] Salisbury's heir, Viscount Cranborne, sat for Hertford and his younger
son, Robert Cecil, for Old Sarum, both subject to the earl's patronage; cf.
M. Keeler, *The Long Parliament*, 51, 71.

ground of feare. . . . Lett many as will despayre: I am one of those, that beleeve [in] an easy and safe way to leade us all [past] this darke and inextricable labyrinth. Lett not feare prevayle above hope, nor reflect on past errors. . . . I am confident, such a beginninge is halfe way to an end. . . .[1]

Delusive hopes! England was swiftly catching fire. To put out the flames, even to contain them, was evidently beyond the power of either the partisans at Westminster or the loyal men at York. Parliament's quest for security against the King, the King's repulsion of parliament's aggression, was ending in the still greater insecurity, the still greater aggression, of a civil war. Weapons to wound and kill were to give the decision, as the sword began to write with its point a scarlet scroll unwound through years.

[1] Cecil MSS., v. 131, ff. 182–3.

10

Conclusion

By one of those singular correspondences that figuratively declare the passing of things, the day Charles I erected his standard at Nottingham was the same 22 August on which his victorious ancestor, Henry VII, won the crown at Bosworth field. The Spirit of the Pities and Spirits Sinister and Ironic, those phantom intelligences shaped by the poet, must have presided at such a coincidence.[1] From the war of York and Lancaster to the war of King and parliament a very long history ran. Yet in a real sense, what began in 1485 was ending in 1642. The Stuart line derived its English title by descent from Henry VII; and through the labours of the first Tudor and his dynasty, it also received a secure inheritance of the realm's subjection to monarchical authority. Charles I would have had to look back from Nottingham more than seventy years before he could descry an army of Englishmen on foot against their sovereign. The quickly vanquished northern rebellion of 1569–70 was the last of its kind.[2] Tudor order prevailed, so that at the close of Queen Elizabeth's reign the Speaker of the Commons in 1601 could eulogize the monarch for 'the happy and quiet and most sweet and comfortable peace, which, under your most happy and blessed government, we have long enjoyed. . . .'[3] But during 1640–2, a revolution liquidated the regime transmitted from the Tudors. An era of kingship expired with the war between Charles I and the Long Parliament.

What was the precipitating cause of the civil war? Despite the prevalence of religious passions at that time, it was not religion. Religion did, indeed, strongly influence the composition of the

---

[1] Cf. Thomas Hardy, *The dynasts. An epic drama of the war with Napoleon.*
[2] The Essex rebellion of 1601 may be overlooked. It was no more than a small riot in London which was immediately quashed.
[3] Cited in J. E. Neale, *Queen Elizabeth I and her parliaments 1584–1601*, 424. Cf. also Bacon's comment on the Elizabethan peace: 'One rebellion there hath been only, but such a one as was repressed within the space of seven weeks, and did not waste the realm so much as by the destruction or depopulation of one poor town,'. *Certain observations upon a libel,* 1592, *Works,* VIII, 157.

parties, but the war itself began over a political-constitutional question. To the Parliamentarians, it was that the King must give securities for what the revolution had already enacted by submitting to the Houses' advice and relinquishing to them the substance of his executive authority; and with these practical demands, embodied in the Nineteen Propositions, the Parliamentarians united a constitutional doctrine that made the Houses the supreme trustee of the commonwealth's safety, invested them with a legislative power as of right, and required the King to conduct himself as the responsible agent of the kingdom's representative body. To preserve, as they believed, popular and parliamentary liberty, the Parliamentarians arrived at the historic decision, a complete reversal of the teaching of English divines and theorists for over a century, that forcible resistance was justifiable.

To the Royalists, the question was the same, only seen from the antithetical angle. It was one of loyalty to the monarchy and the King's person, of acceptance of Charles's previous concessions as sufficient for future security, and of the necessity to withstand an invasion of royal right that subverted the kingdom's constitution and opened the door to change without foreseeable limit; and with this practical opposition to Parliamentarian demands, the Royalists united a doctrine that condemned resistance as sinful and proclaimed the law as the supreme arbiter which had given the kings of England the authority the Houses were illegally challenging.

The role of religion, as the predominant mental and emotional interest of Englishmen, was to dispose them towards one side or the other. Here Puritanism and the other varieties of dissent naturally had a powerful effect. Almost inevitably, anyone who wanted prelacy down and ceremonies abolished, or who desired the reform of liturgy and prayer book, or who cared greatly about a preaching ministry, was likely to be a Parliamentarian. Somewhat more tenuously, perhaps, one can say the same of those with a fanatic and unreasoning hatred of Catholicism, or whose devotion to a rigid, censorious moralism made them unforgiving of the frivolities of a court. On the other hand, affection for the national church as established, solicitude to keep up the bishops as a bulwark against innovation, inclined the possessors of such sentiments towards Royalism for obvious reasons. As for the minority of English Catholics of every degree and condition, they supported the King nearly universally, since only from him and his victory could they expect any lenity towards their faith.

Beyond these considerations, there was no religious issue representing the formulated views of the parties which was set forth at the commencement of the war. That the King would maintain the authority of bishops, and at most consent to some alteration in ceremonies, was clear. That greater change than this must come from parliament was equally clear. The Houses themselves, however, had not yet adopted any model of reform. In the Grand Remonstrance, the House of Commons had promised a further reformation and declared its wish to refer for advice to a general synod of divines. In April 1642 the two Houses repeated this pledge, affirming in a joint resolution that they intended 'a due and necessary Reformation' of church government and liturgy, and 'for the better effecting thereof, speedily to have Consultation with godly and learned Divines. . . .'[1] Here the matter stood at the outset of the war. Although the nomination by the Houses of members to a national synod began promptly,[2] that body itself, which became the Westminster Assembly, did not meet until July of the following year.

2

Two general features characterized the revolution from its inception to the early part of the civil war. The first was that the revolution occurred and developed into an armed conflict not because of a class struggle, but in consequence of a revolt within the governing class against the crown. The second, resulting directly from the first, was that the revolution in its initial stages was not at war with the prevailing form of society, of which the leaders of both parties were equally the beneficiaries. In taking a final view we may consider these in turn, and notice also the factors which threatened to drive the revolution onward in a more radical direction.

We have already seen how the conflict between the Court and the Country, overshadowing the political scene in the years preceding 1640, was the polarity in which the revolution had its beginning. That conflict expressed the opposition to the royal government of a part of the governing class, and in 1640–1, far the larger part, around which a great body of favouring popular sentiment also stood. The Country's victory completed the first stage of the revolution and left its memorial in the constitutional statutes passed during the spring and summer of 1641. Then ensued the Country's disruption. Its alliance of parliamentary support broke up, a disaffection against its leaders in the House of Commons set in throughout the kingdom, and a new Royalism gradually came into existence. As the revolution moved into its second stage, the earlier opposition of the Court and the Country was superseded by that of Royalist and Parliamentarian. Under the aegis of these two parties the civil war began.

The war at its outset represented a reorientation of judgment and

[1] *C.J.*, II, 515; *L.J.*, IV, 706.   [2] On 20 April 1642; *C.J.*, II, 635.

calculation within the kingdom's established elite. Naturally, each party needed and sought for mass support, but the struggle on both sides was initiated and directed by the sort of privileged persons who had previously governed the English people under the crown. No specifiable set of social or economic characteristics differentiated the leadership of one party from the other. On the contrary, Englishmen started to slay one another at the bidding or suasion of their accustomed governors; and one has to add that the Parliamentarian cause could never have possessed legitimacy in English eyes for a single moment, had it not included numerous representatives of the titular aristocracy and the gentry.

The clearest indication of the nature of the leading strata of the parties comes from the division within parliament itself. In the House of Commons the Parliamentarian members totalled about three hundred and two, the Royalists about two hundred and thirty-six; the stand of a tiny residual handful is undetermined.[1] Between these no significant contrast appeared as regarded status, wealth, or occupation. The gentry naturally dominated in the parties as they did in the House and kingdom; greater and lesser gentry, gentry of 'old' and of 'new' families, were not on different sides; the Houses' seventy-odd lawyers and fifty-odd merchants were also present substantially in both. The only observable distinctions were that the Royalists tended on average to be ten years younger than the Parliamentarian members and to originate more frequently from families with a parliamentary record.[2]

Like the Commons, the House of Lords was also divided, so that the titular aristocracy was prominent in both parties. Perhaps thirty peers became Parliamentarians, perhaps fifty to sixty became Royalists; a remaining (approximate) thirty took no part in affairs because of age, infirmity, or absence from England.[3] Although the Royalist

[1] The figures are those of Brunton and Pennington, *op. cit.*, App. I, table I. Keeler's figures (*op. cit.*, 12) are close: three hundred and ten Parliamentarians, two hundred and twenty-six Royalists.

[2] These are the conclusions of Brunton and Pennington, *op. cit.*, 19–20. The data collected by Keeler are substantially in accord. I have remained unconvinced by Christopher Hill's criticisms of Brunton's and Pennington's findings; cf. his *Puritanism and revolution*, 14–17. The number of lawyers and merchants in the House of Commons is taken from Brunton and Pennington, *op. cit.*, 5, 53, and from Keeler, *op. cit.*, 21.

[3] Exact figures are impossible. Those above come from C. H. Firth, *The House of Lords during the civil war*, 74, 115. Firth gives the total peerage in November 1640 as one hundred and twenty-four and then estimates that half were Royalist, a quarter Parliamentarian, and another quarter non-participant. New creations by the King in 1641, of which there were seven (cf. L. Stone, *The crisis of the aristocracy 1558–1641*, App. III), are thus not included. Also, several of the peers of 1640 were dead by 1642.

noblemen thus preponderated, there was again no pattern of socially relevant traits which they shared to the exclusion of their Parliamentarian opponents. Pre-Tudor, Tudor, and Stuart creations appeared on both sides, as did great wealth. The earl of Northumberland, a magnate whose peerage was one of the oldest and most illustrious, was a Parliamentarian. So were the earls of Pembroke, Salisbury, and Holland, all converts from the Court after 1640. On the other hand, the Royalists contained such oppositionist converts as the marquis of Hertford,[1] the earl of Southampton, and lords Paget and Spencer. If Lord Robartes, whose father bought a peerage from the profits of wool, tin, and money-lending, became a Parliamentarian, lords Craven and Campden, whose peerages also derived from commerce and money-lending in the preceding generation, became Royalists.

A nice balancing of personal interest and political-religious conviction doubtless determined the alignment of the peers. In the long run, however, the progress of the revolution brought the nobility nothing but misfortune as an order. The Royalists, going down to defeat, suffered fines, sequestration or confiscation of estates, and sometimes exile. The Parliamentarian lords, in spite of parliament's victory, saw their influence steadily decline amidst the increasing disunion and fragmentation of their party until in 1649 the new-born republic abolished the House of Lords altogether. These developments were not foreseen, of course, when the war began. At that moment the Parliamentarian noblemen were indispensable to their party. Exemplifying more than other men the currently cherished principles of aristocratic honour and pride of birth, they brought it great political prestige. Moreover, even if only a minority of the peerage, they *were* the House of Lords whilst they attended Westminster. Without their concurrence no ordinances could pass: and these ordinances were effective law in all the districts the Houses controlled. On the military side, the earl of Essex's appointment as general also helped the Parliamentarians greatly because of his personal popularity and his social distinction. Perhaps Clarendon exaggerated only a little when he later wrote that 'it had been utterly impossible for the two Houses . . . to have raised an army then if the earl of Essex had not consented to be general of that army.'[2]

The division of families and generations, of which there were numerous instances, gave further proof of the essential social identity between the upper layers of the warring parties. Lord Feilding, another convert from the Court, where all his family connections lay, became a Parliamentarian commander, to his mother's sorrow; his

---

[1] The oppositionist earl of Hertford was created a marquis in June 1640.
[2] *Rebellion*, V, 33; cf. a similar remark, *ibid.*, V, 116n.

Royalist father, the earl of Denbigh, died of wounds fighting for the King in 1643.[1] The earl of Leicester, after becoming Lord Lieutenant of Ireland in 1641, was distrusted by both parties and refused to serve parliament in executing the militia ordinance in Kent; by contrast, his son and heir, Lord Lisle, a member of the Commons, was a faithful Parliamentarian.[2] The earl of Northumberland took parliament's side, but his younger brother, the courtier Henry Percy, took the King's.[3] The earl of Peterborough raised a regiment for parliament and served under the earl of Essex as general of the ordnance. His son, succeeding to the title in 1643, was a Royalist.[4] In the Holles family, the first earl of Clare, who died before the Long Parliament, supported the Country. His older son, the second earl, though wavering somewhat between the parties, was praised by Clarendon as firmly attached to the principles of monarchy and the King's person. His younger son, Denzil Holles, was, of course, one of the foremost oppositionists and Parliamentarians in the House of Commons. Still another relation, a cousin, Gervase Holles, who also sat in the Commons, was expelled as a Royalist in August 1642.[5]

A pattern of split allegiances was seen as well in some other families with recent oppositionist traditions. Notwithstanding that the earl of Warwick was a Country peer and a zealous Parliamentarian, his son, Lord Rich, knight of the shire for Essex, joined the King's party.[6] The earl of Bedford before his death in 1641 belonged to the Country and was Pym's friend and patron. His son, the fifth earl, began as a Parliamentarian but then went over to the Royalists in 1643. A younger son, John Russell, who represented the family borough of Tavistock, also became a Royalist.[7] The M.P.s Edward

---

[1] *D.N.B.*, *s.v.*, 'Basil Feilding second Earl of Denbigh,' 'William Feilding first Earl of Denbigh.' Lord Feilding was summoned to the House of Lords in his father's lifetime. He was the duke of Buckingham's nephew and his first wife was Lord Treasurer Portland's daughter. In 1634 the King appointed him ambassador to Venice. His mother's letters of grief and remonstrance to him are printed in Cecilia Countess of Denbigh, *Royalist father and Roundhead son*, L., 1915, ch. VIII.

[2] *L.J.*, V, 227; R. W. Blencowe, *Sydney papers*, L., 1825, xxi; *D.N.B.*, *s.v.*, 'Philip Sidney third Earl of Leicester.'

[3] *D.N.B.*, *s.v.*, 'Henry Percy Lord Percy of Alnwick.'

[4] *The letter-book of John Viscount Mordaunt 1658–1660*, ed. M. Coate, *Camden society*, 3rd ser., LXIX, 1945, x.

[5] *D.N.B.*, *s.v.*, 'John Holles first Earl of Clare,' and 'John Holles second Earl of Clare'; Clarendon, *Rebellion*, VII, 153; M. Keeler, *op. cit.*, *s.v.*, 'Gervase Holles.'

[6] *D.N.B.*, *s.v.*, 'Robert Rich second Earl of Warwick.' In 1641 Lord Rich was summoned by the King to the House of Lords.

[7] *Ibid.*, *s.v.*, 'William Russell first Duke of Bedford'; M. Keeler, *op. cit.*, *s.v.*, 'William Lord Russell' and 'John Russell.' Lord Russell, M.P. for Tavistock

noblemen thus preponderated, there was again no pattern of socially relevant traits which they shared to the exclusion of their Parliamentarian opponents. Pre-Tudor, Tudor, and Stuart creations appeared on both sides, as did great wealth. The earl of Northumberland, a magnate whose peerage was one of the oldest and most illustrious, was a Parliamentarian. So were the earls of Pembroke, Salisbury, and Holland, all converts from the Court after 1640. On the other hand, the Royalists contained such oppositionist converts as the marquis of Hertford,[1] the earl of Southampton, and lords Paget and Spencer. If Lord Robartes, whose father bought a peerage from the profits of wool, tin, and money-lending, became a Parliamentarian, lords Craven and Campden, whose peerages also derived from commerce and money-lending in the preceding generation, became Royalists.

A nice balancing of personal interest and political-religious conviction doubtless determined the alignment of the peers. In the long run, however, the progress of the revolution brought the nobility nothing but misfortune as an order. The Royalists, going down to defeat, suffered fines, sequestration or confiscation of estates, and sometimes exile. The Parliamentarian lords, in spite of parliament's victory, saw their influence steadily decline amidst the increasing disunion and fragmentation of their party until in 1649 the new-born republic abolished the House of Lords altogether. These developments were not foreseen, of course, when the war began. At that moment the Parliamentarian noblemen were indispensable to their party. Exemplifying more than other men the currently cherished principles of aristocratic honour and pride of birth, they brought it great political prestige. Moreover, even if only a minority of the peerage, they *were* the House of Lords whilst they attended Westminster. Without their concurrence no ordinances could pass: and these ordinances were effective law in all the districts the Houses controlled. On the military side, the earl of Essex's appointment as general also helped the Parliamentarians greatly because of his personal popularity and his social distinction. Perhaps Clarendon exaggerated only a little when he later wrote that 'it had been utterly impossible for the two Houses . . . to have raised an army then if the earl of Essex had not consented to be general of that army.'[2]

The division of families and generations, of which there were numerous instances, gave further proof of the essential social identity between the upper layers of the warring parties. Lord Feilding, another convert from the Court, where all his family connections lay, became a Parliamentarian commander, to his mother's sorrow; his

---

[1] The oppositionist earl of Hertford was created a marquis in June 1640.
[2] *Rebellion*, V, 33; cf. a similar remark, *ibid.*, V, 116n.

Royalist father, the earl of Denbigh, died of wounds fighting for the King in 1643.[1] The earl of Leicester, after becoming Lord Lieutenant of Ireland in 1641, was distrusted by both parties and refused to serve parliament in executing the militia ordinance in Kent; by contrast, his son and heir, Lord Lisle, a member of the Commons, was a faithful Parliamentarian.[2] The earl of Northumberland took parliament's side, but his younger brother, the courtier Henry Percy, took the King's.[3] The earl of Peterborough raised a regiment for parliament and served under the earl of Essex as general of the ordnance. His son, succeeding to the title in 1643, was a Royalist.[4] In the Holles family, the first earl of Clare, who died before the Long Parliament, supported the Country. His older son, the second earl, though wavering somewhat between the parties, was praised by Clarendon as firmly attached to the principles of monarchy and the King's person. His younger son, Denzil Holles, was, of course, one of the foremost oppositionists and Parliamentarians in the House of Commons. Still another relation, a cousin, Gervase Holles, who also sat in the Commons, was expelled as a Royalist in August 1642.[5]

A pattern of split allegiances was seen as well in some other families with recent oppositionist traditions. Notwithstanding that the earl of Warwick was a Country peer and a zealous Parliamentarian, his son, Lord Rich, knight of the shire for Essex, joined the King's party.[6] The earl of Bedford before his death in 1641 belonged to the Country and was Pym's friend and patron. His son, the fifth earl, began as a Parliamentarian but then went over to the Royalists in 1643. A younger son, John Russell, who represented the family borough of Tavistock, also became a Royalist.[7] The M.P.s Edward

[1] *D.N.B., s.v.,* 'Basil Feilding second Earl of Denbigh,' 'William Feilding first Earl of Denbigh.' Lord Feilding was summoned to the House of Lords in his father's lifetime. He was the duke of Buckingham's nephew and his first wife was Lord Treasurer Portland's daughter. In 1634 the King appointed him ambassador to Venice. His mother's letters of grief and remonstrance to him are printed in Cecilia Countess of Denbigh, *Royalist father and Roundhead son,* L., 1915, ch. VIII.
[2] *L.J.,* V, 227; R. W. Blencowe, *Sydney papers,* L., 1825, xxi; *D.N.B., s.v.,* 'Philip Sidney third Earl of Leicester.'
[3] *D.N.B., s.v.,* 'Henry Percy Lord Percy of Alnwick.'
[4] *The letter-book of John Viscount Mordaunt 1658–1660,* ed. M. Coate, *Camden society,* 3rd ser., LXIX, 1945, x.
[5] *D.N.B., s.v.,* 'John Holles first Earl of Clare,' and 'John Holles second Earl of Clare'; Clarendon, *Rebellion,* VII, 153; M. Keeler, *op. cit., s.v.,* 'Gervase Holles.'
[6] *D.N.B., s.v.,* 'Robert Rich second Earl of Warwick.' In 1641 Lord Rich was summoned by the King to the House of Lords.
[7] *Ibid., s.v.,* 'William Russell first Duke of Bedford'; M. Keeler, *op. cit., s.v.,* 'William Lord Russell' and 'John Russell.' Lord Russell, M.P. for Tavistock

Phelips and Samuel Sandys, both offspring of men who had won great reputation as oppositionists in earlier Stuart parliaments, broke with family tradition to become Royalists. Sir Edward Alford, another M.P. of like political antecedents, did the same.[1]

Royal officials found themselves equally disunited by the civil war. Instead of rallying to the regime that employed them, a not inconsiderable minority became Parliamentarians. The probable reason for this lay in the character of office itself. Since offices (as we have previously stressed) tended at that period to be treated primarily as private property and only secondarily as the exercise of a public function by entrustment from the King, office-holders did not necessarily feel themselves committed to the royal party. There was, furthermore, little of a bureaucratic ethos prevailing in the crown's service; in fact, men belonging to the administrative elite were much more likely to be actuated by the range of interests and convictions that swayed the higher orders as a whole than by considerations of a purely professional nature. On the other hand, the Parliamentarian leaders, despite their condemnation of the apparatus of prerogative rule, had no quarrel with the state's machinery as such. They proposed neither to destroy nor to reconstruct it—objectives, indeed, completely foreign to the perspective of these at-bottom conservative revolutionists.

The administrative elite accordingly gave allegiance to both parties without any distinction referrable to determining social or economic criteria. Most plainly was this the case in the House of Commons where, of some forty-odd royal office-holders, seventeen became Parliamentarians and twenty-two Royalists (the few others were apparently neutrals).[2] Belonging to the former were such men as the Treasurer of the Household and former Secretary of State, Sir Henry Vane senior; his son, Sir Henry the younger, made Treasurer of the Navy in 1639 through his father's influence; Sir Benjamin Rudyard,

---

[1] M. Keeler, *op. cit.*, *s.v.*

[2] G. E. Aylmer, *The King's servants*, Table 46. This work contains the best and fullest discussion of the political stand of officials; cf. ch. VI, 'Office and politics.' Aylmer gives the total number of officials in the Commons as forty-five. I have preferred his figures to those in M. Keeler, *op. cit.*, Table 5, which reckons the total of officials at twenty-seven, of whom about half were Royalists, ten Parliamentarians, and two neutrals. The two sets of figures are not strictly comparable, however, as they do not use identical criteria for office-holders. Keeler has also counted as Parliamentarians several officials who were supporters of the Country but died before the civil war. I have myself, with the aid of the biographies in her book, counted eighteen officials in the Commons who were Parliamentarians in the civil war.

---

until his succession to the earldom, was followed as the borough's representative by his brother, John.

Surveyor of the Court of Wards; Sir Richard Wynn, Treasurer and Receiver-General to the Queen; Sir Robert Pye, Auditor of the Exchequer; Sir Henry Mildmay, Master of the Jewel House; Sir John Trevor, Auditor of the Duchy of Lancaster; Cornelius Holland, Comptroller of the Prince of Wales's Household; and Dr. Thomas Eden, Master in Chancery.[1] Parliamentarian office-holders were scattered through most branches of the royal government. Heavily outnumbered in the Household departments, they were less so in the Exchequer and the offices under the secretaries of State, while in the Court of Wards and the Duchy of Lancaster they actually slightly exceeded the Royalists.[2]

3

What has been said of the groups mentioned thus far was true as well of the overall character of the parties as civil war engulfed the kingdom. Royalist and Parliamentarian did not correspond to a structural differentiation in English society nor were they the vehicle of contradictory class or economic interests. Both reflected, rather, the schism within the aristocratic order and the general political nation, so that 'every county,' a Parliamentarian memoirist wrote, 'had the civil war, more or less, within itself.'[3]

To be sure, Clarendon's *History of the rebellion* has been instanced as containing the opinion that the war was one of classes. He 'makes no bones,' it has been stated, 'about describing the line-up . . . as a class division.'[4] This interpretation of Clarendon's view, however, rests on a misconception. The great Royalist historian did not picture the body politic as formed of antagonistic classes, but as an ordered hierarchy of status and deference. 'Gentleman,' 'person of honour' and of 'quality'—such was the mode of social categorization that came naturally to his mind. His conception of 'interest,' being altogether conditioned by the postulates of a status order, referred to the influence and dependency at the disposal of the aristocracy. So, he wrote in characteristic fashion, the marquis of Hertford was sent by the King to raise forces in the west because there 'his interest and reputation was greater than any man's'; and with Hertford went 'the lord Seymour . . . the lord Pawlett, Hopton, Stowell . . . and some other gentlemen of the prime quality and interest in the western

[1] Cf. these men in M. Keeler, *op. cit., s.v.* and references to them also in G. E. Aylmer, *op. cit., passim.*
[2] Cf. G. E. Aylmer, *op. cit.*, Table 49, a survey of the allegiance of two hundred officials.
[3] L. Hutchinson, *Memoirs of the life of Colonel Hutchinson*, ed. C. H. Firth, 2v., L., 1885, I, 163.
[4] Christopher Hill, *Puritanism and revolution*, 204.

Conclusion

centres held out determinedly for the King. In Lancashire, for example, Manchester was Parliamentarian, but Wigan, which had opposed ship money more than any town in the county, and Preston, were Royalist.[1] Decidedly Royalist too was the city of Chester where 'many Aldermen, Sheriffs ... and common Council-men' were accused by the Houses of being 'violent Fomenters of these unnatural Wars against the Parliament. ...'[2] Newcastle was the greatest of Royalist municipalities.[3] The town corporation announced its loyalty to the King at the outset of the war, helped him with advances of money, and conferred honorary citizenship upon the Royalist commander, the earl of Newcastle. For these offences the House of Commons cited the mayor, Sir Nicholas Cole, and a number of prominent citizens as delinquents.[4] The following year the Newcastle Merchant Adventurers voted the King a loan, and the Company of Hostmen laid an impost on coal to pay the upkeep of the Royalist garrison.[5] In 1644, when the town was under siege by parliament's forces, the mayor and common council continued to proclaim their defiance of the Houses and their loyalty to the King.[6]

Of Parliamentarian cities, London was by all odds foremost, but as has been seen, it contained a good deal of Royalist sentiment in the richer and magisterial sector of the citizenry. Clarendon did not fail to boast of this, in spite of his scathing and snobbish comments on the 'factious humour which possessed most corporations, and the pride of their wealth. ...' The Parliamentarians' strength in London, he remarked, 'consisted of the rabble of the people, far the greatest part of the substantial and wealthy citizens being not of their party. ...'[7] Norwich was another Parliamentarian city that harboured a minority of Royalists in its ruling families.[8] This was also the case in Bristol where the notables of both parties possessed an identical history of office in the civic government and the Society of Merchant Venturers.[9] Bristol's first M.P.s to the Long Parliament, Humphrey Hooke and Richard Long, became Royalists. This was perhaps less remarkable than the fact that on their expulsion from the House of

[1] F. Walker, *Historical geography of southwest Lancashire*, 87–96.
[2] *Acts and ordinances of the interregnum*, I, 876; cf. R. N. Dore, *op. cit.*, 18.
[3] J. U. Nef, *The rise of the British coal industry*, II, 290.
[4] J. Brand, *op. cit.*, II, 461; *C.J.*, II, 774 (20 September 1642).
[5] *Extracts from the records of the Merchant Adventurers of Newcastle*, 133–4; *Extracts from the records of the Company of Hostmen of Newcastle*, 80.
[6] Cf. their declaration in *Reprints of rare tracts*, ed. M. A. Richardson, 4v., Newcastle, 1845–9, I.
[7] *Rebellion*, VI, 271, V, 319.
[8] F. Blomefield, *op. cit.*, III, 383–5; B. Allen, *op. cit.*, 235–6, 250–3.
[9] Cf. the biographical notices of Bristol merchants in *The deposition books of Bristol*, v. I, 1643–7, ed. H. E. Nott, *Bristol record society*, VI, 1935, App. I and P. McGrath (ed.), *op. cit.*, xxvi–xxviii.

Commons, their successors as Bristol's members, John Glanville, the recorder, and John Taylor, the mayor, were also Royalists. The two latter were disabled to sit in 1644.[1] During 1643 while Bristol was occupied by a parliamentary garrison, a number of citizens conspired unsuccessfully to open the city to the King. There were over seventy in the plot, their occupations being such as merchant, soapmaker, cutler, trunkmaker, hatter, vintner, hornmaker, plumber, carpenter, brewer, and mercer—virtually a microcosm of the urban economy.[2]

Whatever side merchants, retailers, and townsmen in general joined, it is altogether doubtful in any case that economic interest was the primary determinant of their party sympathies. The citizen element formed a municipal and provincial, not a national, *bourgeoisie*. Its members possessed neither common material interests nor any consciousness of being a class. Indeed, where commercial or economic considerations apparently influenced party attachment most, the greatest capitalists, such as the customs farmers or some of the members of the East India Company, were as likely as not to be Royalists because of their dependence on trading and financial privileges from the King.[3] A further significant, but separate, factor was the popular opposition which appeared after 1640 in certain towns to the oligarchic power of municipal governing bodies. This unquestionably engendered a disposition towards Royalism, by way of reaction, amongst the magistrates and other citizens of the urban governing class who saw a connection between the preservation of their own authority and the King's.

4

The mood and attitudes prevalent in the early period of the war clearly reflected its character as a division of the political nation and the dominant class. The conflict was unaccompanied by general enthusiasm, and even in enmity the kingdom's governors were rarely actuated by crusading passion for a reckoning. The notes of the time —of 1642–3—were persistent hope of an accommodation and reluctance to see differences carried to an extremity that would render settlement impossible. In the House of Commons sat a body of peace Parliamentarians composed of men like D'Ewes with whose sentiments Pym had to reckon while he laboured to create the machinery

---

[1] D. Brunton and D. H. Pennington, *op. cit.*, 61; J. Latimer, *The annals of Bristol in the seventeenth century*, 156–7.

[2] *The copy of a letter sent from Bristol*, 1643, 7–8.

[3] Cf. *supra*, 132–5; the editor of the East India Company's records has commented on the Royalism in the company and in London's merchant community, *A calendar of the court minutes of the East India Company 1640–1643*, ed. E. B. Sainsbury, Oxford, 1909, xxiv–xxv.

Conclusion

to sustain a war.[1] Nor was Pym himself, as a centrist leader and a master of expediencies, at all opposed to peace, provided only it could be got on secure conditions. 'Distrust,' however, as the veteran diplomat, Sir Thomas Roe, declared, was 'the great impediment.'[2]

The spectacle of violence which fellow subjects practised on each other evoked distress and sorrow. Noting the first engagement of the war, the old earl of Cork, one of the foremost victims of Strafford's Irish rule, wrote in his diary:

The 23 of October, 1642, the lamentable (and ever to be, by all treu english hearts, lamentable) battaile at Edgehill . . . was fought between the English; His sacred Maty being in person in the head of his Armye, and the earle of Essex, generall of the Army of Parliament. . . . God graunt it may be the last battaile that ever may be fought between our own nation.[3]

Although they felt themselves in the grip of fatality, partisans nevertheless sought to preserve some amity towards their opponents. Sir William Waller, parliament's commander in the west, wrote in June 1643 to his Royalist counterpart, Sir Ralph Hopton:

. . . hostility itself cannot violate my friendship to your person, but I must be true to the cause wherein I serve. . . . that great God who is the searcher of my heart, knows with what a sad sense I go upon this service and with what a perfect hatred I detest this war without an enemy. . . . We are both upon the stage and must act the parts . . . assigned us in this tragedy; let us do it in a way of honour and without personal animosities.[4]

Of like tenor were the sentiments which the Yorkshire Parliamentarian, Sir Hugh Cholmley, tendered the House of Commons:

. . . nothing can divert me from serving the Parliament with all fidelity . . . yet . . . it grieves my heart to see how these calamities increase and how I am forced to draw my sword . . . against . . . many near friends and allies some of which I know both to be well affected in religion and lovers of their liberties. And therefore I most humbly beseech the House

[1] On Pym's war leadership, cf. J. H. Hexter, *The reign of King Pym*, ch. II–III and L. Glow, 'Pym and parliament: the methods of moderation,' *Journal of modern history*, XXXVI, 4 (1964).

[2] J. Webb, *Memorials of the civil war in Herefordshire*, 2v., L., 1879, II, 357–8.

[3] *Lismore papers*, 1st ser., V, 216.

[4] H.M.C. *Duke of Somerset*, 65 (June 1643).

*that they will be pleased to lay hold of all occasions that may produce
an accomodation between King and Parliament. ...*[1]

Such feelings were doubtless the cause of the belief often expressed
by moderates on both sides that England would suffer if either party
triumphed completely. '... to see hys Maty come in an absolute
Conqueror,' wrote the Royalist Sir Roger Twysden, '... I was never
Cavalier enough to wish. ...'[2] Lord Savile, another Royalist who had
come over from the Country, declared that he 'would not have the
King trample on the Parliament, nor the Parliament lessen him so
much as to make a way for the people to rule us all.'[3] Sir Thomas
Hutchinson, the Parliamentarian M.P. for Nottinghamshire, was
described by his daughter-in-law as 'infinitely desirous' that differences should rather be 'composed by accomodation, than ended by
conquest. ...'[4] And according to John Hotham, who had helped to
preserve Hull for the Houses,

*... no man that hath any reasonable share in the commonwealth can
desire that either side should be absolute conquerors, for it will be then
as it was betwixt Caesar and Pompey, whosoever had the better the
Roman liberty was to have the worse.*[5]

In contrast to these opinions was the conviction of the Parliamentarian earl of Warwick that the war must be waged vigorously. He
told his son-in-law, Lord Mandeville, when the latter was about to
set out with Essex's army against the King in September 1642:

*I am glad to hear the army is to march, I pray stand well upon your
garde both military and politike, for you will never gett the like
oportunity if you slip this. ... and loose not your business with civiltys
and compliment. Give the cavaliers an inch they will take an ell, doe the
worke thourowly. ...*[6]

Warwick's view, however, was not the typical one, nor was Mandeville as a military commander the man to act on it; for as was to
become clear two years later in his quarrel with Oliver Cromwell,

[1] *H.M.C. Portland,* I, 90 (January 1643). Cholmley, M.P. for Scarborough,
became a Royalist in 1643; cf. *D.N.B., s.v.*
[2] *Sir Roger Twysden's journal,* III, 151.
[3] *Camden miscellany,* VIII, 1883, 6.
[4] L. Hutchinson, *Memoirs of Colonel Hutchinson,* I, 167–8.
[5] *H.M.C. Portland,* I, 87. The two Hothams, father and son, went over to
the King in 1643 and were executed for treason for attempting to betray
Hull to the Royalists.
[6] P.R.O. Manchester MSS., 30/15/no. 506.

Conclusion

Mandeville adhered consistently to the belief that the civil war were better ended 'by an accomodation' than 'by the sword.'[1]

One further aspect of the early period of the war, possibly most revealing of all, was the tendency of entire districts to try to preserve neutrality and keep the conflict from their midst. The Yorkshire gentry led the way at the end of September 1642 when the principal personages of both parties in the county subscribed a treaty of pacification and non-assistance to either side. The draftsmen of the agreement were the two knights of the shire, the Parliamentarian Lord Fairfax and the Royalist Henry Belasyse. Next month the Lancashire gentry followed suit. These attempts at neutrality were immediately quashed by the Houses, which condemned the Yorkshire treaty as void of authority and as benefiting only the Royalists to the danger and prejudice of the kingdom.[2]

Despite parliament's disapproval, manifestation of neutralism persisted. The Staffordshire justices and grand jury issued a declaration decrying violence, and in Nottinghamshire the gentry of both parties engaged unsuccessfully in negotiations for a truce.[3] On 8 November at Bristol, the mayor, aldermen, and common council passed a resolution that they were all 'in love and amity one with another, and do desire a friendly association . . . in all mutual accomodation.' With this went an agreement to petition the King and parliament for a reconciliation.[4]

In December a treaty of pacification was also effected in Cheshire between the King's commissioners of array and the Houses' deputy lieutenants. It ordained a cessation of arms except 'ytt bee to resist force, broughte into this Countie,' and included a provision that the representatives of both parties should petition the King and parliament 'for puttinge an end to the great distracions and misery fallen upon this kingdom, by making a speedy peace.' The Houses repudiated the Cheshire agreement, and it was also denounced in a Parliamentarian pamphlet as giving comfort to the Royalists. 'What peace then is this?', asked the author of *Neutrality condemned*:

Unnatural peace, whilst the body of the Kingdome is in danger, so to provide for one member as totally to neglect the rest. . . . Uncharitable peace, to looke on, and not to afford your helping hand to stay the

---

[1] *D.N.B.*, *s.v.*, 'Edward Montagu second Earl of Manchester.' Mandeville succeeded to his father's earldom in November 1642.

[2] Clarendon, *Rebellion*, VI, 257–9; *The Farington papers*, ed. S. M. ffarington, Chetham society, XXXIX, 1856, 80–5; *L.J.*, V, 385–6.

[3] *The committee at Stafford*, xx; L. Hutchinson, *op. cit.*, I, App. VI.

[4] J. Latimer, *Annals of Bristol in the seventeenth century*, 160–1.

downfall of a tottering Kingdome, which may be the sooner ruined by your security. . . .[1]

These expressions of neutralism did not proceed from an absence of political conviction or party sympathy. They testified merely to the superior strength of local attachments and, even more, to the preoccupation of communities with keeping plunder and violence from their doors. It was the extent of such feelings that induced the King and parliament to open peace negotiations in February 1643 at Oxford. The treaty failed, however, and the war went on, nullifying all neutralist tendencies. Yet these latter still continued to break forth sporadically: in Devon and Cornwall in 1643, in Sussex in 1644, and most conspicuously of all, in 1645 in Somerset and Dorset, where the 'club-men' organized themselves in a wide movement to defend their neighbourhoods against the military depredations of both parties.[2]

5

Where, then, in this war begun and directed by the governing class did the potentialities for radicalization lie? Whence arose the pressures that afterward challenged (though unsuccessfully) the reign of inequality and privilege? What soil engendered such growths as the Leveller movement which during the later '40s strove for a democratic liberty altogether beyond the Parliamentarianism of 1642?

The answers are not far to seek. The seeds of radicalism, sown broadcast and ready to bring forth their progeny, lay in the revolution's subversion of authority and in the hopes and passions it released; in the liberal-populist element of Parliamentarian doctrine, easily susceptible of development and adaptation to purposes unthought-of by the framers of the Houses' declarations; finally, in the inflammation of multitudes as the result of the economic dislocation, the hardship and suffering, inflicted by the war.

In 1642, alongside the neutralist reactions which the quarrel evoked, there were also expressions on the Parliamentarian side of a

[1] T. Malbon, *Memorials of the civil war in Cheshire and Lancashire*, ed. J. Hall, *Lancashire and Cheshire record society*, XIX, 1889, 3–34; *C.J.*, II, 916–17; *L.J.*, V, 533; *Tracts relating to the civil war in Cheshire*, ed. J. Atkinson, *Chetham society*, n.s., LXV, 1909, 80.
[2] For Devon and Cornwall neutralism, cf. Clarendon, *Rebellion*, VI, 254–5 and *H.M.C. Portland*, I, 101–2; for Sussex neutralism, cf. Sir William Waller's statement, *Military memoir of Colonel John Birch*, ed. T. W. Webb, *Camden society*, n.s., VI, 1873, 217; for the club-men, cf. Clarendon, *Rebellion*, IX, 50; J. Sprigge, *Anglia rediviva*, 1647, Pt. II, ch. I, III, and H. G. Tibbutt, *The life and letters of Sir Lewis Dyve, Bedfordshire historical record society*, XXVIII, 1948, 68–9.

different spirit of keenest militancy. Welling up from the depths of Puritan faith, it invested the conflict with a burning urgency and summoned Englishmen to warfare against the wicked ungodly. It was religion, affirmed the Puritan Richard Baxter, 'that filled up the Parliaments armies, and put the Resolution and Valour into their Soldiers. . . .'[1] Many saw the crisis between King and parliament as religion's hour of decision. '. . . the vulgar mind,' said Sir Edward Dering, is 'now fond with imaginary hopes. What will the issue be, when hopes grow still on hopes? and one aime still riseth upon another . . . I cannot divine.'[2]

The note of commitment thundered from the Puritan pulpit. At St. Margaret's in Westminster, where the members of the Commons held a solemn fast service monthly, the elite of the Puritan ministry preached fortifying sermons to the congregation of England's elders.[3] In *Meroz cursed*, a discourse so celebrated that he afterwards delivered it sixty times to different auditories, the Rev. Stephen Marshall denounced the wrath of heaven on neutrals. God acknowledges no 'Neuters,' said Marshall, and

curses all them who come not out to helpe him, as well as those who come to fight against him. And our Saviour at the last day will as well denounce go ye cursed *against them. . . . In this case it is a certaine rule . . . he that is not with me, is against me.*[4]

Another preacher bid the House's members,

by the many Petitions you have had from men, by the solemne Protestations you have made to God . . . by the dependence the Protestant cause abroad hath upon you,

to stand by their holy undertaking.[5] Marshall exhorted his eminent hearers:

. . . go ye on, ye Nobles and Worthies. . . . look and presse to the work which yet remaines: Get the resolution of Zisca that brave Bohemian

---

[1] *Reliquiae Baxterianae*, I, 31.

[2] E. Dering, *A collection of speeches*, 166.

[3] The sermons preached to the House are discussed by E. Kirby, 'Sermons before the Commons 1640–42,' *American historical review*, XLIV, 3 (1939) and H. R. Trevor-Roper, 'The fast sermons of the Long Parliament,' *Essays in British history presented to Sir Keith Feiling*, ed. H. R. Trevor-Roper, L., 1964.

[4] Stephen Marshall, *Meroz cursed*, February 1642, 22–3; *D.N.B.*, *s.v.*, 'Stephen Marshall.'

[5] Thomas Hill, *The trade of truth advanced*, July 1642, 22–3.

Captain, who not only was willing to fight while he lived, but bequeathed his skin when he died, to bee made a drum head for the service of the warre.[1]

Such sermons, delivered with civil war in prospect, were incitements to the godly. They testified to the ferment of hope and ardour that agitated the 'Thundring Legions of praying Christians' amidst the dissolution of the polity.[2]

The most vivid statement of the perspectives which the war opened for the Puritan mind was the Rev. John Goodwin's *Anti-cavalierisme*. Published in October 1642, it was a plea for armed resistance to the King, its title alone indicative of the passions the war was generating. Goodwin, a London minister who was to become one of the foremost pamphleteers of the revolutionary era, addressed himself primarily to the citizens of the capital. With unmeasured rhetoric he urged a fight to the death against the 'bloody' and 'butcherly' Royalists and painted the danger to lives, liberty, and religion from the 'Cavaliers' and their papist confederates. The Parliamentarian cause, to his view, represented a heroic struggle of deliverance from long prevailing spiritual and political tyranny. Men's judgments and conscience had been abased 'by doctrines and tenents, excessively advancing the power of superiours, over inferiours, and binding Iron yokes . . . upon those that were in subjection. . . .' Now, however, anti-Christ's downfall was drawing near and God had revealed to his servants 'the just and full extent of the lawfull liberties of those that live in subiection.' Moreover, it was to be the Christians 'of ordinary ranke and qualitie' who would have 'the principall hand, in executing the judgements of God upon the Whore.' But the issue extended far beyond England. Bleeding Ireland, the brethren in the plantations of America, all the saints in the churches of other kingdoms, were equally concerned in the outcome. Pious men were to see the cause, Goodwin said, as

a great and solemne invitation from God himselfe unto you, to do greater things for the world, at least for the Christian world, than ever you did unto this day; or then ever you are like to do . . . yea then any particular Christian State ever did, or is like to doe, while the world stands.[3]

Goodwin's exultant vision of world emancipation undoubtedly went well beyond the outlook of the mass of zealous men and women

---

[1] *Meroz cursed*, 52–3.

[2] Thomas Hill, *The trade of truth advanced*, Dedication.

[3] John Goodwin, *Anti-cavalierisme*, 2–3, 30–1, 49–51.

who filled the congregations of the Puritan clergy. It was strikingly symptomatic, however, of the driving energies which the war was bringing into play as an offset to neutralism. At the same time, the breakdown of the monarchical constitution was also accompanied by a political debate of unprecedented intensity. The kingdom, according to Thomas Hobbes, whose own masterpiece, *De cive*, appeared in 1642, 'was boiling hot with questions concerning the right of dominion, and the obedience due from subjects, the true forerunners of an approaching war.'[1] The press teemed with writings that probed boldly into fundamentals. Besides the declarations of the King and parliament, which themselves became subjects of controversy, a great publicistic literature dealing with politics appeared. The free-ranging discussion laid open the issues of the war to common eyes and encouraged the vulgar to weigh the claims of the parties in the scale of their own reason.

A few hints can be given about the circulation of these publications. The House of Commons took care to provide for the widest dissemination of its own declarations. It ordered in June 1642 that they should be printed in runs of nine thousand copies, sealed up in packets, and distributed throughout the counties to sheriffs, high constables, and down to the petty constables or tithing men of the hundreds. All who received packets were to give receipts and each declaration was to be publicly read to the people of the town or parish within seven days of its arrival.[2]

A speech by Sir Edward Dering which was printed in January 1642 sold over forty-five hundred copies: 'never any thing sold like that,' boasted its author.[3] Productions of the London press went by post or carrier to other parts of the realm. By this means a gentleman in distant Devonshire was able to obtain the current pamphlets from his relations in the capital.[4] A minister in Suffolk bought the London news sheets, making frequent entries from them in his diary. In August 1642 he noted that the differences between the King and parliament 'are extant in multitudes of bookes and papers (unto which God in mercy put an end!). . . .'[5] Later in the '40s, the diary of a Yorkshire yeoman of Parliamentarian sympathies recorded a quite exceptional range of purchase and reading of controversial writings, both religious and political.[6] In London, pamphlets were sold not

---

[1] T. Hobbes, *De cive*, Preface to English translation, *English works*, II, xx. The English edition was published in 1651.
[2] *C.J.*, II, 609, 616.　　　　　　[3] *Proceedings in Kent*, xliii.
[4] *Trevelyan papers*, ed. W. C. Trevelyan and C. E. Trevelyan, *Camden society*, CV, 1872, pt. III, 209, 216, 223.
[5] *Diary of John Rous*, 121.
[6] *Diurnall of Capt. Adam Eyre*, ed. H. J. Morehouse, *Yorkshire diaries*, Surtees society, LXV, 1875, 23, 24, 57.

only by the booksellers, but also by hawkers in the streets.[1] The first parliamentary ordinance to regulate printing, passed in June 1643 (against which Milton wrote *Areopagitica*, his plea for liberty of the press), mentioned the many persons that

have taken upon them to set up sundry private Printing Presses in corners, and to print, vend, publish, and disperse books, pamphlets, and papers, in such multitudes, that no industry could be sufficient to discover or bring to punish all the several abounding Delinquents.[2]

Of the political tracts of 1642, the one that attracted the greatest notice was the Parliamentarian Henry Parker's *Observations upon some of his Majesties late Answers and Expresses*. It was published in July, went through two editions, and besides provoking a swarm of Royalist replies, had the distinction of being denounced in a royal declaration as an attack upon the crown and monarchy itself.[3] According to Richard Baxter, it was the 'principal Writing' on the Houses' side and 'very much prevailed. . . .'[4] Parker's hard, audacious reasoning cut through the ambiguities and quibbles which served to muffle the assertion of sovereignty in the Houses' own manifestoes. He preferred to make out the Parliamentarian case on the basis of fundamental principles. Sovereignty rightly belongs to parliament, he held, and the King must submit his will because parliament is in essence the community itself. With this went a doctrine tracing the origin of power to the people and deriving political society from 'Pactions' and the 'common consent and agreement' of men. He also declared that 'the Charter of nature intitles all Subjects . . . to safetie by its supreame law'; and further, that 'there bee . . . tacite trusts and reservations in all publike commands, though of the most absolute nature, that can be supposed. . . .'[5]

Writing at the beginning of the civil war, Parker had no motive to consider the remoter implications of his and the Houses' principles. But could not their arguments be appropriated to other ends? If power is a trust from the people, then parliament must be as accoun-

[1] Cf. an order of October 1643 by the London common council to suppress the hawkers of pamphlets, Journal, 40, 78b.
[2] *Acts and ordinances of the interregnum*, I, 184.
[3] *An exact collection*, 470.
[4] *Reliquiae Baxterianae*, I, 41.
[5] Henry Parker, *Observations upon some of his majesties late answers and expresses*, 2nd ed., 1642, 34, 1–2, 4. An account of Parker's political ideas is given in J. W. Allen, *English political thought*, 426–35, W. K. Jordan, *Men of substance*, Chicago, 1944, 140–77, and M. Judson, 'Henry Parker and the theory of parliamentary sovereignty,' *Essays . . . in honor of Charles Howard McIlwain*, Cambridge, 1936.

table as the King. A Royalist critic of Parker put the plain consequence in its bearing on the electoral franchise:

The Commons Vote in right of their electors whom they represent; at least nine parts of the Kingdome neither doe nor may Vote in their election . . . all that have not 40.s. per annum free-hold Land, whic h . . . cannot be above a tenth part. . . . Tell me good Sir . . . power being (you say) nothing else but that might and vigour which a society of men contains in it selfe, why should . . . the major part, be over mastred, and concluded by the Votes of those that are deputed by a minor number of the people?[1]

Just here was the point! Parliamentarian theory offered easy ingress to demands for democratic change in the name of much the same principles the Houses and their defenders employed against Charles I. The startling effects of this development would discover themselves before long. One, for instance, whom the Parliamentarian argument persuaded was John Lilburne, religious sectarian and recent victim of Archbishop Laud's repression. In 1642 Lilburne, according to his own account, was convinced by the reasonings in the Houses' declarations and writings such as Parker's *Observations* to take up arms 'in judgment and conscience against the King. . . .'[2] He was presently to become, by a more extended application of these same reasonings aided by an admixture of other ideas, the organizer-in-chief of the Leveller movement and an irrepressible agitator for political justice against parliament itself.

The emergence of a party of radical opposition from among the Parliamentarian rank and file was only possible, however, because of the mass hardship of these years of unsettlement. The civil war began amidst slump and stagnation. Political breakdown destroyed confidence and did severe injury to trade. A pamphleteer wrote in 1641 that 'the decay of trade is in everybody's mouth from the sheep-shearer to the merchant, and even a weak statist, without Galileo's prospective glass, may see both our wealth and safety therewith declining.'[3] The textile industry plunged into another depression, after only barely recovering from the prolonged slump of the '20s. From many parts came the clothiers' threnody that they could find no vent for their cloth, that stocks lay dead on their hands. Widespread

---

[1] Sir John Spelman, *A view of a printed book*, 1643, cited in *Complete prose works of John Milton*, v. II, ed. E. Sirluck, New Haven, 1964, 28–9.

[2] John Lilburne, *The legall fundamentall liberties of the people of England*, 1649, 22–3. Lilburne quoted Parker's *Observations* copiously in *Innocency and truth justified*, 1646.

[3] Cited in B.E. Supple, *op. cit.*, 129.

unemployment set in. A description of the Essex industry in 1642 spoke of the 'poor men, artificers, as weavers, combers and the like, appertaining to the trade of clothworking ... brought (many of them) to beg their bread, and the rest to live upon the parish charge.'[1]

Hard conditions lasted through the whole of the '40s. Money was scarce, credit difficult to obtain. Excise and other taxes created heavy burdens. The necessities of life reached prices beyond living memory. '... things are at that rate,' an Essex clergyman noted in the fall of 1647, 'as never was in our dayes. . . .' And a few months later: 'This time was a sad deare time for poore people, onely their worke beyond expectacion continued plentiful and cheape. . . .'[2] Impoverished tenants were unable to pay their rents. A pamphleteer at the end of the '40s thus described the plight of poor tenants on northern estates:

I have seen multitudes of poor people go bare-footed and bare-legged and scarce a ragge of clothes to cover their nakednesse, or having any bread, or any kind of food to put into their bellies, to keep them from starving. And ask the poor people, whose land they lived in? or who was their Landlord? they would tell us, that it was either the Earl of Northumberland or the Lord Grey. . . .'[3]

The war, too, caused great destruction of property, while plunder and free-quarter added to the widespread misery.[4]

There was no novelty, of course, in poverty and bad times. What *was* in the highest degree novel was the formation of a popular movement that appealed to the victims of the time's oppressions and organized them for independent political action. This was the significance of the Leveller party. The backbone of the party were the small and middle sort of people: shopkeepers, craftsmen, a scattering of agricultural freeholders and tenants, religious sectarians, soldiers of parliament's army, sufferers from excise, monopolies, and debt. They belonged mainly to the inferior strata whose conditions of life had been severely depressed by the war. Already imbued with Parliamentarian doctrines, they responded readily to the agitation of the Levellers. And the party's leaders, taking up their miscellaneous grievances, incorporated them into a programme demanding

[1] *Ibid.*, 12.

[2] *The diary of the Rev. Ralph Josselin 1616–1683*, ed. E. Hockliffe, *Camden society*, 3rd ser., XV, 1908, 45, 46.

[3] Francis Freeman, *Light vanquishing darkness*, 1650, 55–6.

[4] Cf. the account of the depressed conditions of the 1640s in B. Supple, *op. cit.*, 125–31; W. R. Scott, *op. cit.*, I, ch. XII; E. Lipson, *The economic history of England*, III, 315–17; and M. James, *Social problems and policy during the Puritan revolution*, L., 1930, ch. II.

redress through far-reaching political and economic reform. Thus it came about for the first time that a large number of Englishmen strove for a democratic polity and began to talk of natural rights, the liberty of the people, and the establishment of the powers and limits of government by the consent of the governed.

These radical principles pervaded the air of the later '40s. They were asserted against the rich, against privilege and inequality, against parliament itself. '. . . who are the oppressors, but the Nobility and Gentry,' said a Leveller writer, 'and who are the oppressed, is not the Yeoman, the Farmer, the Tradesman, the Labourer . . . ?'[1] When the small masters of the Weavers Company contended for their rights in the gild, they based their case on the natural equality of men and the creation of 'jurisdictive power . . . by a compact and agreement. . . .'[2] More momentous still was the Levellers' call for a parliament chosen by democratic suffrage, a position which one of its advocates justified in permanently memorable words:

> . . . *I think that the poorest he that is in England hath a life to live, as the greatest he; and therefore . . . I think it's clear, that every man that is to live under a government ought first by his own consent to put himself under that government; and I do think that the poorest man in England is not at all bound in a strict sense to that government that he hath not had a voice to put himself under. . . .*[3]

All this is another story, beyond the scope of the present work. But it serves to illustrate the continuity of political development over the 1640s and to show how Leveller democracy and popular opposition to entrenched privilege grew directly from the earlier stages of England's revolution.

[1] Laurence Clarkson, *A general charge*, 1647, 11.
[2] Cf. G. Unwin, *Industrial organization in the sixteenth and seventeenth centuries*, Oxford, 1904, 205.
[3] Col. Rainsborough's words in October 1647 at the Putney debates; cf. A. S. P. Woodhouse, *Puritanism and liberty*, L., 1938, 53.

Index

Index

Index

Petty, Sir William, 24
Phelips, Edward, 335
Phelips, Sir Edward, 79, 82, 86, 87
Philip IV, 1, 4
Pindar, Sir Paul, 133, 135
Pleydall, William, 323
Ponet, John, 195
Portugal, 1, 2
Prerogative, doctrine of, 84–5
Press (*see also* Newspapers)
  secret printing, 193; freedom,
  203–6; pamphlet circulation,
  347–8
Preston, 339
Preston, John, 63, 65, 66, 174, 176
Protest of twelve bishops, 277
Protestation, 223
Providence Island Company, 101,
  103
Prynne, William, 192, 193, 194, 226
Public opinion
  1620s, 106–8; 1641–2, 203–6,
  228–9, 258, 347
Puritanism
  and Elizabethan parliaments, 76–
  7; in the peerage, 93–6; term
  'brother', 107; and London
  oppositionists, 141–3; Newcastle, 150; Norwich, 153–4;
  definition, 157–8; and separatism, 158–9; evolution of,
  159–63; ministers retain hold
  in the church, 163–70; laity in
  the governing class, 101, 170–
  181; ecclesiastical patronage,
  177–81; laity in the inferior
  order, 181–5; and social structure, 185–7; conflict with Arminianism, 188–92; and the
  Country, 191–2; repression of,
  192–5; and right of resistance,
  195–7; and church reform
  1641–2, 226–41; and civil war,
  330, 345–7
Pye, Sir Robert, 210, 266, 336
Pym, John
  and political terminology, 39;
  enters parliament, 80; and

1628 parliament, 82; and fundamental law, 83–4; and privilege of parliament, 86; and
earl of Bedford, 95; holds
office, 97; and Buckingham's
impeachment, 98; and elections to the Long Parliament,
100; and Providence Island
Company, 101, 103; and Puritanism, 102; and Scottish
Rebellion, 104–5; leader of
Long Parliament, 200–1, 202;
committee against Strafford,
203; speech on grievances,
207; and Sir Henry Vane
junior, 208–9; and office, 214,
215, 216, 272; and army plot,
219; and Strafford's trial,
220–1; policy on church reform, 237, 238, 239, 241;
distrusts King, 247, 248; committee for the recess, 250; 251,
demands parliamentary control of councillors, 259–60;
and Grand Remonstrance,
262–3, 263, 269, 270–1; accused of treason, 278; appeals
for peers' cooperation, 298;
and Parliamentarian party,
306–7, 316, 341; committee of
safety, 321

Rainton, Nicholas, 140, 290
Ranke, L. von, 5
Rebellion (*see also* Revolution),
  13, 15, 111, 115–16, 187,
  329
Representation, idea of, 86–7
Resistance, right of, 111–12, 144–5,
  195–7
Revolution
  mid-seventeenth century, 1, 2–5;
  American, 5; English, 5–8, 13,
  331; 'great revolutions of the
  West', 5; French, 5, 9, 11–13;
  Marx on, 7–8, 11–12; 'bour-
  geois', 7–8, 120; concept and
  terminology, 10–18; Russian, 6,

Perez Zagorin

Perez Zagorin, Professor of History at the University of Rochester, was born in Chicago in 1920. He was previously Professor of History at McGill University, and he has lectured at Oxford, Manchester, the University of Toronto, the University of Pittsburgh, and Johns Hopkins. A leading historian of English sixteenth- and seventeenth-century history and of the early modern period in the United States, Professor Zagorin is the author of *A History of Political Thought in the English Revolution* (1954).